The Priesthood of All Believers and the *Missio Dei*

Princeton Theological Monograph Series
K. C. Hanson, Charles M. Collier, D. Christopher Spinks,
and Robin A. Parry, Series Editors

Recent volumes in the series:

Stanley S. MacLean
*Resurrection, Apocalypse, and the Kingdom of Christ:
The Eschatology of Thomas F. Torrance*

Brian Neil Peterson
*Ezekiel in Context: Ezekiel's Message Understood in Its Historical
Setting of Covenant Curses and Ancient Near
Eastern Mythological Motifs*

Amy E. Richter
Enoch and the Gospel of Matthew

Maeve Louise Heaney
Music as Theology: What Music Says about the Word

Eric M. Vail
Creation and Chaos Talk: Charting a Way Forward

David L. Reinhart
*Prayer as Memory: Toward the Comparative Study
of Prayer as Apocalyptic Language and Thought*

Peter D. Neumann
Pentecostal Experience: An Ecumenical Encounter

Ashish J. Naidu
*Transformed in Christ:
Christology and the Christian Life in John Chrysostom*

Alexandra S. Radcliff
*The Claim of Humanity in Christ: Salvation and
Sanctification in the Theology of T. F. and J. B. Torrance*

The Priesthood of All Believers and the *Missio Dei*

A Canonical, Catholic, and Contextual Perspective

HANK VOSS

Foreword by Daniel Treier

◆PICKWICK *Publications* · Eugene, Oregon

THE PRIESTHOOD OF ALL BELIEVERS AND THE MISSIO DEI
A Canonical, Catholic, and Contextual Perspective

Princeton Theological Monograph Series 223

Copyright © 2016 Hank Voss. All rights reserved. Except for brief quotations in critical publications or reviews, no part of this book may be reproduced in any manner without prior written permission from the publisher. Write: Permissions, Wipf and Stock Publishers, 199 W. 8th Ave., Suite 3, Eugene, OR 97401.

Pickwick Publications
An Imprint of Wipf and Stock Publishers
199 W. 8th Ave., Suite 3
Eugene, OR 97401

www.wipfandstock.com

PAPERBACK ISBN: 978-1-4982-8329-8
HARDCOVER ISBN: 978-1-4982-8331-1
EBOOK ISBN: 978-1-4982-8330-4

Cataloguing-in-Publication data:

Names: Voss, Hank | foreword by Treier, Daniel.
Title: The priesthood of all believers and the *missio dei* : a canonical, catholic, and contextual perspective / Hank Voss.
Description: Eugene, OR: Pickwick Publications, 2016 | Series: Princeton Theological Monograph Series 223 | **Includes bibliographical references and index.**
Identifiers: ISBN 978-1-4982-8329-8 (paperback) | ISBN 978-1-4982-8331-1 (hardcover) | ISBN 978-1-4982-8330-4 (ebook)
Subjects: LSCH: Priesthood, Universal. | Mission of the church.
Classification: LCC BV4525 V7 2016 (print) | LCC BV4525 (ebook)

Manufactured in the U.S.A.   10/20/16

Unless otherwise indicated, all English Scripture quotations are from the ESV® Bible (The Holy Bible, English Standard Version®), copyright © 2001 by Crossway, a publishing ministry of Good News Publishers. Used by permission. All rights reserved.

To Johanna

You have helped me more than any other to live what I believe.

Thank you.

> We affirm that Christ sends his redeemed people into the world as the Father sent him, and that this calls for a similar deep and costly penetration of the world.
>
> —Lausanne Covenant, 1974

Contents

Illustrations and Tables | x
Foreword by Daniel Treier | xi
Preface | xv
Acknowledgments | xvii
List of Abbreviations | xxi
Introduction | 1
    Defining Terms | 3
    The Big Picture | 13

Part I: The Royal Priesthood in Scripture's Script

1   Royal Priests: Actors in the New Testament's Story | 27
      A Radical Change in the Priesthood | 41
      What is Christian Priesthood? | 45

2   The Story's Script: Isaiah's Royal-Priestly Servant and His Royal-Priestly Seed | 51
      Jesus as the Priestly Servant of God (*'ebed* Yahweh) | 52
      The Servant's Royal and Priestly Seed (*'ebedîm*) in Isaiah 54–66 | 60

3   Matthew's Jesus as Isaiah's Servant: The Royal Priesthood's High-Priestly King | 72
      Matthew's Priestly Servant and His Priestly Disciples | 74
      Isaiah's Priestly Seed Elsewhere in the New Testament | 91

Part II: From Actors to Audience and Back Again: The Royal Priesthood's Story across the Centuries

4   Defrocking the Royal Priesthood:
    The First Paradigm Shift | 103

> Temple Troubles: Clement of Rome and the Hierarchicalization of Temple Service (a.k.a. "Ministry") | 106
>
> Sharing the Sacrifice? Cyprian and the Rise of the "Third" Christian Priesthood | 112
>
> Royal Priesthood versus Roman Citizenship: Baptism, Constantine, and the Rise of Christendom | 117

5   Reforming the Royal Priesthood: Luther and the Priesthood of All Believers | 129

> Luther's Doctrine of the "Priesthood of All Believers" | 130
>
> A Systematic Account of Luther's Priesthood of All Believers | 135
>
> Assessing Luther's Doctrine of the Believer as Priest | 144

6   Sending the Royal Priesthood: Karl Barth, Lesslie Newbigin, and Missional Theology | 155

> Karl Barth and the Priesthood of All Believers | 156
>
> Lesslie Newbigin and a Missionary Priesthood of All Believers | 170

Part III: The Royal Priesthood in Today's World

7   The Priesthood of All Believers in Trinitarian Perspective | 181

> Christocentric-Only or Christocentric-Trinitarian? | 183
>
> Responding to the Triune God | 187
>
> Protestant Perils and the Priesthood of All Believers | 199

8   The Practices of a Priestly People: Baptismal Ordination and the Offering of Spiritual Sacrifices | 209

> The Royal Priesthood's Practices | 210
>
> Baptism: The Royal Priesthood's Practice of Ordination | 218
>
> Spiritual Sacrifices as Practices: Romans 12:1–2 and the Royal Priesthood's Worship, Work, and Witness | 224
>
> The Lord's Supper as Consummation of the Royal Priesthood's Spiritual Practices | 236

Conclusion | 241

Appendix: Significant Figures and Events for the Royal Priesthood: First through Twenty-first Centuries | 247

Bibliography | 269

Subject Index | 297

Scripture Index | 303

Illustrations

Figure 1: Structural Diagram of Isaiah 66:18b–21 | 68
Figure 2: Tabernacle Graded Holiness | 97
Figure 3: The Royal Priesthood in Trinitarian Perspective | 186

Tables

Table 1: Psalm 2:7 and Isaiah 42:1 in Matthew 3:16–17 | 76
Table 2: Pseudo-Dionysius's Celestial and Ecclesiastical Hierarchies | 111
Table 3: Three Models of Divine Mediation and Sacred Kingship after Constantine | 119
Table 4: Luther's Functions of the Priesthood of All Believers | 142
Table 5: Architecture of Barth's Christological Ecclesiology | 157
Table 6: Parallel Lists of Church Practices | 216

Foreword

Daniel Treier
Blanchard Professor of Theology,
Wheaton College

THIS MONOGRAPH IS A constructive project in evangelical theology. Accordingly, its vision is fundamentally integrative in two distinct and important senses. First, it is "formally" integrative, we might say: it integrates canonical, catholic, and contextual perspectives. Or, in other words, it follows the formal principle of the Protestant Reformation. It addresses Scripture as its fundamental authority, but it interprets Scripture with respect for the tradition of all orthodox Christian churches and with awareness of all their contemporary contexts. Second, this monograph is "materially" integrative: it integrates two previously independent domains of theological discussion. Or, more precisely, it integrates one domain of recent discussion, missional theology, with another domain suffering substantial scholarly neglect: the priesthood of all believers.

To begin with the formal integration: Dr. Voss structures his proposal with an appeal to recent "theodramatic" models. Thus, Chapters 1–3 in Part One anchor the concept of "royal priesthood" in the script of Scripture. This anchor involves substantial theological exegesis of 1 Pet 2:4–9. All believers are God's temple people and, accordingly, priests through Christ Jesus. They are now called to offer spiritual sacrifices. Dr. Voss demonstrates that recent emphasis upon the communal dimensions of their priestly identity does not mitigate the personal dimensions of this calling. The classic Protestant emphasis upon personal access to God follows from the calling believers have to offer spiritual sacrifices—themselves, no less, according to Romans 12—through Christ. This identity as royal priests helps to fulfill the hope of Isaiah's royal-priestly Servant in royal-priestly descendants; accordingly the rest of the New Testament frequently manifests this fulfillment.

In Part Two, Chapters 4–6 address the movement from the church's actors to its audience and back again by treating how the royal priesthood was understood across the centuries. Three major episodes come to the forefront of this narrative. One is the patristic shift from all baptized believers' royal priesthood, as anticipated in the New Testament, toward a hierarchical clergy. Dr. Voss clearly views this shift with concern, but he attempts to trace its gradual development with appropriate understanding. A second crucial episode follows in Martin Luther's recovery of the priesthood of all believers, set in its late medieval context. Dr. Voss does not follow Luther uncritically, but he attempts to recover Luther's account with more careful attention and exegetical sympathy than either recent neglect or alternative treatments.

Missional theology then comprises the third, most recent episode in the career of the church's royal priesthood. Hence, in Part Three, Chapters 7–8 treat Karl Barth and Lesslie Newbigin as key dialogue partners for developing Dr. Voss's own account of the royal priesthood in today's world. Turning to that account leads us to the material integration accomplished in this monograph.

Appealing to the *missio Dei* directs our attention to the doctrine of the Trinity, crucial to Barth's theology generally and to Newbigin's ecclesiology in particular. Mission is participation in the work of God, not a work of independent human initiative. Mission in a sense comprises all that the church does, not just one independent facet of that work. And mission comprises more than work, for being sent is integral to the church's identity, to her very being. Dr. Voss suggests that even many Protestant versions of believers' royal priesthood are missionally inadequate: some still monopolize priestly access to God for the clergy; others lose robustly personal priestly access to God in excessively individualistic or collectivist accounts; still others neglect the Spirit of priestly access.

But if missional theology with its Trinitarian focus helps to revitalize proper attention to the priesthood of all believers, then their integration can also move in reverse: The priesthood of all believers helps to refine missional theology. Dr. Voss demonstrates this integrative movement by rooting believers' royal priesthood in baptism, the initiatory rite that ordains them to priestly service through participation in the ministry of Christ. Thus the Lord's Supper is the ongoing rite that sustains believer-priests in their ministry through giving them anticipatory consummation of their shared participation in Christ. The priestly ministry to which believers are called then involves worship, work, and witness—prayer and *lectio divina* as the bi-directional movements of worship; service and church discipline as temple work; and proclamation of the gospel as the heart of witness. All of these activities—from baptism to the Lord's Supper and everything in between—are not independent episodes of individual life with God, but integrated practices by which members of Christ's community bless one another and a watching world as they are empowered by the Spirit.

The integrative contribution of this monograph is therefore clear. Formally, it integrates theological exegesis of authoritative Scripture with disciplined yet constructively critical appropriation of the church's interpretative traditions as well as contextual appreciation of the Spirit's contemporary mission. Materially, it appropriates and refines missional theology by bringing it into fruitful conversation with the priesthood of all believers. The latter doctrine has been frequently misunderstood, often presented with misleading slogans and still more frequently treated with historical neglect and scholarly disdain. Dr. Voss makes a significant contribution to its recovery.

Like missional theology in general, Dr. Voss's monograph will not command universal agreement at every point—what ecclesiological contribution can?—particularly with respect to how it narrates Christendom and approaches the sacraments. Yet *The Priesthood of All Believers and the Missio Dei* helps to recover what the magisterial Protestant Reformers actually said and why they said it, given their context. Still more importantly, Dr. Voss helps us to return to the biblical roots of Protestant ecclesiology, reform that account as necessary, and then revitalize our understanding of its implications in conversation with an important contemporary movement.

Preface

IT IS IMPORTANT TO acknowledge the "hermeneutical spaces" from which this book arises. It was researched and written between two United States zip codes: 90011 (South Central Los Angeles) and 60187 (Wheaton, IL). Its concerns are shaped by questions rising from both contexts. In some ways these contexts are very different, yet both are western. Pastors and theologians making use of this research should be aware that much of the language in Part One is shaped by conversations in western biblical studies. I have tried to temper this dependency by listening carefully to writers from other cultures and centuries (e.g., Tertullian, Origen, Ephrem, and Luther). Part Two focuses on the doctrine's development in western theology, and afterward largely restricts discussion to Protestant theology. Western conversations are also especially evident in Part Three where discussion of the *missio Dei* and church practices takes place. I hope, however, that the proposals made are clear enough to be critiqued and built upon by those serving the church in diverse global contexts. Recognizing that these theologians may not have access to the West's literary wealth, I have tried whenever possible to reference early (*ANF, NPNF¹ NPNF²*), medieval (*ST*), and Reformation (*CC*) church sources freely available from the Christian Classics Ethereal Library (www.CCEL.org). I have coauthored a more popular book on the doctrine of the Priesthood of All Believers with Uche Anizor, *Representing Christ* (IVP 2016). It assumes many of the theological judgements that are argued for here. For those familiar with Kevin Vahoozer's *Drama of Doctrine* metaphor, my hope is that this book will resource the church's dramaturges and directors while *Representing Christ* will resource the church's diverse actors. My hope for both books is that they will contribute to a greater display of Christ's beauty through his bride.

Los Angeles
Advent, 2015

Acknowledgments

THERE ARE NUMEROUS FRIENDS and family members to acknowledge for debts I will not be able to repay, but for whom I am very grateful. Both forming new friendships and strengthening existing ones were deeply rewarding aspects of this project. Our church, small group, and friends (especially Craig and Anna Miller and Peter and Elizabeth Hubbard) blessed and served our family in countless ways. My Wheaton PhD cohort and the members of the Global Theology Discussion Group provided much encouragement.

This book's original form was birthed from a doctoral dissertation completed at Wheaton College. I am grateful for the generosity of more than fifty individuals, families, and churches that gave to make this study leave possible. Special thanks to our extended family who were incredibly supportive including David and Carla (for providing use of their writer's cabin), Isaac, Abi, Brad, Kiki, David, Jamie, Jon, Matt, Corrie, Mark, Tim, Mary, and Aaron (for support in many ways), and Mom, Dad, John and Donna (for investing in grandchildren while Johanna and I were committed elsewhere). I am grateful to the leadership at World Impact and The Urban Ministry Institute (TUMI) for their long-term vision which made this study possible. Special thanks to Rev. Tim Goddu, Rev. Efrem Smith, Rev. Dr. Don Davis, and World Impact's National Board.

My research into the priesthood of all believers has extended over some twenty years and has left me with many debts. Initial interest and research on this topic was done under the supervision of Professors Bill Heth (1996–98) and Clint Arnold (2001–03). I owe them a deep debt for raising critical questions and providing early encouragement. Arriving at Wheaton, I found an ideal research environment, surpassing my high expectations for doctoral studies. I can only partially acknowledge my gratitude here. While working on Part One, I was especially helped by feedback from Rev. Dr. Matthew Patton, Professor Jon Laansma, Dr. Stephanie Lowery, Dr. Carmen Imes, Professor Mike Kibbe, Professor Ben Ribbens, Professor Richard Schultz, Professor Gregory Thellman, Rev. Dr. Jeremy Treat, Rev. Dr. Dan Brendsel, Professor Grant Osborne, and Professor Daniel Owens.

On Part Two, I was especially helped by feedback from Dr. Jordan Barrett, Professor Michael Goheen, Professor Kevin Hector, Professor Amy Hughes, Dr. Robbie Crouse, Professor John Thompson, and Professor Ashish Varma. Thanks to David Orr, OSB for providing a copy of his dissertation; to Rev. Nathan Essela for help on the history of Bible translation; to Professors John Flett and Jeppe Nikolajsen for making their dissertations available prior to publication; to Professor Malcolm Yarnell for providing a copy of his ThM thesis and for allowing me to read a pre-publication copy of his Oxford monograph. Thanks to Professor Uche Anizor for providing access to his prepublication manuscript and unpublished research on Luther's priesthood of all believers. Finally, thanks to Professor Darrell Guder for providing a copy of his unpublished translation of Barth's "Die Theologie und die Mission in der Gegenwart."

In Part Three, I remain indebted for feedback provided by Professor James Gordon, Professor Jon Hoglund, Professor Isaac Voss, Professor Kevin Vanhoozer, and Rev. Ryan Carter. Timely aid came from various Wheaton professors, including Keith Johnson, David Lauber, Gene Green, Clint Schaffer, John Walton, and Chris Vlachos.

A special place must be reserved for the doctoral committee who strengthened this final product through a careful reading and constructive critique of the original manuscript: Daniel Block, Jeff Greenman, Darrell Guder, and Daniel Treier. Professor Block was my first instructor at Wheaton, and he has always provided wise counsel. Professor Greenman is now President of Regent College. He has given generously of his time both before and after my student days at Wheaton. Professor Guder offered wise feedback at my defense and encouraged me to publish this work. Professor Treier's example as a mentor, writer, and teacher surpassed my expectations. He has raised my personal standard for excellence in the classroom, and I cannot imagine a more helpful *Doktorvater* or a more generous friend. His feedback was always careful, concise, and timely. While the work's faults remain my own, it has been purged of countless more through Professor Treier's gentle questions and patient conversations. His care and concern have continued long after graduation, and I especially appreciate his willingness to write the preface for this book.

While Wheaton provided a hospitable space for the vast majority of this book's research and writing, it would never have seen the light of day without the support of Wipf and Stock's editors. Special thanks to my editor, Chris Spinks, for quick and helpful responses to various inquiries.

Finally, I have received extraordinary support from my wife and children. Thanks to Samuel, David, Renee, and Isaiah for all your encouragement, cards, and prayers. Thank you especially to my best friend, Johanna.

You carried far more than your share during our Wheaton years—even while completing a graduate degree of your own. Your love, support, prayer, and patient friendship are God's great gift to me—a taste of Eden's delight. My respect and gratitude for you continues to deepen, and I dedicate this book to you as the one who more than any other has helped me learn how to live as a member of Christ's royal priesthood. Writing this book has taught me much about divine grace; I pray those reading it will experience the Triune God's grace more deeply as they participate in the royal priesthood's Worship, Work, and Witness.

Abbreviations

AB	Anchor Bible
ABD	Anchor Bible Dictionary
AF^3	*The Apostolic Fathers: Greek Texts and English Translations*, edited by Michael Holmes. 3rd ed. Grand Rapids: Baker Academic, 2007
ACW	*Ancient Christian Writers*
ALD	*Aramaic Levi Document.* Edited by Jonas Greenfield, Michael Stone, and Esther Eshel. Boston, 2004
ANF	*Ante-Nicene Fathers.* Electronic ed. Edited by Alexander Roberts and James Donaldson. Buffalo, 1885–1896. 10 vols. Repr. Peabody, 1994
ATR	*Anglican Theological Review*
BBR	*Bulletin for Biblical Research*
BC-T	*The Book of Concord.* Edited by Robert Kolb and Timothy J. Wengert. Minneapolis, 2000.
BECNT	Baker Exegetical Commentary on the New Testament
BGBE	Beiträge zur Geschichte Der Biblischen Exegese
BHS	*Biblia Hebraica Stuttgartensia.* Edited by Karl Elliger and Wilhelm Rudolph. Stuttgart: Württembergische Bibelanstalt, 1983
BSac	*Bibliotheca Sacra*
BTB	*Biblical Theology Bulletin*
BZNW	Beihefte zur Zeitschrift für die neutestamentliche Wissenschaft
CBH	Comentario Biblico Hispanoamericano

CBQ	*Catholic Biblical Quarterly*
CC	*Calvin's Commentaries*. 44 vols. Edinburgh: Calvin Translation Society, 1844–1856. Reprinted in 22 vols. Grand Rapids: Baker, 1981.
CCEL	Christian Classics Ethereal Library
CD	Karl Barth, *Church Dogmatics*. Edited by G. W. Bromiley and T. F. Torrance. 4 vols. In 13 parts. Edinburgh: T&T Clark, 1956–75. Reprint Peabody: Hendrickson, 2010
CL	Karl Barth, *Christian Life*. Translated by Geoffrey Bromiley. Grand Rapids, 1981
CNTC	*Calvin's New Testament Commentaries*. Edited by David W. Torrance and Thomas F. Torrance (various translators). 12 vols. Grand Rapids: Eerdmans, 1959–1972
CSCO	Corpus scriptorum Christianorum Orientalium
CTR	*Criswell Theological Review*
d.	died
DEC	*Decrees of the Ecumenical Councils*. Edited by Norman Tanner. 2 vols. Washington DC
Diss.	Dissertation
DI	Deutero-Isaiah
ECNT	Exegetical Commentaries on the New Testament
EKKNT	Evangelisch-katholischer Kommentar zum Neuen Testament
ERT	*Evangelical Review of Theology*
EstBib	*Estudios bíblicos*
ET	English Translation
FC	Fathers of the Church
FKD	Forschungen zur Kirchen- und Dogmengeschichte
GDT	*Global Dictionary of Theology*. Edited by William Dryness et. al. Downers Grove, 2008
IBMR	*International Bulletin of Mission Research*
ICC	International Critical Commentary

IJST	*International Journal of Systematic Theology*
IMC	International Missionary Council
Int	*Interpretation*
ITC	International Theological Commentary
ITG	*Irish Theological Quarterly*
JBL	*Journal of Biblical Literature*
JBTM	*Journal for Baptist Theology and Ministry*
JCBRF	*Journal of the Christian Brethren Research Fellowship*
JETS	*Journal of the Evangelical Theological Society*
JR	*Journal of Religion*
JSHJ	*Journal for the Study of the Historical Jesus*
JSJ	*Journal for the Study of Judaism in the Persian, Hellenistic, and Roman Periods*
JSNT	*Journal for the Study of the New Testament*
JSNTSup	Journal for the Study of the New Testament: Supplement Series
JSOT	*Journal for the Study of the Old Testament*
JSOTSup	Journal for the Study of the Old Testament: Supplement Series
KKVC	Kirche und Konfession: Veröffentlichungen des Konfessionskundlichen
KD	*Die Kirchliche Dogmatics*. 4 vols. In 13 parts. Munich: Kaiser, 1932 and Zürich: TVZ, 1938–65
LCL	Loeb Classical Library
LHBOTS	Library of Hebrew Bible / Old Testament Studies
LNTS	Library of New Testament studies
LW	*Luther's Works*. Edited by Jaroslav Pelikan and Helmut T. Lehmann. 56 vols. St. Louis: Concordia; Philadelphia: Fortress, 1955–1986
LXX	Septuagint.

LXXR	*Septuaginta.* Electronic ed. Edited by Alfred Rahlfs. Stuttgart: Württembergische Bibelanstalt, 1979
MCN	*Making Christ Known: Historic Mission Documents from the Lausanne Movement, 1974-1989.* Grand Rapids: Eerdmans, 1997
MR	*Modern Reformation*
MT	Masoretic Text
NA27	*Novum Testamentum Graece.* Electronic ed. Edited by Barbara Aland et al. 27th rev. ed. Stuttgart: Stuttgart: Württembergische Bibelanstalt, 2001
NAC	New American Commentary
NCCR	*National Christian Council Review*
NICNT	New International Commentary on the New Testament
NICOT	New International Commentary on the Old Testament
NIDNTT	New International Dictionary of New Testament Theology. Edited by C. Brown. 4 vols. Grand Rapids, 1975–1985
NIDOTTE	New International Dictionary of Old Testament Theology and Ethics
NIGTC	New International Greek Testament Commentary
NovT	*Novum Testamentum*
NovTSup	Novum Testamentum Supplements
NPNF[1]	*Nicene and Post-Nicene Fathers*, Series 1. Electronic ed. Edited by Philip Schaff. New York, 1886–1889. Reprint, Peabody, MA, 1994
NPNF[2]	*Nicene and Post-Nicene Fathers*, Series 2. Electronic ed. Edited by Philip Schaff and Henry Wace. New York, 1890. Reprint, Peabody, MA, 1994
NSBT	New Studies in Biblical Theology
NSBT	New Studies in Biblical Theology. Edited by D. A. Carson. Downers Grove: InterVarsity
NTS	*New Testament Studies*
OChT	Outstanding Christian Thinkers

OECT	Oxford Early Christian Texts
OHECS	*The Oxford Handbook of Early Christian Studies*. Edited by Susan Harvey and David Hunter. New York, 2008
OTL	Old Testament Library
PBYM	Paternoster Biblical and Theological Monographs
PG	Patrologia Graeca [= Patrologiae cursus completes: Series graeca]. Electronic ed. Edited by J.-P. Migne. 162 vols. Paris, 1857–1866
PI	Proto-Isaiah
PL	*Patrologia latina*. Electronic ed. [=Patrologiae cursus completes: Series latina] Edited by J.-P. Migne. 217 vols. Paris, 1844–64
PMS	Patristic Monograph Series
PNTC	Pillar New Testament Commentaries
PP	Popular Patristics
PRSt	*Perspectives in Religious Studies*
PTM	Princeton Theological Monographs
RevExp	*Review and Expositor*
SBLSP	*Society of Biblical Literature Seminar Papers*
SC	*Sources chrétiennes*. Paris: Cerf, 1943–
SCH	Studies in Church History
SCSS	Septuagint and Cognate Studies Series
SBJT	*Southern Baptist Journal of Theology*
SJT	*Scottish Journal of Theology*
SNTPV	*The Syriac New Testament Translated into English from the Peshitto Version*. 1893 ed. Gorgias Reprint Series 18. Piscataway, NJ: Reprint, Gorgias Press, 2001
SST	Studies in Sacred Theology
ST	Thomas Aquinas, *Summa Theologiae*. 61 vols. New York: McGraw-Hill, 1964–1981.

STh	Wolfhart, Pannenberg, *Systematic Theology*. Translated by Geoffrey W. Bromiley. 3 Vols. Grand Rapids: Eerdmans, 1991
STDJ	Studies on the Texts of the Desert of Judah
SwJT	*Southwestern Journal of Theology*
TDOT	*Theological Dictionary of the Old Testament*. Edited by G. J. Botterweck, H. Ringgren, and Heinz-Josef Fabry. Translated by J. T. Willis, G. W. Bromiley, D. E. Green, and D. W. Stott. 15 vols. Grand Rapids: Eerdmans, 1974–2006
TDNT	*Theological Dictionary of the New Testament*. Electronic ed. Edited by G. Kittel and G. Friedrich. Translated by G. W. Bromiley. 10 vols. Grand Rapids: Eerdmans, 1964–1976
Tg(s).	Targum(s)
THNTC	The Two Horizons New Testament Commentary
ThTo	*Theology Today*
TI	Trito-Isaiah
TJP	*Targum Jonathan to the Prophets: The Jewish Literary Aramaic Version of the Prophets from the Files of the Comprehensive Aramaic Lexicon Project*. Edited by Stephen Kaufman, CD-ROM. Cincinnati, OH: Hebrew Union College, 2005
TNTC	Tyndale New Testament Commentary
TS	*Theological Studies*
TT	*Tracts and Treatises on the Doctrine and Worship of the Church*. Translated by Henry Beveridge. Grand Rapids, 1958
TynBul	*Tyndale Bulletin*
TZ	*Theologische Zeitschrift*
VT	*Vetus Testamentum*
WA	*D. Martin Luthers Werke: Kritische Gesamtausgabe*. 97 vols. In 112 parts. Weimar: Böhlau, 1883–1985
WBC	Word Biblical Commentary
WCL	*Wyclif's Latin Works*. Edited by Johann Loserth, 23 vols. London, 1883–1922. Reprint New York: Johnson, 1966
WSA	*Works of Saint Augustine*. Edited by John E. Rotelle and Boniface Ramsey, Hyde Park, NY: New City, 1990–

WTJ	*Westminster Theological Journal*
WMANT	Wissenschaftliche Monographien zum Alten und Neuen Testament
WUNT	Wissenschaftliche Untersuchungen zum Neuen Testament
WUNT2	Wissenschaftliche Untersuchungen zum Neuen Testament 2.
WW	*Word and World*
ZAW	Zeitschrift für die alttestamentliche Wissenschaft

Introduction

> The Protestant Church is the church of the universal priesthood—or it is nothing.
>
> —Hans Martin Barth[1]

> The priestly people need a ministering priesthood to nourish and sustain it. Men and women are not ordained to this ministerial priesthood in order to take priesthood away from the people but in order to nourish and sustain the priesthood of the people.
>
> —Lesslie Newbigin[2]

THE PRIESTHOOD OF ALL believers is foundational for Protestant ecclesiologies. I grew up in a church that embodied this belief. It had been planted by Peninsula Bible Church, which at the time was pastored by Ray Stedman—a strong advocate of the idea that every member of Christ's body is called to participate in ministry.[3] Early in my formal theological studies, I learned that my experience with the priesthood of all believers was far more controversial than I had suspected.[4] Later, after graduating from seminary I served on a team which planted *Sembrando una Esperanza*, a Spanish speaking church in South Central Los Angeles. During the first two years of the church's existence, the majority of its members were undocumented

---

1. "Evangelischeleithart Kirche ist Kirche des allgemeinen Priestertums—oder sie ist nicht" (Barth, *Einander Priester sein*, 103).
2. Newbigin, *Gospel in a Pluralistic Society*, 235.
3. Stedman, *Body Life*.
4. For a critique of Stedman see Dever, "Priesthood of All Believers," 85–116.

immigrants from Mexico, El Salvador, and Guatemala. In many ways their lives were similar to a group of Israelite slaves who first heard the words "you shall be to me a kingdom of priests" (Exod 19:6). It was while serving with *Sembrando una Esperanza* that I became especially impressed with the importance of a royal and priestly identity for the people of God. It was also in that context that a number of ideas related to the *missio Dei*, or the missionary nature of God, became important to me.

Lesslie Newbigin's statement from the 1952 IMC conference at Willingen, Germany, is illustrative of these missionary ideas. At the conference he wrote, "there is no participation in Christ without participation in His mission to the world" (John 20:21).[5] Newbigin elsewhere related this missionary emphasis to the priesthood of all believers. He focuses on the royal priesthood's witness in the world.[6] This book follows Newbigin's lead and aims to provide a Protestant definition of the priesthood of all believers in light of the *missio Dei*. It secondarily seeks to establish the doctrine as a foundational component of Protestant ecclesiology.

At the outset, it is important to acknowledge that evangelical Protestant ecclesiologies are in poor health. Brad Harper and Paul Metzger lament that the National Association of Evangelicals' statement of faith fails to mention the church.[7] Their concern is not new, but it is symptomatic of a significant problem even at a more theoretical level.[8] The doctrinal foundations of Protestant ecclesiology need a fresh examination, and the doctrine of the priesthood of all believers provides crucial resources for a Protestant *ressourcement*.[9] This book addresses the current ecclesial confusion through an investigation of the doctrine of the priesthood of all believers.

The book makes a contribution to contemporary conversations on ecclesiology generally and specifically to the North American missional church conversation by providing a robust definition of the Protestant doctrine of the priesthood of all believers. The doctrine can be defined as the believer's sharing in the Son's royal priesthood through faith and baptism,

---

5. Goodall, *Missions Under the Cross*, 190.

6. Newbigin, *Gospel in a Pluralistic Society*, 229.

7. Harper and Metzger, *Exploring Ecclesiology*, 15.

8. Stackhouse, *Evangelical Ecclesiology*; Husbands and Treier, *Community of the Word*.

9. Both Roman Catholic and Orthodox monographs on the church have included chapter-length treatments of the priesthood of all believers. Surprisingly, no recent Protestant monographs on ecclesiology have given the doctrine significant discussion. Many do not even mention the doctrine. See Küng, *Church*, 363–87; Afanasiev, *Church of the Holy Spirit*, 1–79. Saucy is a Protestant exception (*Church in God's Program*, 38–44).

and thus in the *missio Dei* through "Worship," "Work," and "Witness."[10] This reframing of the doctrine will rest upon biblical, historical, and dogmatic claims. The remainder of the Introduction defines important terms, describes the book's method, and provides a brief overview.

Defining Terms

This section first identifies four conceptual terms referring to a single ontological reality: the priesthood of all believers.[11] It then identifies four other terms closely related to the royal priesthood in some way. Finally, it explains how this book uses terms related to the *missio Dei*.

Four Conceptual Terms for One Theological Judgment

In a seminal article David Yeago argues that it is essential "to distinguish between *judgments* and the *conceptual terms* in which those judgments are rendered."[12] His counsel needs to be heeded when articulating a contemporary doctrine of the priesthood of all believers. In English alone, there are over twenty conceptual terms used to describe the New Testament (NT) doctrine of the royal priesthood. Often these terms do not refer to the same theological judgments because they are part of different ecclesial conversations.[13] If this level of misunderstanding is taking place in English, one can imagine the magnitude of miscommunication possible when the doctrine is considered in its catholic context (i.e., across centuries and cultures). There are four primary conceptual terms used for the doctrine of the royal priesthood: 1) the royal priesthood (biblical); 2) priesthood of the baptized (traditional Orthodox); 3) priesthood of the faithful (traditional Roman Catholic); and 4) priesthood of all believers (traditional Protestant). This book will primarily use royal priesthood and priesthood of all believers, but each of the four terms is helpful.

---

10. These are technical terms when capitalized in this book. In short, they respectively refer to those activities of the royal priesthood especially directed toward God, other believers, and the world. See note sixty below for further discussion.

11. "Ontology and ecclesiology are quite inseparable, at least for the N. T. writers" (Minear, "Ontology and Ecclesiology," 91).

12. Yeago, "New Testament," 93, emphasis original.

13. Ibid., 94–95.

Royal Priesthood

The conceptual term which best captures the biblical language is "royal priesthood."[14] Ernest Best proposes "general priesthood" as the preferable term.[15] He rejects "priesthood of the church" as overemphasizing the corporate nature of the doctrine, and "priesthood of believers" as overemphasizing its individualistic nature. Best is correct to be concerned about overemphasis on corporate or individualistic aspects. But "general priesthood" is inferior to the biblical "royal priesthood" on two counts. First, it obscures theological content toward which the biblical language points. The ecclesial "royal priesthood" is directly related to the Christological "Priest-king." The NT language is preferable because it irrevocably links the priesthood of believers with the royal priesthood of Christ (Psalm 110). Secondly, "general priesthood" is too easily confused with "natural priesthood," a term related to but distinct from the NT's royal priesthood. Thus "royal priesthood" best captures the canonical concept.

Priesthood of the Baptized

Tertullian (d. 220) is the first early church writer to explicitly link baptism with "ordination" to the royal priesthood.[16] The first extant baptismal rite, Rome's *Apostolic Tradition* (ca. 215–250), also describes baptism as an ordination.[17] Nicolas Afanasiev reports that "the Orthodox baptismal rite

---

14. See βασίλειον ἱεράτευμα, "royal priesthood" (Exod 19:6 LXX; 1 Pet 2:9); ἱεράτευμα ἅγιον, "holy priesthood" (1 Pet 2:5); βασιλείαν, ἱερεῖς τῷ θεῷ καὶ πατρὶ αὐτοῦ, "a kingdom and priests to his God and Father" (Rev 1:6); τῷ θεῷ ἡμῶν βασιλείαν καὶ ἱερεῖς, καὶ βασιλεύσουσιν ἐπὶ τῆς γῆς, "a kingdom and priests to our God, and they shall reign on the earth" (Rev 5:10); ἀλλ' ἔσονται ἱερεῖς τοῦ θεοῦ καὶ τοῦ Χριστοῦ καὶ βασιλεύσουσιν μετ' αὐτοῦ [τὰ] χίλια ἔτη, "they will be priests of God and of Christ, and they will reign with him" (Rev 20:6). An additional variable relates to First Peter's use of the LXX while the author of Revelation relies upon the MT when each cites Exod 19:6; hence in First Peter we have "priesthood" and in Revelation we have "priests." Cf. Vanhoye, *Old Testament Priests and the New Priest*, 241–64; Elliott, *Elect and the Holy*, 50–120. Unless otherwise noted, ETs of Scripture come from the ESV, NT Greek references from the NA27, LXX references from LXXR, and OT Hebrew references from BHS.

15. Best, "Spiritual Sacrifice," 297.

16. See discussion of Tertullian in Chapter 4. By "ordination" I mean a public commissioning to participation in the royal and priestly ministry of Christ. Baptismal ordination does not negate the necessity of a public commissioning, an "ordination," with laying on of hands, for those called to serve as church officers.

17. *Apostolic Tradition* 21. See Bradshaw et al., *Apostolic Tradition*, 112–35; esp. discussion in Afanasiev, *Church of the Holy Spirit*, 25–26.

preserves to this day the idea of the ordination of the laics."[18] Similarly, Sebastian Brock writes that the connection between baptism and ordination to the royal priesthood is "found uniformly in Latin, Greek and Syriac writers of the early Church."[19] Thus the preferred Orthodox term is the "priesthood of the baptized," and the tradition is clear: "there is no such thing as non-ordained persons in the church."[20] "The "priesthood of the baptized" is also commonly used in the Roman Catholic tradition, and both Luther and Barth emphasized the relationship between baptism and the public ordination of believers to the ministry of the royal priesthood.[21]

Priesthood of the Faithful

The classic Roman Catholic term is the "priesthood of the faithful," closely related to the early church's "spiritual priesthood."[22] Paul Dabin treated 348 theologians in the most comprehensive historical study on the priesthood of the faithful ever completed.[23] Some fifteen years later, Vatican II's *Lumen Gentium* became the first conciliar document to use the phrase "*sacerdotium commune fidelium*."[24] While (common) priesthood of the faithful is usually preferred, it is now normal to find Roman Catholic writers using the traditional Protestant term, the "priesthood of all believers."[25]

Priesthood of All Believers

While Martin Luther did not coin "priesthood of all believers"—the closest he comes is the "general priesthood of all baptized believers"—he is clearly

---

18. Ibid., 25.

19. Brock, "Priesthood of the Baptized," 15.

20. Zizioulas, *Being as Communion*, 215–16.

21. Luther, *LW* 44:127; Barth, *CD* IV/4, 201. For Roman Catholic essays see Wood, *Ordering the Baptismal Priesthood*.

22. Henri De Lubac's discussion of "spiritual priesthood" or "internal priesthood" cites Tertullian, Origen, Ambrose, Augustine, Leo the Great, Isidore, Damion, and Aquinas (*Splendor of the Church*, 134–44); Cf. Oden, *Corrective Love*, 119–21. Closely related to "spiritual priesthood" is Origen's "priesthood of your soul" *HomLev* 4.6.2 (*FC* 83:78).

23. Dabin, *Le Sacerdoce Royal*. Dabin was influential on Congar, De Lubac, and Küng.

24. Orr, "Giving of the Priesthood," 72.

25. For example, Michalski, *Relationship Between the Universal Priesthood*, 12; 24–28; 37.

the most important source for the Protestant understanding.[26] Luther referred to believers as priests hundreds of times using at least eight different terms for the doctrine. Building on Luther's understanding, as well as the larger catholic tradition, the doctrine can be defined as the believer's sharing in the Son's royal priesthood through faith and baptism resulting in participation in the *missio Dei* and spiritual sacrifices of Worship, Work, and Witness.

The NT's doctrine of the royal priesthood can be described by all three terms above: "priesthood of the baptized," "priesthood of the faithful," and "priesthood of all believers." The doctrine, however, is often confused with four related terms reviewed below.

Four Terms Related to the Royal Priesthood

Four terms that are not the focus here often cause conceptual confusion with the doctrine of the royal priesthood: the Melchizedekian Royal Priesthood, the Levitical Priesthood, the Natural Priesthood, and the Ministerial or Ordained Priesthood. They are outlined below to prevent confusion.[27]

Melchizedekian Royal Priesthood

The first time the word priest appears in the canon it describes Melchizedek, the original priest-king of Jerusalem. Melchizedek is next mentioned in Psalm 110, where the Lord swears to David's greater son: "You are a priest forever after the order of Melchizedek." This text, and its wider context in Psalm 110 (LXX 109), was the most important Scripture for the royal priesthood in the first century. Psalm 110, the song of the Priest-king, is cited or alluded to as many as thirty-three times in the NT,[28] often in hymnic material.[29] The importance of psalms, hymns, and spiritual songs for understanding the theology of the early Christian communities has often been neglected, and this also seems to be the case for the NT doctrine of

---

26. *LW* 13:332.

27. A fifth term is the priesthood of the firstborn, or the "primogenitural priesthood" which preceded the Levitical priesthood (e.g., Exod 19:22). Its first example was Adam, but it was ultimately fulfilled in Christ. See Hahn, *Kinship by Covenant*, 136–55.

28. Hay, *Glory at the Right Hand*, 15, 163–66.

29. See for example Gourgues' discussion of Ps 110:1 in Rom 8:34 and Eph 1:20 (*A la droite de Dieu*, 45–57; 63–73).

the royal priesthood.[30] In contrast, Martin Luther gave greater attention to Psalm 110 than any other.[31] Similarly, the apostolic church "not only spoke but often thought in terms of the psalm's wording and imagery."[32] The Psalm also played a central role in how Jesus perceived his mission leading up to his royal and priestly offering on the cross.[33] John Goldingay writes that "the particular distinctive insight of Ps 110 is that the king is also priest," and this insight, more than any other, funds the NT doctrine.[34]

When the early Christians "sang in alternate verses a hymn to Christ as to a god,"[35] Psalm 110 was a favorite as illustrated by its use across the NT's genres.[36] If we become like what we worship, then the liturgical attention given by the first Christians to Jesus as their Priest-king is significant.[37] Douglas Farrow is correct to emphasize the importance of Psalm 110 for understanding early Christian theology: "the Melchizedek typology . . . is the most comprehensive typology available and the only one that does justice to the new thing God has done in Christ."[38] The apostolic understanding can only be grasped in relation to its identification of Jesus as the eschatological Melchizedekian Priest-king. The royal priesthood shares in Christ's royal priesthood as his seed and siblings (Isaiah, Hebrews) not separate from Christ's Melchizedekian priesthood, but sharing in his one office as the eschatological Priest-king of Israel's narrative. This one Melchizedekian priesthood in which believers participate must be distinguished from the Levitical priesthood, the natural priesthood, and the ministerial priesthood.

---

30. Waltke, et al., note that Larry Hurtado's study of early worship of Jesus (*Lord Jesus Christ: Devotion to Jesus in Earliest Christianity*, is "exhaustive, except for the surprising lacuna of any reference to their hymnic and liturgical character" (*Psalms as Christian Worship*, 486).

31. *LW* 13:225–348.

32. Hay, *Glory at the Right Hand*, 160.

33. See discussion of Matt 22:41–46; 26:64 in Chapter 3. Psalm 110 is the twin of Psalm 2, and the two psalms are closely linked by Hebrews (1:1–4; 5:5–6). This makes the use of Psalm 2 at Jesus' baptism theologically relevant for the Royal Priesthood. See Fletcher-Louis, "Jesus as the High Priestly Messiah: Part 1," 173–75.

34. Goldingay, *Psalms: 90–150*, 299.

35. Pliny's description is ca. 105–110 A.D. Pliny, *Letters*, 2:403. Radice translates *carmenque* as "to chant." Pliny, *Letters, and Panegyricus*, 2:288–89.

36. Hay, *Glory at the Right Hand*, 163–66.

37. See discussion of Isaiah 6 in Beale, *We Become What We Worship*.

38. Farrow, "Melchizedek and Modernity," 287.

Levitical Priesthood

Hebrews describes the Levitical priesthood as completed in Christ's Melchizedekian royal priesthood.[39] Insight into Christ's royal priesthood can be gained typologically by study of the Levitical priesthood. Similarly, the Levitical priesthood can be typologically related to the royal priesthood through believers' participation in Christ. Paul may be the oldest extant witness to the new royal and priestly privilege of believers. He applies formerly exclusive Levitical privileges to every member of Corinth's Christian community, and elsewhere he applies those same Levitical privileges to himself, even though he is a Benjaminite.[40]

A minority within the catholic tradition followed Paul's lead, while a larger group reduced Paul's typological reading to a higher and holier caste within the Christian community having elite priestly privileges. The minority tradition is represented by Tertullian, Origen, and Luther. Tertullian argued that if all believers are priests, then all believers are called to priestly discipline as reflected in the high standards for Levitical priests.[41] Origen argued similarly; his *Homilies on Leviticus* provide dozens of examples of how Levitical priestly privileges and responsibilities can be applied to the whole people of God. In his preface to the Pentateuch, Luther counseled readers to think about Christ when they read about the High Priest, but about themselves when they read about the High Priest's sons—all of Luther's readers were sharers in Christ's royal priesthood.[42] More recently, this way of reading is best illustrated by Paul Dabin and Scott Hahn.[43] In the church of the apostles and apologists, Levitical typology was often used to emphasize the priestly nature of the whole eschatological body of Christ, but as the centuries wore on a reductionist typology emerged limiting Levitical imagery to clergy. Chapter Four will document this decline narrative with special attention to Clement of Rome, Origen, Tertullian, Cyprian, Constantine, Eusebius, Augustine, and Pseudo-Dionysius.

---

39. Hahn, *Kinship by Covenant*, 175.

40. See his use of Isa 52:11 in 2 Cor 6:17 and his use of Levitical terms for his own ministry (Rom 15:16).

41. "Exhortation to Chastity," (*ANF* 4:54 [*CCEL* 4:126–27]).

42. *LW* 35:247.

43. Dabin, *El Sacerdocio Real*, 141–46; Hahn, *Kinship by Covenant*, 136–75; 278–331.

Natural Priesthood, Priests to Creation, and Soul Competency

In his prelapsarian state, Adam was given responsibility to serve as a royal priest for all creation. This royal and priestly responsibility has been labeled "natural priesthood."[44] Timothy George makes a similar judgment when he speaks of a "priesthood of all human beings."[45] He describes this as "soul competency," a term coined by Baptist theologian E. Y. Mullins.[46] George's primary aim is to distinguish such soul competency from the priesthood of all believers. His theological instincts are correct; the natural priesthood must be distinguished from the royal priesthood of Christ in which believers participate, yet two dimensions of the natural priesthood should be recognized.

First, the natural priesthood is rooted in theological anthropology, suggesting that responsibility for ecological stewardship is a shared human task. All humans bear God's image, and as such represent God to creation. In this sense, all humans are "priests of creation."[47] If this is true for the natural priesthood, then it is doubly true for the members of the royal priesthood who through faith and baptism have been united with the royal and priestly ministry of Christ.[48] Second, the concept of natural priesthood, especially as developed by "soul competency," means that every human will ultimately give account for his or her actions to God. The natural priesthood's eschatological *telos* is unmediated interaction with the triune God at the Parousia.

Ministerial or Ordained Priesthood.

The fourth term closely related to the royal priesthood of believers is the "ministerial priesthood." This term is primarily used within Roman Catholic and Orthodox communions to refer to those members of the royal priesthood who have been commissioned to the office of *episkopos* or *presbyteros*. The story of the rise of the ministerial priesthood cannot be told here, but

---

44. Congar, *Lay People in the Church*, 121; Bordeianu, "Priesthood Natural," 405–33. Congar's understanding of the natural priesthood overlaps with the primogenitural priesthood identified above.

45. George does not equate soul competency with the category of "natural priesthood" as used in Orthodox and Roman Catholic sources. As far as I am aware, this book is the first to connect these two concepts (George, "Priesthood of All Believers," 86).

46. Mullins, *Axioms of Religion*, 15, 25–26; 69–76; 79–80; 93–115.

47. Bordeianu, "Priesthood Natural," 407–11.

48. Ibid., 412.

a few early turning points are discussed in Chapter 4.[49] Suffice it to say that the decision to refer to the ordained leaders of the church as "priests" has not been without difficulties. Largely because of these difficulties, the only other major Christian community which uses cultic terminology for its ordained leaders is the Anglican communion.[50]

Most Protestant churches have chosen to follow the apostolic practice of reserving priestly language for Christ, and through him to all believers equally. They are all a high priestly race. Since the NT does not use cultic language to distinguish within the one priestly body of Christ, Protestants have been hesitant to use terms such as "priest" as an exclusive way to refer to the ordained leaders within the one royal and priestly body. They prefer to use biblical terms (*episkopos, presbyteros, diakonos, poimēn*), usually in vernacular translation. Since Paul himself makes analogies between church leaders and the Levitical priesthood, Protestants should not be absolutely opposed to the use of cultic vocabulary for their leaders.[51] Yet history reveals the need for great caution when a Christian communion takes this route; it has often had a negative effect on the royal priesthood. The relationship between the ministerial priesthood and the royal priesthood is not the focus of this study, but some implications for their relationship are summarized in Chapter 8.

Having defined four conceptual terms for the biblical doctrine of the royal priesthood, and four closely related terms, a final selection of terms relating to the *missio Dei* needs clarification.

The missio Dei *and Missional Theology*

The priesthood of all believers is an important assumption of the missional church discussion.[52] Darrell Guder points out that the "first resources" for a missional theology "can be traced in Luther's vision of the priesthood of all believers."[53] But the relationship between missional theology and the priesthood of all believers is a two-way street. Missional theology is more than

---

49. See further Noll, *Christian Ministerial Priesthood*; Bulley, *Priesthood of Some Believers*; Stewart, "'Priests of My People.'"

50. For example the chapter epigraph by Newbigin. See also Webster, "Ministry and Priesthood," 285–96.

51. Rom 15:16; 1 Cor 9:13–14; cf. Rom 1:9.

52. In North America, the missional church conversation has centered in the Gospel and Our Culture Network. It has produced a substantial literature as illustrated by recent Eerdmans' series: The Gospel and our Culture (seven volumes as of 2013) and Missional Church (five volumes as of 2013).

53. Guder, "Church as Missional Community," 122.

just another adjectival theology. Guder notes that "every classical theme in ecclesiology . . . will be drawn into and redefined by the foundational vocation of the church to be Christ's witness."[54] Missional theology is a comprehensive way of reading Scripture and viewing the church and the world. It is a rethinking of all theological topics in light of the *missio Dei*, and can be distinguished from "theology of mission/s" which focuses on explaining or justifying theologically the practice of missions.[55] This book's most exciting contribution is gleaned from its newly proposed interaction with missional theology: the royal priesthood's earthly vocation is witness in the world. Thus it is important to define the terms *"missio Dei," "mission/s,"* "missional," "missionary," and "Christendom."

The missio Dei

The received history of the modern development of the *missio Dei* concept usually begins with a 1932 lecture given by Karl Barth on the relationship between the Trinity and mission.[56] Barth's contribution was then supposedly popularized through the 1952 IMC conference at Willingen.[57] Whatever the actual history, Willingen is significant in that it was the first major ecumenical gathering to dogmatically locate mission in a trinitarian context rather than its traditional locus within ecclesiology or soteriology.[58]

The *missio Dei* is not so much about the Gospel's geographic spread as it is about the nature of Godself. God is a missionary God. Stephen Holmes explains:

> The fundamental difference between asserting that God has a mission and asserting that God is missionary is that in the former case the mission may be incidental, disconnected from who God is; in the latter case, mission is one of the perfections as God, as adequate a description of who he is as love, omnipotence or eternity.[59]

If the royal priesthood worships a missionary God, then it too is called to be missionary. This basic assumption about God must inform the study of the royal priesthood.

---

54. Ibid., 128.
55. See especially the distinctions drawn by Conner, *Practicing Witness*, 11–42.
56. Barth, "Die Theologie," 189–215.
57. Cf. Flett, *Witness of God*, 24.
58. Bosch, *Transforming Mission*, 389–93.
59. Holmes, "Trinitarian Missiology," 89.

Mission/s, Missionary, and Missional

If the royal priesthood is called to participate with God in God's own mission, how should this mission be understood? In general we can understand the *mission* of the royal priesthood as offering spiritual sacrifices through the Son, in the Spirit, to the Father. These spiritual sacrifices especially consist of Worship (*latreia*), Work (*diakonia*), and Witness (*martyria*).[60] Within Christendom, the word *missionary* has often been closely tied to colonial projects. In some contexts, the post-colonial critique has resulted in calls for a moratorium on all "missionary" efforts. As a result of these negative connotations, many theologians have begun to use "mission partners" rather than missionary. The word *missional* has also exploded in popularity since the publication of a seminal book in 1998.[61]

Missional is used to emphasize the theological truths pointed to by the *missio Dei*. Since God is missionary or missional, all who worship him are also called to be missionary or missional. As a member of a missionary community, I am not advocating that we jettison the word "missionary."[62] I do, however, welcome the arrival of the adjective missional to the theological conversation, as it calls attention to the fact that Christendom theologies have tended to ignore mission.[63] The implications of the missional nature

---

60. "Spiritual sacrifices" are best understood as the entire lives of the royal priesthood's members—every thought, word, and action, when these are directed to the glory of the Father through the Son by the Spirit. In this book these thoughts, words, and actions are understood as the ministry of the royal priesthood. This ministry possesses three directions: a ministry of Worship toward the triune God, a ministry of Work (upbuilding) toward other members of the royal priesthood, and a ministry of Witness toward the world. Understanding ministry as thought, word, and actions is consistent with both Augustine and Luther's understanding of spiritual sacrifices. See Augustine's well-known discussion of spiritual sacrifices in *City of God* 10.6 (FC 14:125) and *The Trinity* 4.14 (FC 45:155). For a summary and synopsis of Luther's understanding see Pelikan, "Once for All the Sacrifice of Himself (Heb 9:26)," 238–54. The royal priesthood's practice of offering spiritual sacrifices provides the content of Chapter Eight.

61. Guder, *Missional Church*, 11–12; Guder, "Church as Missional Community," 114–17; Wright, *Mission of God*, 22–25; Goheen, *A Light to the Nations*, 3–6; Conner, *Practicing Witness*, 11–42.

62. My rationale is similar to Newbigin's concern for retaining the plural "missions" in addition to the singular "mission." According to Newbigin, mission is "the entire task for which the church is sent into the world" (*Gospel in a Pluralist Society*, 121). Missions is a particular dimension of the church's mission in which the aim is to make Christ known where he is not known. The distinction between mission and missions builds upon the distinction between "missionary dimension" and "missionary intention." All of the church's activities have a missionary dimension, but not all have a missionary intention. See Newbigin, *One Body*; Goheen, *Lesslie Newbigin's Missionary Ecclesiology*, 275–76.

63. Flett, *Witness of God*, 31.

and vocation of the royal priesthood will be especially explored in the book's final chapters.

Christendom

David Bosch understands Christendom historically as the "symbiotic relationship between church and state" that began in the West at the time of Constantine.[64] Since every society will be informed by some cultural framework and religious beliefs, it seems reasonable for Christians to work and pray for some type of Christendom project as they await the Parousia, at which time all political theologies will simply bow their knee before Christ the King.[65] Historically, however, Christendom has been most problematic when it has married Christianization and colonization or used political power to force citizens to bow their knee against their conscience to a particular understanding of Christ or doctrine.[66]

Christendom's use of compulsion to force issues of conscience began soon after Constantine's conversion, and has been problematic for western Christians ever since. This study makes use of the Christendom paradigm as a tool to reflect upon the development of the doctrine of the royal priesthood—especially its missional dimension. One result of Part Two's historical analysis is the recognition that societies where all citizens were compelled by force to follow the doctrinal commitments of the political ruler of the land (*cuius regio, eius religio*) almost always have anemic versions of the doctrine of the royal priesthood. Baptism on pain of death loses its ordination powers.

The Big Picture

During my doctoral studies I had the privilege of working with Professor Kevin Vanhoozer for a three year period while we were both at Wheaton College. Scattered across Vanhoozer's numerous books and essays are a number of significant references to the priesthood of all believers. In one programmatic essay, Vanhoozer describes the nature of Protestant theology

64. Bosch, *Transforming Mission*, 274. Cf. Nichols, *Christendom Awake*, 1.

65. I share Newbigin's ambivalent attitude toward the West's historical forms of Christendom (Goheen, *Lesslie Newbigin's Missionary Ecclesiology*, 192–97). The many benefits must be weighed against a number of significant flaws.

66. Cf. Kreider's wider definition: "Christendom is a civilization in which (a) Christianity is the dominant religion and in which (b) this dominance has been backed up by social and legal compulsions" (*Origins of Christendom*, viii) has led some to define the concept more narrowly; e.g., O'Donovan, *Desire of the Nations*, 195.

as involving two distinctive commitments, *sola scriptura* and the priesthood of all believers.⁶⁷ The priesthood of all believers is thus a foundational assumption of Vanhoozer's larger project. Vanhoozer is aware of unsatisfactory versions of the doctrine (see especially his discussion of the novel *Wieland*), but in general he sees it as an essential element of his canonical-linguistic approach.⁶⁸ As far as I am aware, no one has yet challenged Vanhoozer's version of the priesthood of all believers, yet Vanhoozer has often been taken to task for failing to provide specific examples of how his canonical-linguistic approach works in practice.⁶⁹ One way to view this book, then, is as an attempt to put Vanhoozer's methodology into practice by focusing on a particular doctrine of foundational importance.

At the risk of oversimplification, we can summarize Vanhoozer's theological program under three slogans: attend to canon sense, appraise with catholic sensibility, and advance with contextual sensitivity.⁷⁰ By *canon sense* we refer to Vanhoozer's concern that Protestants take Scripture's ontology seriously.⁷¹ Scripture is thus the royal priesthood's script, and it must be carefully attended to as a whole in light of the one text's divine author. By *catholic sensibility* we refer to the royal priesthood's need to recognize "that it takes many interpretive communities spanning many times, places and cultures in order fully to appreciate the rich, thick meaning of Scripture."⁷² In order to develop a catholic understanding it is imperative to listen carefully to how the doctrine has been understood across centuries and across cultures. Especially important is appraising the church's performance of the doctrine in light of masterpiece performances found in the Great Tradition and regional performances found in various confessions and denominations.⁷³ Finally, *contextual sensitivity* refers to the performative nature of theology. All theology is to be lived wisely in particular times and places as the people of God advance into the world.⁷⁴ With this last emphasis,

---

67. Vanhoozer, "Voice and the Actor," 85–86. Cf. McGrath, *Christianity's Dangerous Idea*.

68. Vanhoozer, *Drama of Doctrine*, 122–24; Vanhoozer, *First Theology*, 331.

69. Meadors, *Four Views*, 204, 209, 213, 285–86.

70. Vanhoozer, "Theological Method," *GDT,* 896; Vanhoozer, "Drama-of-Redemption Model," 198.

71. This means attending to both human and divine *authorship* as well as the unique nature of the canonical *text* as both one book and many. See Vanhoozer, *Is There a Meaning in This Text?*.

72. Vanhoozer, "Theological Method," 896.

73. Vanhoozer, *Drama of Doctrine*, 445–57.

74. Ibid., 399–444.

Vanhoozer is helping especially evangelical Protestants make the "cultural turn," a turn to ecclesial practices.

Another way of understanding three levels of tradition also shapes the study's priorities. Don Davis' prolific theological output, primarily written in service to the urban poor, is based upon a tripartite prioritization: the Authoritative Tradition (Canon), the Great Tradition (Creeds and Councils through AD 450), and specific church traditions (esp. founders of denominations and orders).[75] Davis is an advocate of retrieval theology, a way of "going forward by looking back."[76] Thus, three methodological concerns are reflected in the three parts of the book. Part One, "The Royal Priesthood in Scripture's Script," describes the canon sense of the doctrine. Part Two, "From Actors to Audience and Back Again: The Royal Priesthood across the Centuries," appraises the doctrine's performance in various theatres across the centuries. Finally, Part Three, "The Royal Priesthood in Today's World," proposes a canonically normed and catholically informed contextual performance of the doctrine, consisting of seven ecclesial practices.

Part One: The Royal Priesthood in Scripture's Script

A canonical understanding requires a robust biblical theology of the royal priesthood.[77] The most comprehensive one produced to date is Paul Dabin's nearly five-hundred-page tome.[78] In the seventy years since its publication, no other work has rivaled its scope.[79] Still, other monographs have updated portions of its larger biblical theology. John Elliott's 1966 monograph on 1 Peter 2:4–9 has been the most influential, and his conclusions have often been uncritically accepted.[80] The most important treatment of the royal priesthood in Revelation and in the third part of Isaiah was published by Elizabeth Schüssler Fiorenza (1972).[81] This was followed by John Scholer's

---

75. Davis, *Sacred Roots*, 35–47.

76. Ibid., 27.

77. The biblical theology in Part One is done with a missional aim and framework. See Hunsberger, "Proposals for a Missional Hermeneutic: Mapping a Conversation," 310–14.

78. The work was first published in a two-volume Spanish translation, followed by the one-volume French edition. See Dabin, *El Sacerdocio Real*.

79. See bibliographies in Chrupcała (*Kingdom of God*, 479–88); and monographs listed below.

80. Elliott, *Elect and the Holy*.

81. Schüssler Fiorenza, *Priester für Gott*, 1972.

important 1991 monograph on the royal priesthood in Hebrews.[82] Jo Bailey Wells' monograph (2000) was the first of the studies surveyed here to give serious consideration to the royal priesthood in Ezekiel and Genesis.[83]

More recently (2004), Philip Davies produced the most extensive study to date on Exodus 19:6.[84] He also considers intertextual parallels in the OT, and is the first in modern times to give significant attention to Numbers, Hosea, and Zechariah. That same year, G. K. Beale published his biblical theology of *The Temple and the Church's Mission*.[85] Beale's work highlights Adam as a royal priest and thus roots the biblical theology of the royal priesthood in the protology of Genesis 1 and 2. Beale's claims find support in two other recent studies. Martha Himmelfarb (2006) examines Exodus 19:6 in light of second temple literature and finds "that the idea it expresses and the tensions it hints at are of central importance to Jews during that period."[86] Especially Himmelfarb's reading of *Jubilees* endorses the conclusions about protological priesthood for which Beale argues. Scott Hahn (2009) provides an important discussion of primogeniture and priesthood—thereby offering additional insight into Beale's claims for a patriarchal priesthood. Hahn also develops the relationship of the Levitical priesthood to the royal priesthood through careful readings of Exodus, Ezekiel, Jeremiah, and Hebrews.[87]

In the 1950s and 1960s Thomas Torrance, Cyril Eastwood, and Earnest Best each produced important article or chapter-length summaries.[88] More recently, similar summaries have been written by Malcolm Yarnell, Uche Anizor, and N. T. Wright.[89] Wright's is the first in recent history to begin a biblical theology of the royal priesthood with Adam (citing Beale).[90]

---

82. Scholer, *Proleptic Priests*.

83. Wells, *God's Holy People*. Wright builds on Wells and Davies in his *Mission of God*.

84. Davies, *Royal Priesthood*. Since I largely agree with Davies' conclusions, I do not treat Exod 19:6 in depth. This provides space to build on his work and describe the intertestamental development of Exod 19:6 in Isaiah 56—66. The few places where I disagree with Davies on Exod 19:6, usually in agreement with Christopher Wright and Jo Bailey Wells, are noted in the book.

85. Beale, *Temple and the Church's Mission*.

86. Himmelfarb, *Kingdom of Priests*, 1. See also 2 Macc 2:17.

87. Hahn, *Kinship by Covenant*, 136–75; 278–331.

88. Torrance, *Royal Priesthood*; Eastwood, *Royal Priesthood of the Faithful*; Best, "Spiritual Sacrifice."

89. Yarnell, "Priesthood of All Believers," 221–45; Anizor, "Royal Priesthood of Readers," 34–65; Wright, *After You Believe*, 73–100.

90. The Syriac church has recognized Adam as a priest-king since at least the fourth century. See discussion and art in Brock, "Priesthood of the Baptised," 16–18.

In light of the larger systematic aims of this book, Part One examines this literature selectively. A full biblical theology of the royal priesthood needs to be written, but that larger project cannot be done here. Instead, Part One explores three neglected aspects. First, Chapter One examines the two most important New Testament texts in order to demonstrate that the doctrine has clear biblical warrant. Chapter 2 then shows that these two NT texts are not isolated proof texts, but are deeply rooted in Isaianic expectations of a democratization of the priesthood in the eschaton. Chapter 3 builds on the previous chapters to show how Jesus, the Anointed One, is the Priest-king (Psalm 110) who fulfills Isaiah's eschatological expectations, inaugurating the royal priesthood described in Isaiah 54–66. Briefly, each of the chapters does the following.

Chapter One examines two central NT texts upon which the apostolic doctrine of the royal priesthood rests: 1 Pet 2:4–9 and Rom 12:1. From these passages the chapter argues that the royal priesthood is a significant theme in the NT, its scope far greater than the four texts to which it is often limited (1 Pet 2:5–9; Rev 1:6; 5:10; 20:6). It first identifies three major strands of scriptural evidence (temple, sacrifice, and priestly vocabulary) providing warrant for the claim that every member of God's eschatological people has been granted priestly status. Secondly, it identifies the offering of spiritual sacrifices, especially temple-service and proclamation, as the primary functions of the royal priesthood.

Chapter 2 looks back in time to ask how the apostolic theologians interpreted the OT in order to maintain their claim that they were an eschatological royal priesthood. Two OT passages were of primary importance: Psalm 110 and the second half of Isaiah. Psalm 110's description of a son of David who would be both priest and king lies in the conceptual background of the royal and priestly Servant described in Isa 52:13—53:12. The book of Isaiah provided a script of current events for the first Christian theologians, and Jesus was understood as Isaiah's Suffering Servant, the Davidic Priest-king whose climactic self-offering ushered in democratized priestly holiness and privilege. The arrival of Isaiah's royal and priestly Servant (*'ebed Yahweh*) marked the turning point of world history. Isaiah's Servant would suffer, but he would afterward lead a New Exodus and bring a new priesthood with a new covenant. In Isaiah, the result of the Servant's priestly self-offering was the reward of a royal and priestly seed (Isa 53:10), and this royal and priestly Servant-seed—the *'ebedîm*—becomes the main theme of Isaiah 56–66. They fulfill the promise given at Sinai (Exod 19:6), surprisingly including those formerly disqualified from priestly service, namely, women, the maimed, and the alien.

Chapter 3 builds upon earlier chapters to argue that at the heart of the NT doctrine is Jesus, the anointed Melchizedekian priest-king. Matthew's narrative portrayal of both Jesus' life and teaching presents Isaiah's sacral-servant-king whose inheritance includes a servant seed from all nations, a royal priesthood. The chapter examines Jesus' baptism, an event which publicly ordains Jesus to ministry as Isaiah's Servant and David's Son. After his baptism Jesus begins his ministry as Israel's Melchizedekian Priest-king. By serving Jesus, Matthew's disciples share in a new priestly-temple service (Matt 12:1–8); like Jesus they have received a royal-priestly role. For Matthew, Jesus leads his siblings into Edenic access to the Father, a royal-priestly privilege not seen since Yahweh walked with his son, Adam (Genesis 3; cf. Luke 3:38). The second half of Chapter 3 illustrates that Matthew is not alone. In addition to 1 Peter (Chapter 1) and Matthew (Chapter 3), the priestly characteristics of Isaiah's eschatological servant-seed are found in Paul's letters, the Johannine literature, and Hebrews. In sum, Part One finds strong biblical warrant for the priesthood of all believers. The doctrine resonates in its canonical cave.[91]

Part Two: From Actors to Audience and Back Again: The Royal Priesthood across the Centuries

A catholic sensibility recognizes that the rich canonical development of a doctrine is best appreciated through a dialogue with its performances across cultures and centuries. "God has spoken to previous generations through his Word, and we need to hear what God said to them as well as the original readers."[92] The priesthood of all believers is no exception. Each culture has received its own gifts from the Holy Spirit, but also possesses vice. For Luther, the most important text on the royal priesthood was Psalm 110, rarely considered by most contemporary biblical theologies. Appraising Luther's performance of the doctrine helps us become aware of ways our own performance might be challenged and enriched.

Attending to the doctrine in history requires some criteria of selectivity.[93] Hans Küng's adaption of Thomas Kuhn's paradigm theory provides a helpful periodization for theology;[94] a periodization used by David Bosch

---

91. Hays, *Echoes of Scripture*, 21.

92. Vanhoozer, *First Theology*, 202.

93. Cf. Appendix One's "annotated bibliography" of the doctrine's significant figures and events.

94. Küng, "What Does a Change of Paradigm Mean?," 215.

in his most important book *Transforming Mission*.[95] This book modifies Küng's proposal, viewing church history through three paradigms: pre-Christendom, Christendom, and post-Christendom.[96] It makes a contribution by explicitly using the Christendom paradigm for identifying how the doctrine of the royal priesthood has been shaped historically.[97] Attention to Christendom also highlights how the missional dimension has been affected by its cultural context in the West. Broadly speaking, these three paradigms shifts trace how the NT doctrine fared as it entered Christendom (Chapter 4), at the beginning of Protestant Christendom (Chapter 5), and at the beginnings of Christendom's demise (Chapter 6). Other heuristics could be chosen, but the doctrine's shifts are well illustrated by these periods' turning points. During them the church has undergone seismic changes and been especially forced to reflect on its ecclesial identity.[98]

Obviously other periodization schemes could have been chosen, and this study's choice is only one of several possible ways to narrate the doctrine's historical performances. If this portion of the book "inspires others to think about why the [paradigms and] turning points found here are not as important as other possibilities, it will have been successful."[99] Other possible periodization schemes have been proposed by Paul Dabin, Cyril Eastwood, James Leo Garrett, Kenan Osborne, and Malcolm Yarnell. Before summarizing Part Two, it is helpful to review alternative proposals.

The story has been told in greatest detail by Paul Dabin whose research reveals the rich weight of tradition behind the doctrine.[100] His treatment of the western development of the doctrine also identifies three "paradigm shifts": 1) the Patristic Period (175–1157); 2) the Scholastic and Post-scholastic Period (beginning with Peter Lombard, 1160–1757); and 3) a "Contemporary" Period from 1820 until Pope Pius XII (d. 1958). Unfortunately, the conventions of the pre-Vatican II era in which Dabin wrote resulted in his project's exclusion of Luther and all Protestant theologians.

---

95. Bosch, *Transforming Mission*, 181–89.

96. In using the Christendom paradigm, I am following the lead of Kreider ("Beyond Bosch," 59–68).

97. On the vocabulary and perils of "paradigm" language, see Küng, "Paradigm Change in Theology," 3–33.

98. While Torrance does not use a Christendom periodization scheme, he does identify parallel periods (patristic, Reformation, and the present era) as being the most important developmentally for ecclesial identity. He claims that "there was no significant monograph on the church between Cyprian' *De Unitate* and Wycliffe's *De Ecclesia*" ("A New Reformation?," 266).

99. Noll, *Turning Points*, 14.

100. Dabin, *Le Sacerdoce Royal*, 64–65, 639–42.

More recently, Franciscan theologian Kenan Osborne suggested six periods in which the doctrine developed, especially as it relates to the issue of lay ministry.[101] His six periods are: 1) Early Church to AD 325; 2) Emergence of the Clerical Church from AD 325–1000; 3) First Resurgence of the Lay Person: AD 1000–1600; 4) From 1600 to the French and American Revolutions; 5) From French and American Revolutions to Vatican II; and 6) Contemporary Lay Involvement in the Church.[102] Osborne's emphases on the significance of Constantine's conversion and Luther's Reformation are developed in this work, but his other periods do not play a central role.[103]

Among Protestant theologians, Thomas Torrance, Cyril Eastwood, Hans-Martin Barth, and Peter Leithart do not attempt to periodize the historical development of the doctrine of the royal priesthood. Torrance works directly from biblical texts and does not provide a historical narrative. Eastwood's two-volume study remains the most comprehensive Protestant treatment of the doctrine's history but, as Malcolm Yarnell notes, the work is marred by unwarranted historical selectivity.[104] Thus, while Eastwood's work remains invaluable, it is best viewed as a collection of helpful essays.[105] While neither Barth nor Leithart suggests a larger historical periodization, each spends a chapter describing "the" turning point. For Leithart it is the papacy of Gregory VII (d. 1085) and the Investiture Struggle of the eleventh century; for Barth, it is the Reformation and Luther's "allgemeine Priestertum der Gläubigen."[106]

In contrast, Baptists James Leo Garrett and Malcolm Yarnell have each proposed a periodization scheme.[107] Garrett does not focus on the

---

101. Osborne, *Ministry*, 115–21. Vastil Istavridis provides an Orthodox perspective and suggests a threefold periodization: 1) Ancient church history, AD 100–800; 2) Middle church history, AD 800–1453; 3) Modern church history, AD 1453 to present ("Orthodox World," 276–97).

102. Elsewhere, Osborne treats twelve major theological events from the contemporary period affecting the royal priesthood, among these events is the global growth of various forms of liberation theology (Osborne, "Envisioning a Theology," 195–227).

103. Osborne does not confine himself to these six periods. In his *Orders and Ministry*, he makes use of a fourfold periodization scheme (179–91).

104. Eastwood, *Priesthood of All Believers*; Eastwood, *Royal Priesthood of the Faithful*; Yarnell, "Priesthood of All Believers," 233n40.

105. See extended treatments of particular theologians (e.g., Cyprian, Augustine, Wycliffe, Luther, Calvin, Owens, Wesley), movements (e.g., monasticism, mysticism), and periods (e.g., Early Church, Middle Ages, British Reformation).

106. Leithart, *Priesthood of the Plebs*, xv, 223–48; Barth, *Einander Priester sein*, 29–53.

107. Yarnell builds upon Garrett's work ("Priesthood of All Believers," 233n40).

Christendom paradigm, but his latest proposal is similar: 1) the Patristic era;[108] 2) the era of the Protestant Reformers; and 3) the Contemporary Period.[109] More recently, Malcolm Yarnell has emphasized the "Believers' Church" dimension of the doctrine's development.[110] He proposes five historical "paradigms": 1) the "Catholic Sacramental Priesthood" initially proposed by Cyprian; 2) the "Caesarean Sacred Kingship" expressed by Constantine; 3) Luther and the "Reformation Universal Priesthood";[111] 4) John Smyth and the "Congregational Nature of Royal Priesthood";[112] finally, 5) E. Y. Mullins and the "Modern Libertarian Priesthood."[113] Spatial constraints will not permit fully defending the choice of the Christendom periodization scheme, yet its use helpfully illuminates how the missional dimension of the priesthood of all believers has been affected by its host culture. Theological discussions on the missional church in North America have also found the Christendom model helpful. They have helped illuminate the western churches' historically anemic commitment to participation in the *missio Dei*. A robustly missional understanding of the priesthood of all believers flourished before Christendom, and could once again flourish as we enter an increasingly post-Christendom period.[114] Part of the explanation for this relationship may be the importance of proclamation. As later chapters illustrate, where the ministry and proclamation of the royal priesthood is emphasized, the doctrine has flourished. Similarly, its rediscovery has often resulted in significant advances for evangelism and mission (e.g., John Wycliffe, Nicholas Zinzendorf, William Carey, Lesslie Newbigin).

---

108. Broken down further by Garrett and Hinson. Garrett suggests that Cyprian's writings "constitute a major turning point" for the doctrine and that Chrysostom's essay on priesthood may have "opened a succeeding epoch" in the doctrine's history (Garrett, "Priesthood of All Christians," 22, 33). See Garrett, "Pre-Cyprianic Doctrine," 45–62. Hinson's fivefold periodization distinctively emphasizes the role of the barbarian conquests. His five periods are: 1) Cyprian to Constantine (248–313); 2) Constantine to Odovacer (313–476); 3) Odovacer to the Carolingians (476–741); 4) Carolingians to the Renaissance (741–1300); 5) Renaissance and Reformation (1300–1600) ("Pastoral Authority," 6–21).

109. Garrett, *Systematic Theology*, 557–63. See also Tie, "Priesthood of All Believers," 19–21.

110. Garrett, *Concept of the Believers' Church*, 5.

111. Yarnell, "Reformation Development of the Priesthood of All Believers."

112. Yarnell, *Royal Priesthood*; Yarnell, "Changing Baptist Concepts," 236–52; Yarnell, "Congregational Priesthood," 110–35.

113. For an overview of these five paradigms, see Yarnell, "Priesthood of All Believers," 233–39.

114. For example, Newbigin's "priesthood in the world," discussed in Chapter 6.

Part Two identifies only a few of the historical turning points through which this doctrine has passed, but it provides important context for the systematic proposals made in Part Three. Chapter Four narrates a decline. To defrock is to remove one's priestly credentials, and there can be no doubt that the royal priesthood was gradually defrocked during the church's first millennium and a half. Every tale of the doctrine of royal priesthood must include some account of this decline. In short, the royal priesthood was gradually defrocked of its priestly privileges through hierarchicalization, sacralization, and politicization. While the members of the royal priesthood had once been players in the divine drama, their role was gradually reduced to passive audience.

Chapter 4 looks at Clement of Rome, Cyprian, and Constantine, all associated with significant ecclesial "firsts," each its own turning point. Clement was the first to distinguish church leaders from laypersons (*plebs*), initiating hierarchicalization within the church.[115] Cyprian was the first to reserve the title "priest" exclusively for the clergy, and to give to the clergy special sacerdotal powers at the Eucharist, thereby contributing to the sacralization of the hierarchy and the desacralization of the plebs.[116] Finally, Constantine's conversion as the first Christian emperor meant a new relationship for church and empire, a relationship with significant political repercussions on baptism, citizenship, and the doctrine of the royal priesthood.

Chapter 5 explores the development of Luther's doctrine, provides a systematic account of it, and assesses its positive and problematic aspects.[117] Luther's doctrine provided a basic pillar for the emerging ecclesiologies of the Magisterial, Anabaptist, and Anglican churches in the sixteenth century. His doctrine centers on the Christian's participation in the royal priesthood of Christ made possible through the new birth and baptism. Believers exercise their priesthood by preaching the word, praying, and offering spiritual sacrifices, thereby representing God to one another and each other to God. Luther's doctrine was not without its problematic dimensions, especially significant was its failure to develop implications for mission, a realization championed some four hundred years later by Karl Barth.

---

115. Clement's text was translated into Latin toward the middle of the second century and λαϊκοῖς was translated as *plebeius*. See Faivre's discussion, "The Scruples of a Latin Translator" (*Emergence of the Laity*, 21–22).

116. By "clergy" I refer to a leader of the church who has been ordained to ecclesial office.

117. Luther provides a Christendom version of the priesthood of all believers as Christendom remained largely the same for the Magisterial reformers.

Hans Küng suggests that Barth pioneered a new paradigm for contemporary theology.[118] Chapter 6, explores how Barth's contribution enriches a contemporary understanding of the priesthood of all believers. The chapter examines the *Church Dogmatics'* three explicit discussions of the priesthood of all believers (§§67, 69, 72) and its twenty-five uses of 1 Pet 2:9. This careful reading lays the groundwork for a discussion of the three most important elements of Barth's doctrine: election, baptism as ordination, and emphasis on witness as the royal priesthood's vocation. The chapter concludes with discussion of Lesslie Newbigin's "priesthood in the world," a version of the priesthood of all believers illustrating the paradigmatic changes suggested by Barth's Christological and missionary ecclesiology.

Part Three: The Royal Priesthood in Today's World

The rediscovery of Trinitarian doctrine and a turn to culture are two boons of contemporary theology. Part Three examines both developments, exploring their contribution to a contemporary understanding of the priesthood of all believers. Chapter 7 examines the priesthood of all believers in light of recent discussions about the Trinity. It first builds upon Newbigin's Christocentric-Trinitarian ecclesiology to develop a version of the priesthood of all believers informed by the *missio Dei*, and it then describes how members of the royal priesthood relate in especially appropriate ways to the Father (*latreia*), the Son (*diakonia*), and the Holy Spirit (*martyria*). The final section identifies three inadequate forms the doctrine has taken within Protestantism.

Chapter 8 raises the question of how the priesthood of all believers is to be performed today.[119] It argues that a canonically and catholically informed doctrine leads to particular ecclesial practices. The first section introduces how the seven "Central Practices" of the royal priesthood relate to contemporary discussions about ecclesial "practices." These seven Central Practices are 1) Baptism; 2) Prayer; 3) *Lectio Divina* (divine "reading"); 4) Ministry; 5) Church Discipline, 6) Proclamation, and 7) the Lord's Supper. The next section introduces Baptism as a "Constitutive Practice," ordaining the royal priesthood to mission and ministry. The third section returns to the spiritual sacrifices of the royal priesthood as Worship, Work, and Witness. These offerings are examined through the lens of the five "Core Practices": Prayer,

---

118. Küng calls him the "Initiator of a 'Postmodern' Paradigm in Theology" (*Theology for a New Millennium*, 271–75).

119. Vanhoozer, *Drama of Doctrine*, 399–444.

Lectio Divina, Ministry, Church Discipline, and Proclamation. The chapter concludes with a second Constitutive Practice, the Lord's Supper, the seventh and consummative practice of the royal priesthood.

If you have read this far you now have a good overview of the book's structure and arguments. The conclusion includes an even briefer summary in the form of eight theses advanced by the book's eight chapters. For now, we turn to Part One, the royal priesthood's canonical story as described in Scripture's script.

Part I

The Royal Priesthood in Scripture's Script

Royal Priests: Actors in the New Testament's Story

> Theologians must therefore keep a wary eye on the foundations they build on, lest their castles be left up in the air . . . theological thinking should grow from the bottom up.
>
> —Bruce Chilton, Introduction to *The Isaiah Targum*

> I am a priest of the Lord, and to him I serve as a priest; And to him I offer the sacrifice of his thought. For neither like the world, nor like the flesh is his thought, nor like those who serve in a fleshly way. The sacrifice of the Lord is righteousness, and purity of hearts and lips.
>
> —A Syrian Christian Hymn, ca. AD 100

THE INTRODUCTION IDENTIFIED THE need for a clear articulation of the Protestant doctrine of the priesthood of all believers. No reader should be surprised that this *Protestant* articulation commences with three chapters on the doctrine's biblical foundations. Two categories of texts are especially relevant to the NT doctrine: texts focusing on Christ as a royal priestly figure (Priest-king) and texts applying priestly or royal-priestly terminology to every member of Christ's body. Chapter 1 focuses on the latter, while Chapters 2 (OT) and 3 (NT) address both categories.

This chapter examines two central NT texts upon which the apostolic doctrine of the royal priesthood rests.[1] Here I argue that the royal priest-

---

1. By apostolic "doctrine" of the royal priesthood I mean, in Jaroslav Pelikan's well-known formula, "what the Christian church believed, taught, and confessed" between roughly AD 60 and 100. This "doctrine" would be rooted in the διδαχή of the apostles

hood is a significant theme across the NT, its scope far greater than the four texts to which it is often limited.² The chapter first identifies three major strands of scriptural evidence (temple, sacrifice, and priestly vocabulary) for the claim that every member of God's eschatological people (λαός) has been granted priestly status. Secondly, it identifies the offering of spiritual sacrifices, especially understood as the work of temple-service and proclamation, as the primary function of the royal priesthood.

Did the NT's authors and the first Christian theologians share a common doctrine of royal priesthood? Are the handful of NT references to Exod 19:6 randomly mined proof texts, or part of a larger motif relating to eschatological priesthood? What are we to make of the NT's unique appropriation of cultic language? Are all believers in Jesus "priests"? With these questions we turn to Peter and to Paul, important NT witnesses to the doctrine.³

Temple, Priesthood, and Sacrifice in 1 Peter 2:4–9

The first-century concept of the royal priesthood is rooted in the conceptual triad of priest-king/royal-priesthood, temple, and sacrifice. Neglecting one of these three components can lead to a distorted understanding of the NT's use of cultic vocabulary. For Bruce Chilton and Robert Daly, sacrificial language is paramount;⁴ for Gregory Beale and Nicholas Perrin the temple provides the leading concept.⁵ In this study, royal priesthood is central. But these three cultic concepts must be held together, and one contribution made by this chapter is carefully attending to the cultic concepts of temple and sacrifice while describing the NT's doctrine of the royal priesthood. Through the Anointed (ὁ Χριστός), every believer is a priest, an actor in an eschatological drama, called to offer acceptable spiritual sacrifices in a temple being built by God.

(Acts 5:28; 17:19) and the διδασκαλία of the church's teachers (Rom 12:7; 2 Tim 4:3; Tit 1:9; 2:1; cf. Matt 23:8; John 13:13; Acts 13:1; 1 Cor 12:28; Eph 4:11; James 3:1).

2. 1 Pet 2:5–9; Rev 1:6; 5:10; 20:6.

3. The first-century view of the priesthood was far simpler than today's critical reconstructions (Leuchter, "Priesthood in Ancient Israel," 100–10). I work with a canonical approach to the priesthood building on recent studies by Leithart (*Priesthood of the Plebs*) and Hahn (*Kinship by Covenant*). As neither Leithart nor Hahn address 1 Pet 2:4–9 or Rom 12:1–8 this chapter further advances their line of investigation.

4. Chilton, *Temple of Jesus*, ix; Daly, *Sacrifice Unveiled*; Daly, *Christian Sacrifice*.

5. Perrin, *Jesus the Temple*; Beale, *Temple and the Church's Mission*; Congar, *Mystery of the Temple*.

Peter provides one of the clearest NT examples of this conceptual triad by weaving together "spiritual sacrifices" (1 Pet 2:5), temple (οἶκος πνευματικὸς, 2:4–8), and "holy/royal priesthood" (2:5, 9).[6] For 1500 years, the nearly unanimous history of interpretation found here a clear articulation of the doctrine of the royal priesthood.[7] Recently, however, the atomization of biblical studies has provided opportunity for scholars to construct novel interpretations by isolating texts from their canonical contexts, a trend illustrated by John Elliott's exegesis of 1 Pet 2:4–9.[8]

While Elliott has made an unsurpassed contribution to contemporary Petrine scholarship, he has also continually crusaded against a "priesthood of all believers" interpretation of 1 Pet 2:4–9.[9] According to Elliott, and others who have followed his lead, the one thing we can be sure about in 1 Pet 2:4–9 is that individual believers are *not* priests. Beginning in 1966 with his published doctoral dissertation,[10] Elliott attempted to demonstrate that Peter's "believers" (2:6–7) are neither a temple of the Holy Spirit (1 Pet 2:5) nor believer-priests (1 Pet 2:5–9) who personally share in the priestly service of the "Anointed One."[11] A full rebuttal of Elliott's claims is not possible here (although see the summary of key points below) but, by attending to Peter's cultic triad and its early Jewish-Christian context, it becomes clear that Elliott's revisionist interpretation is ultimately unconvincing (as the recent scholarship cited here increasingly demonstrates). The believers that Peter describes are *priests* serving in an eschatological *temple* offering *spiritual sacrifices*.

---

6. On Petrine authorship see Jobes, *1 Peter*, 5–19.

7. As far as I am aware, the first to deny the royal priesthood to the laity was Thomas Murner in a 1520 attack on Luther's interpretation of 1 Pet 2:4–9 (*An den Grossmechtigsten und Durchlüchtigsten adel tutscher nation das sye den christlichen glauben beschitmen / toyder den zerstorer des glaubens christi /Martinum Luther eine verfierer der einfeltigen christen* [Strasbourg]). See Bagchi, "'eyn Mercklich Underscheyd,'" 156. Also see Dabin, *Le sacerdoce royal des fidèles*, 382; Leithart, *Priesthood of the Plebs*, 231.

8. On this trend, see Hahn, *Kinship by Covenant*, 333.

9. As far back as 1966, Elliott saw the priesthood of all believers as a "theological slogan" needing "elimination" (*Elect and the Holy*, xiii, xiv).

10. Elliott, *Elect and the Holy*; Elliott, *1 Peter*, 406–55.

11. First Peter refers to Jesus as the anointed twenty-two times. For readers of the LXX, the "Anointed Ones" were: 1) High Priests (Lev 4:3, 5, 16; 6:15 LXX [ET 22]; although other priests were also anointed; Exod 30:30); 2) Davidic kings (Psalm 2; cf. Dan 9:25–26; exception in Isa 45:1); and 3) the *'ebed Yahweh* (Isa 61:1; cf. Acts 4:27). See Grundmann, "χρίω, χριστός, ἀντίχριστος, χρῖσμα, χριστιανός," 497–579 esp. 562, 579.

God's "Temple-People"

Peter begins this passage with προσέρχομαι ("to draw near"), a word which "in the LXX regularly connotes cultic activity,"[12] and in Hebrews and 1 Peter "is used in a purely cultic sense."[13] Just as Levitical priests approached the Holy Place, *believers* (ὁ πιστεύων, 1 Pet 2:6, 7) are now to draw near to Jesus, the Anointed, the cornerstone of the new eschatological temple being built by God (οἰκοδομεῖσθε, v. 5).[14] Believers are *living* stones in the house God is building (cf. ζῶντα in Rom 12:1), and Peter here builds on combined allusions to two OT texts (Ps 118:22; Isa 28:16). Peter's choice of a "Temple Psalm" (Psalm 118) is significant, as is his use of the Isaiah text in a manner nearly identical to Paul (Rom 9:33)—one of many hints that the two letters' cultic conceptions are harmonious.

Cultivating a cultic identity was fundamental to basic Christian catechesis. God is building the believers into a "spiritual house" (οἶκος πνευματικὸς), an exact phrase used nowhere else in either the LXX or the NT (1 Pet 2:5).[15] The closest parallels in vocabulary come from Paul's letters, especially 1 Cor 3:16 (cf. Rom 8:9a, 11).[16] The verse's "do you not know" implies that the concept of believers as the new temple of God (ναὸς θεοῦ), the place where God's Spirit dwells (οἰκεῖ), was a fundamental component of the apostolic instruction.[17] This is confirmed by Eph 2:18–22, where the conceptual and linguistic parallels to 1 Peter are striking.[18] All *believers* (Eph 2:8) have priestly access to God *through* Jesus (Eph 2:18). They are now "members of the household of God" (Eph 2:19; "οἰκεῖοι τοῦ θεοῦ") being built into a

---

12. Scholer, *Proleptic Priests*, 90, cf. 90–149.

13. Schneider, "προσέρχομαι," 2:684.

14. Cf. Eph 2:20; 4:12, 16; 1 Cor 14:26; Matt 16:18 (Leithart, *Priesthood of the Plebs*, 152. See also: Flusser, "The Eschatological Temple," 207–13).

15. In the LXX temple and tabernacle are referred to as the οἶκος of the Lord over 250 times. See eschatological use in Zech 6:12 "the man whose name is the Branch . . . he shall build the οἶκον κυρίου" (Also 6:14, 15, 14:20, 21; Isa 66:20; Ezek 44:4; Joel 4:18). Likewise significant is Ps 118:26 (οἴκου κυρίου, LXX 117:26), because Ps 118:22 is cited in 1 Pet 2:4 and 2:7. See further Achtemeier, *1 Peter*, 156.

16. First Cor 3:16 reads, "Οὐκ οἴδατε ὅτι ναὸς θεοῦ ἐστε καὶ τὸ πνεῦμα τοῦ θεοῦ οἰκεῖ ἐν ὑμῖν."

17. So Corriveau, *Liturgy of Life*, 47. See esp. Corriveau's extended studies of fifteen words with cultic connotations for the royal priesthood.

18. If Ephesians, 1 Peter, and Romans were all written within the same decade, in the same city, by members of the same minority group, we should not be surprised to find parallels in cultic vocabulary. See Brown and Meier, *Antioch and Rome*, 188–91; Hagner, *Use of the Old and New Testaments*, 237, 354.

holy temple (ναὸν ἅγιον) where Jesus is the Cornerstone.¹⁹ The Ephesian metaphor, like Peter's, is even mixed so that the temple is portrayed as alive and growing (Eph 2:21; cf. Eph 4:16); believers are "being built together into a dwelling place for God by the Spirit" (Eph 2:22).

A third significant Pauline parallel describes believers (πιστοις) as a temple (2 Cor 6:15–18), and applies priestly/Levitical functions to them.²⁰ After calling believers "the temple of the living God," Paul concisely cites four OT quotations,²¹ at least one suggesting that "the Church forms a kind of neo-Levitical or priestly people" (Isa 52:11).²² Also significant is his citation from 2 Sam 7:14 (LXX), a passage which reveals that the Son of David will build a house for Yahweh's name and will receive an eternal throne." (2 Sam 7:13).²³ First Peter's reference to God's temple-people is deeply rooted in the narrative world of the LXX and apostolic teaching (διδασκαλία).²⁴

While Elliott has argued substantially against understanding 1 Pet 2:5's οἶκος πνευματικὸς as a temple,²⁵ the majority of interpreters recognize that the grammar, use of the early Christian tradition,²⁶ and theological logic support a cultic understanding of the term as the temple of the Holy Spirit.²⁷ With others, we note that the best explanation for Peter's understanding is the teaching of Jesus.²⁸ Gillespie summarized Peter's point well, describing all God's servants as "temple-people."²⁹

Temple people (i.e., royal priests) do temple service (i.e., "Ministry") by building up the living stones that make up the temple. Each member of

19. Goetzmann, "House," 2:249.

20. So Gupta, "Which 'Body' Is a Temple," 530. Gupta helpfully documents the importance of not bifurcating individual and corporate understandings of cultic NT cultic imagery.

21. Lev 26:11 = 2 Cor 6:16; Isa 52:11 = 2 Cor 6:17; Ezek 20:34 = 2 Cor 6:16; 2 Sam 7:14 = 2 Cor 6:18.

22. Isa 52:11 describes functions previously limited to Israel's priestly caste, which Paul now applies to all believers (Corriveau, "Temple, Holiness, and the Liturgy," 154).

23. "οἰκοδομήσει μοι οἶκον τῷ ὀνόματί μου, καὶ ἀνορθώσω τὸν θρόνον αὐτοῦ ἕως εἰς τὸν αἰῶνα." On David's eschatological son as temple-builder see Leuchter, "Priesthood in Ancient Israel," 102.

24. Cf. 1 Pet 4:17; Ezek 9:4 (Elliott, 1 Peter, 797–800; Bauckham, "James, 1 Peter, Jude and 2 Peter," 163).

25. Elliott, Elect and the Holy, 149–59; Elliott, 1 Peter, 414–21.

26. Peter is making extensive use of the primitive Christian tradition. Ernest Best lists twelve examples from the passage ("1 Peter 2:4–10," 279–82).

27. Achtemeier, 1 Peter: A Commentary on First Peter, 149–56; Best, "I Peter 2:4–10: A Reconsideration," 280; Jobes, 1 Peter, 148–50.

28. Selwyn, First Epistle of St. Peter, 291.

29. Gillespie, "Laity in Biblical Perspective," 327.

the royal priesthood is called to do "a work of service, for the building up of the body of Christ" (Eph 4:12).[30] It is especially in the work of mutual edification, where each uses their gift "to serve one another," that royal priests engage in temple service (1 Pet 4:10).

Priests *through* Christ Jesus

The second of Peter's three cultic concepts in 1 Pet 2:4–9 is priesthood; a concept intimately tied to both sacrifice and temple.[31] The temple is the locus of God's presence on earth—the place where the faithful long to go to meet with God[32]—yet in the OT, the priests alone are privileged to serve in Yahweh's temple as his intermediaries.[33] Peter has this basic relationship in mind as he moves from the house of God to those who serve in it. He makes three important claims about believers as a new priesthood: 1) as holy priests they offer spiritual sacrifices; 2) as royal priests they proclaim their King's wonderful acts; and 3) as a holy priesthood their identity is found only *through* Jesus' priestly mediation.

The exercise of priestly functions is no longer primarily associated with ancestry, but is now based upon belief in Jesus,[34] resulting in a new birth (1 Pet 1:3, 23), and a complete identification with the Anointed One (ὁ Χριστός) through baptism.[35] In 1 Peter 2:5, the chief priestly function of believer-priests, who through baptism share in the ministry of the Anointed One, is the offering of spiritual sacrifices. Writing from the same Roman minority community as Peter, Justin Martyr (d. 165) clarifies further. Believers in the Anointed One (ὁ Χριστός) share in their High Priest's ministry:

> We are the true high priestly race of God, as even God himself bears witness, saying that in every place among the Gentiles sacrifices are presented to him well-pleasing and pure. *Now God receives sacrifices from no one, except through his priests.*[36]

---

30. My translation.

31. Greek etymology suggests the intimate relationship between priest (ἱερεύς) and temple (ἱερόν). See Congar, *Lay People in the Church*, 133.

32. Pss 5:7 (LXX 5:8); 23 (LXX 22); 27:4 (LXX 26:4). Augustine develops this theme, connecting 1 Pet 2:9 and Ps 84:10 (LXX 83:11) in *City of God* 17.5 (LCL 415:261).

33. Leithart, "Attendants of Yahweh's House," 3–24.

34. First Peter 1:5, 7, 8, 9, 21; 2:6, 7; 4:19; 5:9 (also *LW* 30:62). On the tension between ancestry and merit in first-century Judaism see Himmelfarb, *A Kingdom of Priests*. Unfortunately, Himmelfarb does not discuss 1 Pet 2:4–9.

35. On 1 Pet 3:21 and baptism as a "fundamental presupposition and reference point" see Elliott, *1 Peter*, 34; Selwyn, *First Peter*, 368–466.

36. Justin Martyr, *Dialogue with Trypho*, 116 (FC 3:174); emphasis added. Justin

Justin's remarks clarify how 1 Peter's words would fall on first-century ears. If the elect and holy readers of 1 Peter are the ones offering spiritual sacrifices, then they are indeed "priests to God" (Rev 1:6).

In 1 Pet 2:5 believer-priests offer sacrifices, but a second function is emphasized in 2:9. As a holy and priestly family, the believers' chief function is mediating God's good news to the world. The priesthood's purpose is heralding their King to those in darkness.[37] Luther understood this functional component of priesthood, and he draws attention to believers' mediatorial role in priestly proclamation of their Lord's excellence (ἀρετὰς). "We see that the first and foremost duty we Christians should perform [as priests] is to proclaim the wonderful deeds of God."[38]

Disappointingly, many recent commentators—though not all—disagree with Luther's exegesis here. Jo Bailey Wells is typical when she states that 1 Pet 2:4-9's priesthood "is not a literal conveyance to every believer of priestly rights and functions,"[39] but rather an understanding "the Reformation imposed on this passage . . . nowhere in the NT is this the understanding."[40] Wells overstates her case, creating a false dichotomy by denying priesthood to individual believers. While the *emphasis* of 1 Pet 2:4-9 is on the corporate nature of the believer-priests' life together, this corporate emphasis does not *exclude* individual believers (ὁ πιστεύων; v. 6) from offering spiritual sacrifices through Jesus Christ (2:5), or from functioning as priestly mediators when they "proclaim the wonderful deed God has performed" on their behalf.[41] The sacrifices of believers (1 Pet 2:5), like their proclamation (1 Pet 2:9), service and speaking (1 Pet 4:11) are priestly

---

argues from Zechariah 3 and Mal 1:11 (cf. Isa 66:21).

37. Here ὅπως indicates purpose (Elliott, *1 Peter*, 439). For a discussion of 1 Pet 2:9's "light" in relation to the "light" of the holy of holies, see Barker, *Great High Priest*, 186.

38. *LW* 30:64–66.

39. Wells, *God's Holy People*, 218. Also denying the priesthood of all believers in 1 Pet 2:4-9: Harink, *1 & 2 Peter*, 69; Green, *I Peter*; Jobes, *1 Peter*, 160–61; Elliott, *1 Peter*, 37:451–54; Achtemeier, *1 Peter*, 152; 156; Green, *1 Pedro Y 2 Pedro*, 133. A number of commentaries uphold the traditional reading.

40. Wells, *God's Holy People*, 218.

41. Far from being an individualistic Reformation innovation, early Syriac and Ethiopian translations support the idea of believers as priests: "And ye . . . are builded and become *spiritual temples* and *holy priests* for the offering of spiritual sacrifices. . . . *officiating as priests* of the kingdom" (SNTPV, 427, emphasis added). Ancient Ethiopian versions also support a "priesthood of all believers" interpretation in 1 Pet 2:5, 9 (*Book of Jubilees* [ed. Charles], 116).

only because each one (ἕκαστος; 1 Pet 1:17; 4:10; cf. Rom 12:3) serves the Father through (διὰ) Jesus Christ (2:5; 4:11) in the temple (1 Pet 2:4–8).[42]

Peter's clarity about priestly identity is rooted in the OT's narrative. Our story provides our indicative, giving authority and clarity to the imperatives.[43] The *Magna Carta* of Israel's peoplehood given at Sinai (Exod 19:6) "presents the rest of the Pentateuch from a new perspective, namely the *unique identity of the people of God.*"[44] Peter's multiple allusions to Exod 19:6 (1 Pet 2:5, 9) recall Israel's story where the role of God's people "is to be a priestly and holy community in the midst of the nations."[45]

Similarly, Peter's adaptation of Isa 43:21, "the people whom I formed for myself that they might declare my praise,"[46] is rooted in the eschatological framework of Isaiah. In Isaiah's story, a stream of nations (Isaiah 2)[47] would one day return to Jerusalem in a New Exodus[48] following the sacrificial Passover offering of the *'ebed Yahweh*, and in *that* day the elect of the nations would be made into priests, ministers, and Levites (Isa 61:6; 66:21) in order that they too might serve in God's eschatological house for all nations (Isa 56:6–7).[49] Peter understood that Isaiah's vision of the thrice Holy God (Isa 6:1–8) leads ultimately to his vision of an eschatologically holy and priestly people (1 Pet 2:5). While modern commentators seem comfortable reading 1 Peter largely independent of this larger canonical narrative,[50] for Peter, Israel's story, culminating in Jesus, provided the elementary education of the faith.[51] It provides the priestly indicative authorizing the proclamatory imperative.[52]

---

42. Believers are both individually and collectively united to Christ through faith and the public event of baptism. Similarly, in the OT the Levitical priesthood could be considered as a collective, but this did not negate individual members from serving as priests.

43. Wright, *Mission of God*, 58–61.

44. Wells, *God's Holy People*, 34; emphasis original. See also Wright, *Mission of God*, 255–57.

45. Citation from Christopher Wright; on this point his and Wells' position is superior to that of Davies (Wright, *Mission of God*, 256; also 224–24, 255–57, 329–33, 369–73; Wells, *God's Holy People*, 56–57; Davies, *Royal Priesthood*, 238).

46. Achtemeier, *1 Peter*, 166.

47. For how Isaiah's eschatological stream of nations was understood by first-century Jews see Ware, *Mission of the Church*, 59–71.

48. Bauckham, "James, 1 Peter, Jude and 2 Peter," 161. Cf. 1 Cor 5:7.

49. *'ebed Yahweh* and *'ebedim*, discussed in Chapter 2, are technical terms transliterated for emphasis.

50. An exception is Boring, "Narrative Dynamics in First Peter," 8, 35.

51. Minear, "House of Living Stones," 243–44.

52. Cf. narratives in Acts 2 and 8:26–39.

Peter's first-century readers possessed a priestly *identity*. Because they are the royal-priests of Isaiah's New Exodus, they are commanded to proclaim the good news about their Priest-king to the Gentiles (1 Pet 2:9, 12; 3:15). Their social identity as priests transforms their "identity vis-à-vis how they approach the world . . ." and "offers a perspective of priesthood that reinforces their peculiarity as the priest-people of God, but describes their task as one of mediation and witness."[53] This priestly identity is affirmed from the very first sentence of the letter where they are described as "consecrated" by the Spirit (ἐν ἁγιασμῷ πνεύματος).[54] As Gupta notes, "the idea of consecration, however, also implies the notion of being set apart *for a particular task*."[55] This task is described as "obedience to Jesus Christ and for sprinkling with his blood" (1 Pet 1:2). Sprinkling (ῥαντισμὸν) with blood was an important part of the consecration of Aaron and his sons when they were ordained to priesthood.[56] From the very beginning of his letter, Peter is seeking to shape the identity of his readers with reference to their priestly consecration through Christ's blood (1 Pet 1:2; 2:5).[57] Revelation 7:14 describes a similar situation. Saints are dressed in robes dipped in the Lamb's blood. Like Levitical priests, the blood covering now permits them to serve day and night as priests in the temple (Rev 7:15).[58] Peter's readers, like John's, are a royal and priestly people.

Finally, while royal priests offer spiritual sacrifices and proclaim the glorious deeds of their divine King, their identity as a *holy* priesthood is found only *through* Jesus' priestly ministry. The essence of priesthood is mediation (Heb 5:1) and, for both Peter and Paul as for the author of Hebrews,[59] "there is one mediator between God and man—Christ Jesus" (1 Tim 2:5).[60] While Jesus is not explicitly called "priest" as in Hebrews, or "mediator" as in Paul, he does fulfill both roles in 1 Pet 2:5. Believers offer spiritual sacrifices to God only *"through* [διὰ] Jesus Christ."[61]

---

53. Gupta, "Spiritual House," 62, 68.

54. The Greek word is "more accurately understood as 'consecration'" (ibid., 63).

55. Ibid., emphasis original.

56. Exodus 29:1, 21; Lev 8:30; cf. Exod 32:29.

57. Gupta, "Spiritual House," 65.

58. Ibid., 65. Osborne finds here a reference to "the priesthood of all believers" (*Revelation*, 327).

59. Hebrews 8:6; 9:15; 12:24.

60. This verse provides "the closest approach to the priestly idea" in Paul (Vos, *Teaching of the Epistle to the Hebrews*, 93.

61. "[τῷ] θεῷ διὰ Ἰησοῦ Χριστοῦ," 1 Pet 2:5. See also 1:21; 3:21; 4:11 cf. 1:2 (alluding to Exod 23:3–8); 2:24; 3:18; 2 Pet 1:3.

The logic is the same as elsewhere in the NT. Only in light of God's mercy, accessible through Jesus Christ, can believers offer living, holy, and acceptable sacrifices (Rom 12:1).[62] As Calvin notes, Heb 13:15 relates Christ's priesthood to the sacrifices of believers, which are only offered *through* (διὰ) Christ.[63] The same logic is also found in Rev 1:6 where the blood of Jesus has made priests to God "ἐποίησεν ἡμᾶς βασιλείαν, ἱερεῖς τῷ θεῷ." Christ's royal and priestly mediation (Psalm 110) is foundational to Peter's understanding of the royal priesthood's priestly mediation to the world.[64] His vindicated offering[65] and present high priestly ministry (1 Pet 3:22) give believers the priestly right of access to the Father. Peter's understanding of priestly mediation is rooted in an OT narrative world, especially centering on the Servant of Isaiah 53.[66] In that world, the '*ebed Yahweh* and Moses are the two most important mediatorial figures;[67] when "the majority fails to meet God's claim, the mediator stands in the breach, first in intercession, then in substitutionary self-offering."[68] For Peter, Jesus has stood in this breach once for all (ἅπαξ) as a substitute; he has "suffered once for sins, the righteous for the unrighteous, that he might bring us to God" (1 Pet 3:18).[69] Jesus is the priest through whom all believers exercise their royal priesthood.[70]

Spiritual Sacrifices: *Public Praise and a Eucharistic Life*

Moving to Peter's third cultic term, spiritual sacrifices (πνευματικὰς θυσίας), we build on previous discussions. If believers serve in a temple and offer

---

62. Compare 1 Pet 2:5's διὰ Ἰησοῦ Χριστοῦ with Eph 2:18's "ὅτι δι' αὐτοῦ ἔχομεν τὴν προσαγωγὴν οἱ ἀμφότεροι ἐν ἑνὶ πνεύματι πρὸς τὸν πατέρα." See also Paul's eighteen uses of διὰ with reference to Jesus in Romans (esp. Rom 5:2).

63. Calvin, *CNTC*, 259–60.

64. Peter identifies Jesus as Psalm 110's Priest-king (1 Pet 3:22). Psalm 110 is the most cited Psalm in the NT, and its significance for the NT doctrine of the royal priesthood has been largely ignored since Luther. See esp. Matt 22:41–46; Acts 2:33, 34; Rom 8:34; Eph 1:20; Heb 1:3 and 5:5–7; Farrow, *Ascension and Ecclesia*, 27; 275–77; Hay, *Glory at the Right Hand*; Gourgues, *A la droite de Dieu*.

65. First Peter 1:2–3, 19–21; 3:18–21.

66. Elliott identifies five citations and five allusions to Isaiah's Servant Songs; citations in 1 Pet 2:22 (Isa 53:9); 2:23 (Isa 53:6, 12); 2:24a (Isa 53:4, 5, 12); 2:24d (Isa 53:5); and 2:25 (Isa 53:6); and allusions in 1 Pet 1:18 (Isa 52:3); 2:9 (Isa 42:12); 3:13 (Isa 50:9); 3:18b (Isa 53:11 LXX), and 1:19 (Isaiah 52–53). See Elliott, *1 Peter*, 13–15.

67. Oepke, "μεσίτης, μεσιτεύω," 4:611.

68. Ibid., 4:614. cf. Exod 32:11–14, 30–34; 33:12–23; 34:8–9; with Is 53:12, 4–10.

69. On ἅπαξ see Heb 9:26, 28. Cf. Rom 6:10; Heb 7:27; 9:12; 10:10.

70. Hill, "'To Offer Spiritual Sacrifices,'" 59.

sacrifices, they are priests.[71] These priests offer acceptable spiritual sacrifices (note the plural) only through the priestly mediation of Jesus Christ.[72] Hans Küng explains:

> If then *all* believers have, in this particular way, to offer sacrifices through Christ, this means that *all* believers have a priestly function, of a completely new kind, through Christ the one high priest and mediator. The abolition of a special priestly caste and its replacement by the priesthood of the *one* new and eternal high priest has as it's strange and yet logical consequence the fact that *all* believers share in a universal priesthood.[73]

Peter's sacrificial theology is rich, perhaps, as some have suggested, the most "comprehensive" in the NT.[74] It involves the whole person, especially emphasizing activities of proclamation.

What then is the nature of the "acceptable spiritual sacrifices" which Peter's believer-priests are to offer to God? Jobes surveys six proposals before concluding that spiritual sacrifices are best understood as "all behavior that flows from a transformation of the human spirit by the sanctifying work of the Holy Spirit (1:2)."[75] With Jobes we affirm that Peter's spiritual sacrifices encompass all of life, thanksgiving offerings in response to God's mercy. We explore this holistic understanding of spiritual sacrifices further below (Rom 12:1-8). But here in 1 Pet 2:5, the context indicates that "spiritual sacrifices" especially consist of priestly witness in the world.[76]

Believer-priests offer spiritual sacrifices when they live holy lives before God (*coram Deo,* 1 Pet 3:12) and before the world. Their good works (καλῶν ἔργων) are a witness bringing glory to God (1 Pet 2:12). Even when holy conduct is performed without a word (1 Pet 3:1), it may win the unbeliever to the Anointed One. This is not to say that sacrificial witness avoids verbal proclamation (1 Pet 2:9); it is continuously (ἀεί) prepared to speak

---

71. In *Priesthood of the Plebs,* Leithart argues that this is not the case because the patriarchs offered sacrifices and were not priests (56). But compare how Genesis was read in the first century. See for example *Jubilees* 3:18; 4:7, 25; 6:1-3, etc. which views the patriarchs as priests (Wintermute, "Jubilees," 35-142).

72. ἀνενέγκαι "to offer up" is a cultic term, also used with cultic connotations in Heb 7:27(2×); 9:28; esp. 13:15; Jas 2:21; cf. 1 Pet 2:24. Similarly, εὐπρόσδεκτος is used with a cultic sense as in Rom 15:16 (discussed below).

73. Küng, *Church,* 370; emphasis original.

74. Daly, *Christian Sacrifice,* 250.

75. Jobes, *1 Peter,* 151.

76. 1 Pet 1:15-16; 2:9; 2:12 (Daly, *Christian Sacrifice,* 256; Elliott, *Elect and the Holy,* 179-85).

about Christ's holy-heart work *within* the believer.[77] Thus, the spiritual sacrifices in 1 Pet 2:5 include all holy works done by believers, but especially those sacrificial words and deeds offered to God for the sake of winning others from darkness to the light (1 Pet 2:9, 12; 3:1).

The closest parallels to Peter's redefinition of sacrifice are neither Hellenistic writers nor Qumran sectarians,[78] but four Christian epistles associated with Rome in the AD 60s (Romans, Ephesians, Philippians, and Hebrews). These epistles share not only cultic vocabulary, but also unique Christian adaptations of cultic concepts. While Clement develops these cultic concepts in a new direction, his use of these five epistles some thirty years later (ca. AD 96) shows their continued influence on the Roman churches.[79]

Just as Peter's holy and royal believer-priests offer spiritual sacrifices by proclaiming the good deeds of their King, so Paul in Romans identifies himself as a priest whose cultic activity consists of missionary service to the Gentiles (Rom 1:9; 15:16).[80] As a missionary theologian, he is a member of the "priesthood unto the Gentiles."[81] Like 1 Pet 2:4–9, Paul "redefines the nature of sacrifice and priestly service in terms of the gospel, its service and fruit."[82] Both the spiritual sacrifices offered (ἀναφέρω) by Peter's believer-priests as they proclaim their King's marvelous works and Paul's missionary offering (προσφορὰ) of Gentiles are pleasing (εὐπρόσδεκτος) to God (Rom 15:16; 1 Pet 2:5).

Similarly, in Paul's letter to the Philippians, the believers' missional service as those who "hold forth[83] the word of life" (Phil 2:16) qualifies them as priests. Careful exegesis of Phil 2:14–18 leads James Ware to conclude that Paul sees the Philippian believers as a "community of priests. . . . lights and priests for the world," holding out good news to those in darkness.[84]

---

77. So 1 Pet 3:15: "κύριον δὲ τὸν Χριστὸν ἁγιάσατε ἐν ταῖς καρδίαις ὑμῶν . . . περὶ τῆς ἐν ὑμῖν ἐλπίδος."

78. This is not self-evident in many commentaries. For example, Jobes mentions parallels to 1 Pet 2:5's πνευματικὰς θυσίας at Qumran, but not conceptual parallels in Rom 12:1, Heb. 13:15–16; Eph 5:2, or Phil 2:16–17 (*1 Peter*, 150–51).

79. Hagner, *Use of the Old*, 246, 314, 327.

80. Schlier, "Die 'liturgie,'" 248.

81. Barth, *Epistle to the Romans*, 530.

82. Hess, "Serve, Deacon, Worship," 3:552.

83. With the KJV, NIV1, and NJB, against the ESV, NIV2, NASB2, and NRSV's "holding fast." See Ware's discussion of ἐπέχω in Phil 2:16a (*Mission of the Church*, 256–70). For a weak version of "holding fast" see Poythress, "'Hold Fast' versus 'Hold Out,'" 45–53. Ware's argument would be further strengthened by noting 2 Tim 4:5–6.

84. Ware, *Mission of the Church*, 272, 273.

Like 1 Peter, Paul's theological logic for the priesthood of the Gentiles is rooted in both the work of the 'ebed Yahweh (Isaiah 53; Phil 2:4–11) and in Isaiah's eschatological and democratized priesthood (Isaiah 54–66).[85] For Paul, as for Peter, it was especially the missionary service and holy lives of believers which constituted the spiritual sacrifices and offerings marking their eschatological priesthood.

Finally, Hebrews also expects its priestly readers to offer spiritual sacrifices (Heb 13:15–16). These sacrifices are offered through Jesus (Δι' αὐτοῦ; Heb 13:20–21), especially praise, "doing good" (εὐποιΐας),[86] and sharing (κοινωνίας) with one another. Hebrews 12:28 previously explains that acceptable worship is based upon a grateful response to the priestly kingdom believers have *already* received. The "already," made possible by the blood of Christ, permits believers to serve as priests offering thanksgiving sacrifices.[87] While the immediate emphasis of Hebrews 13 is on priestly ministry to God and one another, there are also "missiological strains in 13:15–16."[88] The siblings of the High-priestly King share in his royal and priestly ministry "on behalf of men in relation to God" (Heb 5:1),[89] thus sharing a mediatorial role to the unbelieving world.[90]

In sum, believers' offerings of spiritual sacrifices through Christ testify to their sharing in his royal priesthood. In 1 Peter and the rest of the NT, spiritual sacrifices are offered by all believers in all of life—presupposing a priestly identity in the one making the offering.[91] In 1 Peter and other NT writings, they are especially associated with words and deeds bearing witness to God before the world. Only through the mediation of the Anointed One can believers offer acceptable spiritual sacrifices and serve as eschatological priests to God. Only when built upon Christ the cornerstone can believers contribute to the new eschatological temple being built by God. In 1 Peter, temple, sacrifice, and priesthood have been reinterpreted by the Anointed One's royal and priestly offering.

---

85. Ibid., 57–159.
86. Note parallels in 1 Pet 2:15, 20; 3:6, 17; 4:19.
87. O'Brien, *Letter to the Hebrews*, 503, 515, 526–29.
88. Laansma, "Hebrews and the Mission," 343.
89. Ibid., 341–43.

90. Aspects of Jesus' High Priestly ministry were unique, a once-for-all event (ἐφάπαξ, Heb 7:27; 9:12, 26, 28; 10:10), but other aspects serve as examples (e.g., teaching, pronouncing forgiveness, blessing, teaching, intercession). See Cullmann: "an imitation of Christ is possible only when we are first of all aware of the fact that we are not able to imitate him" (*Christology of the New Testament*, 100). On Christ's priestly ministry on earth according to Hebrews, see Scholer, *Proleptic Priests*, 85–89.

91. Gupta, "Spiritual House," 62.

Summary: Why Luther Was (Mostly) Right and Elliott Is (Largely) Wrong: Believers as Priests in 1 Peter 2:4–9

John Elliott presents a false dichotomy when he claims that because priesthood (ἱεράτευμα) means something like "brotherhood" and is "a *collective* noun designating the believing community as a whole," it therefore *cannot* mean a group of individual priests.[92] Elliott's logic suggests that a body of slaves excludes an individual slave; a body of ambassadors, an individual ambassador; a body of craftsmen, an individual craftsman. An English parallel would be a "brotherhood" excluding "brothers." Just as the fact that we are a *sanctorum communio* simultaneously identifies individual members as saints, so the fact that believers are a holy and royal priesthood does not exclude individual members from functioning as priests but identifies them as such.[93]

This logic would have been as nonsensical to Peter as it is today.[94] Elliott can only deny that individual believers function as priests by 1) rejecting the fact that 1 Pet 2:4–9 refers to believers as a temple;[95] 2) ignoring the fact that believers (vv. 6, 8) are individually baptized (i.e., commissioned or "ordained") into the royal priesthood;[96] 3) downplaying the significance of the "spiritual sacrifices" (v. 5) offered by individuals, not just a corporate body;[97] 4) denying any reference to Christ's priestly role in 1 Peter, and thereby failing to recognize the *priestly* nature of the *Anointed One*;[98] 5) downplaying

---

92. Elliott, *1 Peter*, 452; Elliott, *Elect and the Holy*, 63–70. In addition to the argument presented above, see extensive critiques of Elliott from Schüssler Fiorenza, *Priester für Gott*, 53–59, 99–101, and Best, "1 Peter 2:4–10," 286–87.

93. Elliott seems to contradict himself when asserting that "body of functioning priests" may be the most "adequate" translation of ἱεράτευμα (*Elect and the Holy*, 69). Here again Gupta's documentation of a bias in contemporary NT scholarship against the individual provides helpful context ("Which Body is a Temple," 518–36).

94. For Greek parallels see Selwyn, *First Peter*, 160.

95. Elliott, *1 Peter*, 414–18. If believers are being portrayed as temple-servants, then it becomes very difficult to deny that they are functioning as priests.

96. But note 1 Peter's emphasis on baptism in Elliott, *1 Peter*, 33–34.

97. Ibid., 421–23; cf. Rom 12:1; Heb 13:15–16.

98. Discussing spiritual sacrifices (1 Pet 2:5), Elliott claims that "in 1 Peter, Christ is nowhere depicted as a priest" (421), yet in a later comment on διὰ Ἰησοῦ Χριστοῦ in the same verse he writes "*through Jesus Christ* expresses the mediatorial role of Jesus Christ" (*1 Peter* 423; emphasis original). While 1 Peter is not as explicit as Hebrews, the same cultic logic is at work. Jesus is portrayed as priest in his role as unique Mediator between the Father and humanity (1 Pet 2:5; also 1:3; 3:21; 4:11; cf. 1 Tim 2:5), as the priestly "Suffering Servant" (1 Pet 2:21–25; cf. Peter's speeches: Acts 3:13, 26; 4:27, 30), and as the head of a priestly temple-family, believers who are "in Christ" (1 Pet 3:16; 5:10, 14; cf. 4:14, 16–17). Union with Christ, the Priest-king, is not only collective, but

the canonical significance of Exod 19:6;[99] 6) arguing that cultic concepts in 1 Pet 2:4–9 are "alien" to the Pauline Epistles and Hebrews where individual believers are often called upon to exercise priestly activities;[100] 7) failing to attend to the larger canonical story, especially Jesus' relation to Israel with its restoration eschatology and expectations of a universal priesthood in the last days (e.g., Isaiah's priestly "Servant seed").[101]

Luther was correct to uphold the classic tradition and find reference to the priesthood of all believers in this text; his exhortation still rings true: "You must remain with the pure word of God. What it calls priests, you, too, must call priests."[102] This does not mean that Peter's doctrine cannot be abused. Yet abuse does not negate proper use. Fear of abuse has led many recent commentators, even those in baptistic traditions, to deny that believers are priests.[103] But emphasizing corporate unity while denying priesthood to individual members is as dangerous as emphasizing individual priesthood while denying need for the corporate body.[104] Peter would agree with Paul's balance in Rom 12:1–8 (e.g., 1 Pet 4:10–11). The individual's priestly offering (Rom 12:1–2) cannot be separated from her service within the priestly body of Christ (Rom 12:3–8).[105]

A Radical Change in the Priesthood

There are good reasons to closely compare the cultic language of 1 Pet 2:4–9 with the cultic vocabulary of the rest of the NT, especially the language and theological concepts found in Paul and Hebrews.[106] A radical "change in the priesthood" was achieved in Christ's incarnation (Heb 7:12, NRSV). All NT documents share a view of the priesthood that differs fundamentally

---

also an individual experience.

99. For example he denies that Isa 61:6 is an intertextual reference to Exod 19:6 (Elliott, *1 Peter*, 452; Elliott, *Elect and the Holy*, 59). In contrast to Elliott, see the extensive arguments of Himmelfarb who finds the concept of Exod 19:6's royal priesthood to be "of central importance" to first-century Jews (*Kingdom of Priests*, 1).

100. Elliott, *1 Peter*, 453.

101. See Isaiah 54–66; Zechariah 6, 14; Mal 1:11, etc. Cf. Bauckham, "James, 1 Peter, Jude and 2 Peter," 163.

102. *LW* 30:62.

103. For an example of such a denial see Harink, *1 & 2 Peter*, 69.

104. See further the helpful article by Newell, "Many Members," 413–26.

105. As ἑκάστῳ in verse three indicates, "each one" is responsible for the offering of sacrifice, not simply the corporate body as a whole.

106. Daly, *Christian Sacrifice*, 493.

from both the Jewish priesthood and the pagan priesthoods dominant in Greco-Roman life.[107]

A New Priesthood across the Roman Empire

A shared view of priesthood is especially evident in four Pauline letters (Romans, Philippians, Ephesians, 2 Timothy), 1 Peter, and Hebrews—all six letters associated with the Roman church in the second half of the first century.[108] These letters, while containing unique melodies, harmonize around a common core of apostolic teaching (διδασκαλία) concerning an eschatologized temple, priesthood, and sacrifice. The combined witness of this Roman corpus shows that by the sixth decade of the first century, a new *priesthood* was offering new *sacrifices* in a new *temple*. The eschatological promises of Isa 56:6–8 and 66:21 were being fulfilled in Rome. Yahweh was appointing priests from all twelve tribes of Israel and from the Gentiles to minister and to offer sacrifices in his house of prayer for all nations. Rome had new priests.

A Syriac poet-theologian, writing around AD 100 in the region of Antioch, illustrates the widespread consensus on this new conception of priesthood.[109] In a hymn now known as *Ode* 20, the poet describes his understanding of the "priesthood of all believers":

> I am a priest of the Lord, and to him I serve as a priest; And to him I offer the sacrifice of his thought. For neither like the world, nor like the flesh is his thought, nor like those who serve in a fleshly way. The sacrifice of the Lord is righteousness, and purity of hearts and lips.[110]

According to Michael Lattke, the priest described in *Ode* 20 is not a Stoic or Jewish Levitical priest, but one standing "in the line from Exod 19:6 to 1 Pet 2:5, 9 (ἱεράτευμα) or from Isa 61:6 to Rev 1:6; 5:10; 20:6 (ἱερεῖς)."[111] *Ode* 20 demonstrates that first-century Jewish-Christians in the region of Antioch perceived themselves as individual priests offering spiritual

---

107. *Contra* Elliott, *Elect and the Holy*, 174.

108. These six (with 1 and 2 Corinthians) are used in Clement's Corinthian epistle (ca. AD 95).

109. The *Odes of Solomon*, the first Christian hymnal, best fits the genre described in Col 3:16 and Eph 5:19 (Lattke, *Odes of Solomon*, 13). Charlesworth argues "that the Odes were probably composed sometime around AD 100 ("Odes of Solomon," 727).

110. Lattke, *Odes of Solomon*, 285. Cf. Charlesworth, "Odes of Solomon," 753.

111. Lattke, *Odes of Solomon*, 286.

sacrifices, with language remarkably parallel to that used by Roman believers in the latter half of the first century.[112]

Romans 12:1–8 as Paradigmatic Example of the Believer Priest

Peter's understanding of believers as priests (1 Pet 2:4–9) was widely shared by first-century Jewish Christians. Paul's understanding of believers as eschatological priests in Rom 12:1–8 provides an additional example. He sees members of Christ's body as priests, free to offer eschatological sacrifices. Before turning to the passage, we make two contextual observations.

First, the epistle is bookended by Paul's self-identification as a priest engaged in offering acceptable sacrifices to God (Rom 1:9; 15:16).[113] Like 1 Pet 2:4–9, this priestly ministry is especially concerned with missional proclamation to the nations. For Jewish readers, however, an obvious question would be: How can Paul—from the tribe of Benjamin (Rom 11:1; Phil 3:5)—claim to be a priest, when this is the exclusive prerogative of Levi's tribe? The answer is that "Paul assumes an eschatological transformation of the OT cultic ministry . . . Paul did not, then—as some Hellenistic Jews did—'spiritualize' the sacrifices; he 'eschatologized' them."[114] Paul saw himself as a member of the eschatological priesthood promised by Isaiah, Zechariah, and Malachi, a priesthood which did not exclude Levites, but now included members from all the tribes and even Gentiles (Isaiah 54–66; Zechariah 14; Mal 1:9).

Second, note the placement of Rom 12:1–8 within the epistle's larger argument. These verses are a hinge upon which the book turns. The reader has followed Paul's logic from the universal plight of sin (chs. 1–3), to faith in Christ (chs. 3–4), to hope of union with Christ and the believers' complete identification through baptism (chs. 5–7), to new life in the Spirit (ch. 8), and the relation of the eschatological people of God (believers in Christ) to the Jews (chs. 9–11). Therefore, the imperative in Rom 12:1–2 assumes the indicative of the preceding eleven chapters. To those who *through* faith now have priestly access to God,[115] to those who have identified themselves

---

112. Romans 12:1–2; 1 Pet 2:4–9; Heb 10:15–16.

113. See significance of λατρεία in both texts with its LXX background. Thus Paul's priestly activity offers a seventh parallel (between Rom 1:8–15 and 15:14–33) to add to six others identified by Moo, *Epistle to the Romans*, 886.

114. Ibid., 890–91.

115. προσαγωγή in Rom 5:2. Campbell bases his understanding of Paul's "priesthood of all believers" on Rom 5:1–2 ("Priesthood of All Believers," 20). As Eph 2:18 makes clear, this access to the divine is associated with the temple. It is available through

with Jesus' death, burial, and current priestly ministry,[116] to these believers, Paul begins his exhortation with priestly language. He exhorts them to live as the eschatological priests they already are, but only by virtue of the indicative (union with Christ; chs. 1–11) can Paul command the imperative (offer acceptable sacrifices as spiritual worship; Rom 12.1).

Priestly identity is foundational to Paul's self-understanding and vocation (Rom 1:9; 15:16), so it is also fundamental to Rome's believer-priests.[117] Paul begins the parenetic portion with emphasis on the priestly responsibility of each member to offer his or her own sacrifice (Rom 12:1–2; cf. ἑκάστῳ in 12:3; 14:12). Just as the entrance (through confession) and ordination (through baptism) of royal priests is done individually,[118] so is the offering of each priest's daily sacrifice.[119] But while every believer is a priest, each (ἕκαστος; Rom 12:3b, cf. 1 Pet 4:10) member of the royal priesthood must exercise (πρᾶξις; Rom 12:4) his or her priesthood as a member of the priestly body of Christ.[120] An individualistic claim to Christian priesthood by one who has rejected the priestly family of God is invalid; neither Peter nor Paul endorses an "atomistic" priesthood.

Romans 12:1–8 illustrates the NT's balance between identifying believers as eschatological priests (Isa 61:6) and at the same time rejecting an atomistic priesthood. Romans 12 does not exclude the priestly imperative of proclamation emphasized by Paul and Peter elsewhere,[121] but here focus is on "temple service" *within* the body.[122] Paul is describing the service of saints to one another, for which his first choice is cultic language.[123] For

---

Jesus Christ (Eph 3:12). Peter uses the verbal cognate to express the same idea (1 Pet 3:18; cf. Heb 10:19).

116. Rom 8:34; cf. 1:9; 1 Tim 2:1. Intercession is an important function of the mediatorial priesthood (e.g., Aaron [Exod 28:29–30] and the 'ebed Yahweh [Isa 53:12]). Christ, as High Priest, "is able to save to the uttermost those who draw near to God through him, since he always lives to make intercession for them" (Heb 7:25).

117. Daly, *Christian Sacrifice*, 246.

118. See esp. ch. 7, "La Iniciacion Individual Del Sacerdocio Real," in Dabin, *El Sacerdocio Real*, 2:125–52.

119. Rom 12:1; cf. 1 Pet 2:5; Heb 10:11.

120. Rom 12:4–8; cf. "λίθοι ζῶντες" in 1 Pet 2:5–6.

121. Rom 1:9; 15:16; Phil 2:17; 1 Pet 2:9. Paul bases his priestly evangelistic ministry (Rom 15:16) on the work of the Suffering Servant (Rom 15:21 = Isa 52:15).

122. Rom 15:31; 2 Cor 6:16–7:1; 9:12; Eph 5:1–2; Phil 2:25, 30; 3:3; 4:18; 2 Tim 4:6.

123. Paul uses six cultic terms in Rom 12:1: παραστῆσαι "to offer" as a sacrifice is a cultic term in the LXX (Deut 10:8; 17:12; 18:5, 7; 21:5; Judg 20:28); priests are the ones who offer sacrifices θυσίαν (cf. 1 Pet 2:5; Heb 13:15–16); ἁγίαν recalls the fact that believers are only holy because the Holy Spirit indwells them—making them the temple of the living God (I Cor 6:19; 2 Cor 6:16; Rom 8:9–16, 23; Eph 2:19–22); εὐάρεστον is

Paul, all service by the ἁγίοις is temple-service, for it is all done through/in Christ. Thus, like 1 Peter, he uses priestly language for every member of God's household—all of whom can offer sacrifices (1 Pet 2:5). Paul uses cultic language for his own temple-service, but not in a way distinctive from that of other members of Christ's priestly body. Therefore, whether service is expressed as ministry (λειτουργός),[124] worship (λατρεία),[125] or service (διακονία),[126] the work of all "called to be saints"[127] is a priestly ministry. James Dunn's conclusions regarding Paul are equally applicable to other NT authors; they "saw all ministry and service on behalf of the gospel as priestly ministry, ministry which all believers could engage in and which was not limited to any special order of priests."[128]

What is Christian Priesthood?

In this chapter's final section, we offer three preliminary conclusions about Christian priesthood.

1. Christian priesthood is royal priesthood, founded upon familial union with the eschatological Priest-king—Jesus the Anointed One.

2. The primary function of the royal priesthood is the offering of spiritual sacrifices (especially temple service and proclamation).

3. Every member of the royal priesthood has an active ministerial role to play; there are no passive priests in God's house.

Each thesis is elaborated below.

---

a cultic word in the LXX (Phil 4:17 cf. εὐπρόσδεκτος in 1 Pet 2:5; Rom 15:16); λογικὴν has cultic conotations when used in 1 Pet 2:2 (although its meaning in Rom 12:1 is debated); and λατρείαν (Rev 7:15) is rooted in LXX usage relating to tabernacle and temple service. In sum, Rom 12:1 describes "Christian life in terms of cultic service" (Daly, *Christian Sacrifice*, 246).

124. Rom 15:16; cf. 15:27.

125. Rom 12:1; cf. 1:9; Rev 7:15. See also Luter, "'Worship' as Service," 335–44.

126. Especially Rom 12:4; 11:13; 15:31; cf. 1 Cor 16:15; 2 Cor 4:1; 5:18; Eph 4:12; 1 Tim 1:12; 2 Tim 4:5. John Collins's conclusions have been helpfully critiqued by Andrew Clarke; however, if διακονία is recognized as eschatological temple service, then Collins's mediatorial aspect (as a "go-between") becomes more palatable, for it is mediatorial work done by all the ἅγιοι (Eph 4:12). See Collins, *Diakonia*; Clarke, *Serve the Community*, 233–45; Clarke, *Pauline Theology*, 63–66; Bulley, *Priesthood of Some Believers*, 46.

127. Rom 1:7. On this phrase see Procksch, "ἅγιος—ἁγιάζω—ἁγιασμός ἁγιότης—ἁγιωσύνη," 1:107.

128. Dunn, *Theology of Paul the Apostle*, 546.

The Royal Priesthood and the Melchizedekian Priest King

The foundation of the royal priesthood is its familial union with the eschatological Priest-king, Jesus the Anointed One. It is often claimed that there are three priesthoods in the NT: pagan priesthoods, the Levitical priesthood, and Christ's royal priesthood. Christ's priesthood is Melchizedekian, and it is his royal priesthood in which believers share.[129] Congar explains:

> If there is one truth everywhere proclaimed in the gospel and Paul, it is that Christ is the firstborn among a great multitude of brethren, and that he communicates to many what he has accomplished for all. . . . He is priest and sacrifice, but the faithful are priests and sacrifices with him—this is attested in more than fifteen passages of the New Testament.[130]

The uniqueness of Christian priesthood needs emphasis, since it is often confused and its distinctiveness obscured. Christian priesthood is radically eschatological. For NT believers, the eschaton had already dawned. It is a new age in which the Holy Spirit has been poured out on all men and women. All have access to Yahweh's Holy Place, called as temple servants. The Holy Spirit has gifted each of the Father's children; all are oblates. The roots of this understanding of a democratization of priesthood can be found in both OT protology and eschatology: the one drawing from the priesthood of primogeniture (Adam), and the other from the royal priesthood of eschatological promise (Melchizedek and Isaiah's Royal Servant). These OT expectations and their relationship to the apostolic doctrine of the royal priesthood are explored further in Chapters 2 and 3.

Offering Spiritual Sacrifices as the Basic Function of the Christian Priesthood

Christian priesthood is royal priesthood, rooted in the office of the Priest-king, Jesus Christ. But what about his brothers and sisters who now share in his office? How are they identified, and what are their priestly tasks? In sum, *the primary function of the royal priesthood is the offering of spiritual sacrifices, especially understood as temple service and proclamation.*[131]

---

129. Jesus "μένει ἱερεὺς εἰς τὸ διηνεκές" (Heb 7:3). See Demarest, *History of Interpretation*, 136.

130. Congar, "Different Priesthoods," 75.

131. There is no consensus on the central function of the priesthood. Leuchter emphasizes the teaching and mediatorial role ("The Priesthood in Ancient Israel," 100). Leithart rejects mediation and instead argues that "access to Holy Place and altar was

First, just as Jesus the Priest-king offered his life as a sacrifice, so members of the royal priesthood offer their lives in thanks as spiritual sacrifices (Rom 12:1; Eph 5:1–2). All of life is to be offered to the Father, through Christ (Rom 12:1; 1 Pet 2:5; Rev 1:6). Believers are to live unto the Lord, whether working as slaves (Eph 6:5–8), obeying their parents (Eph 6:4), or using their gifts to build up the body (Eph 4:12). Because the eschatological age has arrived, all the royal priesthood's offerings are sacrifices of praise and thanksgiving (Heb 13:15).

Second, by "temple service" I refer to every believer-priest's ministry as a living stone in the Lord's temple-body. Jesus, Paul, and Peter make use of a Temple Psalm (118) to indicate that Christ is the cornerstone of the long-awaited eschatological temple. This temple is not made with human hands, but consists of living stones. All believers are part of this temple, and are called as temple servants to a priestly ministry to one another (Rom 12:1–8). All are called to build up the body, to teach one another, to pronounce forgiveness to one another, to intercede for one another and the world, and to use their spiritual gifts for service.[132] Eschatological priests are anointed and taught by the Holy Spirit in order to instruct one another, proclaiming truth to each other and the world.[133]

Finally, every believer-priest is called to proclaim the glorious deeds of Yahweh (1 Pet 2:9). In the OT, priestly proclamation was especially focused on Torah instruction for God's people.[134] Teaching one another remains a responsibility for the NT's royal priests (Heb 5:12; Col 3:16), but there is now also emphasis on proclamation to the world. This priestly proclamation is a light shining in darkness (Phil 2:14–18). Both words and deeds are to be marked by priestly holiness so that those who see the good deeds are pointed to God (Matt 5:16, 1 Pet 3:1–2, 15). Through proclamation royal priests mediate God's word and presence to the world. This understanding is rooted in the OT's portrayal of priesthood. Deborah Rooke has helpfully described the relationship between OT priestly functions and priesthood:

---

the specifically priestly privilege, and the priestly task was service to Yahweh in the inner chambers of his house" (Leithart, *Priesthood of the Plebs*, 70; cf. 58; 55–71). Rooke's definition, cited below, provides the working definition for this book.

132. Eph 4:12; Col 3:16; Jas 5:16; Matt 18:18; Col 4:3; 1 Pet 4:10–11.

133. John 16:13; Acts 5:32; 6:10; 13:2; Rom 8:14; 1 Cor 2:13; Eph 4:4; Heb 10:15; 1 Pet 1:12; Rev 2:7. On these texts, see Witmer, *Divine Instruction*, esp. 178–83.

134. OT texts speaking of a teaching ministry for priests include: Lev 10:10–11; Deut 27:14–26; 31:9–11; Isa 2:3; Mic 3:11; 4:2; Jer 18:18; Ezek 7:26; 22:26; 44:23; 2 Kings 17:27–28; Ezra 7:10; Hag 2:11–13; Zech 7:3; Mal 2:7–9. Second Temple texts include: 1 Esdr 8:3, 7, 8, 9; 9:7, 39–42, 48; Sir 45:17, 26. See Scholer for further examples (*Proleptic Priests*, 18, 25–26).

> Priesthood is the responsibility of *acting as a mediator* between the human and divine within a given context of ritual, and it appears in the biblical records with two main characteristics: priesthood is primarily about *doing things*, about carrying out rituals and procedures [especially oracular consultation, blessings, and sacrifice]. . . . This leads on to the second major characteristic of the priesthood which appears through the records from the earliest periods, namely, its *involvement with sanctuaries*.[135]

In 1 Pet 2:4–9 and the Pauline letters discussed above, believers meet all three of Rooke's characteristics for priesthood: 1) they are functioning in a mediatorial way, especially between God and those who live in darkness (1 Pet 2:9); 2) by offering spiritual sacrifices they are *doing* what priests do; and 3) all of this service is done as God's temple-people—or from within the cultic context of God's eschatological house, the new temple, of which Christ is the cornerstone.

To sum up, every Christian priest has a threefold task: a vertical ministry of Worship to the Father through Jesus in the Spirit; a horizontal Work of service to other temple servants, and a priestly role of Witness to those living in darkness. Christian priesthood is service to the Lord, one another, and the world.

Cast or Caste: Where are the Cultic Professionals?

Every member of the royal priesthood has an active ministerial role; there are no passive priests in God's house. While the NT applies priestly language to Jewish priests, pagan priests, Christ, and the members of his royal priesthood, it never applies the term to a specialized caste of priestly professionals within the body of Christ. For the NT theologians, the only presently valid priesthood is Christ's, a priesthood shared with each member of his body. Hence, while there were Levitical priests among the early Christian communities, they did not necessarily have a privileged position (Acts 4:36; 6:7). The absence of an ongoing hierarchical priesthood is one of the most remarkable developments in early Christianity. As Yoder notes, "the specialized purveyor of access to the divine has been out of work since Pentecost."[136]

---

135. Rooke, "Kingship as Priesthood," 188–89, 191; emphasis added. Cf. 192n13. While I cannot agree with all of her conclusions (e.g., a low view of priestly election), she is correct in her basic description of this relationship.

136. Yoder, *Body Politics*, 56. See Yoder, *The Fullness of Christ*, Schüssler Fiorenza, "Cultic Language in Qumran and in the NT," 168.

The radical and scandalous nature of this void is easily missed today. A new religion lacking a professional priesthood would be like starting up a charter school for the children of engineers and scientists at Pasadena's Jet Propulsion Labs, but neglecting to include math and science in the curriculum. James Dunn notes that a new religion lacking professional priests, animal sacrifices, and a geographical temple "must have seemed like a plain contradiction in terms, even an absurdity" to most members of the first century.[137] The revolutionary tone of the early Christian vocabulary could be compared to those today who refer to the baptized as "oblates."[138] In the western church, oblate is a word traditionally reserved for those whose whole life has been monastically offered to God. But for Paul, every believer's life is to be a self-oblation, and thus the normal Christian life is participation in a community of oblates.[139]

Kevin Vanhoozer provides a *play-full* way to conclude. He suggests a helpful metaphor for the church: the sacred assembly is a dramatic "company of the gospel."[140] Thus, the priesthood of all believers could be construed as the "playerhood of all believers. . . . every member of the church is a player: a Spirit-endowed agent with a role to play, a gift to contribute."[141] Vanhoozer follows the first Christian theologians well. The royal priesthood is a priestly cast. Every actor in the company offers a sacrifice, serves in the temple, proclaims the excellence (ἀρετὰς) of God, has access to the holy of holies, and is "holy unto the Lord." Peter, Paul, and the author of Hebrews leave no room for a priestly caste within the priestly cast. Members of the company of the gospel are priests who have an active role/part to play by offering spiritual sacrifices, ministering in the temple, and proclaiming the gospel of Jesus, the Anointed, before the world.

Chapter Summary: A Proleptic Priesthood's Temple-Service and Spiritual Sacrifices

To sum up, we might imagine that the television game show, Jeopardy, was set in the first century. In this gameshow, the host gives the contestants clues in the form of an answer, and the contestants must respond with a

---

137. *The Theology of Paul the Apostle*, 548.

138. From the Latin *oblatus* and the Greek προσφορά. See Dabin, *El Sacerdocio Real de los Laicos y la Accion Catolica*, 2:153, 229.

139. "la del nuevo sacerdocio real consiste esencialmente en la auto-oblacion de sus miembros" (Dabin, *El Sacerdocio Real de los Laicos y la Accion Catolica*, 2:153).

140. Vanhoozer, "Evangelicalism and the Church," 86–87.

141. Ibid., 88.

question. As the host, the apostle Peter tells his contestants the answer, and they must reply with the correct question. Peter says, "If the the answer is, 'A person who continually works in a *temple* and daily offers *sacrifices*,' What is the answer?" Before the theme music began to play, all buzzers would have sounded. All the contestants, indeed all members of that first-century audience would already know the correct question, "What is a *priest*?" The relation between temple workers, sacrifice and priest was obvious. As Justin Martyr assumes, only priests offer sacrifices.[142]

In the already-not-yet kingdom, there is an already-not-yet priesthood. All born anew through Christ (1 Pet 1:2, 5) participate in a proleptic priesthood. United with Christ, they are now priests who offer spiritual sacrifices in the new eschatological temple of the Holy Spirit. All believers are saints, oblates, whose whole lives are devoted to temple service. But while they serve in the new temple, their priestly job description includes proclamation of their King's mighty deeds. The priests' sacrificial witness may necessitate suffering, as the example of their High Priest has shown,[143] but ultimately their *telos* is to serve unhindered in an Edenic temple-city where they will walk with God and worship him forever.[144]

In this chapter we surveyed two of the NT's most significant texts on the royal priesthood (1 Pet 2:4–9 and Rom 12:1–8), describing its foundation and function. The next chapter examines Isaiah's Royal and Priestly Servant (Isaiah 40–53) and then the Servant's promised royal-priestly seed (Isaiah 54–66). Here the promise of Exod 19:6's royal priesthood is eschatologized and renewed. Chapter Three explores how Matthew portrays Jesus as Isaiah's priest king, the one who "makes many righteous" (Isa 53:11) and brings forth the long-awaited royal priesthood (Isa 61:6).

---

142. Justin Martyr, *Dialogue with Trypho*, 116 (FC 3:174).
143. 1 Pet 2:21–24; Heb 3:14; 12:2.
144. Rev 1:5–6; 5:9–10; 7:15; 20:6; 21:3–4; 21:22–26; 22:3.

The Story's Script: Isaiah's Royal-Priestly Servant and His Royal-Priestly Seed

> From Judah a king will arise and shall found a new priesthood in accord with the Gentile model and for all nations. His presence is beloved as a prophet of the Most High, a descendant of Abraham, our Father.
>
> —*Testament of Levi* 8:14b–15, ca. 100 BC

> For I tell you that this Scripture must be fulfilled in me: 'And he was numbered with the transgressors.' For what is written about me has its fulfillment.
>
> —Jesus, citing Isa 53:12 (Luke 22:37)

IN THE LAST CHAPTER we saw Peter's clear articulation of a doctrine of the royal priesthood, a belief shared throughout the apostolic writings. But where did this doctrine originate? For the NT authors, the foundational event underwriting the NT doctrine is the royal and priestly ministry of Isaiah's Servant. Isaiah's Servant is understood as a Davidic Priest-King, whose seed will be a royal priesthood. The Servant will lead God's people in a New Exodus, and his seed will finally fulfill their destiny as the royal priesthood described in Exod 19:6—destined to bless the whole world (Gen 12:1–3).

The logic of this chapter proceeds in two movements. The first section describes the NT's identification of Jesus as Isaiah's Servant, best understood as a Davidic and messianic figure, specifically, a Priest-king along the lines of Psalm 110. Secondly, Isaiah's Servant is promised "offspring" (Isa 53:10), and these descendants share in their progenitor's identity. As the Servant (*'ebed Yahweh*) is the major character in Isaiah 40–55, the servants (*'ebedîm*) are the major actors in Isaiah 56–66. The Servant is a Priest-king, and his servant-seed is a royal priesthood. Throughout Isaiah 54–66, the eschatological descendants of the Servant are described as Yahweh's priests and temple servants. In sum, Isaiah depicts a Davidic Priest-king who brings about a democratized state of priestly purity for the whole people of God, thus making possible the realization of Exod 19:6.

Jesus as the Priestly Servant of God (*'ebed Yahweh*)

Over fifty years ago, Thomas Torrance and Cyril Eastwood wrote significant monographs on the royal priesthood. Their first chapters center on Christ as Suffering Servant and Great High Priest.[1] For Torrance, the "wonderful climax" of the OT is the "doctrine of the Suffering Servant" while, for Eastwood, the "Servant of the Lord" is one of three OT concepts necessary to interpret the royal priesthood.[2] Torrance and Eastwood were right to begin with "the heart of New Testament Christology."[3] Yet much has happened in biblical studies during the last fifty years. The recent "Servant of the Lord" literature is prodigious, continuing to grow rapidly. This chapter can do little more than sketch some recent developments in order to build upon Torrance and Eastwood's work.

One thing unchanged during the last fifty years is the importance of the *'ebed Yahweh* theme, an image John Mackay called the "most significant symbol in the Bible and the Christian religion."[4] The Servant's significance contributes to the Servant Songs' categorization as some of the "most debated texts of the Old Testament."[5] The controversy goes back at least to the second century and Justin Martyr's (d. 165) debate with Trypho the Jew.[6] While disagreement is not new, recent NT scholarship has largely rejected Bultmann and Hooker's denial of Jesus' self-identification with the vocation of the *'ebed Yahweh*.[7]

---

1. Torrance, *Royal Priesthood*, 6–22; Eastwood, *Royal Priesthood*, 9–15. Failure to treat the *'ebed Yahweh* is one of the few lacunaes in Dabin's encyclopedic study (*La Sacerdoce Royal des Fidéles dans les Livres Saints*).

2. Torrance, *Royal Priesthood*, 6; Eastwood, *Royal Priesthood*, 1.

3. Cullmann, *Christology of the New Testament*, 51.

4. Cited by Schultz, "Servant, Slave," 1189.

5. Their existence and boundaries are debated (Reventlow, "Basic Issues," 23).

6. Bailey, "'Our Suffering and Crucified,'" 324–417.

7. Bultmann, *Theology of the New Testament*, 28–31; Hooker, *Jesus and the*

Reading Isaiah with the First Christian Theologians

Charles le Brun's (d. 1690) portrayal of Jesus learning Hebrew from an Isaiah scroll open to chapter seven may not be as naive as some imagine.[8] Ancient authors often expected their work to be memorized by their readers (2 Macc 2:25), and Isaiah was a text inscribed on Jesus' heart.[9] The Synoptic Gospels suggest Isaiah was Jesus' favorite book; he cites or alludes to it some thirty-nine times (not counting parallels).[10] No other book comes close to this number; his next most frequently cited books (Daniel, Deuteronomy, and Psalms) have less than half this number. Jesus' words and actions reflect deep meditation upon Isaiah, and his first-century friends were sure that "Isaiah said these things because he saw his glory and spoke of him" (John 12:41).[11] Although given centuries later, Augustine's advice on how to read Scripture provides helpful perspective on ancient reading practices:

> The first rule in this laborious task is, as I have said, to know these books; not necessarily to understand them *but to read them so as to commit them to memory* or at least make them not totally unfamiliar.... *memory is extremely valuable*.[12]

Jesus' apparent memorization of large portions of the Hebrew Scriptures, especially Isaiah, has gone under-appreciated for much of the twentieth century.[13] But the situation is now changing. Theologians claim that "the Savior found the blueprint of his mission"[14] in the Servant Songs, and

---

Servant.

8. The painting is entitled *The Holy Family in Egypt* (Sawyer, *The Fifth Gospel*, plate 2).

9. Safrai, "Spoken and Literary Languages," 244; Carr, *Writing on the Tablet*, 258–60, 287–91.

10. R. T. France, *Jesus and the Old Testament*, 259–63. While there are a number of allusions to the Servant in Jesus' teaching (Mark 10:45 // Matt 20:28; Mark 14:24 // Matt 26:28 // Luke 22:20; Mark 9:12; Matt 3:15; Luke 11:22; cf. the predictions of Jesus' suffering—France explores seventeen passages), the only explicit application of a Servant Song by Jesus to himself is from Isa 53:12, a Song referring to an individual (114–116; Luke 22:37).

11. See for example Matt 5:34–35; 11:5, 23; 12:1; 13:13–15; 15:7–9; 20:28; 21:13; 24:29–30; Luke 4:17–27; 22:37; cf. John 12:8; 13:1–17; 15:7.

12. Augustine, *De doctrina Christiana*, 2:30–31 [2:9]; 70–71; emphasis added.

13. Here I am basically making the same claims for Jesus that Wagner makes for Paul: "Paul in particular was raised in a culture that deeply valued an intimate acquaintance with Israel's Scriptures. In such an environment, the memorization of large portions of scripture was probably the norm" (*Heralds of the Good News*, 21).

14. For example, Blocher, *Songs of the Servant*, 17.

many NT scholars agree that "Jesus' understanding of his mission had been shaped by his reading of Isaiah."[15] If Jesus' self-understanding was shaped by Isaiah's Servant figure (esp. Isa 52:13–52:12), then it becomes imperative to listen closely to the message of Isaiah as read in the first century.[16]

Richard Schultz provides a starting place for understanding the *'ebed Yahweh* theme used by Jesus and the first Christian theologians: "It is best to understand the *'ebed* as one who is dependent on another and accordingly carries out his will or acts for his benefit."[17] Schultz clarifies this comment in relation to *Yahweh* by explaining that the *'ebed Yahweh* "is applied most frequently to Moses (37x) and David (38x)."[18] As *'ebed Yahweh* they 1) have been sent by God "to carry out a crucial task for him;" and 2) "are exemplary in their obedience to him and in their sense of dependence on him."[19]

When considering the *'ebed Yahweh* within Isaiah, it is essential to understand the term within the book's overall structure. Isaiah is often divided into three parts: chapters 1–39 called Proto-Isaiah (PI), chapters 40–55 called Deutero-Isaiah (DI), and chapters 56–66 called Trito-Isaiah (TI).[20] Although these divisions helpfully identify major divisions in content within the book, recent scholarship is moving away from treating the three sections in isolation. After a hundred-year slumber, an emphasis on the book's unity has re-emerged.[21] Both the importance of the three sections and the unity of the one book are illustrated by Isaiah's careful use of the *'ebed Yahweh* theme.[22]

Schultz is thus right to conclude that "only in the context of the thematic development of the book of Isaiah as a whole can the identity and work of the 'servant of the Lord' in Isaiah 40–55 be understood correctly."[23] He

---

15. Freyne, "Jesus and the 'Servant Community,'" 118. Watts notes the influence of Isa 50:6 on Mark 10:33–44 (Matt 20:18–19 // Luke 18:31–33) and especially the impact of Isa 53:3–12 on Mark 8:31; 9:31; 10:45; Matt 16:21; 17:22–23; 20:28 // Luke 9:22. Cf. Luke 4. See his "Isaiah in the New Testament," 219.

16. Isaiah's significance is illustrated by its 450 citations and allusions in the NT (e.g., Watts, *Isaiah's New Exodus*).

17. Schultz, "Servant, Slave," 1184.

18. Ibid., 1190. See Isa 37:35.

19. Ibid., 1191.

20. I use DI and TI as a scholarly convenience without endorsing complex authorship. My aim is to read Isaiah with the first Christian theologians, who were unanimous in assuming a single historical author. Cf. Schultz, "How Many Isaiahs," 150–70; Carr, "Reading Isaiah," 188–218; and Seitz, "Isaiah and the Search," 113–29.

21. Isaiah's three parts have been emphasized since Duhm's 1882 commentary. See Williamson, "Recent Issues," 21; Ausín, "El Espíritu Santo," 98–99.

22. Schultz, "King in the Book of Isaiah," 141–65.

23. Schultz, "Servant, Slave," 1196.

ascribes "theological" significance to thirty-three of the book's thirty-nine uses of *'ebed*, the most important of which take place in DI and TI.[24] DI introduces four Servant Songs of great significance to the *'ebed Yahweh* concept.[25] The final Servant Song (Isaiah 52-53) becomes the climatic turning point for the theme, a turning point which promises a seed to the Servant. In Isaiah 54-66, the seed—the *'ebedîm*—become Isaiah's central characters.

From 'ebed (Servant) to 'ebedîm (servantS)

Identifying the fourth Servant Song as the climatic turning point of Isaiah's Servant theme requires careful attentiveness. Within Isaiah 40-55 (DI), *'ebed* occurs in the *singular* (twenty times) with the final singular use occurring in the final Servant Song (Isa 53:11). After the fourth Servant Song, there is one additional appearance of *'ebed* in DI, but this final reference, is now in the plural (*'ebedîm*).[26] In Isaiah 56-66 (TI) the remarkable transformation of the Servant concept begun in Isa 54:17 continues; all ten appearances of *'ebed* are now *plural* (*'ebedîm*).[27]

W. A. M. Beuken provides further insight into Isaiah's developing Servant theme. The Servant will see his "seed" (זֶרַע; σπέρμα) after offering his life as a "guilt offering" (Isa 53:10, אָשָׁם; δῶτε περὶ ἁμαρτίας).[28] Apparently, what the corporate Servant (Israel) was unable to do (e.g., Isa 43:10), the individual Servant of Isaiah 52-53 accomplishes through a priestly

---

24. In PI *'ebed* appears in 14:2; 20:3; 22:20; 24:2; 36:9, 11; 37:5, 24, 35. It may be significant that PI's final use of *'ebed* is the only place in Isaiah where David is called "my Servant." PI thus ends with a promise of deliverance "for the sake of my servant David" (Isa 37:5).

25. Isa 42:1-9; 49:1-6 (7-13?); 50:4-9; and 52:13-53:12). The actual phrase *'ebed Yahweh* only appears in 42:19. On the starting and ending points of the first three songs, see Watts, *Isaiah*, 2:107-8; 113-15; Smith, *Isaiah 40-66* 152-59.

26. Isa 54:17. *'ebed* appears exclusively in the singular elsewhere in DI: 41:8, 9; [42:1]; 42:19 (x2); 43:10; 44:1, 2, 21 (x2), 26; 45:4; 48:20; [49:3, 5, 6, 7]; 50:10; [52:13; 53:11]. Servant Songs are in brackets. At times *'ebed* refers to the nation of Israel (41:8-9; 42:19; 43:10; 44:1-2; 44:21; 44:26; 45:4; 48:20) and at other times he appears to be an individual or group distinguished from Israel (49:5-6; 52:13-12). Schultz only finds nineteen occurrences of the singular *'ebed* in DI ("Servant, Slave," 1195).

27. Isa 56:6; 63:17; 65:8, 9, 13 (3x), 14, 15; 66:14.

28. "Before the fourth Servant Song Israel is addressed as 'the seed' of the patriarchs (Abraham: Isa 41:8; cf. 51:2; Jacob-Israel: 45:19), which will itself have offspring (Isa 43:5; 44:3; 49:19), but from Isa 53:10 on the promise of posterity regards the Servant and the new city (Isa 54:3)" (Beuken, "Main Theme of Trito-Isaiah." Followed by Childs, *Isaiah*; Blenkinsopp, *Isaiah 56-66*.

self-offering.[29] The Servant provides the way for his eschatological seed to be the holy people and royal priesthood they were originally called to be.[30] The Servant's seed continues elements of the Servant's priestly work in TI's eschatological age (temple service, light-bearing, teaching, offering sacrifices). They become the central theme of the third part of Isaiah. Beuken's essay demonstrates "that in his whole work, TI is occupied with the question of the servants of YHWH, until the last place where the term is found in this corpus (Isa 66:14); indeed, that this question is the centre of his interest."[31] Jesus' teaching as captured by the NT authors reflects attentiveness to Isaiah's subtle development of the Servant theme.

Turning Point: The Servant as Priest-King in Isaiah 52–53

The Servant's characteristics are essential for understanding his seed. Early Christian reflection on the priestly work of the *'ebed Yahweh* led to an understanding of Jesus as the great hight priest (ἀρχιερέα μέγαν).[32] Cullmann rightly recognizes that a priestly ministry is at the core of the Servant's work; "the concept of High Priest is closely related to that of the Suffering Servant."[33] Since Cullmann, a number of writers have presented a strong case that the Servant of Isaiah 53 is not simply a high-priestly figure, but a royal-priestly figure.[34] He is a Davidic Priest-King according to the order of Melchizedek, fulfilling both the Davidic and Levitical covenants and initiating a new-covenant priesthood.[35] This interpretation provides Isaiah 53's Servant with both royal and priestly qualifications. The Davidic *'ebed Yahweh* is a Priest-king.[36]

---

29. Watts, "Isaiah 40–55," 55.

30. Exod 19:6. See use of זֶרַע in Isa 53:10. C.f. 59:21; 65:9; 66:21–22.

31. Beuken, "Main Theme of Trito-Isaiah," 68.

32. Heb 4:14; 7:27; 9:28. The high priestly office contains the idea of sacrifice; the *'ebed Yahweh*, the idea of self-sacrifice (Cullmann, *Christology of the New Testament*, 83; 91–92).

33. Ibid.

34. Petterson, *Behold Your King*, 240; Hahn, *Kinship by Covenant*, 13–14; Block, "My Servant David,"17–56; Motyer, *Prophecy of Isaiah*, 13–16.

35. Hebrews 7:12; 2 Cor 3:6; cf. Jer 30:1–33:26, esp. 31:31–34; Psalms 110 and 89:20, 26–28 (on Psalm 89 see Hahn, *Kinship by Covenant*, 175). Cf. *T. Levi* 8:14b–15.

36. On the Davidide as Priest-king see Block, "My Servant David," 33–36; Merrill, "Royal Priesthood," 50–61; Rooke, "Kingship as Priesthood."

While arguments have been made for the Servant's identification with a "prophet like Moses" (Deut 18:14),[37] a Davidic Priest-King along the lines of Psalm 110 best fits Isaiah's conceptual background.[38] This also resonates with a canonical perspective[39] where David is the more important figure "theologically," since in the majority of the servant references to "David (23x), it is God himself who calls David 'my servant.'"[40] Yet we may be able to acknowledge that both Moses and David serve as royal-priestly types for the *'ebed Yahweh*. Both are priestly,[41] having a special intercessory relationship with Yahweh;[42] both play central roles in the formation of covenants between God and his people; both are instrumental in establishing new places and practices for the worship of Yahweh (tabernacle, temple); and both are in some sense "royal."[43]

Schultz sees evidence of prophetic, priestly, and royal characteristics in the final Servant Song, but claims that the priestly function is emphasized.[44] In Isa 52:15, the Servant "sprinkles" many nations.[45] He offers himself as a

---

37. So Hugenberger, but he separates evidence for the Servant as a royal figure (114–18) from evidence for the Servant as a priestly figure (118–19). This is an unnecessary bifurcation if a priest-king is in view ("Servant of the Lord," 105–40).

38. See Ezekiel, Jeremiah, and Zechariah's development of Isaiah's Servant figure as a Davidic Priest-king. The three most frequently cited texts in the OT are messianic (Isa 52:13–53:12, Daniel 7, and Psalm 110), and the NT authors believed all three described a Davidic Priest-king, the Anointed One (ὁ Χριστός).

39. For example, Ezekiel's temple vision provides canonical warrant for the priority given to the Davidic Priest-king. When considering the context of Ezek 37:20–29, Levenson identifies a surprising absence of the high priest from Ezekiel's eschatological temple and suggests he has been replaced by the Davidic Priest-king (*Theology of the Program of Restoration of Ezekiel 40–48*, 143). See also Block, "Bringing Back David," 183–88.

40. Schultz, "Servant, Slave," 1191. See Isa 37:35 and Schultz's discussion of the *'ebed Yahweh* in the Psalms, where 26 of its 29 occurrences are singular.

41. See Ps 99:6 and Wells's argument that Moses is the archetypical priest (*God's Holy People*, 127). David's role as Priest-king is clearest in Psalm 110.

42. For Moses, see Exod 15:25–26; 17:10–13; 32:11–14; 33:11, etc. For David, note the function of "inquire" (לִשְׁאֹל) in 1 Sam 23:1–3; 30:8; 2 Sam 2:1; 5:19, 23; 1 Chron 14:10, 14 and compare its usage with the negative example of Saul in 1 Sam 14:35–37; 28:6–7. Second Samuel 16:23 seems to imply that "inquiring of God" was a priestly function. Cf. Jehoshaphat's question in 1 Kgs 22:7.

43. Moses is associated with royalty at his birth and functions as a royal figure in the Pentateuch, modeling the royal qualities described in Deut 17:15–20. Philo portrays him as an ideal Priest-king (*De vita Mosis*).

44. Schultz, "Servant, Slave," 1196. By way of comparison, Beaton argues that Matthew's citation from the first Servant Song (Isa 42:1–4) emphasizes the royal aspect of the Servant (*Isaiah's Christ*, 192).

45. There is a textual issue with the NLT and NRSV preferring "startle" over the "sprinkle" of the ESV, NIV, NASB, and HCSB. "Sprinkle" is to be preferred; cf. Exod

sacrificial lamb,[46] and his life as a guilt offering (אָשָׁם Isa 53:10). The LXX translates guilt offering (אָשָׁם) as "given for sin" (δῶτε περὶ ἁμαρτίας), and this is most likely why Paul can say that Christ's death for our sins was "according to Scripture."[47] His death will make "*many*" righteous, which underlies Jesus' words at the Last Supper: "this is my blood of the covenant, which is poured out for *many*."[48] Perhaps most significantly, the final line of the poem testifies that the Servant continues to engage in priestly work, since "he makes intercession for the transgressors."[49]

The MT emphasizes the priestly nature of the Servant, and this emphasis is magnified in the second-century *Targum of Isaiah*.[50] Since Jesus most likely taught in Aramaic, it "must be consulted" when studying first-century interpretations of Isaiah 53.[51] The Targum especially emphasizes three priestly functions of the Servant, who is portrayed as a new Moses or

---

29:21; Lev 4:1–21; 5:9; 14:7; Heb 9:13–21; 10:22; 11:28; esp. 12:24 and 1 Pet 1:2.

46. Isaiah 53:7; cf. Acts 8:26–40; cf. Jeremias' observation that the NT's "Lamb of God" and "Servant of the Lord" vocabulary are linked in Aramaic. This overlapping conceptual usage becomes especially important in the Johannine literature. "In Aramaic the word אַיְלָט has the twofold significance of a. lamb and b. boy or servant. Probably an Aramaic אָהְלָאד אַיְלָט in the sense of הוֹהִי דְבַע underlies the Greek ὁ ἀμνὸς τοῦ θεοῦ, the original reference thus *being to Jesus as the servant of God*" ("ἀμνός, ἀρήν, ἀρνίον," 1:339; emphasis added). So also Wenschkewitz, *Die Spiritualisierung der Kultusbegriffe*, 159.

47. 1 Cor 15:3–4, cf. "prolong his days" in Isa 53:10.

48. Mark 14:23 (cf. Matt 26:28). See use of πολλοῖς in Isa 53:11, 12 (x2). See Betz, "Jesus and Isaiah 53," 86; Watts, "Isaiah in the New Testament," 219. Luke places special emphasis on Jesus as the Servant (22:24–27), and Jesus explicitly identifies himself with the Servant as he approaches the cross (Luke 22:37 = Isa 53:12c). Another ancient application of Isa 53:12c to Jesus' death on the cross is preserved in the textual variant found at Mark 15:28.

49. Isa 53:12 עָגַפ; cf. 59:16; Rom 8:24; Heb 7:25. Contra Cullmann: "Deutero-Isaiah gives us no details about the future work the '*ebed* will accomplish in glory" (*Christology of the New Testament*, 77).

50. Ådna dates the Targum to AD 132–35. Most scholars agree that it preserves many first-century readings ("Isaiah 52:13—53:12," 197).

51. Betz, "Jesus and Isaiah 53," 71. Chilton writes that "the most evident [NT] coincidences with the Targum appear in the sayings of Jesus" (Chilton, *Isaiah Targum*, xxvi). Note Jesus' Aramaic citation of Ps 22:2 in Mark 15:34; cf. Matt 27:46. See also Chilton's discussion of Mark 4:12 and *Tg. Isa.* 6:9–10; Matt 26:52 and *Tg. Isa.* 50:11; Mark 9:48 and *Tg. Isa.* 66:24; Matt 7:2 and *Tg. Isa.* 27:8.

David: 1) the Servant's intercession (יְעַבִי) brings forgiveness;[52] 2) he builds the temple (אַשְׁדְקִמ תִיב);[53] and 3) is a "teacher of the law."[54]

The priestly emphasis is especially illustrated when verse five of the Targum is compared with the MT:

MT וְתִרְבְחָבוּ וִילָע וְנֻמוֹלִשׁ רֹסוּם וְנִיתָנוּעִם אָכָדָם וְנִעְשָׁפִם לְלָחֵם אוּהִן וְנָל־אָפַרְנ[55]

ET But he was wounded for our transgressions; he was crushed for our iniquities; upon him was the chastisement that brought us peace, and with his stripes we are healed.

TG הִיגְפַלְאֲבוּ אָנָתָיָוֵעָב רְסַמְתָא אָנָבוֹחָב לְחַתִיאָד אַשְׁדְקָם תִיָב יָנְבִי אוּהִן[56] :אָנָל וְוקְבַתְשִׁי אָנָבוֹח יְהוֹמַגְתָפֵל יְהוֹנִיתָנְדִיבוּ אָנָלָע יָגְסִי יָמָלְשׁ

ET And he *will build the sanctuary which was profaned* for our sins, *handed over* for our iniquities; and *by his teaching his* peace *will increase* upon *us,* and in *that we attach ourselves to his words our sins will be forgiven us.*[57]

The Targum's emphasis on the Servant's threefold priestly ministry (building the sanctuary, teaching, bringing forgiveness) magnifies the MT's emphasis on the priestly ministry of the Servant.

A close reading of Isaiah 52–53, with its first Christian interpreters and the *Isaiah Targum,* suggests that a priestly interpretation of the *'ebed Yahweh* was present in first-century Palestine.[58] After the Servant's priestly

52. Isa 53:4, 11, 12. According to Ådna, "When it says that forgiveness occurs 'for his sake' (4, 6, 12), that is to be understood as a reference to his intercession, which here corresponds to the priestly atonement ritual in Leviticus 4–5 and Numbers 15" ("Isaiah 52:13–53:12," 218).

53. Isa 53:5; cf. 56:5, 7. The Servant/Son of David as temple builder is a major OT motif. David's son *par excellence* is the temple builder (1 Chron 17:11–14 // 2 Sam 7:11–16; 2 Chron 28:6–10). Stephen Dempster describes the Tanakh as a story with a beginning (Genesis), middle, and end (Chronicles). Almost twenty chapters at the end are devoted to David, Solomon, and the building of the temple (1 Chron 22—2 Chron 10:1). Yet the destruction of Solomon's temple leaves Chronicles' readers hungry for a son of David who will rebuild Yahweh's temple. Dempster notes: "The goal of the canon [Tanakh] is clearly the great house of God, which is as inclusive as the globe" (*Dominion and Dynasty,* 46, 227).

54. Isa 53:5 (Ådna, "Isaiah 52:13–53:12," 197–223).

55. Isa 53:5. The LXX of Isa 53:5 generally follows the MT: "αὐτὸς δὲ ἐτραυματίσθη διὰ τὰς ἀνομίας ἡμῶν καὶ μεμαλάκισται διὰ τὰς ἁμαρτίας ἡμῶν, παιδεία εἰρήνης ἡμῶν ἐπ᾽ αὐτόν, τῷ μώλωπι αὐτοῦ ἡμεῖς ἰάθημεν."

56. Targum of Isa 53:5. Targum references come from *TJP*.

57. Chilton, *Isaiah Targum,* 104; emphasis original.

58. In addition to the Isaiah Targum, Heb 9:28 relates Jesus' role as high priest to

work, his seed will continue aspects of his priestly ministry (Isaiah 54–66). This servant-seed matches the description of the "royal priesthood" promised to Moses in Exod 19:6.

The Servant's Royal and Priestly Seed ('*ebedîm*) in Isaiah 54–66

Following the Servant's priestly self-offering in the final Servant Song, Isaiah's emphasis moves to the Servant's seed—the '*ebedîm*. In Isaiah 54–66, we find at least five texts attributing priestly titles and/or activities to the eschatological descendants of the Servant.[59] The early church understood their post-Pentecost communities as already experiencing the realities promised by Isaiah in these five texts. They were Isaiah's priestly servants. For example, Paul saw himself participating in Isaiah's narrative as one of the Servant's '*ebedîm*.[60] The new priestly privileges of the eschatological '*ebedîm* can be seen in the Gentile eunuch, who formerly disqualified from entering the ἐκκλησίαν κυρίου (Deut 22:2 LXX), could now minister in God's house and joyfully offer sacrifices because of the Servant's self-sacrifice.[61] In Acts, the "Isaianic New Exodus program provides the structural framework for the narrative" and supplies "the foundation story through which the identity of the early Christian movement can be constructed."[62] We now move to these five passages.

---

the priestly offering of the Suffering Servant in Isaiah 53 (cf. 1 Pet 2:24). For more on the priestly nature of the Servant see Koch, "Messias und Sündenvergebung in Jesaja 53," 137–48 esp. 144. Cf. Ådna, "Isaiah 52:13–53:12," 223.

59. Isa 54:11–17; 56:1–8; 59:21–60:3; 61:1–11; 66:18–21. These texts do not exhaust the theme in TI. The '*ebedîm* have greater access to the Holy One than is found in the temple (Isa 57:15; see Wells, *God's Holy People*, 152–55). Sommer identifies a possible reading of Isa 60:7 where "foreigners will be accorded priestly privileges that even regular Israelites do not have in priestly law" (*Prophet Reads Scripture*, 148). Hanson finds a reaffirmation of "the early Yahwistic, egalitarian notion of a nation of priests" in Isa 60:21 (*People Called*, 255). Laansma makes connections between Isa 66:1–6, Hos 6:6, and Jesus' claim to be greater than the temple in Matt 12:6 ("I Will Give You Rest," 231–32).

60. Isaiah 54–66. As argued by Gignilliat, *Paul and Isaiah's Servants*; Ware, *Mission of the Church*; Bauckham, "God Crucified," 1–59. Cf. Wagner, *Heralds of the Good News*, who holds a slightly different view of Paul's relationship to Isaiah's Servant.

61. Isaiah 53; 56:1–8; Acts 8:26–40. See Pao, *Acts and the Isaianic New Exodus*, 140–42.

62. Ibid., 250.

The Eschatological Seed's Priestly Access to Yahweh (Isaiah 54:11–17)

Isaiah's first use of the plural *'ebedîm* takes place in Isa 54:17.[63] The eschatological "inheritance" of Yahweh's *'ebedîm* (Isa 54:17) includes the promise that "all your children will be taught by Yahweh."[64] This promise "envisions a situation of eschatological divine instruction in Jerusalem."[65] Divine instruction is an eschatological reality in the "last days" (Isa 2:2–3), a benefit of the covenant established by the Servant.[66]

There is an important intertextual development of Isaiah's theme in Jeremiah's Book of the Covenant (Jer 31:31, 33b–34):

> Behold, the days are coming, declares the Lord, when I will make a new covenant with the house of Israel . . . I will put my law within them, and I will write it on their hearts. And I will be their God, and they shall be my people. And no longer shall each one teach his neighbor and each his brother, saying, 'Know the Lord,' for they shall all know me, from the least of them to the greatest.

Isaiah's promise that Yahweh will make "his instruction accessible" to every member of the *'ebedîm*,[67] and Jeremiah's knowledge of Yahweh "from the least of them to the greatest" (Jer 31:34), become major themes for the first Christian theologians. Witmer shows that divine instruction, whether by Jesus or the Holy Spirit, plays an important role in the writings of John, Paul, and Matthew.[68] Although Witmer does not address Hebrews' use of Jer 31:32–34, the new covenant reality described in Hebrews 8–12 also fulfills this vision.

---

63. Beale has noted that Rev 21:18–21 develops Isa 54:11–17, providing canonical evidence that Isaiah 54 may point toward the eschatological temple (*Temple and the Church's Mission*, 132). Cf. Smith, *Isaiah 40–66*, 489.

64. Isa 54:13, my translation; in agreement with LXX, "καὶ πάντας τοὺς υἱούς σου διδακτοὺς θεοῦ." Witmer prefers "And all your sons (will be) disciples of Yahweh, and great will be the peace of your sons" (*Divine Instruction*, 21). This eschatological reality was prophesied in Isa 2:3, but only becomes a reality after the Servant's priestly offering.

65. Ibid., 21.

66. Isa 49:8; cf. 54:10; 55:3; 56:6.

67. Witmer, *Divine Instruction*, 27.

68. He discusses 1 Thess 4:9; 1 Cor 2:13; Matt 23:8–10; John 6:45–46; 1 John 2:20, 27 (ibid., 81–85; 94–95; 116–22; 131–52; 153–78). See also Yieh, *One Teacher*, 7–93, esp. 89.

Through Christ all of God's people have an entirely new level of priestly access to Yahweh and his divine instruction.[69] Whereas under the old covenant access to Yahweh and divine instruction were mediated through the tribe of Levi, in the New Covenant every member of the royal priesthood holds these privileges. In the eschatological age, the veil is torn and the Holy of Holies is accessible to all God's children (Heb 10:19–24).[70]

The Priestly Seed Includes Eunuchs and Foreigners as Temple Servants (Isaiah 56:1–8)

Both the prologue (Isa 56:1–8) and the epilogue (Isa 66:18–21) of Isaiah 46–66 (TI) promise a new level of eschatological access to Yahweh. The *'ebedîm*'s democratized priestly ministry serves as an inclusio in TI. Cultic service is not only characteristic of the *'ebedîm* in TI's first use of the term,[71] but priestly service also marks their final description (Isa 66:14–21). Thus, it is not surprising that many have identified a chiastic structure within TI.[72]

> A—Isaiah 56:1–8: The *'ebedîm* Includes Foreigners as Temple-Servants
>
> > B—Isaiah 56:9–12: Description of the Wicked
> >
> > > C—Isaiah 57–60: Various Proposals
> > >
> > > > D—Isaiah 61:1–11: All Will Be Priests and Ministers
> > >
> > > C'—Isaiah 62–65: Various Proposals
> >
> > B'—Isaiah 66:15–17: Description of the Wicked
>
> A'—Isaiah 66:18–24: The *'ebedîm* Includes Foreigners as Priests

The chiastic structure identifies Isaiah 61 (with its intertextual echo of Exod 19:6 and description of the *'ebedîm* as ministers and priests) as the "theological core" of Isaiah 56–66.[73]

---

69. Hebrews 4:14–16; 5:12; esp. 10:19–25. See discussion in Chapter 3, and Scholer, *Proleptic Priests*.

70. Küng, *Church*, 373; Isa 56:6.

71. Isa 53:6. שָׁרֵת is the normal verb of Levitical service. See cultic use in Isa 60:7, 10, esp. 61:6.

72. Details of the chiasm vary (see Smith, *Isaiah 40–66*, 520–22), but its presence is widely acknowledged.

73. Oswalt, *Book of Isaiah*, 534; Stromberg, "Inner-Isaianic Reading," 269; Ausín, "El Espíritu Santo," 98–99.

Secondly, in TI's prologue we learn that Yahweh's *ʿebedîm* will include *both* eunuchs and foreigners. Luke's narrative skillfully emphasizes both aspects: the Ethiopian eunuch's discovery of the true meaning of Isaiah 53 frees him to be joyful in Yahweh's eschatological temple.[74] In Acts, the content of baptismal catechesis consists of teaching on Isaiah's eschatological royal priesthood. Acts 8:26–39 fulfills Isaiah 56 and illustrates how foundational the Isaianic narrative was to Luke-Acts.[75] In these last days Isaiah's democratization of the Spirit has taken place within Luke's eschatological community.[76]

Finally, the prologue to Isaiah 56–66 shockingly reveals that in the eschatological era Gentiles and eunuchs will engage in cultic service within Yahweh's house.[77] In TI's first use of *ʿebedîm*, the servants are described with priestly vocabulary and astoundingly will include those previously unfit for temple service. Like the Servant, the *ʿebedîm* will present acceptable burnt offerings and sacrifices, and their divine service will be offered in the temple.[78] It would be difficult to make the priestly service of the Servant's seed more explicit.

The Seed Shares the Servant's Priestly Anointing (Isaiah 59:21—60:3)

Beuken's identification of the *ʿebedîm* as the main theme of Isaiah 56–66, is strengthened by recognizing an aposiopesis in Isaiah 56:9—63:6, in which the character of the servants is "slowly but surely constituted without mention of their name."[79] The theological center of TI is found within these chapters, with two passages especially important for understanding the priestly nature of the Servant's seed.[80]

---

74. Isaiah 56:7 and Acts 8:39 (Pao, *Acts and the Isaianic New Exodus*, 140–42).

75. Mallen explains that the Servant motif in Luke provides a "job description or outline for Jesus' mission and that of his followers" (*Reading and Transformation*, 207. Mallen does not interact with Beuken.

76. Pao, *Acts and the Isaianic New Exodus*, 116. See Isa 32:14–17 and 59:21.

77. This "shock value" of foreigners performing cultic service "seems to have been so repugnant to the scribe of 1QIsa that he omitted it [תִּירֹשׁ]" (Oswalt, *Isaiah*, 459, 460). See Corriveau on Isa 56:6–7 and LXX cultic vocabulary (*Liturgy of Life*, 30–35).

78. Isa 56:7: עוֹלֹתֵיהֶם וְזִבְחֵיהֶם לְרָצוֹן עַל־מִזְבְּחִי. The LXX terms here are discussed below. See Beuken, "Main Theme," 85.

79. Beuken, "Main Theme" 68.

80. Isa 59:21–60:3; 61:1–11.

The first passage, Isaiah 59:21—60:3, reveals that the seed will be anointed with the Spirit just as the Servant himself was anointed.[81] In the OT, the privilege of anointing belonged to priests and kings. Here the anointing is part of Yahweh's covenant with the Servant's seed (Isa 59:21). Verse twenty-one sums up themes from Isaiah 56–59. Its reference to covenant "is obviously linked to the programmatic occurrence in 56:6-7, addressed to God's servants."[82] In the power of Yahweh's Spirit the *'ebedîm* are now invited to share in the Servant's mission of bringing "justice"[83] and "light"[84] to the nations. A major transition takes place in the opening verses of Isaiah 60; portions of the Servant's functions are transferred to the people of Zion.[85]

In mediating the light of Yahweh to the nations, the Servant's seed is now imitating the Servant by exercising a *priestly* function.[86] The nations in darkness receive Yahweh's light through the witness of the *'ebedîm*.[87] By faithfully following the Servant's example and sharing in his priestly work, Isaiah's eschatological people will bring radiant joy to both Jew and Gentile.[88] Paul develops this principle explicitly in Phil 2:14-18. The Philippian believers are a "community of priests" who shine as lights holding forth the gospel to the world.[89] Isaiah's prophecy has been realized in the Philippian community; the *'ebedîm* now share the Servant's priestly responsibility of bringing light to the Gentiles.

---

81. Isa 42:1; 59:21; cf. 61:1-11; Luke 3:22; 4:1, 14, 18; Acts 1:8; 2:4, 38-39; 10:36-38.

82. Childs, *Isaiah*, 490. Cf. Isa 59:6; Jer 31:32-34.

83. On justice as a responsibility of priests see Lev 17:8-13; cf. Isa 42:1-9 and 58:8, 10.

84. Isa 42:1-6; 49:6; 60:1-3; Cf. Luke 2:32; 11:31; Acts 13:46-47; Phil 2:14-18; 1 Pet 2:9. On light bearing, the temple, and priests see Barker, *Great High Priest*, 186. Karl Barth also emphasizes the royal priesthood as light bearers (see ch. 6 below).

85. Beuken, "Main Theme," 70.

86. Martens ("Impulses to Mission," 236) and Elliott (*Elect and the Holy*, 61) emphasize the Servant's mediatory role.

87. Whether the light functions in a centripetal way (come), "a light *for* the nations" (lighthouse), or a centrifugal way (go), "offered *to* the nations" (torch, flashlight), is a secondary issue (Martens, "Impulses to Mission," 227, 237).

88. On "light" and "joy" see Isa 42:6; 49:13; 60:5; 61:7; Acts 13:47-48; Phil 2:14-18; esp. Isa 56:7 and Acts 8:39.

89. Ware, *Mission of the Church*, 272-73.

The Seed Shares the Servant's Priestly Mission (Isaiah 61)

The second passage in the aposiopesis, Isaiah 61, has received much attention from Christian theologians since at least the first century when Luke, the evangelist-theologian, records Jesus announcing its fulfillment in his own ministry.[90] Isaiah and Luke were both concerned with a "redefinition of the people of God" in a new era following the pattern provided by the Exodus paradigm, the primary difference being that for Isaiah the new era was in the future, and for Luke it had proleptically arrived.[91] Given the importance of the Exodus narrative to Isaiah, it is not surprising that Exodus' climatic statement about the royal priesthood of God's people (Exod 19:6) plays a central role in Isaiah's description of the eschatological remnant (Isa 61:6). In both passages, the priesthood received by Yahweh's chosen people is for the nations.

Isaiah 61:6 is the second most important OT text on the royal priesthood.[92] It makes the royal priesthood in Exod 19:6 the focal point of Isaiah's New Exodus narrative.[93] Israel's identification as a royal priesthood comes at a very significant point in the literary structure of Exodus, and the same is true for Isaiah.[94] Exodus provides a paradigmatic example of how God works with his people, and Isaiah "eschatologizes" the promise that one day Israel would be Yahweh's royal priests.[95]

Isaiah 61 begins with three verses referring back to the Servant figure of Isaiah 40–53. Childs comments that "in the speaker of chapter 61 the offspring of the 'suffering servant' of chapter 53 is embodied, who can be an individual as well as a collective entity."[96] Jesus' claim of Isa 61:1–3's fulfillment is a statement not only about his own identity, but also about the

---

90. Luke 4:17–21. Origen connects Isa 61:6 with 1 Pet 2:9 to instruct Alexandrian Christians on their status as "priests of God" (*Homélies Sur Le Lévitique*, SC 286:180). See Luther, *LW* 17:329; Calvin, *CC* 4:311; Childs, *Isaiah*, 507–08; Pao, *Acts and the Isaianic New Exodus*, 70–84.

91. Pao, *Acts and the Isaianic New Exodus*, 58.

92. Elliott, *Elect and the Holy*, 59–63; Davies, *Royal Priesthood*, 212–17; Schüssler Fiorenza, *Priester für Gott*, 155–66; Oswalt, *Isaiah*, 571–72.

93. Recall TI's chiastic structure in which Isa 61:6 falls at the exact center. Fifty years ago Elliott denied an intertextual relationship between Exod 19:6 and Isa 61:6, but only one interpreter has followed his lead. For refutations of Elliott see Davies, *Royal Priesthood*, 16n88, 212–17; Schüssler Fiorenza, *Priester für Gott*, 158–60.

94. Davies, *Royal Priesthood*, 103–69.

95. Pao, *Acts and the Isaianic New Exodus*, 56.

96. Childs, *Isaiah*, 503.

Servant's seed.⁹⁷ As Ausín notes, Isaiah 61 (and Luke 4:17–21) focuses on the eschatological community receiving the titles "Priests of Yahweh" and "ministers of our God" (Isa 61:6). Their priestly status is "the new condition of those who received the anointing of the Spirit. They, all of them, are priests who exercise their functions in relation to the pagans."⁹⁸

Isaiah 61 emphasizes the priestly status and ministry of the eschatological seed.⁹⁹ Davies has provided a summary of the textual evidence, which includes: 1) a reference to the anointed royal and priestly Servant (Isa 61:1–3; cf. Ps 110:4) whose seed now shares a similar anointing (Isa 59:21); 2) royal and priestly clothing for the Servant's seed identifying them with the clothing of Yahweh himself;¹⁰⁰ 3) the Servant's seed receiving the titles *"priests of Yahweh"* and *"ministers of our God"*;¹⁰¹ 4) a return of the privilege of the primogenital priesthood, for the Servant's seed now receives the double portion of the firstborn;¹⁰² and 5) the seed receiving its priestly office alongside an everlasting covenant, bringing to mind earlier examples of the relationship between priesthood and covenant.¹⁰³ In sum, chapter 61 provides Isaiah's clearest statement of the priestly status of the *'ebedîm*, priestly status emphasized in Isaiah 56–66.¹⁰⁴

---

97. Ibid., 503; Gignilliat, *Paul and Isaiah's Servants*, 120.

98. *"sino la nueva condición de los que recibirán la unción del espíritu. Ellos, todos, serán sacerdotes que ejercerán sus funciones en relación con los paganos"* (Ausín, "El Espíritu Santo," 117; cf. 97).

99. Isaiah 56–66 emphasizes the priestly status of the *'ebedîm*, but the royal dimension is present (cf. Isa 55:3–5; 60:14, 21; Schüssler-Fiorenza, *Priester für Gott*, 164–66; Davies, *Royal Priesthood*, 213).

100. Isa 61:3, 10; cf. רֹאשׁ in 60:7.

101. Isa 61:6; emphasis added. Davies writes, "the use of כֹּהֲנֵי and יְתָרְשָׁמ together is only otherwise associated with cultic contexts, and some extended cultic metaphor seems unavoidable. That is, Zion . . . will come to occupy, an analogous relationship to Yahweh as that enjoyed by the Levitical priests" (*Royal Priesthood*, 216).

102. Isa 61:7. Davies does not note the link to primogenital priesthood. Although a number of commentators identify the relationship between the double portion and the privilege of the firstborn (e.g., Oswalt, *Isaiah*, 572), none relate this observation to primogenital priesthood. Yet the priestly privilege emphasized in the preceding verse (Isa 61:6), the presence of primogenital priests in the literary context of Exod 19:6 (vv. 22, 26), and the Pentateuch's emphasis on the relationship between priesthood and the firstborn suggests a primogenital priesthood (cf. Exod 4:22–23; 12:29; 13:2–16; Num 3:11–13; 40–51; 8:14–19; Deut 21:15–17). Barth comes close to this insight (*CD* IV/1, 169–71).

103. Isa 61:8. So Davies, *Royal Priesthood*, 216; Hahn, *Kinship by Covenant*, 136–75.

104. Among writers on the royal priesthood and Isa 61:6, only Schüssler Fiorenza recognizes the larger "Kultmotiv in Tritojesaja" (*Priester für Gott*, 162–64). She discusses Isa 56:4–8, 61:1–11, and 66:20–21. Cf. Hahn, *Kinship by Covenant*, 168–69.

Finally, Isaiah 61's royal priesthood, like that of Exod 19:6, is for the nations.[105] The nations or the peoples are mentioned four times in chapter 61, and the ultimate purpose of the Servant's priestly seed relates to Yahweh's action of causing "righteousness and praise to sprout up before all the nations."[106] A "priesthood for the nations" reading of Isaiah 61 receives further canonical warrant when the two interpolations (Isa 42:7a and Isa 58:6d) in Luke's citation of Isa 61:1–3 (Luke 4:18–21) are examined in their original Isaianic context.[107] Jesus' exposition of Isaiah 61 with reference to Elijah and Elisha's ministry toward two Gentiles also indicates his understanding of the text's missional orientation (Luke 4:26–27). The Servant's seed will share in the Servant's mission as a priestly "light to the nations" (Isa 42:6e).[108]

The Eschatological Seed's Priestly Office (Isaiah 66:18–21)

Isaiah 66:18–21 is the final text establishing a priestly ministry for the Servant's seed. It summarizes previous themes while serving as a double inclusio,[109] concluding both the eschatological stream of nations from PI's prologue and the radical democratization of priestly privilege (including eunuchs and Gentiles) from TI's prologue.[110] Beuken has shown that Yahweh's *'ebedîm* play a fundamental role between Isa 56:1 and 66:14. In all of TI "there is no passage, except 63.1–6, in which the theme does not play a central part."[111] While the *'ebedîm* may suffer in eschatological tension, they will ultimately be vindicated in an Edenic new creation.[112]

When we turn to the summary statement found in Isa 66:18–21, Beuken's work on the *'ebedîm* as the main theme of Isaiah 56–66 provides

---

105. Gen 12:1–3. *Contra* Davies, *A Royal Priesthood*, 217; with Wells, *God's Holy People*, 153, 157–58; Wright, *Mission of God*, 339, 487; and Schüssler Fiorenza, *Priester für Gott*, 160–62.

106. Isa 61:11; vv. 6, 9 (2x), 11. See Martens, "Impulses to Mission," 232–35.

107. Ibid.

108. Küng, *Church*, 380–82.

109. Childs, *Isaiah*, 542; Smith, *Isaiah*, 520; 696–99; 725–26; Blenkinsopp, *Isaiah*, 313; Sommer, *Prophet Reads Scripture*, 146–48, 278, 331; Oswalt, *Isaiah*, 683; Brueggemann, *Isaiah*, 259.

110. Isa 2:1–5; 56:1–8, esp. v. 6. Cf. Zech 14:16–21. Ware cites twenty-seven OT references of Gentiles streaming to the Temple (*Mission of the Church*, 60). Bryan (*Jesus and Israel's Traditions*, 153–55) develops the relationship between Zechariah 14 and Isaiah 66. The democratization of holiness is also seen in Jub 4:26 and 1 En. 10:22.

111. Beuken, "Main Theme," 85. The *'ebedîm* reappear with emphasis in ch. 65 (7x).

112. Isa 57:1; 63:6–64:12; 66:22–24; cf. Genesis 1–3; Revelation 21–22.

insight into a passage whose unclear referents (they/them) have left many commentators confused.[113] Picking up from where Beuken's article ends (Isa 66:14c), note that immediately following this final appearance of the *'ebedîm* there is mention of Yahweh's enemies, "and the hand of the Lord shall be known to his *servants* [*'ebedîm*], and he shall show his indignation against his *enemies*" (Isa 66:14c–d, emphasis added).

Could the verses that follow Isa 66:14 provide a final summary of Beuken's main theme? If so, then verses 15–17 provide concluding commentary on the fate of Yahweh's *enemies*, while verses 18–21 provide similar commentary on the fate of Yahweh's *'ebedîm*. This could also explain why the final three verses of the book again compare the fate of the Servant's seed (מְבָעֲרֵי) with the fate of the rebellious (Isa 66:22–24).[114]

If Isa 66:18–21 provides a final description of Yahweh's *'ebedîm*, we would expect the description to be consistent with both the character of the Servant (Isaiah 40–53) and the character of his seed (Isa 54:1—66:14). In fact, this is exactly what we find. Like DI's Servant and TI's *'ebedîm*, the "saved ones" (σεσῳσμένους, LXX) in Isa 66:18–21 have a priestly role. This priestly role is democratized and twofold: they first have a missional and mediatorial role to the nations,[115] and they secondly have priestly access and responsibilities before Yahweh in his temple.[116] Figure 1 illuminates this twofold mediatorial responsibility:

v. 18 ... the time is coming to gather
all nations and tongues ....

 v. 19 And **from them** (מֵהֶם) *I will send* saved ones (פְּלֵיטִים)
   to the nations (הַגּוֹיִם) ....
    And they shall declare my glory among the nations (הַגּוֹיִם).
    And they shall bring all your brothers from all the nations
    (הַגּוֹיִם) as an offering to the Lord ... to my holy mountain
    Jerusalem ... just as the children of Israel bring their grain
    offering in a clean vessel to the house of the Lord.
 v. 21 And *even* **some of them** (מֵהֶם) *I will take* for priests and for Levites ...

Figure 1: Structural Diagram of Isaiah 66:18b–21

---

113. Westermann (*Isaiah 40–66*, 423–28) and Blenkinsopp (*Isaiah*, 315) can only make sense of the passage by insisting that v. 20 is an interpolation. Cf. Oswalt, *Isaiah*, 683.

114. On "your seed" as the "seed of the Servant" see Beuken's comments on Isa 61:9 ("Main Theme," 72).

115. Isa 66:19–20; cf. 42:1–7; 52:15; 56:6–7; 60:3; 61:1–11.

116. Isa 66:21; cf. 53:4–12; 54:11–17; 56:6–7; 57:15; 59:21; 61:1–11; 66:1–3.

The passage is laden with theological fruit, but three are especially relevant. First, because of the sin of Yahweh's foes (Isa 66:14d–17), Yahweh is about to gather "all nations and tongues" (v. 18). From this larger group Yahweh will choose a remnant of "saved ones" for special mediatorial purposes. Beuken's demonstration of the centrality of the *'ebedîm* in TI makes it difficult to imagine that the "saved ones" (Isa 66:19) could refer to any group other than the *'ebedîm* (cf. Isa 66:14, 22), a group already shown to include foreigners.[117] To sum up, the best candidates for the identity of "them" (מֵהֶם), those Yahweh sends on mission to the nations (Isa 66:19–20) and those he chooses to serve as "priests and Levites" (Isa 66:21), are the *'ebedîm*.

Secondly, Yahweh will *send* his "saved ones" on mission to the nations (vv. 19–20). We have already seen that both Yahweh's Servant and his *'ebedîm* serve as a light for the nations. Isaiah 66:19–20 develops this missional theme by predicting that in the eschatological age Yahweh will send the *'ebedîm* to preach (נָגַד; ἀναγγέλλω, LXX) to the nations (centrifugal motion).[118] The missionary work of the "saved ones" is described as an "offering," a priestly or cultic activity.[119] Yahweh gathers all nations (Isa 66:18) and *sends* "saved ones" from this group as missionaries to the nations (Isa 66:19–20).

Finally, in addition to *sending* saved ones, Yahweh will *take* "some of them" from the nations to serve in his temple as "priests and Levites" (Isa 66:21). As Blenkinsopp notes, "the only possible antecedent of *mēhem* ('some of them') is the phrase the 'nations of every tongue.'"[120] Both TI's prologue and epilogue make the provocative claim that "some" from the Gentiles will serve as priests in Yahweh's temple.

Who are these "some" chosen by Yahweh to be priests? Unless Isaiah is introducing a radically new theme, the best candidates for the "some" (מֵהֶם) *taken* by Yahweh (v. 21), like the "some" (מֵהֶם) *sent* by Yahweh (v. 19), are the Servant's seed. These *'ebedîm* have priestly access to Yahweh (Isa 54:11–17), include Gentiles as temple servants (Isa 56:6–7), share in the Servant's priestly anointing (Isa 59:21–60:3), serve as a "light to the nations" (Isa 60:3), and have received the titles "priests of Yahweh" and "ministers of

---

117. Isa 56:6–7; cf. 45:20, 22.

118. Note use of נָגַד in Isa 48:20 and Ps 22:31 (MT v. 32). The same emphasis is found in Matt 28:19 and 1 Pet 2:9. Cf. ἀναγγέλλω in 1 Pet 1:12 and 1 John 1:5.

119. The identity of the "brothers" (Isa 66:20) as Jews or an ethnic mixture is not germane to our argument.

120. Blenkinsopp, *Isaiah*, 314. Sommer adds, "the phrasing '*even*, from them' suggests that the more surprising of the options is more likely–that the prophet does anticipate priestly service performed by foreigners" (*Prophet Reads Scripture*, 148, emphasis original).

our God" (Isa 61:6). In short, Yahweh's humble and righteous *'ebedîm* are the "some" who receive the titles "priests and Levites" in Isa 66:21.

Some Christian commentators have argued that verse 21's "priests and Levites" should now be understood exclusively as church officers, but this seems unlikely. For example, Calvin proposed an influential reading of Isa 66:21 based on his earlier exegesis of Rom 15:16. For Calvin, the "priests and Levites" refer to the "priesthood of the gospel";[121] like the "Papist" priests they too offer a unique sacrifice, only their priesthood consists of offering "men in sacrifice to God, by bringing them to the obedience of the gospel."[122] More recently, Gary Smith has suggested a similar hierarchical possibility for Isa 66:21 based on his exegesis of Num 8:19, Ps 68:18, and Eph 4:7–12.[123]

The problem with both Calvin's and Smith's readings is that they fail to take account of the democratization of the priesthood emphasized in Isaiah 56–66. Throughout these chapters, emphasis is on fulfillment of Exod 19:6's promise of royal priesthood for the whole nation. The "some" from the nations are not the officers of the church but the *'ebedîm*. All the *'ebedîm* have direct access to Yahweh's instruction (Isa 54:13); serve in the temple (Isa 56:6–7); receive a priestly anointing (Isa 59:21—60:3); receive the primogenital privilege of being called ministers and priests (Isa 61:6–7); and are taken by Yahweh as priests and Levites (Isa 66:21). A sacerdotal division within the *'ebedîm* does not fit the eschatological reality described in TI.

Isaiah's messianic Servant, the Davidic Priest-King, will bring forth a royal and priestly seed. The *'ebedîm* are a priestly family whose access to Yahweh is even greater than that of Levi's family. Later prophetic books such as Jeremiah (esp. the "Book of Consolation," Jeremiah 30–33) and Zechariah build upon Isaiah's prophecy of a suffering Priest-king who receives an eschatological seed.[124] The next chapter demonstrates that Isaiah's prophecy of the arrival of an eschatological priestly seed following the self-offering

---

121. Calvin, *CC* 4:435. The problem is not with a "priesthood of the gospel," but with limiting this priesthood to ordained ecclesial teachers. Cf. *CNTC* 3:251.

122. Calvin, *CNTC* 8:310. Calvin states earlier on the same page, "The one who offers in sacrifice the people whom he obtains for God makes himself a priest or celebrant in the ministry of the Gospel." Cf. Rev 1:6; Num 8:18.

123. Gary Smith, "Paul's Use of Psalm 68:18," 187; Smith, *Isaiah 40–66*, 751n692.

124. Other relevant texts discussed in the literature include Ezekiel 40–48; Dan 7:13–14; Hos 4:4–9; Joel 2:17, 28–29; Mic 4:8; Zeph 3:10; Haggai 2; and Mal 1:11; 2:1–9. For example, Levinson argues that Ezekiel 40–48's vision of an eschatological future where all Israel is free to devote itself to cultic worship provides "a constitution for the 'kingdom of priests and a holy people'" described in Exod 19:6 (*Theology of the Program of Restoration of Ezekiel 40–48*, 130).

of the royal and priestly Servant is a fundamental component of the NT authors' doctrine of the royal priesthood (Rom 16:26).

Chapter Summary

The book of Isaiah provided a script of current events for the first Christian theologians. Jesus the Christ was Isaiah's Suffering Servant, the Davidic Priest-King whose climactic self-offering ushered in an eschatological age of democratized priestly holiness and privilege. The arrival of Isaiah's royal and priestly Servant marked the turning point of world history. Isaiah's Servant would suffer, but he would afterward lead a New Exodus and bring a new priesthood with a new covenant. As a result of his priestly self-offering, the Servant would receive a priestly seed (Isa 53:10). This seed fulfills the promise of royal priesthood given at Sinai (Exod 19:6), but Isaiah's surprising revelation, confirmed by Zechariah (14:20), is that the eschatological priesthood includes those formerly disqualified: the maimed, the foreigner, the alien. Isaiah's eschatological promise was sure: all the 'ebedîm would have priestly access to God and would serve as priestly lights for the nations. Isaiah warned that this priestly witness would be costly. Like the 'ebed Yahweh, the 'ebedîm would suffer, but they would eventually be vindicated in an Edenic new creation (Isa 66:22–24).

The next chapter concludes our survey of the NT's doctrine of the royal priesthood. It explores how Isaiah's narrative shaped Matthew's portrayal of Jesus and his disciples. Matthew identifies Jesus as the Davidic Priest-king, the royal and priestly 'ebed Yahweh, who received a priestly seed (the 'ebedîm). Matthew follows Isaiah in assigning priestly characteristics to the disciples, and by extension to the readers of his gospel. For Matthew, the call to discipleship is a call to imitate the divine service of the Priest-king. The chapter concludes by showing that the priestly characteristics of disciples in Matthew's gospel are present across the NT.

3

Matthew's Jesus as Isaiah's Servant: The Royal Priesthood's High-Priestly King

> Jesus . . . becomes conscious at the moment of his baptism that he had to take upon himself the *'ebed Yahweh* role.
>
> —Oscar Cullmann, *Christology of the New Testament*

> We have this as a sure and steadfast anchor of the soul, a hope that enters into the inner place *behind the curtain*, where Jesus has gone as a forerunner on our behalf, having become a *high priest* forever *after the order of Melchizedek*.
>
> —Heb 6:19–20, emphasis added

THE APOSTOLIC DOCTRINE OF the royal priesthood is firmly rooted in Jesus as the protagonist of Israel's ancient story. He plays the first part in the narrative and the plot centers on him. Theologians and biblical scholars are asking "new" questions about Jesus' relationship to first-century priesthoods.[1] These questions have important implications for the doctrine of the royal priesthood. For example: did Jesus think "of himself in terms of Israel's true priesthood? . . . Did he prepare his disciples for a revelation of his Melchizedekian aspirations?"[2] Or equally important, "Does contemporary historical-critical reconstruction of the Jesus of the Gospels support

---

1. See surveys in Levering, *Christ and the Catholic Priesthood*; O'Collins and Keenan Jones, *Jesus our Priest*.

2. Fletcher-Louis answers in the affirmative based on his reading of Mark 1–6 ("Jesus as the High Priestly Messiah: Part 1" 155–75; Fletcher-Louis, "Jesus as the High Priestly Messiah: Part 2" 57–79).

the portrait of Christ the priest that the letter to the Hebrews offers?"[3] This chapter suggests an affirmative answer to these questions, but it also asks several more. Why is Psalm 110 the most quoted Psalm in the NT? Does it provide insight into how Jesus might have been able to consider himself a priest? Does Matthew portray Jesus's disciples as a new priesthood? What about readers of Matthew's gospel? Finally, what about NT readers in general: is there a widespread implicit assumption that believers function as a royal priesthood?

To answer these questions we first turn to Matthew's gospel. Why Matthew? Whatever the literary relationship between the four gospels, the church placed Matthew first as a transitional and catechetical gospel. It provides a reasonable place to explore the final step in the three-tiered argument which has made up Part One. Namely, 1) first-century Christians recognized a democratization of priesthood in the eschaton (Chapter 1); 2) the primary source for this understanding was provided by Isaiah's royal and priestly Servant (the 'ebed Yahweh) who would suffer and receive a royal priestly *seed* (the 'ebedîm) as his inheritance (Chapter 2); 3) Jesus understood himself to be Isaiah's Servant, the Melchizedekian Priest-king (Psalm 110), whose sacrifice would bring about a New Exodus and Isaiah's promised eschatological royal and priestly community (Exod 19:6; Isa 61:6).

The chapter's first half explores the life of Jesus and his disciples as presented by Matthew. It begins by examining Jesus' baptism, an event publicly ordaining Jesus to ministry as Isaiah's Servant and David's Son. After his baptism Jesus begins his ministry as Israel's Melchizedekian Priest-king. But if Jesus' Melchizedekian kingship is informed by Isaiah's Servant, then he would expect a *seed* (Isa 53:10) who would continue his royal and priestly work (Isaiah 54–66). In the Gospels "the priestly traditions of Israel are being replaced by the community of Jesus' followers."[4] Thus next we explore the disciples as Israel's new priesthood. The chapter's second half surveys additional NT evidence in order to illustrate that Matthew is not alone in applying the priestly characteristics of Isaiah's eschatological 'ebedîm to Jesus' first-century followers.

---

3. Levering argues "yes" (*Christ and the Catholic Priesthood*, 67–68).
4. Broadhead, "Jesus and the Priests," 144.

Matthew's Priestly Servant and His Priestly Disciples

Isaiah's eschatology is a dye coloring all of Matthew.[5] Jesus understood his ministry as fulfilling the royal and priestly vocation of Isaiah's Suffering Servant.[6] At his baptism, Jesus is commissioned as David's Son and Isaiah's Servant. He is thus the Davidic and Melchizedekian Priest-King whose self-offering institutes a new and permanent priesthood. As Isaiah foretold, Jesus believed his disciples to be the eschatological first-fruits of a new royal priesthood extended to all nations. The promised eschatological priestly characteristics of Isaiah's servant-seed (Isaiah 54–66) are assigned to the disciples in Matthew's gospel.

Baptism: Commissioning of the Royal Priest (Matthew 3:13–17) and the Royal Priesthood (Matthew 28:16–20)

Jesus' life marks the turning point in Israel's history, and his baptism is the turning point in his own life (Matt 11:11–13). Matthew uses Isaiah's script to triangulate the baptism with the history of Israel and the ministry of John the Baptist.[7] John was a priest whose "baptism functioned as an alternative" to the sacrifices in the Temple by mediating forgiveness to the people.[8] Robert Webb notes that John's baptism was distinct from all other known baptisms in Second Temple Judaism. It was the only baptism not self-administered; hence John's nickname, "the Baptizer."[9] John's performance of baptism functioned as a "parallel to the mediatorial role of a priest in performing a sacrifice to mediate forgiveness in the sacrificial system."[10] Yet Webb makes no comment on why John's baptism took the form it did; he surprisingly even denies that John was a priest.[11]

While some look to Jewish proselyte baptisms or Qumran for the origin of John's baptism, a better case can be made that it was rooted in Israel's own history. Peter Leithart agrees that nearly all ritual washings in the OT were

---

5. Beaton, "Isaiah in Matthew's Gospel," 76.

6. The second Servant Song calls Isaiah's Servant to a dual mission: to restore the "tribes of Jacob" and to serve as a "light to the nations" (Isa 49:6). Jesus' ministry reflects this prioritization (Matt 10; 28:19–20). See Blenkinsopp, *Opening the Sealed Book*, 132.

7. Matt 3:13–17 // Mark 1:9–11 // Luke 3:21–22; cf. John 1:29–34.

8. Webb, "Jesus' Baptism by John," 120. In Matthew, John explicitly condemns the temple leadership—the Sadducees (Matt 3:7).

9. Ibid., 114.

10. Ibid., 116.

11. Ibid., 127. Cf. Wright, *Jesus and the Victory of God*, 160–61.

self-administered, adding the observation that most were often-repeated due to various types of impurity, not once-for-all like John's baptism. But Leithart moves beyond Webb by suggesting that "the OT is the primary context for answering the question, why did Johannine and Christian baptism take *this* form?"[12] Examining Israel's history, Leithart finds only one bath administered by someone else: the washing that takes place during the consecration and ordination of Israel's priests.[13] John's baptism appears to have received its form from these Aaronic ordination rights. Although using the form, he is not ordaining to an Aaronic priesthood. Rather, he is initiating people into the eschatological priesthood.[14] If John was calling all of Israel to enter a state of priestly purity in preparation for the eschaton, then his ministry fits well with other first-century Jewish restoration movements working to prepare an eschatological priesthood (e.g., Pharisees, Qumran).[15]

Why then did Jesus receive John's baptism? There are a number of answers to this question, none of which is wholly adequate on its own.[16] But at least one important component of Jesus' baptism was its role in publicly ordaining Jesus to royal and priestly ministry.[17] At his baptism, Jesus is washed, anointed with the Spirit, and commissioned to ministry, all mirroring Aaronic ordination rites. Yet Jesus' ministry is greater than the Aaronic; "by his preaching and at the baptism, John, a priest of the order of Aaron and Zadok, pays homage to Jesus, as Levi did to Melchizedek."[18] Or, as the author of Hebrews puts it, Jesus is "a *high priest* forever *after the order of Melchizedek*" (Heb 6:20). At his baptism, Jesus is anointed and inducted not into a Levitical high-priesthood, but as the eschatological Anointed One (Χριστός), the High-priestly King.[19] He is the faithful royal priest Israel had originally been called to be (Exod 19:6).

12. Leithart, *Priesthood of the Plebs*, 95. Emphasis original.

13. Ibid., 95. Exodus 29:4; 40:12; Lev 8:6. Elsewhere λούω in the LXX refers to a self-washing in every place except Ezek 16:9—a divine washing. Cf. Heb 10:22, John 13:10; Rev 1:6 v.r. NA26.

14. Exodus 19:6 and Isa 61:6; cf. 1 Sam 2:35; Matt 3:3. (Webb, "Jesus' Baptism by John," 118).

15. Wright, *Jesus and the Victory of God*, 160–61; 434–36.

16. Rae follows John Chrysostom in identifying five reasons for Jesus' baptism. Jesus' baptism as ordination fits best with his fifth reason ("the inauguration of Jesus' ministry"). Unlike Chrysostom, Rae does not make the royal and priestly aspect of Jesus' ordination explicit ("Baptism of Christ," 132).

17. Leithart, *Priesthood of the Plebs*, 112; Hagner identifies a relationship to Psalm 2 and Isaiah 42, but does not emphasize the ordination/coronation theme (*Matthew*, 1:57–59).

18. Ibid., 115. Cf. Heb 7:4–10.

19. For other options, see Fletcher-Louis, "Jesus as the High Priestly Messiah: Part 1," 171.

Ordained by the Father and Anointed by the Spirit

No greater warrant for Jesus' public ordination to a royal and priestly ministry could be provided than the Father's own voice. He endorses Jesus' ordination using a benediction that combines the coronation Psalm of David's Son (2:7) with the ordination song of the royal and priestly *'ebed Yahweh* (Isa 42:7; see Table 1). The theological logic of the OT pairing in Matt 3:16–17 is similar to Heb 5:5–8, where Psalm 2 and Psalm 110 are paired to demonstrate that Jesus is Jerusalem's High-priestly King.[20] Especially relevant, however, is Heb 5:5's claim that Jesus was made a High-priestly King when the Father quoted Ps 2:7 to him: "Christ did not exalt himself to be made a high priest, but *was appointed by him who said to him*, 'You are my Son, today I have begotten you.'"[21] The first time the Father publicly quotes Ps 2:7 to Jesus is at his baptism.[22] Combined with what we have already seen about John's *baptism* as consecration to priestly ministry, Hebrews suggests that Jesus was appointed as the eschatological High-priestly King at his Baptism.[23]

		Notes
Matt 3:16–17	καὶ εἶδεν [τὸ] πνεῦμα [τοῦ] θεοῦ καταβαῖνον ὡσεὶ περιστερὰν [καὶ] ἐρχόμενον ἐπ' αὐτόν· οὗτός ἐστιν ὁ υἱός μου ὁ ἀγαπητός, ἐν ᾧ εὐδόκησα	Cf. Matt 17:5; Mark 1:11; 9:7; Luke 3:22; 9:35; John 1:34; esp. 2 Pet 1:17.
Psalm 2:7	πρός με Υἱός μου εἶ σύ	Note "χριστοῦ αὐτοῦ" in Ps 2:2.
Citation of Isa 42:1 in Matt 12:18	ἰδοὺ ὁ παῖς μου ὃν ᾑρέτισα, ὁ ἀγαπητός μου εἰς ὃν εὐδόκησεν ἡ ψυχή μου· θήσω τὸ πνεῦμά μου ἐπ' αὐτόν, καὶ κρίσιν τοῖς ἔθνεσιν ἀπαγγελεῖ.	Cf. esp. ἀγαπητός in Zech 12:10 and LXX Psa 44:1 and descent of Spirit in Matt 3:16; Luke 3:22; 4:18.

Table 1: Psalm 2:7 and Isaiah 42:1 in Matthew 3:16–17[24]

---

20. Hebrews makes extensive use of the Psalm 2/Psalm 110 pairing. See the chiastic structure of Hebrews' exordium (pairing Ps 2:7 with Ps 110:4), and Heb 1:5–13 where Pss 2:7 and 110:1 serve as bookends for seven OT quotations.

21. Ferguson's *Baptism in the Ancient Church*, 101–02.

22. Heb 5:7 shows that the "ἡμέραις τῆς σαρκὸς αὐτοῦ" are being described.

23. Oden cites numerous patristic authors in support of this reading (*Classic Christianity*, 342–43). Also relevant is *T. Levi* 8:14–15's promise of a priest who would arise from the tribe of Judah. See parallels in *T. Levi* 18 and *ALD* 4:7; 5:5–6; 11:6–7; 13:16.

24. See Beaton (*Isaiah's Christ*, 123–32) and Bauckham (*Jude, 2 Peter*, 205–10; 218–21) for textual issues.

Both the royal-Anointed One (Χριστός) of Psalm 2 and the Servant-king of Isaiah 42 are later revealed to possess a *priestly* mission (Psalm 110; Isa 52:13—53:12), as Jesus' use of Psalm 110 and Isaiah 53 during Passion week demonstrates (Matt 22:42; Luke 22:37).[25] As the Anointed One, the Father's beloved Son is not anointed with oil, but with the Holy Spirit.[26]

The baptism is only the first of the Father's three affirmations of his Son's royal-priestly service.[27] From a literary viewpoint, all three of the Father's appearances in Matthew's script affirm his Son's royal-priestly ministry. The Father's first appearance reveals that Edenic access to heaven has been opened to Jesus, the High-priestly King (Matt 3:16). In a similar way, the Father's final appearance to rip the inner veil of the Temple from top to bottom reveals that Eden's sword has been removed through Jesus for all his siblings.[28] If Jesus' ministry and priestly sacrifice mediate eschatological access to God, then his baptism represents his public ordination to this royal-priestly work.

Baptism, the Son, and Eternity

What exactly happened at the baptism? Against adoptionism, Jesus did not become the Son of God.[29] He was conceived by the Spirit, and his life before the baptism reflects fullness of the Spirit (Luke 2:46–52; cf. Isa 11:1–3). Thus the conception, not the baptism, is the "archetype to our birth in the Spirit."[30] At his baptism Jesus was publicly anointed to his messianic (royal-priestly) task. Kilian McDonnell's words are apt: "Before the baptism Jesus is not the Christ. The baptism is a clear messianic boundary."[31] Prior to baptism, Jesus was already the Father's unique "beloved" Son.[32] Baptism thus does not represent a change in Jesus' ontological status; rather it publicly announces the

---

25. Davies and Allison are correct in identifying an allusion to LXX Ps 2:2 in Matthew's use of συνάγω in 22:41 cf. Matt 26:3; 26:57; 27:62; "whom *you* anointed" Acts 4:26–27. See also χριστός in Matt 22:42; 26:63, 68; (*Gospel According to Matthew*, 3:251). See below on Matt 22:41–46.

26. Cf. "χριστοῦ αὐτοῦ" in Ps 2:2; also Acts 10:38.

27. Matthew 3:17 = Baptism; 17:5 = transfiguration; 27:51 = rending of the veil (note the divine passive).

28. Gurtner, *Torn Veil*, 143, 191, 194.

29. A father cannot adopt his own son (see Aquinas, *ST* 3.23.4).

30. Habets, *Anointed Son*, 129.

31. McDonnell is here summarizing the teaching of Irenaeus (*Baptism of Jesus in the Jordan*, 118).

32. ἀγαπητός is only used three times in Matthew: the baptism (Matt 3:17); in the citation of Isa 42:6 (Matt 12:18); and at the transfiguration (Matt 17:5).

commencement of his service as Israel's High-priestly King. Closely related is his anointing with the Holy Spirit, which signals both his commissioning and empowering for mission (Cf. Matt 26:6–13).

Jesus' baptismal ordination as Israel's High-priestly King also sheds light on a later conversation with the chief priests of Israel. When these priests ask Jesus who gave him the authority to come into Yahweh's house and do what only a priest is supposed to do (teach, guard temple purity), he responds with a question about John's baptism (Matt 21:25).[33] Jesus' priestly ordination at John's baptism has given him authority to act as the eschatological High-priestly King of Israel.[34]

Jesus' Baptism Is the Basis of His Disciples' Baptism

Every worldview requires an answer to the question, "What time is it?"[35] The age of the prophets ended as Jesus went under the waters of baptism. John was the last and greatest prophet of that era of salvation history: "among those born of women there has arisen no one greater than John the Baptist. . . . all the Prophets and the Law prophesied until [him] . . . he is Elijah who is to come."[36] Just as Samuel's ministry midwifed a new priesthood and kingship for Israel, so does John and his baptism.[37] A new eschatological age and kingdom are publicly inaugurated as a meek and Melchizedekian King rises from the consecrating waters of baptism. The early church fathers unanimously ascribed great significance to Jesus' baptism for liturgical practice. Given that nations tend to celebrate what they deem most important, it is noteworthy that the "Holy Nation's" second oldest annual celebration is the festival of Jesus' baptism.[38] To this day the Feast of Epiphany, especially in the Eastern Church, celebrates the public commencement of the royal and priestly mission of Jesus for the world.[39]

---

33. This is the only mention of baptism between Jesus' baptism in Matthew 3 and Jesus' command to baptize in Matt 28:19.

34. Leithart, *Priesthood of the Plebs*, 120.

35. Wright, *Jesus and the Victory of God*, 138–44; 467–72.

36. Matt 11:11–14, cf. 17:12; 21:25; Acts 10:37–38. Note that Mark's gospel begins with John's baptism.

37. 1 Sam 2:35. See Leithart, *Priesthood of the Plebs*, 115; Levinson, "On the Promise to the Rechabites," 513. In Jesus' Melchizedekian priesthood, the Levitical priesthood has been fulfilled (Matt 3:15; 5:17; 26:54).

38. McDonnell, *Baptism of Jesus*, 246.

39. Chrysostom argued that at the baptism, not his birth, Jesus' mission was first understood by himself and John the Baptist (*On the Baptism of Christ* 2 [PG 49.365]).

New Testament authors identified both Jesus' baptism and their own as ordination to priestly service.[40] Later chapters discuss Luther's and Barth's endorsement of this early consensus.[41] The command to baptize is certainly to be obeyed (Matt 28:19-20), but the command finds its *basis* in the historical event of Jesus' own baptism. Thus the Great Commission does not present a radically new message when it prescribes baptism as a normative practice for Jesus' disciples. Rather it summarizes and repeats what has already been a central theological theme for Matthew. Jesus' disciples follow the life and teaching of their Master, their path of public royal-priestly ministry beginning with baptism. As baptism ordained Jesus to royal and priestly ministry, so it ordains the believer to divine service as a member of the royal priesthood.[42] Immediately following baptism, Jesus was led by the Spirit into the wilderness to begin his ministry. Like baptism, *imitatio Christi* is also true here for the believer. The life of the baptized disciple is a life of ministry and mission lived in the power of the Spirit.[43]

To sum up, Jesus' baptism provides the foundation for Christian baptism. When Jesus (Ἰησοῦς) was baptized in the Jordan River, he was revealed as the eschatological Joshua (Ἰησοῦς) who would lead his people into the promised land of milk and honey (Josh 1:1, cf. Zechariah 3). At his baptism, he was anointed with the Spirit and publicly commissioned to ministry as Isaiah's Servant, Israel's High-priestly King. Jesus began his royal and priestly ministry after his baptism; so do his disciples—the *'ebedîm* of Isaiah's long-awaited eschatological royal priesthood.

Jesus as Isaiah's Servant and David's Son: A Startling High-Priestly King

A textual variant of Isa 52:15 describes the Servant as one who will "startle many nations." Even the greatest of OT prophets, John the Baptist, is surprised by the long-awaited Coming One (Matt 11:2-15). Despite his meek status, Matthew's Anointed One fulfills Israel's multifaceted expectations. He is Isaiah's Servant-king, but also David's greater Son, the Priest-king of Psalm 110. The genius of Matthew's gospel is to show how Isaiah's meek-servant

---

40. For example, Heb 10:19-25 (cf. Psa 110). See Leithart (*Priesthood of the Plebs*, 87-132); McDonnell (*Baptism of Jesus in the Jordan*, 111-27); Ferguson (*Baptism in the Ancient Church*, 113-31); and Dabin (*Le Sacerdoce Royal*). Ferguson's tome would be strengthened by engaging Leithart and Dabin.

41. WA 51:111; *CD* IV.4, 50-68.

42. Cf. Rom 6:3-4; Mark 10:38-39; Beasley-Murray, *Baptism in the New Testament*, 64.

43. Witness involves many priestly ministries (Barth, *CD* IV/3.3, 854-901).

King enriches the glory of David's Melchizedekian Son. Douglas Farrow is correct, Melchizedekian typology "is the most comprehensive typology available and the only one that does justice to the new thing God has done in Christ."[44] Following Zechariah's lead, Matthew portrays David's Son as a surprising Priest king, humble and meek like Isaiah's Servant. We now turn to four passages in Matthew's gospel where Jesus' surprising identity is revealed.

Jesus as Isaiah's Royal and Priestly Servant (Matthew 12:15–21)

Matthew's longest OT quotation (Matt 12:18–21 cf. Isa 42:1–4) from the first Servant Song is not careless proof texting. Rather as Richard Beaton argues, Matthew's overall aim for citing Isaiah is "to demonstrate that Jesus is indeed the Servant of Isa 42:1–4."[45] Israel's King has arrived in the person of Jesus, but he is unexpectedly humble and meek.[46] Immediately following Jesus' identification with the Servant (Matt 12:18–21), Matthew has the crowd ask if Jesus could be the "Son of David" (Matt 12:23). Matthew wants readers to understand that "the Son of David is the lowly Servant of the Lord."[47] He is not only interested in helping readers make these connections regarding Jesus' identity, but he also wants them to see that the beloved Son's baptismal commissioning as the Servant (Isa 42:1; cf. Matt 3:17; 17:5) will lead to his priestly self-offering (Isaiah 53).[48] This offering will bear much fruit: an inheritance including Matthew's readers (Isa 53:12; Matt 12:21).

Psalm 110 and the Priest–King Question (Matthew 22:41–46)

The motif of Jesus as Priest-king becomes clearest as Jesus enters Jerusalem, "the city of the great king" (Matt 5:35). Matthew 22:41–46 is a Christological turning point: for the first time Jesus publicly makes explicit his identity as the Anointed One of Psalm 2 via a riddle about his identity from Psalm 110, the Psalm of the Priest-king. He enters Jerusalem as Zechariah's

---

44. Farrow, "Melchizedek and Modernity," 287. Farrow notes that Hebrews and Revelation undertake "daring large-scale expositions of Psalm 110" (281). Psalm 110 is also weighty in Matthew.

45. Beaton, *Isaiah's Christ*, 196.

46. Good, *Jesus the Meek King*, 61–93.

47. Laansma, "I Will Give You Rest," 212, 245.

48. Isa 52:13–53:12; Matt 8:17; cf. Matt 26:28, 63, 67; Luke 22:37.

Priest-king[49]—the one bringing eschatological priesthood and purity to all of God's people.[50] He brings this eschatological gift to the ones who at that moment are lauding him with words from Psalm 118, a song of praise to the builder of a restored temple (Matt 21:9, 15).[51] Jesus demonstrates royal-priestly authority as he cleanses the temple (Matt 21:12–13),[52] and his use of Isa 56:7 implies that the temple-servants in the purified temple will include Gentiles.[53]

Jesus engages in a number of controversies during Passion Week, but he is the instigator of only one (Matt 22:41–46). As he teaches (a priestly task), he cites Ps 110:1 (Matt 22:44). This text reveals that God's holy nation is to be led by a King who is also a priest.[54] It refers to the very first "priest" mentioned in the OT (Gen 14:18), Melchizedek, the most significant king of Jerusalem until the time of David. An ancient rule of canonical exegesis places great weight on a term's first appearance in Scripture, and this rule applies to "priest." Jesus' citation of Ps 110:1 as a *pars pro toto* refers not only to the whole of Psalm 110, but also to the larger canonical narrative in which Melchizedek—the first priest king of Jerusalem—plays an important typological role.[55]

Was Jesus' identity as he moved through Passion Week really shaped by Psalm 110's promised Priest-king? Evidence to the affirmative is provided by Jesus' next use of Psalm 110 during the high drama of his interview with the so-called "High Priest" of Israel.[56] There the question posed by the characters' staging is: "Who is the real High Priest in Israel's temple?"[57] On

---

49. Matt 21:4–5; Zech 6:9–15; 9:9–10. See Moss, *Zechariah Tradition*, 61–80.

50. Zech 3:1–9; 14:16–21. See Davies, *Royal Priesthood*, 218–37; Bryan, *Jesus and Israel's Traditions*, 153–56; Perrin, *Jesus the Temple*, 54.

51. Psalm 118 is cited or alluded to five times during Passion Week, closely tied to Jesus' work in the temple—work he is qualified to do as David's greater son (Psalm 110).

52. Wright, *Jesus and the Victory of God*, 417; Perrin, *Jesus the Temple*, 105.

53. See Chapter 2's discussion of Isa 56:7. Cf. Jer 7:4–11; Jesus, like Jeremiah, called attention to a *new* locus of God's presence (Jer 31:31–34) found in a new eschatological temple.

54. The promised Priest-king of Psalm 110 is David's descendant. This theme of David's seed being greater than David himself is also found in the messianic Ps 132:10–12. Cf. Levenson, "On the Promise," 514n25; Acts 2:30; Matt 12:6, 41, 42; and the "Jesus-is-greater-than x" theme in Hebrews.

55. Fletcher-Louis, "Jesus as the High Priestly Messiah: Part 1," 174; Dodd, *According to the Scriptures*, 126.

56. Matt 26:57–69. See Himmelfarb, *Kingdom of Priests*, 162.

57. The staging is the same as Jesus' later face-off with Pilate in Matt 27:11, where the question is, "σὺ εἶ ὁ βασιλεὺς τῶν Ἰουδαίων"; and the emphasis is on the *kingly* contrast between Jesus and Pilate. In Matt 26:63 the High Priest's explicit question is

one side is the Anointed One (ὁ Χριστὸς), the silent high-priestly Servant;[58] on the other Caiaphas, the Sadducee High Priest.[59] The only confession Jesus makes during his trial is his identity as Daniel's royal-priestly "Son of Man," the Davidic Priest-king at the "right hand" of Yahweh (Psalm 110).[60]

Jesus' Interpretation of his Priestly Sacrifice (Matthew 26:26–30)

At his baptism, Jesus was commissioned to ministry as David's Son and Isaiah's Servant, a messianic ministry Matthew unites in Jesus (Matt 12:15–21, 23). As Jesus entered Jerusalem, he explicitly embraced the identity of Zechariah's meek-King, who would suffer for his people. Further, Jesus' dialogues with Pilate and the High Priest show that he understood himself to be both the true High Priest and the true King of Israel. Given these facts, it is not surprising that a Servant Christology underlies Matthew's narration of the institution of the Lord's Supper.[61] What has been written about Jesus in John is also true for Matthew: "during the Last Supper *Jesus enacted Isaiah 53:12*: He identified himself with the Servant who 'poured out his soul to death' and 'bore the sins of many.'"[62] Matthew's unique contribution to the institution narrative is his report that Jesus' blood is "for the forgiveness of sins" (Matt 26:28).[63] Forgiveness of sins is a divine right mediated through the priesthood, and within first-century Judaism, especially through the work of the High Priest when he makes atonement for the sins of the people behind the veil in the most Holy Place.[64]

"Are you the Anointed One?", but the literary context emphasizes the *priestly* contrast between Jesus and Caiaphas. In first-century Palestine, the high priest above all others served as the "anointed one" (Exod 29:4–9; Lev 4:3, 5, 16; 6:13; Sir 45:15; Josephus *Ant.* 3.8.2). The contrast between Jesus as true priest-king versus false priests and kings was a theme already introduced in Matthew 1–2. Cf. Heb 2:17; Josephus, *Jewish Wars* 1.2.8.

58. Matt 26:63 and 27:14 allude to the fourth Servant Song (Isa 53:7). Matt 26:67 and 27:30 allude to the third Servant Song (Isa 50:6).

59. Even a false High Priest can speak as a divinely inspired prophet by virtue of his office (John 12:49–52; cf. Matt 13:57; 14:5; 16:14; 21:11, 46; 23:37).

60. Matt 26:64; cf. Matt 27:11, 42. It is beyond this project's scope to demonstrate the relationship of Daniel's "Son of Man" to Psalm 110's Davidic Priest-king, but see Lucass, *Concept of the Messiah*, esp. 169–71; 173–74; 197.

61. Daly, *Christian Sacrifice*, 222.

62. Otto Betz, "Jesus and Isaiah 53," 86; emphasis original. See John 13 and 17.

63. Hagner, *Matthew*, 773; Davies and Allison, *Matthew*, 3:469, 473; esp. Gurtner, *Torn Veil*, 127–37; 1 Cor 15:3.

64. Lev 16:12, 30–34; cf. Num 18:7; Lev 16:2; Figure 1 below. The "*vellum schissum* means the ending of the cultic separation of holy and less holy" (Gurtner, *Torn Veil*,

There are at least two significant points of contact between Isaiah 52–53 and Matthew's description of the Last Supper. First, Jesus identifies himself with the priestly Servant who offers himself as sacrificial lamb[65] and guilt offering (אָשָׁם, Isa 53:10). Secondly, the Servant's death will make *"many"* righteous (Isa 53:11, 12 [x2]), a promise alluded to by Jesus' words, "This is my blood of the covenant, which is poured out for *many* for the forgiveness of sins."[66] At his final meal, Jesus interprets his earthly ministry as the priestly action of Isaiah's Servant. He ritually helps his disciples recognize that his death will accomplish a New Exodus. He will lead his people across the Jordan into his Father's kingdom. There he will baptize his disciples with the eschatological Spirit and they will all serve as Yahweh's temple-servants. They will celebrate the Servant's work and remember his sacrifice around an eschatological table (1 Cor 11:20–34).

The Father's Confirmation of the Great High Priest's Sacrifice (Matthew 27:51)

"And behold, the curtain of the temple was torn in two, from top to bottom" (Matt 27:51). What was publicly inaugurated at the baptism is publicly completed on the cross.[67] The verse's divine passive reveals the final of three acts in Matthew's gospel by which the Father confirms the royal-priestly identity and mission of his beloved Son. Matthew states this narrative detail without comment, leading scholars to one of two positions. Either Matthew was mindlessly parroting the tradition, or the logic of the temple veil's tearing was so obvious that it did not need explaining.[68] Church tradition sees Hebrews as accurately interpreting the event's theological significance.[69] While his term may be anachronistic, Hagner's theological judgment is consistent with the Evangelist's when he writes, "The death of Jesus establishes the priesthood of all believers."[70]

188; see also 63–70).

65. Isa 53:7. Jesus' offering took place at Passover when every devout family brought a lamb to Jerusalem to sacrifice. Recall also that "lamb" and "servant" were homonyms in first-century Aramaic.

66. Matt 26:28. Betz, "Jesus and Isaiah 53," 86; Watts, "Isaiah in the New Testament," 219.

67. See Kupp's discussion of Matthew's narrative framework (chs. 1–2 and 27:51–28:20) in *Matthew's Emmanuel*, 50–52; 100–08.

68. For discussion see Gurtner, *Torn Veil*, 1.

69. Heb 6:19; 9:3, 8; 10:19–20 (Luz, *Matthew*, 1989), 3:595–66n56; Gurtner, *Torn Veil*, 2–28).

70. Hagner, *Matthew 14–28*, 849.

While avoiding the term "priesthood of all believers," Daniel Gurtner champions Hagner's theological claim in an important monograph on Matt 27:51.[71] His study compares three elements linked by the evangelist: the temple, the death of Jesus, and the tearing of the veil.[72] He shows that the inner curtain before the Holy of Holies was torn.[73] It had Cherubim woven onto it (Exod 26:31), and Cherubim guard Eden once it is lost to the first Priest-king (Gen 3:24).[74] There "inaccessibility to the presence of God is first seen in biblical tradition."[75] In Second Temple Judaism, the Garden of Eden was known as the Holy of Holies.[76] The veil was often associated with the firmament of Gen 1:6, its tearing removing the physical barriers to entering God's presence in the eschaton.[77] Unlike Mark 1:10, the connection between the *vellum schissum* and Jesus' baptism is not primarily between the rent veil and the rent heavens. Rather it is between Jesus' commissioning for priestly mission by the Spirit at his baptism (Matt 3:16) and the departure of the Spirit as the anointed Priest-king completes his messianic mission at death.[78]

Gurtner finds two significant conclusions from the *vellum schissum* for Jesus' death. First, like the baptism, "it occasions an apocalyptic opening of heaven . . . depicting the sovereignty of God."[79] Second, the tearing of the curtain "depicts the cessation of its function, which . . . is generally to separate God from people. Its rending then permits accessibility to God in a manner not seen since Genesis 3."[80] This access to Yahweh is also seen in Matthew's unique Emmanuel Christology, for Jesus alone ("Ἰησοῦν μόνον," Matt 17:8) makes Yahweh's presence accessible.[81]

---

71. Gurtner, *Torn Veil*.

72. Ibid., 97.

73. Ibid., 47–71.

74. Ibid., 57–60. On Adam as a Priest-king in Eden's sanctuary see Beale's *Temple and the Church's Mission*, 75–76.

75. Gurtner, *Torn Veil*, 71.

76. Ibid., 193. *Jub.* 3:12–14; *Test. of Levi* 18:10–11a.

77. Ibid., 96, 189.

78. Ibid., 176. This fact has priestly implications for the disciples when they are baptized/anointed with the Spirit at Pentecost. In the background of the Acts 2 Pentecost event are both the holy-nation-forming covenant at Sinai—where Israel is first named a "royal priesthood" (Exodus 19–24)--and the dedication of Solomon's Temple where fire came down from heaven (1 Kings 8:10–11; 2 Chron 7:1–2). See Perrin, *Jesus the Temple*, 61–65.

79. Gurtner, *Torn Veil*, 138.

80. Ibid.

81. Ibid., 200.

In conclusion, I acknowledge that the algebraic equation I have argued for, in which Matthew's Anointed One (Χριστός) is identified with Isaiah's Suffering Servant, David's Son, and the Melchizedekian priest king (as described in Psalm 110 and Hebrews) might make some biblical scholars nervous. Undoubtedly, some will ask about illegitimate totality transfer (I-TT). But I am more concerned about the widespread abuse of illegitimate identity denial (I-ID). Too often modern scholarship separates what the canonical authors found to be united "in Christ." Matthew's Anointed One cannot be fragmented; he is both Isaiah's priestly 'ebed Yahweh and the Davidic Priest-king.

The Siblings/Disciples of the Priest-King as Royal Priests

In Chapter 2, we saw that the Servant-king's priestly ministry (Isaiah 52–53), would result in a new eschatological age for his royal and priestly seed (Isaiah 54–66). The previous section showed how this Isaianic sub-structure undergirds Matthew's portrayal of the Messianic identity of Jesus; the next section shows its relevance for the identity of Jesus' disciples/siblings.[82] Matthew's gospel makes a significant contribution to the apostolic doctrine of the royal priesthood; for the twelve and for Matthew's ideal readers, *discipleship and royal priestly ministry are irrevocably linked*.

Priestly Service to Jesus: Priest, Temple, and Sacrifice (Matthew 12:1–8)

Approximately one hundred years after Matthew was written, Irenaeus—a spiritual grandson of the Apostle John—argued that Jesus was a priest who shared his office with his disciples. In *Against Heresies* (ca. 185), Irenaeus commented on Matt 12:1–8 to argue:

> For all the righteous possess the priestly order [*sacerdotali ordinem*]. And all the apostles of the Lord are priests, who do inherit here neither lands nor houses, but serve God and the altar continually. . . . [they] had a priesthood of the Lord . . .[83]

---

82. Contra Blenkinsopp who, while acknowledging Matthew's intensive engagement with Isaiah, finds only one allusion to the disciples as Isaiah's 'ebedîm (Matt 20:27–28; *Opening the Sealed Book*, 202, cf. 147–68).

83. Irenaeus, *Against Heresies*, IV.7.3 (*ANF* 1:471 [*CCEL*: 1:1179], translation modified). When John of Damascus (d. 749) cites this passage he limits exercise to the king's royal priesthood, reflecting Eastern Caesaropapism. More likely the earlier Latin

Irenaeus describes the disciples as priests who share in the priesthood of the Lord. How did he reach this conclusion from Matthew 12?

In Matt 12:1–8, Jesus builds on earlier interaction with the Pharisees (Matt 9:9–13), to make a profound point about temple, sacrifice, and priesthood. Others have identified the Markan parallel as a place where Jesus displays his "bold claims to a high priestly consciousness" and the "belief that he bears a priestly ontology."[84] For Fletcher-Lewis, this pericope is one of six in Mark 1–6 where Jesus makes a claim to "high priestly identity as the 'holy one of God' (1.24), with a high priestly contagious holiness (1.40–45; 5.25–34;[85] 5.35–43), freedom to forgive sins (2.1–12) and the embodiment of divine presence in a Galilean cornfield (2.23–28)."[86]

Similarly, Broadhead identifies this confrontation with the Pharisees as one of five scenes in Mark where "Jesus does what a priest should be doing."[87] All five episodes are included in Matthew.[88] Spatial constraints prevent discussing them, but in at least the "cornfield" confrontation Matthew not only adopts but embellishes Mark's priestly emphasis. Matthew 12:6 adds Jesus' saying, "something greater than the temple is here"; he adds the example from the priestly profaning of the Sabbath in the temple (Matt 12:5); and he cites Hos 6:6 on sacrifice.

Jesus was part of a first-century "minority tradition" which saw the eschaton bringing obviation to the priestly code and a democratization of priestly purity and holiness. This eschatological age was publicly inaugurated at Jesus' baptism.[89] Within this context, the narrative logic of Jesus' argument in Matt 12:1–8 becomes clearer. David, the servant of the Lord, served Israel as a royal-priestly figure (Psalm 110); Jesus now serves Israel

---

translation is original, given its pre-Constantinian setting and Irenaeus' later comment, "In the preceding book I have shown that all the disciples of the Lord are Levites and priests" (*Against Heresies*, 5.33.3 [*ANF* 1:564; *CCEL* 1:1386]) See also his equation of discipleship with all believers (*Against Heresies*, 4.33.1 [*ANF* 1:506; *CCEL* 1:1259]). *Contra* Bulley (2000), 154–55.

84. Fletcher-Louis, "Jesus as the High Priestly Messiah: Part 2," 63. Cf. Matt 15:1–20 = Mark 7:14–23, discussed by Broadhead ("Jesus and the Priests of Israel," 133).

85. Matthew adds that the unclean woman touches the κρασπέδου τοῦ ἱματίου αὐτοῦ. Fletcher-Louis writes, "In wearing these tassels the whole nation is 'a kingdom of priests' (Exod 19:6). So, although Jesus does not wear the high priest's full regalia he does wear garments by which the laity are identified with the high priest" ("Jesus as the High Priestly Messiah: Part 1," 70).

86. Fletcher-Louis, "Jesus as the High Priestly Messiah: Part 2," 57.

87. Broadhead, "Jesus and the Priests of Israel," 133.

88. Mark 1:39–45 = Matt 8:2–4; Mark 2:1–13 = Matt 9:2–8; Mark 2:23–28 = Matt 12:1–8; Mark 3:1–7 = Matt 12:9–14; and Mark 7:14–23 = Matt 15:17–20.

89. Bryan, *Jesus and Israel's Traditions*, 148–56.

in a similar but greater way.⁹⁰ As David's men served David, or as Levitical priests serve in the temple/tabernacle, so Jesus' disciples demonstrate faithful cultic eschatological service when they practice ἔλεος (דֶסֶח in Hos 6:6) to the one greater than the temple (Matt 12:6).⁹¹ Bruce Chilton and Jacob Neusner understand the "profound argument" Jesus is making; when he claims rank over the temple, "He and his disciples may do on the Sabbath what they do *because they stand in the place of the priests in the Temple*: the Holy Place has shifted, now being formed by the circle made up of the master and his disciples."⁹²

Jesus himself has replaced the temple; service to him constitutes new priestly service on the part of his disciples.⁹³ Where Jesus is "in that place there is the transcendent liturgical space and time of the true temple *in which his disciples can legitimately act as priests* for whom the Sabbath prohibition against work does not apply."⁹⁴ As we saw above, Jesus' implicit claims to priestly identity will be made explicit when he stands opposite a competing high priest of Israel and confesses his true identity (Ps 110:1; Matt 26:64).

Discipleship as a Priestly Task in Matthew

Later developments in Matthew's gospel suggest that Jesus thought of his followers as the "seed" of the Suffering Servant.⁹⁵ In Matt 20:28 Jesus refers to himself as a servant (cf. Isa 53:10, 12) for the purpose of emphasizing the servant nature of those who follow him.⁹⁶ Similarly, in Matt 23:8–12, Jesus makes clear that his followers are all *servants* (διάκονος) and *siblings* (πάντες ἀδελφοί ἐστε). Only the Anointed One (ὁ Χριστός) is distinct among the Father's children; he alone is the teacher (ὁ διδάσκαλος), the instructor (καθηγητής); all others follow his example and obey his divine teaching

---

90. Matt 1:1, 6, 11, 16; 3:13–17; 22:41–46; 26:57–69. See Schultz, "Servant, Slave," 1190, 1191.

91. Chilton and Neusner, *Judaism in the New Testament*, 142. In basic agreement are: Perrin, *Jesus the Temple*, 60–61; Wenschkewitz, *Die Spiritualisierung der Kultusbegriffe*, 94. Cf. Wright *Jesus and the Victory of God*, 390–96.

92. Chilton and Neusner, *Judaism in the New Testament*, 142; emphasis added.

93. Davies and Allison, *Matthew*, 2:313–15; Osborne, *Matthew*, 453–54; Perrin, *Jesus the Temple*, 60.

94. Fletcher-Louis, "Jesus as the High Priestly Messiah: Part 2," 77; emphasis mine.

95. Paul was already arguing this way ca. AD 55 when he wrote 2 Cor 5:14–6:10 (Gignilliat, *Paul and Isaiah's Servants*). See also Matt 8:17.

96. Matthew's placement of the episode as the penultimate event before Jesus' royal entry points to the uniqueness of Jesus' kingship. Cf. Osborne, *Matthew*, 742.

(Matt 23:8–10; cf. Isa 54:13).[97] Jesus' teaching provides explanation for the remarkable discovery described in Chapter One: disciples have no priestly *caste* but are a *cast* of priests. They play different roles, some as leaders (Peter) and others in the background (the seventy). Yet within Jesus' sibling group, there is no elite group of priests who mediate access to Yahweh (as the Levites did in the Temple). Isaiah's promise of the Servant's eschatological priestly seed (Isa 53:10; 54–66) was being fulfilled through the firstborn of the family, the Davidic and Melchizedekian Priest-king (Psalm 110).

According to Joseph Hellerman, the most significant difference between modern western kinship systems and family systems in Mediterranean society is that, for the latter, sibling solidarity was "the central relational priority."[98] Our cultural situatedness can leave us blind to the radical community Jesus envisions, one "for which membership depends upon obedience to God, not upon one's patriline," upon ethical quality over ethnic pedigree.[99] Echoing description of the righteous in Isaiah 56–66 (esp. Isaiah 58 and Matt 25:31–46), the one who does the Father's will is Jesus' sibling (*adelphos*), not necessarily his own blood relatives.[100] Jesus refers to his followers as siblings fifteen times in Matthew's gospel;[101] thus Jesus does not eat the Passover meal with his biological family, but with his "siblings" (Matt 12:49–50; Exod 12:3–27). Related to this spiritual kinship emphasis is Jesus' teaching about his Father; for example his sermon on community ethics (Matthew 5–7) refers to God as Father seventeen times.

The social implications of Matthew's equation are staggering, scandalous and subversive.[102] If Jesus is the Priest-king of Psalm 110, Isaiah 52–53, and Zechariah 9, then his brothers and sisters are royal-priestly siblings. All siblings share in his priestly ministry and mission (Matt 10:40).[103] All receive priestly access into the secret mysteries of Yahweh (Matt 13:11).[104] All share access to the keys, which represent eschatological priestly powers

---

97. Yieh, *One Teacher*, 289; Stephen Witmer, *Divine Instruction in Early Christianity*, 166–72, 183; cf. Clement of Alexandria, "Instructor" (*ANF* 2:207–98).

98. Hellerman, *Ancient Church As Family*, 35.

99. Ibid., 66; Yieh, *One Teacher*, 292. On cultic implications of the Good Samaritan (Luke 10:29–37) see Bryan, *Jesus and Israel's Traditions*, 177–87.

100. Isa 56:1–8; 57:15; 66:2; Matt 12:49–50.

101. Matt 5:22–24 (x4), 47; 7:3–5 (3x); 12:49–50 (x2); 18:15, 21, 35; 23:8; 25:40; 28:10. Cf. Hebrews (8x).

102. Yieh, *One Teacher*, 290.

103. Cf. Bruner, *Christbook*, 1:403–05.

104. Matt 13:16, 23, 51–52.

(Matt 16:13–20),[105] authority to bind and loose (Matt 18:15–20).[106] All are equally servants of Yahweh; there is no elite caste with exclusive temple access among Jesus' followers (Matt 23:8–12). Like the Johannine version of the Great Commission (John 20:21–23), all are given a priestly mission and ministry (Matt 28:18–20).

To sum up, Matthew's narrative portrayal of both Jesus' life and teaching presents Jesus as a new Priest-king. His inheritance includes a servant seed from all nations, an eschatologized royal priesthood.[107] By serving Jesus, Matthew's disciples share in a new priestly-temple service; like Jesus they have received a royal-priestly role. For Matthew, Jesus is the anointed Davidic Priest-king who leads siblings into eschatological and Edenic access to his Father, a royal-priestly privilege not seen on earth since Yahweh walked with his son, Adam (Genesis 3; Luke 3:38).

The Implied Readers of Matthew's Gospel as Priestly Disciples

Matthew's gospel most likely originated around Antioch, the same region which produced the *Odes of Solomon* some thirty to fifty years later.[108] It seems to have had significant impact on the author of the *Odes*—whose liturgical imagination led him to compose the line "I am a priest of the Lord, and to him I serve as a priest."[109] Was the author of Ode 20 simply guilty of "personal enthusiasm" and "Protestant individualism" or was he faithfully following Matthew's lead?[110]

Every author has an implied audience. Biblical scholars use narrative criticism to reconstruct the implied audience from the text's own clues. Thus a working definition is "the reader presupposed by the narrative. . . . [who] responds appropriately to the text's rhetorical devices and thus fulfills the goals of the text."[111] Thinking about the implied reader and the goals of

---

105. See also John 20:22–23. Matthew 16:18–19 is controversial, and I can only state my position without defending it. Peter is representative of the twelve, and the twelve are representative of all disciples. See Wilkins, *Discipleship in the Ancient World*, 198; 185–99; Barth, *CD* II/2, 442.

106. Kupp, *Matthew's Emmanuel*, esp. 181, 187, 236, 240–44. As for Tertullian, Matt 18:20 is central for Anabaptist ecclesiology.

107. Freyne, "Jesus and the 'Servant Community.'"

108. Yieh, *One Teacher*, 263.

109. Lattke, *Odes of Solomon*, 285.

110. *Contra* Farrow's straw man characterization of all Protestant accounts of the priesthood of all believers ("Melchizedek and Modernity," 295).

111. Brown, *Disciples in Narrative Perspective*, 36, 123.

the text helps identify an important question: "Should the implied reader identify with the priestly privileges and responsibilities given by Jesus to the disciples?"[112]

At least three options present themselves; the reader could decide that 1) no one in his or her community should identify with the disciples in Matthew's narrative; 2) only the leaders of the Christian community should identify with the disciples in Matthew's narrative;[113] 3) all followers of Jesus should identify with the disciples in Matthew's narrative. Of these three, surely the last is most faithful to the text.

> Matthew presents Jesus' disciples as a paradigm of discipleship. As characters in the story, their interaction with Jesus functions as a mirror allowing the readers to evaluate their own relationships with Jesus.[114]

Matthew's discipleship ideal encompasses more than his narrative characterization of the twelve; it also includes the teaching and model of Jesus.[115] Matthew's distinctions are drawn between Jesus and others, or between his disciples and others; they are not drawn within the church (ἐκκλησίᾳ) itself.[116] The removal of the expectation of discipleship from all followers of Jesus is a later chapter in Christian history; it is unfortunate that some anachronistically read it back into Matthew's gospel where all believers are called to discipleship (Matt 16:24–27; 18:20) and priestly ministry. After all, "in Antioch the disciples were first called Christians" (Acts 11:26c; cf. 1 Pet 4:16).

To sum up, Matthew's motif of discipleship suggests that the royal-priestly status of the disciples also applies to the readers of Matthew's gospel. The disciples are the paradigmatic examples of those who follow the great Priest-king.[117] Matthew's readers can be assured that the same priestly access to the Father, the same priestly service to Jesus' siblings (*adelphoi*), and the same priestly mission to the Gentiles are now their privilege and responsibility.

---

112. Matt 12:1–8; 13:11, 16, 23, 51–52; 18:15–20; 28:19–20.

113. Illustrated by Minear, "Disciples and the Crowds," 41. Far better is Wilkins' reading (*Discipleship in the Ancient World*, 170).

114. Yieh, *One Teacher*, 302. See Osborne, *Ministry*, 48–113.

115. Brown, *Disciples in Narrative Perspective*, 145–46.

116. Matt 18:17; 23:8–12.

117. Yieh, *One Teacher*, 284–301, 304; Brown, *Disciples in Narrative Perspective*, 138–42, 145; Wilkins, *Discipleship in the Ancient World*, 143, 228–33.

Isaiah's Priestly Seed Elsewhere in the New Testament

Before ending our study of the apostolic doctrine of the royal priesthood, it is helpful to review. Chapter 1 revealed a radically new vision of temple, sacrifice, and priesthood within the Christian communities (1 Pet 2:4–9; Rom 12:1–8). Chapter 2 described the role Isaiah's prophecy played by describing a Davidic Son who would lead a New Exodus and bring his family (seed) into a new eschatological age where all would be priests (Isa 61:6). This chapter has examined Matthew's gospel and found that Jesus understood himself to be David's Son and Isaiah's Servant. Jesus' ministry resulted in his spiritual family receiving the eschatological priestly privileges foretold by Isaiah: access to the mysteries of God (Matt 13); the power of pronouncing forgiveness of sins (Matt 18:18); access to Yahweh through the presence of Jesus in their midst (Matt 18:20; 27:51; 28:20); and a priestly ministry of mediating Jesus' presence and teachings to the nations (Matthew 10; 28:19–20). This chapter concludes with samples from diverse NT genres. They reveal that the doctrine of the royal priesthood was neither "insignificant" nor "altogether useless" to the first Christian theologians.[118] To the contrary, the Pauline letters, the Johannine literature, and Hebrews provide weighty testimony to the royal priesthood.

Priestly Servants in the Pauline Literature

Within twenty years of Jesus' death, the apostle Paul was writing letters about its theological import to the churches. While Paul nowhere explicitly calls Christ, himself, or believers a "priest,"[119] this does not mean that the doctrine of the royal priesthood is absent from his corpus.[120] We find a wealth of testimony to the priestly functions and status of the "holy ones" who receive his letters. Raymond Corriveau undertakes a careful exegeti-

---

118. Elliott's description of the doctrine (*Elect and the Holy*, xiii).

119. Paul applies priestly functions to Jesus, and the Pauline corpus includes five allusions to Jesus fulfilling Priest-king functions (Rom 8:34; 1 Cor 15:25; Eph 1:20; Eph 2:6; Col 3:1). See Hay, *Glory at the Right Hand*, 131–34, 164; Moo, *Romans* 542–43.

120. Why did Paul not make more explicit use of ἱερεῖς and cognates? While we cannot know for sure, it seems to have been a foundational assumption in his ministry, never an issue for those receiving his occasional letters. Just as the rending of the veil (Matt 27:51) did not need explanation by Matthew, neither did Paul need to remind his readers they were a royal priesthood. The evidence suggests that Paul would have agreed with Hebrews portrayal of Jesus as the Priest-king and Peter and John's description of believers as royal priests.

cal examination of fifteen Pauline texts in order to demonstrate that cultic vocabulary is frequently used by Paul to describe the praxis (πρᾶξις) of daily life for those "in Christ" (Rom 12:4).[121] He also explores Paul's understanding of temple[122] and sacrifice,[123] both having important implications for the apostolic doctrine of the royal priesthood. Paul believed that to be a new creation in Christ meant to participate in Isaiah's eschatological priesthood (2 Cor 5:17–6:4).

Although Rom 12:1 was discussed in Chapter 1, we can now observe that it follows the same priestly logic found in Matt 12:1–8. Those who have believed (Romans 3) and identified with Christ (through baptism, Romans 6) are commissioned to priestly service (offering of living sacrifices, Rom 12:1). Space prohibits discussion of many texts relevant to Paul's view of the eschatological royal priesthood, but for the sake of illustration we briefly explore two (Phil 2:16b–18 and 2 Corinthians 6).

Philippians 2:16b–18 was treated in Chapter 1's discussion of spiritual sacrifices.[124] Here we note that Paul's theological logic is based upon his eschatological reading of Jesus as Isaiah's Servant, who has brought forth a priestly seed. James Ware has carefully described the Isaianic background to Philippians, concluding that "the Philippians' identity as priests also reflects Paul's conviction that the eschatological time of renewal had dawned in Christ Jesus. . . . Paul's use of this imagery thus depicts the Philippians as priests to the surrounding pagan world."[125] Ware demonstrates that Paul's understanding of the priestly nature of the Philippian community is rooted in Isaiah's "Servant of the Lord" motif[126] and the scroll's mediatorial implications for God's people in the eschaton.[127] For Paul, the Philippians were a "community of priests."[128]

---

121. While Corriveau's *Liturgy of Life* does not interact with Exod 19:6, 1 Pet 2:9, Rev 1:6; 5:10, or 20:6 (cf. Isa 61:6 [1x]), it does discuss in detail Paul's cultic vocabulary in 1 Thes 1:9; 2 Cor 6:16–7:1; 1 Cor 3:16–17; 1 Cor 6:19–20; 1 Cor 5:6–8; 2 Cor 2:14–15; 2 Cor 9:12; Phil 4:18; Phil 2:17; Rom 1:9; Rom 15:16; Rom 12:1; Eph 2:20–22; 5:1–2; 5:25–27.

122. 1 Cor 3:16–17; 6:19–20; 2 Cor 6:16–7:1; and Eph 2:20–22. See also Gupta, "Which 'Body,'" 518–36.

123. Rom 12:1 and Phil 2:17. See extensive study of Paul's cultic vocabulary, some 150 pages (examining Rom 3:25, 6:3, 1 Cor 10:16; 11:23; Eph 2:14–16; 5:2, 25–27; and Rom 12:1), in Seidensticker, *Lebendiges Opfer (Röm 12, 1)*. Seidensticker's study also begins with the Suffering Servant.

124. The following builds upon Ware, *Mission of the Church*, 271–84.

125. Ibid., 273; see also 237.

126. Ibid., 78–89.

127. Ibid., 114–17; 124–27; 137–43; 151.

128. Ibid., 272; Herbert, *Kenosis and Priesthood*, 101; 75–104.

Second Corinthians, written about twenty-five years after Jesus' death, provides a second example of Paul's identification of himself and believers as priestly servants of the Servant. Chapter 1 already described Paul's cultic claims in 2 Cor 6:15–18, but the immediately preceding passage, where Paul identifies himself as a servant of the Servant (2 Cor 5:14–6:10), is also relevant.[129] Paul quotes from the second Servant Song (Isa 49:8 = 2 Cor 6:2): the passage's "hermeneutical key. . . . the tip of the iceberg revealing the passage's underlying Isaianic logic."[130] He sees Jesus as Isaiah's Servant (Isaiah 40–53),[131] and the identity of himself and his readers as "wrapped up in the servant followers of the Servant who continue to suffer in righteousness as heralds of the message" (Isaiah 54–66).[132]

Given this identification with Isaiah's 'ebedîm (Isaiah 54–66), it is not surprising that elsewhere in 2 Corinthians Paul attributes priestly status and functions to believers. At the beginning, he refers to God's anointing of Corinthian believers to a royal and priestly ministry like Christ's.[133] The anointing here seems similar to the anointing mentioned in 1 John 2:20 and 27, suggesting priestly access to Yahweh for all believers.[134] Later, in 2 Cor 2:14–17, he describes his service to God as a "cultic offering."[135] In so doing Paul provides a specific example of the priestly offering to which he calls all baptized believers in Rom 12:1.[136] God has made Paul, and the Corinthians who are all part of the new creation (2 Cor 5:17–20), competent as ministers of a new covenant (2 Cor 3:6). Leithart relates these New Creation ministers to the priestly ministers portrayed in Heb 10:19–22. There "the baptized are priests and beyond priests, welcomed into the inner chambers where only High Priests once dared enter. Exposure to glory is no longer limited to office-bearers."[137] For all priestly ministers of the New Covenant, "the veil is removed" (2 Cor 3:16).

---

129. I am now summarizing Gignilliat, *Paul and Isaiah's Servants*.

130. Ibid., 57, 60.

131. Ibid., 60–107.

132. Ibid., 54. See 108–52.

133. Syriac biblical scholar, John Chrysostom, recognized that the anointing in 2 Cor 1:21 refers to believers' commissioning to participation in messianic ministry as prophets, priests, and kings (*NPNF2* 12:290).

134. So Witmer, *Divine Instruction in Early Christianity*, 131–52; Leithart, *Priesthood of the Plebs*, 121–31; Bulley, *Priesthood of Some Believers*, 46–47.

135. Daly, *Christian Sacrifice*, 251.

136. See Phil 4:18; Eph 5:2; 1 Cor 9:13–14; and Bulley, *Priesthood of Some Believers*, 24–25.

137. Leithart, *Priesthood of the Plebs*, 130.

Priestly Disciples in the Johannine Literature

Having briefly reviewed Paul's testimony to the royal priesthood, this section touches on two examples from the Johannine corpus. The most well-known references to the royal priesthood in the Johannine literature are found in Revelation. There "priest" is only used three times, but all uses refer to the royal priesthood.[138] Especially noteworthy is the first reference (Rev 1:6). The aorist tense of ἐποίησεν reminds readers that they have already been "made" "priests to God,"[139] through the cleansing of Christ's blood (Rev 1:5).[140] In Revelation, to be a disciple is to be a royal priest.

The larger context of Rev 1:6's reference to readers as "a kingdom, priests to God" includes Christ as Melchizedekian Priest-king standing between seven lampstands in the Holy Place, where only priests are allowed to be.[141] He is "one like a son of man, clothed with a long robe and with a golden sash around his chest" (Rev 1:13; cf. Daniel 7). Some commentators see Jesus depicted as a high priest[142] but, as "ruler of kings" (Rev 1:5), he is more likely portrayed as a High-priestly King.[143] In the OT priests tended the lampstands in the tabernacle and temple; now Jesus, the High-priestly King, tends his lampstands "in order to secure the churches' fitness for service as lightbearers in a dark world."[144] Also significant is the frequent description of Jesus as the "Lamb of God" (27x), a name closely tied to the 'ebed Yahweh figure.[145] The Jesus of Revelation is a Priest-king, and Revelation's readers are a royal priesthood (Rev 1:6; 5:10; 7:15; 20:10).

---

138. Revelation 1:6, 5:10, and 20:10. Believers are also described as priestly kings in Rev 7:15 and 22:3–4. See Beale, *Book of Revelation*; Osborne, *Revelation*; Wright, *After You Believe*, 78–79.

139. Use of ἐποίησεν for installation of persons into offices finds parallels in both the LXX and the NT. See 1 Kings 12:31 where Jeroboam "made" priests from the non-Levitical tribes (cf. 1 Sam 12:6); Mark 3:14 where Jesus "made twelve; and Acts 2:36 where Jesus is "made" "κυριον" and "χριστον."

140. Jesus' blood in Rev 1:5 probably refers "to the way in which the Aaronic priesthood was consecrated" (Beale, *Revelation*, 194). Cf. Eph 1:7; 2:6.

141. Heb 9:2; Exod 25:31–37; 37:17–24; Num 8:1–4; see Figure 1 below.

142. Schüssler Fiorenza, *Priester für Gott*, 418; cf., Osborne, *Revelation*, 89. See also John 19:23–25 and Jesus' "seamless robe" in conjunction with what Josephus says about the robe of the High Priest (*Ant. 3.161*; cf. Exod 39:29; Rev 15:6).

143. Jonathan, the Hasmonean Priest-king, was given a golden buckle to wear as an honorary identification (1 Macc 10:89). Blount identifies Jesus as both priest and king (*Revelation*, 44), but does not relate to Jesus as Melchizedekian Priest-king (Psalm 110).

144. Beale, *Revelation*, 209. Note the cultic implication of the church's location within the Holy Place—the exclusive domain of the priests. On light bearing see Isa 60:3; Phil 2:15–16; 1 Pet 2:9; Figure 1.

145. Cullmann, *Christology of the New Testament*, 71.

The "beloved disciple" had a personal relationship with the Jewish High Priest (John 18:15), and it should not surprise us that his Gospel also contains special emphasis on Jesus as a High-priestly King.[146] In the Gospel, various texts reveal how John sees the priestly ministry of Jesus being passed on to his disciples.[147] Exegetical discussion is not possible here, but Jesus' washing of the disciples' feet provides a useful closing illustration. Jesus' meek service identifies him with Isaiah's Servant. As Jesus washes his disciples' feet, the apostles are consecrated to priestly service. "Jesus knew that as he was the High Priest over the House of God, the disciples were its priests. . . . The priesthood and servanthood of the disciples were never more cogently expressed than in this dramatic act by the Servant-Priest."[148] If John 13:10's "washed" (λελουμένος) alludes to baptism, then here is yet another connection between baptism and consecration to royal priesthood.

The High-Priestly King and His Royal-Priestly Siblings in Hebrews

Jesus is not a high priest of the Levitical order; rather Hebrews five times emphasizes that Jesus's priesthood is after the order of Melchizedek.[149] This fact more than any other explains why Hebrews is 1 Peter's closest rival for the title, "Epistle of the Royal Priesthood." Hebrews begins with a theologically exquisite exordium (Heb 1:1–5); its "rhetorical artistry . . . surpasses that of any other portion of the New Testament."[150] It is chiastically designed around the Son's mediatorial work (3a–b), and alludes to two Psalms.[151] In 2b there is an allusion to the commissioning of the Davidic king (Ps 2:8), and in 3d there is an allusion to the Davidic Priest-king (Ps 110:1). The author of Hebrews spends the bulk of his letter explaining why Jesus, as Psalm 110's Melchizedekian priest-king, is greater than all Levitical high priests.[152]

A second long sentence (Heb 10:19–25) provides a bridge from the theological reflection on Christ's priesthood (Heb 4:14—10:18), to

---

146. Ibid., 104–07.

147. John 2:13–22; 4:4–42; 13:1–17; 20:19–21; and John 17's "high priestly prayer." See also Exod 28:29–30 and Attridge's comments relating John 17 to the priesthood of all believers ("How Priestly," 14).

148. Eastwood, *Royal Priesthood*, 42; Perrin, *Temple*, 54.

149. Heb 5:6–10 (2x); 6:20; 7:1–17 (2x). Cf. Gen 14:18–20, Ps 110:4.

150. Attridge, *Epistle to the Hebrews*, 36.

151. O'Brien, *Hebrews*, 45–46.

152. Heb 4:14—10:25. Hebrews refers to Christ as mediator (3x), High Priest (5x), and Priest (10x).

exhortation to participate in it (Heb 10:26—13:25).[153] The sentence includes a number of important motifs for the general priesthood: we who have been baptized (λελουσμένοι τὸ σῶμα ὕδατι καθαρῷ)[154] are to draw near (προσερχώμεθα) to the Holy Place, through the "curtain" (καταπέτασμα),[155] by the blood of our great priest Jesus (ἱερέα μέγαν), who is over the "house of God" (τὸν οἶκον τοῦ θεοῦ) and who has "sprinkled" (ῥαντίζω)[156] our hearts so that we can spur each other on to love and "good works" (εὐποιΐα).[157] Ernest Best concludes:

> Those who draw near to God are thus to be regarded as consecrated priests, perhaps as high priests, since they enter through the veil, the privilege restricted to the high priest in old Israel. The Christians are consecrated priests with the blood of Christ and by the water of baptism. . . . the members of the church are thus successors to the Levitical priests.[158]

Best's conclusions are confirmed by the only monograph published to date on the priestly nature of Hebrews' readers. Scholer presents two primary arguments: first, the readers of Hebrews function as priests because they do the things priests do. They "are characterized as 'priests,'" because of the cultic verbs which describe their access to sacred space and "by the sacral activity still attributed to them: sacrifices of praise and acceptable worship."[159] In addition to offering spiritual sacrifices (Heb 13:15–16),[160]

---

153. O'Brien, *Hebrews*, 361.

154. Many find reference to the priestly ordination of Aaron and his sons when Moses "λούσεις αὐτοὺς ἐν ὕδατι" (Exod 29:4) and then sprinkled (ῥαίνω) them with the blood of a lamb (Exod 29:20–21). See Leithart, *Priesthood of the Plebs*, 100; Scholer, *Proleptic Priests*, 129; cf. O'Brien, *Hebrews*, 367–68.

155. The noun appears six times in the NT. Three times it refers to the veil being torn at Jesus' death (Matt 27:51; Mark 15:38; Luke 23:45), and three times to the cultic significance of this event (Heb 6:19; 9:3; 10:20).

156. See 1 Pet 1:2 above; also Floor, "General Priesthood of Believers," 77; Scholer, *Proleptic Priests*, 129–31; Leithart, *Priesthood of the Plebs*, 99–100.

157. εὐποιΐα are later called "spiritual sacrifices" (Heb 13:16). On this sentence as a whole, see O'Brien, *Hebrews*, 360–61; 369–71; 528–29.

158. Best, "Spiritual Sacrifice," 281. See also Leithart, *Priesthood of the Plebs*, 99–101; Origen, *Homilies on Leviticus*.

159. Scholer, *Proleptic Priests*, 204; DeSilva, "Invention and Argumentative Function," 321.

160. See Heb 13:15–16; also 52–56 above.

the use of "to draw near" (προσέρχομαι)[161] and "to enter" (εἰσέρχομαι)[162] indicates that Hebrew's readers have priestly access to the Holy of Holies.

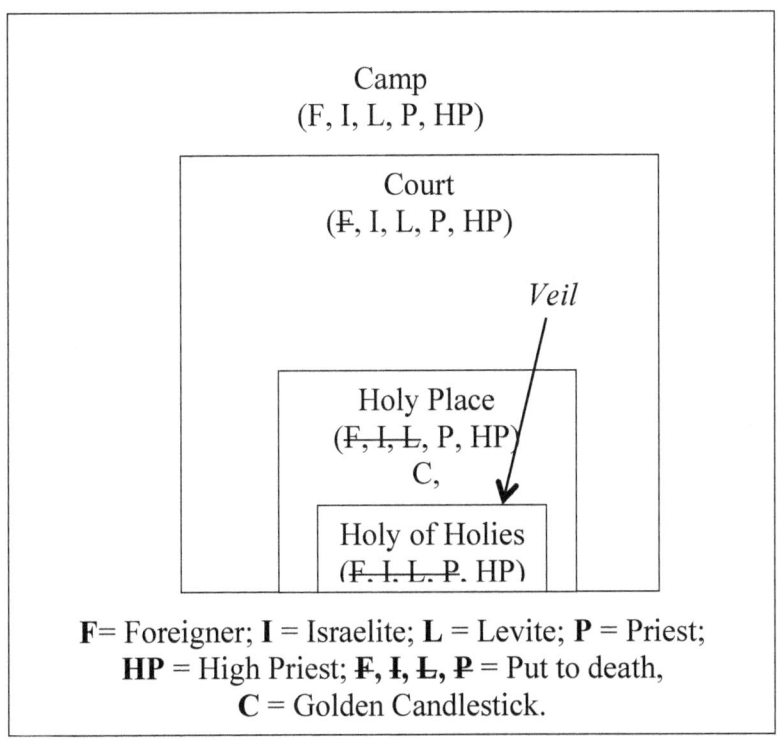

Figure 2: Tabernacle Graded Holiness[163]

Figure 2 reminds us that cultic access was not a privilege to be taken lightly. Five times in Numbers we are told that outsiders approaching the tabernacle court are to be killed.[164] Twice more we are warned that even Levites approaching the Holy Place or touching the holy things are in

---

161. Scholer, *Proleptic Priests*, 91–149; Heb 4:16; 7:25; 10:1, 22; 11:6; 12:18, 22.

162. Ibid., 150–84, esp. 182–84; Heb 6:19–20; 9:12, 24, 25. Note the synonym εἴσοδον in Heb 10:19.

163. Not to scale. The Holy of Holies was a cube (cf. cubic dimensions of the new Jerusalem, Rev 21:16). Diagram adapted from Jenson, *Graded Holiness*, 90.

164. Num 1:51; 3:10, 38; 18:4, 7. Both an inscription from Herod's temple and Josephus testify that death remained a possibility for Gentiles in the first century (Büchsel, "ἀλλογενής," 1:267).

danger of death.¹⁶⁵ The torn veil has brought a new eschatological age; now women, eunuchs, and even Gentiles can enter the most Holy Place through Christ Jesus. Scholer's second argument relates to the importance of kinship relationships (also discussed above). Hebrews' readers have priestly status as seed (παιδία) and siblings (ἀδελφοῖς) of Jesus. Scholer writes:

> By virtue of their relatedness to the high priest, they are entitled to be 'priests' also. . . . Hebrews sees the brothers and παιδία of the 'high priest' as also entitled to hold the priestly office. As a result of Christ's efficacious sacrifice he has set apart his brothers from the rest of the world for God's service.¹⁶⁶

In Hebrews, the Priest-king's siblings share his priestly privileges.

Examples of the priestly identity of the readers of Hebrews could be multiplied. DeSilva recently identified forty-five intratextual links between Hebrews and other priestly canonical texts.¹⁶⁷ This evidence leads some scholars to assume that Hebrews' original recipients were Levitical priests, a conclusion accurately pointing to the priestly *identity* of the original recipients, even if it overstates historical facts.¹⁶⁸ A second example comes from Heb 1:6, where Jesus is called the "firstborn" (πρωτότοκος), a position bringing royal and priestly status (cf. Heb 7:14–17).¹⁶⁹ The term is only used one other time in Hebrews, where believers are called "the church of the firstborn" (Heb 12:23). Hahn accurately observes that "the privileges of the firstborn, namely kingship and priesthood, accrue also in some sense to the individual believer."¹⁷⁰ Finally, Heb 5:11 states that the readers ought to be teachers, a task especially assigned to the priesthood.¹⁷¹

In sum, the priestly identity of Hebrews' readers makes a powerful, although implicit, statement about the royal priesthood. Hebrews' assembly of believers "is a cultic community, not a community with a cult."¹⁷² Jesus' office as Melchizedekian priest-king, with corollary sharing in this royal priesthood by his disciples, was a widely shared doctrine.

---

165. Num 4:15; 16:40; cf. Isa 52:11 in 2 Cor 6:17.
166. Scholer, *Proleptic Priests*, 11, 90.
167. DeSilva, "Priestly Discourse," 317–19.
168. Moe, "Der Gedanke," 163; Floor, "General Priesthood," 72.
169. See Hahn's discussion of priestly primogeniture (*Kinship by Covenant*, 170).
170. Ibid.
171. Scholer, *Proleptic Priests*, 18, 25–26. See also Heb 10:25 and the possible allusion to baptism as a priestly ordination through laying on of hands in Heb 6:2.
172. Marshall, "One for All," 12.

Chapter Summary

Jesus is David's greater son, the Melchizedekian Priest-king. He is Isaiah's meek Servant-king, receiving a royal priestly seed for his sacrificial self-offering (Isa 53:10; 61:6). Jesus' disciples are adopted as siblings into this royal priesthood. First Peter, Matthew, Paul, John, and Hebrews testify to this new reality. In Jesus, Israel's story has come to eschatological fulfillment. The eschaton has begun, and the New Exodus royal priesthood again sings the Song of Moses (Rev 15:3), even as they eagerly await the second coming of their Priest-king in full glory (Heb 9:28).

How was this eschatological view of the royal priesthood received by the church? As we build toward contemporary systematic articulation of the doctrine (Chapters 7 and 8) we pay attention to three "turning points" from the last nineteen hundred years. Chapter 4 examines the "fall" of the apostolic doctrine during the church's first six hundred years. Chapter 5 examines the restoration of the doctrine during the Reformation, along with the "holy egotism" which has hindered it into the present. Finally, Chapter 6 explores the rediscovery of the *missio Dei* in the twentieth century and its implications for the royal priesthood's vocation of witness.

Part II

From Actors to Audience and Back Again:

The Royal Priesthood's Story across the Centuries

4

Defrocking the Royal Priesthood: The First Paradigm Shift

> Or are you ignorant that to you also, that is, to all of the Church of God and to the people of believers, the priesthood was given? . . . you have a priesthood because you are a 'priestly nation,' and for this reason 'you ought to offer an offering of praise to God,' an offering of prayers, an offering of mercy, an offering of purity, an offering of justice, an offering of holiness.
>
> —Origen (d. ca. 254), *Homilies on Leviticus*, 9.1.3

> One could not but be impressed by the prominence which the doctrine of the priesthood of the faithful held in the minds of patristic writers.
>
> —Bishop Laurence Ryan (d. 2003)

FOR THE NON-SPECIALIST, SOME heuristic is necessary for telling a doctrine's history. Part One described what NT churches believed, taught, and confessed. The next three chapters describe a number of "turning points." Broadly speaking, these paradigm shifts trace how the NT doctrine fared before Christendom (Chapter 4), in Protestant Christendom at the Reformation (Chapter 5), and after Christendom's demise (Chapter 6). During these three transitional periods the church has undergone seismic changes and been especially forced to reflect on its ecclesial identity.

This chapter begins with a brief overview of how the royal priesthood developed during the second through fourth centuries. It subsequently narrows its focus onto how the NT's eschatological view of temple, sacrifice, and baptismal priesthood fared. A social move by Clement of Rome (*hierarchicalization*; f. ca. 96) looms large in the first section, as does a theological innovation by Cyprian (*sacralization*; d. ca. 254) in the second. The chapter's final section examines how an understanding of baptism as ordination to the royal priesthood was influenced by political changes in the fourth century. Here the effect of the first Christian emperor, Constantine the Great (d. 337), is explored (*politicization*). Before turning to Clement, Cyprian, and Constantine, we survey development of the doctrine of the royal priesthood in the pre-Constantinian church, with emphasis on Origen.

Toward the beginning of his monograph, Paul Dabin states, "The *unanimous consent of the Fathers*, in matters of faith and morals, constitutes a sure theological argument."[1] Dabin believes that the royal priesthood of the faithful once commanded this kind of Vincentian consensus; more recent scholarship has largely affirmed his conclusion. Earlier we noted a hymn about the sacrifice of a holy life offered by a member of the royal priesthood (*Ode* 20; ca. AD 100).[2] We also discussed Justin Martyr's (d. 165) description of believers as a "high priestly race" (*Dialog with Trypho*, 116)[3] and Irenaeus' (d. ca. 200) description of all the righteous sharing a place in the "priestly order" just like the Lord's disciples (*Against Heresies*, 4.8). Thus the doctrine receives attestation during the second century from across the Roman Empire (Antioch, Rome, and Asia Minor/Lyons).

Overall evidence from the second and third centuries is less comprehensive than that found in the NT. However, Bulley's review from the church's first three centuries "suggests that belief in the general priesthood was fairly constant and general in the whole church of this period."[4] In addition to authors already discussed, we find Melito of Sardis (d. ca. 180) describing believers as those whom Christ has "made a new priesthood and an eternal people for himself."[5] His second-century contemporaries also often use cultic language to describe the ministry of all believers (λειτουργίαι, cf. 1 Clem 41:1). In the third century, testimony is found most strongly in Clement of Alexandria (d. 216), Tertullian (d. 220) and especially Origen (d. 254).

---

1. "Le *consentement unanime des Peres*, en matiere de foi et de moeurs, constitue un argument theologique certain" (Dabin, *Le Sacerdoce Royal des Fidèles*, 13; emphasis original).

2. *Ode* 20's relevance is first recognized by Bulley (2000), but he appears to miss its significance claiming that Justin Martyr is the first non-canonical writer to apply "priest" to all believers (*Priesthood of Some Believers*, 153).

3. Faivre, *Emergence of the Laity*, 31.

4. Bulley, *Priesthood of Some Believers*, 224.

5. "καὶ ποιήσας ἡμᾶς ἱεράτευμα καινὸν καὶ λαὸν περιούσιον αἰώνιον" (Melito of Sardis, *Sur la Pâque* 68 [SC 123:98]).

Origen's writings are voluminous, and his understanding of the priesthood is multifaceted.[6] His thickest extant description of "the priesthood of believers" takes place in his sixteen homilies on Leviticus (ca. AD 240), written ten years after he was ordained.[7] Origen reads Leviticus through Hebrews and 1 Peter, the two foundational NT books for his understanding of Christian priesthood. Although Origen's commentary on Hebrews is lost, the letter's importance is demonstrated by more than one thousand citations found in his extant works.[8] Origen relies upon Hebrews for how the Levitical priesthood relates to the priesthood of Christ. Similarly, 1 Pet 2:9 (cited four times in *Homilies on Leviticus*) provides Origen's basis for "the priesthood of your soul."[9] For Origen, the priestly book of Leviticus is relevant to the whole "priestly race" of believers, since "all who have been anointed with the chrism of the sacred anointing have become priests."[10] Thus, in *Homilies on Leviticus*, Origen applies priesthood to all believers at least a dozen times.[11]

In sum, the apostolic doctrine of the royal priesthood receives consistent witness from the second and third centuries. Syrian, Roman, Egyptian, and African theologians all testify to this "unanimous consent." Yet when Alexandre Faivre wrote his history of the laity in the early church, he described the third century as the century "when the people of God were split in two."[12] We turn now to a brief overview of how the eschatological priestly ministers of the first and second centuries were defrocked.

To defrock is to remove one's priestly credentials, and it is my claim that the royal priesthood was gradually defrocked during the church's first millennium. Every tale of the doctrine must include a story of decline between the second and sixteenth centuries. In the first century, all believers were siblings; by the sixteenth, "brothers" was a term largely reserved for

---

6. Bright describes six ways Origen refers to priesthood ("Priesthood," 179). Stewart focuses exclusively on Origen's hierarchical priesthood, overstating its importance ("'Priests of My People,'" 139–44).

7. While "priesthood of believers" may be anachronistic, Origen uses similar terminology: "Aut ignoras tibi quoque, id est omni Ecclesiae Dei et credentium populo, sacerdotium datum?" (Origen, *Homélies Sur Le Lévitique*, 9.1 [SC 287:72]).

8. Bright, "Priesthood," 179.

9. Origen, *HomLev* 4.6.2 (FC 83:78); 6.2.3 (FC 83:118); 9.1.3 (FC 83:177); 9.9.3 (FC 83:196).

10. Ibid., 9.9.3 (FC 83:196).

11. See also *HomLev* 4.6.5 (FC 83:79); 6.2.6 (FC 83:119); 6.5.6 (FC 83:119), where all believers are called "high priests"; 5.12.9 (FC 83:115); 9.9.4 (FC 83:197); 9.9.6 (FC 83:198); and 13.5.4 (FC 83:243), which emphasizes that "all we who believe in Christ are now a priestly race" (my translation).

12. Faivre, *Emergence of the Laity*, 41.

monastic orders. In Matthew's gospel, discipleship was the norm for all believers, and discipleship remained the norm for Justin Martyr, who speaks of "Christ, and us, his followers . . . his disciples."[13] Yet by the seventh century the "perfect" way of discipleship had been limited to the higher castes of Christians, namely monastic or clerical orders.[14] Franciscan theologian Kenen Osborne describes the overall defrocking of the laity as "disempowering" their priestly ministry:

> 'Disempowering' might not be the correct term, however, and some authors prefer terms such as disenfranchising, displacement, denigrating, diminishment, etc., . . . the overwhelming usage of terms which include a prefix of 'dis' or 'de' and therefore a negative prefix are clear.[15]

While the sections below begin with the ecclesial "firsts" of Clement, Cyprian, and Constantine, each also highlights trajectories set in motion. Hierarchicalization, sacralization, and politicization are the three pillars upon which the royal priesthood's defrocking rests. Each influenced the development of the royal priesthood, through changes in the three major concepts identified in Part One: temple, sacrifice, and baptismal priesthood.

Temple Troubles: Clement of Rome and the Hierarchicalization of Temple Service (a.k.a. "Ministry")

Who gets to serve (λειτουργέω) in the temple? In the OT, the answer was clear: only Aaron's priestly caste possessed this privilege. Temple service, conceived broadly, was the defining function of the Levitical priesthood.[16] But in the eschatological age of the Spirit, brought about by Christ's Melchizedekian royal priesthood, all believers are now priests (Isa 61:6). Peter sums up this eschatological temple service (note οἶκος vocabulary, cf. 1 Pet 2:5) in 1 Pet 4:10–11:

> As each [ἕκαστος] has received a gift, use it to serve [διακονοῦντες] one another [ἑαυτούς], as good stewards [οἰκονόμοι] of God's varied grace: whoever speaks, as one who speaks oracles of God; whoever serves, as one who serves by the strength that God supplies—in order that in everything God may be glorified through

---

13. Justin, *Dialogue with Trypho* 17 (FC 6:173); Faivre, *Emergence of the Laity*, 25–35.

14. Osborne, *Ministry*, 49.

15. Ibid., 115.

16. Leithart, *Priesthood of the Plebs*, 48–86.

Jesus Christ. *To him belong glory and dominion forever and ever. Amen.*[17]

Thus for Peter, Paul, and the other NT writers, there are no laypersons within the one body of Christ;[18] rather, God's whole flock are clergy (κλῆρος, 1 Pet 2:3).[19] All believers are called to engage in priestly ministry within the eschatological temple (Christ's body). Yet this eschatological view of a universal priestly ministry did not endure for more than a few generations after the death of the apostles. In this section we trace the layperson's "fall" from temple service through the hierarchicalization of priestly ministry. As Yoder notes:

> "Fall" or "loss" in this sense is not equivalent to "apostasy".... The term is simply descriptive reference to the fact that, losing the specific and original trait of the primitive community, the church by and large became again subject to the usual anthropologically universal pattern of the single, sacramentally qualified religionist.[20]

A division in cultic competence between leaders and followers is *first* suggested by Clement of Rome. Eusebius then *reduces* priestly ministry primarily to those who govern God's brick and mortar temple, and temple-service is further *ontologically* separated from the laity by Pseudo-Dionysius.

Clement of Rome and the Christian Plebs

Around AD 96, Clement of Rome penned an epistle to the Corinthian church on behalf of the Roman house churches. The letter's second half begins in chapter forty, where Clement becomes the first to describe believers as "laypersons;" categorically different from leaders:

> For to the high priest the proper services [λειτουργίαι] have been given, and to the priests the proper office has been assigned, and upon the Levites the proper ministries [διακονίαι]

---

17. Emphasis added. The doxology, "ἡ δόξα καὶ τὸ κράτος εἰς τοὺς αἰῶνας τῶν αἰώνων, ἀμήν," only appears in one other NT location, Rev 1:6, where believers have been made "priests to God." Origen seems to have noticed the priestly significance of this doxology, using it to conclude fourteen of his sixteen *Homilies on Leviticus*.

18. Cf. ἰδιώτης in 1 Cor 14:16. Fee's interpretation is superior to Faivre (*Emergence of the Laity*, 8; Fee, *First Epistle to the Corinthians*, 672–73; 683–88; Fee, "Laos and Leadership under the New Covenant," 3–13).

19. A church leader is not referred to as κλῆρος until early in the third century (see Faivre, *Emergence of the Laity*, 21).

20. Yoder, *Fullness of Christ*, 18.

have been imposed. The layman [ὁ λαϊκὸς ἄνθρωπος] is bound by the layman's [λαϊκοῖς] rules. Let each of you brothers, give thanks to God with your own group [τάγματι], maintaining a good conscience, not overstepping the designated rule of his ministry [λειτουργίας], but acting with reverence.[21]

Clement is the first in extant Greek literature to use λαϊκὸς in a religious sense, suggesting two ranks (τάγματι) among believers.[22] While Clement distinguishes between the priestly ministries of leaders and followers in order to emphasize proper church order, he still sees all believers as engaged in priestly service (λειτουργίας).[23] Thus his terminology is more problematic than his concepts. Yet Clement's hierarchicalization of ministry was compounded by sociological changes a century later, as churches moved from domestic homes to the *domus ecclesiae* or "house of the church" around AD 200.[24] The beginnings of Christian architecture marked a new moment for the movement, its implications best seen in Constantine's fourth-century building projects.

Eusebius and the Reduction of Temple Service to a Clerical Caste

Clement uses Levitical typology as he appeals to the Corinthian church. The question is not so much whether or not it is appropriate to see church leaders with Levitical typology but, rather, whether it is appropriate to exclude other members of Christ's body.[25] Paul describes all Christians in Levitical terms, assigning duties once limited to Levites and priests (2 Cor 6:16—7:1). In the church of the apostles and apologists, Levitical typology emphasizes the priestly nature of the whole body of Christ. But, as centuries wear on, the eschatological nature of the whole priestly body fades farther and farther into the background.[26] In its place, a reductionist priestly typology limits Levitical types to clergy.

---

21. *First Clement* 40:5–41:1 (*AF3* 99).

22. Faivre, *Emergence of the Laity*, 21; Leithart, *Priesthood of the Plebs*, 182–222.

23. Stewart's failure to recognize this point is a consistent weakness ("Priests of My People," 242–44).

24. White, *Social Origins*, 1:111. White describes a further development around the time of Cyprian to the *aula ecclesiae* ("hall of the church"), the primary predecessor of Constantine's grand basilicas (1:127–39).

25. Paul draws analogies between church leaders and the Levitical priesthood (Rom 15:16; 1 Cor 9:13–14; cf. Rom 1:9).

26. Cyprian's influence is greater in the Latin West, perhaps explaining why the

This reductionist Levitical typology was furthered by a new sociological situation at the beginning of the third century and a new political situation in the first quarter of the fourth century. The beginning of the third century saw the rise of a "Christian material culture," one instance being the first appearances of public buildings set aside permanently for Christian worship.[27] There is a move from home churches to buildings set aside as the home of God. With this move, a new function of Christian leaders is emphasized, care of the physical property of the church: God's house is less an eschatological reference to the living stones of Christ's body[28] than a literal brick and mortar building.[29]

Eusebius is the first in extant literature to call the building (rather than the people) God's "temple."[30] For Hans Thümmel, Eusebius' declaration is illustrative of a "radical innovation" and a "turning point" for the Christian community.[31] Temple service is now associated primarily with specific geographic space, and in this space new functions for church leaders develop. These new functions were explained by a reductive Levitical typology, rather than the Levitical typology used by Paul, Clement of Rome, Justin Martyr, Irenaeus, Tertullian, and Origen who applied it to the priestly nature of the whole body of Christ. Eusebius' reductive Levitical typology matched OT types to the church's new material culture of temple buildings, altar/sacrifice, and clerical priesthood/caste. Stewart sums up the material turn's effect on ecclesial identity:

> With regard to the architectural and artistic developments, a sacred space and the emergence of a more materially defined identity would invite a new understanding of the Church as Culture. It would facilitate a re-conceptualization of the role and function of one who presides over the emerging sacred space and objects as a "priest."[32]

East, at least in principle, retained greater emphasis on the royal priesthood of the baptized (Ryan, "Patristic Teaching," 30).

27. Clement of Alexandria is the first to refer to a building as a "church" (*Christ the Educator* 3.2.79 [FC 23:259]; White, *Social Origins of Christian Architecture*, 2:53).

28. 1 Pet 2:5–9; 1 Cor 3:16; Eph 2:18–22. Cf. Matt 12:6; 18:15–20.

29. Stewart, "Priests of My People," 28–29.

30. Eusebius, *Ecclesiastical History*, 10.4 (LCL 265:395–45); Stewart, "Priests of my People," 231.

31. "In diesen Vergleichen aber geschieht eine *radikale Neuerung*. . . . Wie schnell auch immer man Eusebios gefolgt ist, hier scheint der *Wenderpunkt* zu liegen" (Thümmel, "Versammlungsraum, Kirche, Tempel," 499, emphasis added).

32. Stewart, "Priests of My People," 23, cf. 28.

Stewart calls the church's evolving ecclesiology a "politico-theological ecclesiology" because of its contrast with the Greco-roman *polis* and its continuity with OT Israel.[33] There is nothing inherently wrong, and much that is potentially good, in the material turn during the third and fourth centuries. But uncritical acceptance of these gains would prove problematic. The rise of Christian "temples" contributed to a specialized group of clerical "priests" distinct from the royal priesthood. Emphasis on the clerical "priests" of brick and mortar "temples" contributed to eclipse of the apostolic emphasis on the priestly character of all church members. Other factors were also significant in the hierarchicalization of the church's politico-theological ecclesiology, especially the influence of Pseudo-Dionysius.

Pseudo-Dionysius and the Ontologizing of Hierarchical Distinctions

The Greek philosophy which most influenced early Christianity was Platonism.[34] From its beginnings, Platonism's concept of divinity, especially as developed in Neo-Platonism, was accessible only to the elite. In *Timaeus*, Plato remarks that if it is possible for a philosopher to discover God, "to declare him unto all men were a thing impossible."[35] This hierarchical view of access to God was given great currency by Pseudo-Dionysius (ca. AD 485–528). In AD 529, Emperor Justinian forced the closure of the Neoplatonist Philosophical schools in Athens. Perhaps in part due to this imperial pressure, an innovative pseudonymous writer preserved and popularized a synthesis of neoplatonist philosophy and Christian doctrine under the name of Dionysius the Areopagite. Dionysius was the Athenian philosopher Paul led to Christ (Acts 17:34). By claiming apostolic warrant, Pseudo-Dionysius brought near canonical status to his blend of Neo-Platonism and biblical theology.

Of Pseudo-Dionysius's four surviving treatises, the two most influential on the royal priesthood were *On the Celestial Hierarchy* and *On the Ecclesiastical Hierarchy*. In the former, God interacts with the world only through three levels of tripartite intermediaries; in the latter, the hierarchical intermediaries continue on earth with the tripartite orders of clergy (bishop, priest, deacon) and layperson (monk, faithful, penitent). Table 2 illustrates this hierarchical cosmology where authority moves from left to

---

33. Ibid., 24.
34. Drobner, "Christian Philosophy," 680–82.
35. Plato, *Timaeus* 28c (LCL 234 8:51).

right (bishop higher than deacon) and then from top to bottom (deacon higher than monk).

Seraphim (*Cael. hier.* 7)	Cherubim (*Cael. hier.* 7)	Thrones (*Cael. hier.* 7)
Rulers (*Cael. hier.* 8)	Powers (*Cael. hier.* 8)	Dominions (*Cael. hier.* 8)
Principalities (*Cael. hier.* 9)	Archangels (*Cael. hier.* 9)	Angels (*Cael. hier.* 9)
Bishops (*Eccl. hier.* 5)	Priests (*Eccl. hier.* 5)	Deacons (*Eccl. hier.* 5)
Monks (*Eccl. hier.* 6)	Lay Faithful (*Eccl. hier.* 6)	Penitents (*Eccl. hier.* 6)

Table 2: Pseudo-Dionysius's Celestial and Ecclesiastical Hierarchies[36]

It would be difficult to over-emphasize Pseudo-Dionysius' impact on medieval theology. Aquinas explicitly cites him more than two thousand times. Cooke summarizes the royal priesthood's distancing from God as posited by Pseudo-Dionysius:

> Dionysius crystallized ontologically the clergy/lay division and the superiority of monks within the church, doubly distancing ordinary laity from the God "at the top of the hierarchical ladder." . . . Hierarchy is now considered an ontological reality which, certainly from Dionysius onward, placed people at different levels of proximity to the divine.[37]

In short, Pseudo-Dionysius's hierarchical view of access to God radically reduced the privileges of the royal priesthood, who in apostolic times had access to the Holy of Holies through the eschatological presence of the Holy Spirit.[38] What for Clement had been a difference in *categories*, and for Eusebius was primarily a *functional* difference, became an *ontological* division rooted in creation order. One of Pseudo-Dionysius's six sacraments was the consecration of monks—thus even the laity were ontologically divided. Gregory the Great propagated this hierarchical view of church and world, and the ontological distance between clergy and laity, spiritual and secular,

---

36. Adapted from Drobner, *Fathers of the Church*, 534–35.
37. Cooke, *Distancing of God*, 94, 108.
38. Even for Pseudo-Dionysius, access to the Eucharistic table was available to the laity because of participation in the royal priesthood (*Ecclesiastical Hierarchy* 2.2.7). Cf. Levering, *Christ and the Catholic Priesthood*, 251–72.

continued to grow until reaching its zenith during the papacy of another Gregory some six hundred years later.[39]

The Fundamental Question: Who Are Yahweh's Temple Servants in the Eschatological Age?

Leithart overstates the case when claiming that Luther's great contribution was not so much the doctrine of justification by faith, but rather "when he attacked the Babylonian Captivity of the church and exulted in the 'clerical' status of the baptized."[40] Yet Leithart is correct to identify the return of priestly ministry to the whole people of God as an event of major ecclesial significance: once again eunuchs could shout for joy at their temple access (Isa 56:1-8; Acts 8:26-39). The medieval reduction of temple service to an exclusive clerical caste was a far cry from the apostolic vision of a royal priesthood offering priestly sacrifices in an eschatological temple. Many centuries, events, and theologians played a role in this reduction, and our focus on Clement of Rome, Eusebius of Caesarea, and Pseudo-Dionysius could easily have included others. While removing the privilege of temple service from the laity was an important factor in the defrocking of the royal priesthood, the changing relationship of sacrifice and baptismal ordination to the royal priesthood must also be considered. Having sketched the defrocking implications of the hierarchicalization of temple service, we now turn to a similar reduction of the concept of sacrifice as a result of the sacralization of the clergy.[41]

Sharing the Sacrifice? Cyprian and the Rise of the "Third" Christian Priesthood

While Jewish priesthood especially focused on temple service, Greco-Roman priesthood primarily focused on sacrifice; a priest was a sacrificer (*sacerdote*).[42] Cyprian of Carthage (d. AD 258), more than any other fig-

---

39. For Leithart and Congar the Gregorian reform (ca. 1050–80) marks the decisive shift for the royal priesthood (Congar, "Ministry in the Early Church," 351; Congar, "Sacralization of Western Society," 61–62, in *Sacralization and Secularization*, ed by. Roger Aubert (New York: Paulist, 1969; Leithart, *Priesthood of the Plebs*, 232–47; esp. 234).

40. Leithart, *Priesthood of the Plebs*, 247.

41. For more on hierarchicalization and sacralization see Torjeson, "Clergy and Laity," 391.

42. Plato, *Statesman* 290 C/D (*LCL* 164:121).

ure, is responsible for applying this Greco-Roman concept (*sacerdotos*) to Christian clergy.[43] Cyprian was a popular and gifted church leader.[44] He was the first bishop martyred in Africa,[45] one of the first to write on the church (*The Unity of the Catholic Church*), the first to write an extended reflection on the Eucharist (*Letter* 63), the first to give the bishop exclusive powers to control reconciliation of penitents through the laying on of hands,[46] and the first to assign unique sacrificial powers to clergy. Especially these two final ecclesial "firsts" were problematic for the apostolic doctrine of the royal priesthood. Before Cyprian, the royal priesthood was a consistent feature in patristic doctrine. After Cyprian, with the exception of Augustine, the doctrine receded in the West and exclusive clerical priesthood rose to prominence.[47]

The Origin of the "Third" Christian Priesthood

Tertullian described all believers as a "third race"; in Cyprian we find the origin of a "third" priesthood. Prior to Cyprian, ecclesial teachers spoke of two Christian priesthoods: 1) the Melchizedekian priesthood of Christ, and 2) the royal priesthood of believers, who—through the Spirit—share in Christ's royal priesthood.[48] For Tertullian, ecclesial leaders could be called priests by virtue of the royal priesthood they shared with all believers through baptismal ordination. Cyprian, in his zeal to protect the unity of the church as found in the office of bishop, moves beyond Tertullian and defrocks the laity by reducing priesthood to those men with official ecclesial approval to offer Eucharistic sacrifice. For Cyprian, the bishop is the peoples' priest.[49] This is

---

43. Lang, *Sacred Games*, 258–62.

44. Augustine preached ten sermons on Cyprian (*Sermons* 308A–131F [*WSA* III/9:55–122]) and cites him more than one hundred times. See also Prudentius, *Peristephanon* 13.5.6 [*ACW* 36: xii; cf. 257n1]).

45. Pontius, *St. Cyprian* 19 (*FC* 15:24).

46. Cyprian, *Letters* 15.1.2 (*ACW* 43:91); 16.2.3 (*ACW* 43:94); Brent, *Cyprian and Roman Carthage*, 266–70.

47. Bulley, *Priesthood of Some Believers*, 209; Garrett, "Pre-Cyprianic Doctrine," 22; Eastwood, *Royal Priesthood*, 80–90.

48. Cf. Origen, *HomLev* 8.5; Ryan, "Patristic Teaching," 29–30.

49. BéVenot, for example, argues that Cyprian considered only bishops to be priests ("'*Sacerdos*' as Understood by Cyprian," 414). Bulley's conclusion that Cyprian occasionally included presbyters is more nuanced (*Priesthood of Some Believers*, 115–18, esp. 118). So also Laurance, *Priest as Type of Christ*, 200.

because only the bishop (*sacerdos*) "serves in Christ's place [*uice Christi*]" when he offers the sacrifice of the Eucharist.[50]

While Cyprian seems to have been aware of the doctrine of the royal priesthood, unlike Tertullian he avoids ever calling *plebes* "priests," instead almost exclusively reserving *sacerdotos* for the office of bishop (he twice includes *presbyters*). His defrocking of the laity is especially associated with his innovative view of the bishop's role at the Eucharist. As John Laurance notes, "Cyprian is the first Latin writer to use the term '*sacerdos*' of the leader of the Eucharist."[51] He introduces a "new priesthood" into the church, a "third priesthood" of the president of the Eucharist. Like Plato's priests, this new priesthood has exclusive power to mediate God's forgiveness and to offer Christ's sacrifice to God on behalf of the people.[52] Because this bishop-priest stands in the place of Christ, he is the one *mediator* between God and the people.[53] If his priesthood is invalid, then Christ has "no priest" and the people no "hope of peace and salvation . . . no grace of baptism and the Holy Spirit."[54] In one of his pastoral epistles, Cyprian warns the believers in Carthage of those who would "set up another altar" or appoint a "*sacerdotium nouum*."[55] Yet, somewhat ironically, Cyprian has created a "*sacerdotium nouum*," one standing apart from the priesthood of the faithful. This innovative new priesthood was primarily characterized by its new and exclusive sacrifice.

An Exclusive Priesthood with an Exclusive Sacrifice

The fundamental question raised by Cyprian's creative and contextual theology is, "who in the Christian community can offer acceptable sacrifices"? Hebrews describes two kinds of Christian sacrifices: the once for all sacrifice of Christ (Heb 9:26; 10:12) and sacrifices of praise (Heb 13:15–16). Cyprian's third priesthood offers a third sacrifice, standing between Christ's sacrifice and the sacrifices of believers. Cyprian's nigh exclusive emphasis

---

50. Cyprian, *Letters* 63.14.4 (*ACW* 46:106). See also *Epistle* 59.5.1 (*ACW* 46:72, 243) where Cyprian claims that in each geographical area "there is but one bishop [*sacerdos*] and judge who acts in Christ's stead."

51. Laurance, *Priest as Type of Christ*, 220.

52. Part of Cyprian's agenda was to defrock the martyrs, to centralize the power to pronounce forgiveness of sins solely in the territorial bishop and his designees. See "Cyprian's Case against the Church of the Martyrs" in Brent, *Cyprian and Roman Carthage*, 250–89, esp. 254.

53. Cyprian, *Letters* 66.8.3 (*ACW* 46:121); Cooke, *Distancing of God*, 71.

54. Cyprian, *Letters* 66.5.1–2 (*ACW* 46:119).

55. Ibid., 43.5.1 (*ACW* 44:64).

on this third sacrifice—a sacrifice only the bishop could offer—diminished emphasis on the other two, especially the sacrifices of the royal priesthood.

Cyprian lived in an era when sacrifice was the preeminent issue facing the church; his emphasis on the bishop offering the only true sacrifice is a byproduct of unique tensions in the decade he served as bishop.[56] In AD 248, the year after Cyprian became bishop, Rome celebrated its 1,000-year anniversary, and Emperor Decius (249–251) decreed that every citizen must offer a sacrifice to obtain the peace of the gods for the new millennium. Cyprian's first great challenge as bishop was how to respond to the great number of baptized who in a "millennial panic" compromised themselves in order to obey the imperial edict.

In addition to external challenges, Cyprian's elite patrician background played a significant role in his reduction of sacrifice primarily to the monarchial (patrician) bishop who sacrificed on behalf of the plebs. The burden of Allen Brent's *Cyprian and Roman Carthage* (2010) is to show how Cyprian's view of ecclesial authority was "shaped by the third-century, pagan, environment of Roman Carthage."[57] Brent aims to expose "the unexplored metaphysical assumptions underlying a pagan jurisprudential and political theology that condition Cyprian's model."[58] Cyprian's contextualized ecclesiology used the patrician/pleb distinction typical of his era, and "availed itself of a pagan political discourse that made the ruler the channel of the Logos, or divine order of the world," resulting in a Christian society where "the divine ruler should be both priest and king."[59] Cyprian reduced Peter's concept of the spiritual sacrifices of the royal priesthood (1 Pet 2:5, 9) to an almost exclusive emphasis on the Eucharistic president.[60] Just as the previous section identified a reduction of the NT's concept of temple service, so this section has identified a similar reduction of spiritual sacrifice.

The Medieval Trajectory of the Cyprianic Reduction of Sacrifice

The story of increasing sacralization of the clergy's sacrifice has been told elsewhere.[61] We can only gesture toward the effect changing Eucharistic conceptions had on the doctrine of the royal priesthood. Gregory the Great

56. Brent, *Political History*, 257–60.
57. Brent, *Cyprian and Roman Carthage*, 329.
58. Ibid.
59. Brent, *Political History*, 274. Cf. Hellerman, *Ancient Church as Family*, 182–212.
60. Cf. Garrett, "Priesthood of All Christians," 24n32.
61. E.g., Lang, *Sacred Games*, 205–81; Kilmartin, *Eucharist in the West*.

added a mystical dimension to the clergy's powers of Eucharistic sacrifice which became extremely influential in the medieval period. He was one of the first to claim that Christ was offered again (*iterum*) every time the Eucharistic sacrifice was made.[62] According to Gregory, the Mass can free souls after death from the fires of the damned; it can set a prisoner free of his chains, and can save a man who has been shipwrecked.[63] Paschasius Radbertus (d. 851) built on Gregory's mystical view, and became the first to teach that the Eucharist, after the words of consecration, becomes identical with the body of Jesus born to the Virgin Mary: "We receive in the bread that which hung upon the cross."[64] The priest, whose magical powers made this change possible, "becomes a *ministerial means* to the somatic real presence."[65]

As the centuries progress, it becomes standard for the laity to "buy a mass [sacrifice]" (*missam comparare*) as God's grace is primarily accessible only through the clergy's special sacrifice.[66] By the time of John Duns Scotus (d. 1308) and his later commentator, Gabriel Biel (d. 1495), the priest's power to distribute the fruit of the mass/sacrifice had become highly systematized. Discussions of the spiritual sacrifice of the royal priesthood found little currency among the clergy, but they did find a resurgence in the lay spirituality movements of the fourteenth and fifteenth centuries (e.g., Thomas á Kempis' [ca. 1420] *Imitation of Christ*), which prepared the way for the Reformation's return to the apostolic doctrine.

In sum, Cyprian's sacralization of the clergy is a "watershed,"[67] marking the true "grund 'Schisma'" of church history.[68] According to Garrett, Cyprian "marked the advent of a new era," his teaching constitutes "a major turning point in the history of the concept of the priesthood of all Christians."[69] For Eastwood, Cyprian's move from "the High Priestly Race" to "a High Priestly Class" is "one of the important landmarks in the history of the Church."[70] At the least, Cyprian's exclusive focus on the bishop evolved in an unfortunate

---

62. Gregory the Great, *Dialogues* 4:60 (*FC* 39:273); Kilmartin, *Eucharist in the West*, 22, 76, 88; Lang, *Sacred Games*, 240–46.

63. Gregory the Great, *Dialogues* 4:57, 58, 59 (*FC* 39:266–72).

64. Paschasius, cited by Kilmartin, *Eucharist in the West*, 84; see 82–89.

65. Ibid., 83; emphasis added.

66. Lang, *Sacred Games*, 246–53.

67. Bulley, *Priesthood of Some Believers*, 318.

68. Wess, *Ihr alle seid Geschwister*, 64–65.

69. Garrett, "Pre-Cyprianic Doctrine," 46; Garrett, "Priesthood of All Christians," 22.

70. Eastwood, *Royal Priesthood*, 80, 88.

direction, contributing significantly to the royal priesthood's defrocking during the next millennium.[71]

Royal Priesthood versus Roman Citizenship: Baptism, Constantine, and the Rise of Christendom

The gradual defrocking of the royal priesthood rests upon three pillars. The final pillar was a gradual politicization and decommissioning of baptismal priesthood during the third through sixth centuries. Baptism was initially a believer's ordination to the ministry of the royal priesthood, sharing in Christ's Melchizedekian ministry as the Priest King. For those baptized into Christ Jesus, baptism marked a radically new eschatological and priestly reality (Gal 3:27–28).[72] Yet the situation which met the reformers in the sixteenth century was not a unified nation of priests; but a sea of *getauftes Heidentum*.

How did the saints' *ekklesia* move from *baptized priests* to *baptized pagans*? Like the hierarchicalization and sacralization of the clergy, the politicization and decommissioning of the baptismal priesthood was a gradual process. Just as Clement of Rome and Cyprian of Carthage played important initial roles, so also did Constantine the Great. Constantine's contribution cannot be separated from the new era Christianity entered when Rome's *Pontifex Maximus* joined the royal priesthood. The deleterious effects upon the apostolic doctrine of the royal priesthood were twofold: 1) the reduction of the royal priesthood's priestly responsibilities by the addition of a fourth Christian priesthood, the Caesarean sacral kingship; and 2) the disassociation of baptism from priestly ordination as imperial decree gradually, and eventually definitively (AD 529), equated baptism with Roman citizenship. When all citizens were compelled by imperial might to accept baptism, the waters slowly lost their powers of ordination. We begin this part of the story with Constantine as the first Christian representative of the Caesarean sacral kingship.

---

71. Cyprian's theological judgment can be more conducive to participation by the royal priesthood than is illustrated by the medieval period. Working to do so in the Roman Catholic tradition is Orr, "Educating for the Priesthood," 437–57. See also Orr, *Gift of the Priesthood to the Faithful*.

72. Leithart, *Priesthood of the Plebs*, 102–08.

Constantine as a Christian Priest-King and Enforcer of the Divine Will

When Constantine died on May 22, 337 he died as an ordained member of the royal priesthood (by virtue of baptism), but also as the Roman Empire's *Pontifex Maximus*.[73] Since Constantine waited until his deathbed to be baptized, his service to the church as emperor falls under the latter priesthood rather than the former. The title *Pontifex Maximus*, or "Greatest High Priest," may have come from the Latin roots *pons* (bridge) and *facere* (to make); literally, a "bridge-builder."[74] Beyond etymology, the Emperor served as a mediator between the gods and the citizens; his divine empowerment enabled him to maintain the *pax romana*.

As the first Christian *Pontifex Maximus*, Constantine's unique priestly role was recognized by Eusebius, who called him the "bishop of externals" (*episkopos ton ektos*), "another apostle," even a type of Christ, a "Savior."[75] The sacral role of the Emperor was not uncontested in the fourth century but, following Constantine's death, one of three variations of sacred kingship remained the norm in Christendom for over 1,500 years (until 1776). To a degree, Constantine's non-clerical priestly leadership might be seen as movement back toward the eschatological royal priesthood found in the NT. But Constantine's sacral kingship was not the proleptic priesthood of 1 Peter, Revelation, and Hebrews; it was rather a realized eschatological priesthood unique to sacral kings. It found warrant in Israel's kings and Arius' Christ, not in the eschatological priestly seed promised to Isaiah's Servant (Isa 53:15; 61:6).[76]

Kenan Osborne's research suggests that beginning with Constantine, the ministry of the royal priesthood was further reduced by a new division within the people of God. The emperor or king, between Constantine and Gregory VII, is not cleric, layperson, or monastic, but rather a fourth class who has special access to the divine just like the cleric and the monk. Osborne identifies three historical models for relationships between emperor, clergy, monks, and laity (Table 3). In all of them, after Constantine, the laity

---

73. Aufhauser, "Die Sakrale Kaiseridee in Byzanz," 531–42.Leithart, *Defending Constantine*, 308–09.

74. The title was first held by Augustus (d. AD 14) and eventually surrendered by Gratian (d. AD 383) however, a sacral role for emperors and kings remained for more than a millennium.

75. See "Constantine as Christ," in Bardill, *Constantine*. Cf. Leithart, *Defending Constantine*, 147–67.

76. Cf. Williams, "Christology and Church-State Relations: Part I," 8–14.

were again removed one step further from the sacrifices and temple service of the royal priesthood.

Papal Monism	Imperial Monism	Dualism	
Pope (Clergy)	Emperor/King	Emperor/ King	Pope (Clergy)
Emperor/King	Pope (Clergy)		
Monks	Monks	Monks	
Laity (and Penitents)	Laity (and Penitents)	Laity (and Penitents)	

Table 3: Three Models of Divine Mediation and Sacred Kingship after Constantine[77]

Prior to Constantine, Christian theologians associated the Roman emperor with creation order. After Constantine, the emperor was often associated with the order of salvation. As *Pontifex Maximus* the Roman emperor was expected to be a mediator of the divine will. Beginning with Constantine, Christian emperors used this sacral expectation to compel citizens to accept particular confessions and ecclesial practices. One practical implication was that the mission of the church dissolved into the acids of empire. The expansion of Christianity became synonymous with the expansion of empire—a legacy of Christendom that especially plagued the churches of the Holy Roman Empire and the magisterial Reformation, with its ghost haunting the missionary movement into the present.

Augustine, Infant Baptism, and the Royal Priesthood's Priestly Ordination

While Constantine's sacral kingship did affect the doctrine of the royal priesthood, its influence is dwarfed by comparison with another fourth-century change—from post-conversion to *infant* baptism—the latter's widespread acceptance almost singlehandedly wrought by Augustine's influence. Robert Wilken speaks for an ecumenical consensus when he describes early Christian baptism "as a ritual for adults, not infants . . . a moral as well as

---

77. See Osborne for "papal monism," "imperial monism," and "dualism" (*Ministry*, 196–216).

a spiritual experience."[78] Thus, Justin Martyr claims, "At our first birth we were born of necessity without our knowledge," but as Christians we are reborn through our "free choice and knowledge."[79] It was not infant baptism *per se* but the sixth-century imperial degree requiring infant baptism for all citizens of the Roman Empire which was especially problematic.[80]

For Tertullian, Christians are a people "made, not born."[81] Once they were like other peoples, but baptism has now made them a priestly people—just as Aaron's ordination once made him a priest.[82] Believers are "true priests" who offer prayer as their sacrifice through Christ, "the Pontiff of the priesthood of the uncircumcision."[83] As priests, baptized believers are expected to live lives of priestly holiness,[84] and to do the work of God's "priest and advocate before men," namely, "preaching the gospel of God."[85] In sum, for Tertullian, baptism is for the converted, representing ordination to royal and priestly ministry.[86]

---

78. Wilken, *Spirit of Early Christian Thought*, 37. On the ecumenical consensus: "While the possibility that infant baptism was practiced in the apostolic age cannot be excluded, baptism upon personal profession of faith is the most clearly attested pattern in the New Testament documents" (*Baptism, Eucharist, Ministry*, 4).

79. Justin Martyr, *1 Apol.* 61; so also Cyprian, *Ad Quirinum* 3.52 (*ANF* 5:547 [*CCEL* 5:1304]).

80. This subsection is not intended as polemic against infant baptism, other biblical arguments can also be made. Thus, David Wright and Peter Leithart, both committed paedobaptists, have also argued for significant baptismal reform. Leithart opposes believers' baptism for the children of believers, yet states that "the century long farce of schizophrenic paedobaptism is hardly preferable" ("Infant Baptism in History," 262). Whether one holds to believers baptism (as I do) or to paedobaptist (as do Leithart and Wright), there is desperate need for baptismal reform. See further Wright, "Baptism: Where Do We Go From Here?," 377–84.

81. Tertullian, *Apology* 18.4 (*ANF* 3:32 [*CCEL* 3:56]). See also Tertullian, *On Baptism* 18 (*ANF* 3:677–78 [*CCEL* 3:1512]).

82. Tertullian, *On Baptism* 7 (*ANF* 3:672 [*CCEL* 3:1496]).

83. Tertullian, *On Prayer* 28 (*ANF* 3:690 [*CCEL* 3:1549]); *Five Books against Marcion*, 5.9 (*ANF* 3:448 [*CCEL* 3:979]).

84. "Are not even we laics priests? . . . if you have the right of a priest in your own person, in cases of necessity, it behooves you to have likewise the discipline of a priest whenever it may be necessary to have the right of a priest" (Tertullian, *Exhortation to Chastity* 7 [*ANF* 4:45; *CCEL* 4:126]).

85. Tertullian, *On the Resurrection*, 61 (*ANF* 3:592 [*CCEL* 3:1327]).

86. Tertullian, *Five Books against Marcion*, 5.9 (*ANF* 3:448 [*CCEL* 3:979]). See further Cramer, *Baptism and Change*, 48, and discussion of Tertullian's use of *sacramentum* in relation to Christian baptismal vows and the sacred military vows of Rome's legionnaires (63); Justin Martyr, *Apology* 1:61.

Tertullian viewed baptism as an ordination service for the converted; with few exceptions, this remained the standard view until the fifth century.[87] Thus nearly all fourth-century church leaders who grew up in Christian homes were baptized as young adults: Ambrose, Augustine, Basil the Great, Gregory Nazianzen, Gregory of Nyssa, Jerome, John Chrysostom, Paulinus of Nola, Rufinus of Aquileia, and others.[88] Baptismal liturgies indicate that "adult baptism very early became the model for Christian initiation."[89] Edward Yarnold's study of the fourth-century baptismal homilies of Cyril, Ambrose, and Chrysostom led him to conclude that "adult baptism was normal, almost unvariable even in Jerusalem, Milan, and Antioch."[90] David Wright's study of the Nicene Creed's "one baptism for the remission of sins" led him to conclude that the phrase adopted by the 150 bishops gathered at Constantinople in 381 "could not have been understood to encompass the baptism of babies."[91] Similarly, all nine baptisms mentioned by Augustine in *Confessions* are post-conversion.[92]

According to Leithart, "the church was rescued from Baptist theology and practice by Augustine."[93] Infant baptism became important to the later Augustine when it became his defeater of all things Pelagian. Infant baptism was essential for infant salvation; the unbaptized infant of Christian parents would burn in hell.[94] Thus the focus moved from ordination to the royal priesthood through union with Christ's Melchizedikian priesthood onto exorcism from original sin. In Augustine's baptism, "the rite loses all its ethical color: instead of something done by the candidate, it becomes something done to him."[95] Augustine himself maintained apostolic emphasis on baptism as ordination to Christ's royal priesthood.[96] Explaining Rev 20:6 and 1 Pet 2:9, he writes, "we call them all priests insomuch as they are members

---

87. Tertullian is the first to explicitly argue against infant baptism.

88. Wright, "At What Ages Were People Baptized in the Early Centuries?," 65.

89. Leithart, "Infant Baptism," 251. But note David Wright's criticism: "Leithart fails to draw the obvious conclusion from this evidence, that infant baptism can never have been the norm in this early period" (*What Has Infant Baptism Done to Baptism?*, 8). Leithart blames the apostolic church's "fall" from infant baptism to post-conversion baptism on the alien influence of mystery religions. He does not acknowledge the significance of Jesus' baptismal example for the early church.

90. Yarnold, *Awe-Inspiring Rites of Initiation: The Origins of the RCIA*.

91. Wright, "Meaning and Reference," 57.

92. Wright, "Augustine and the Transformation," 71.

93. Leithart, "Infant Baptism in History," 258.

94. Wright, "Augustine and the Transformation," 84–86.

95. Cramer, *Baptism and Change*, 113. See further 87–129.

96. Augustine, *Expositions of the Psalms* 26.2 (*WSA* III/15:274–75).

of the One Priest."⁹⁷ Augustine states the responsibility of all the baptized, those "consecrated in the name of God and vowed to God," to offer their whole lives as to God through Christ.⁹⁸ When expounding Rom 12:1–2, Augustine defines the royal priesthood's "true sacrifices" as "works of mercy done to ourselves or our neighbor and directed to God."⁹⁹

Yet Augustine's insistence on an exclusive practice of infant baptism, when combined with Constantine's "Christianization" of the Roman Empire, "affected a massive baptismal reductionism" and "set in motion a far broader transformation that determined the contours of the Christianity of Christendom, in large measure to the present day."¹⁰⁰ Universal infant baptism was legally required of all Roman citizens less than one hundred years after Augustine's death. In 529, Emperor Justinian decreed that anyone within the empire who failed to have his household's infants baptized would have his property confiscated; any Christian (i.e., baptized person) who reverted to paganism would be executed; Jews were forbidden to testify in court; and, as noted in the discussion of Pseudo-Dionysius, the philosophical schools in Athens were closed.¹⁰¹ The unhappy marriage between Constantine's sacral Caesarean kingship and Augustine's version of infant baptism led to politicization and decommissioning of the baptismal priesthood in the fourth through sixth centuries.

The Monastic Monopolization of Discipleship: Spiritual and Secular Lay Siblings

Within decades of Constantine's legalization of Christianity, monasticism began to rapidly expand.¹⁰² Neither its complex historical origins nor its many laudable accomplishments can detain us; we must concentrate on the curious connection between the flourishing of monasticism following Constantine and the parallel, widespread replacement of baptized priests with baptized pagans. By way of foreshadowing, we note the interesting historical accident that in the same year Emperor Justinian issued his edict requiring

---

97. Augustine, *City of God* 20:10 (FC 24:280–81).
98. Ibid., 10:6 (FC 14:125–26).
99. Ibid. (FC 14:126–27). See also *Trinity* 4.14.19 (FC 45:155–56).
100. Wright, "Augustine and the Transformation," 88.
101. See discussion of *Codex Iustinianus* 1.11.10 in Kreider, "Beyond Bosch," 2005.
102. The first recorded mention of a Christian "monk" refers to a man named Isaac mentioned in a parchment dated June, 324. More well-known monks include Pachomius (d. 346), Antony (d. 356), Basil of Caesarea (d. 379), Augustine (d. 430), John Cassian (d. 435), and Benedict (d. 547). See further Harmless, "Monasticism," 494–517.

all citizens to be baptized at birth (529), St. Benedict founded his monastery on Mt. Cassino; these two related events would heavily influence Christendom for a millennium.

In Chapter 3 above, Matthew's community of disciples were shown to possess priestly characteristics; all members of the community are oblates.[103] They were a community of siblings who through identification with Jesus had become priestly servants in a Temple greater than that found in Jerusalem (Matt 12:6). Baptism was a definitive mark of these disciples, the first and last exhortation given by their "one Teacher" (Matt 3:15 and 28:19; cf. Matt 23:8). Baptism commissioned disciples to share in the continued ministry and mission of Jesus through the Holy Spirit (Acts 1:8). Richard Hays describes the ethics of Matthew's community as consisting of three components: 1) a communal ethic of perfection; 2) a hermeneutic of mercy; and 3) a tension between discipline and forgiveness.[104] With Justinian's decree requiring the entire Empire to be baptized, it became extremely difficult to maintain the "perfect" community of disciples envisioned by Matthew, and instead a "perfect" group of professionals was substituted. Jesus became the pattern for religious professionals; the patriarchs became the model for secular laity.[105]

Constantine's embrace of Christianity did not cause two-level discipleship within the church, but imperialized and expanded it. In the pre-Constantinian church, the Didache's "two ways" doctrine typified believers' self-understanding: "There are two ways, one of life and one of death, and there is a great difference between these two ways."[106] Believers lived one way, unbelievers another. By Constantine's time, the hierarchicalization of the church had resulted in a *new* "two ways" doctrine. Witness Eusebius:

> *Two ways* of living were thus given by the law of Christ to his church. The one . . . devotes itself to the service of God alone . . . performing the duty of a priesthood to Almighty God for the whole race, not with sacrifices of bulls and blood . . . but with right principles of true holiness. . . . Such then is the perfect

---

103. Matthew was the primary catechetical gospel in the early church. Clement of Alexandria's extant works cites it over five hundred times, two hundred times more than the next most cited canonical book.

104. Hays, *Moral Vision*, 96–104.

105. Ambrose, *Duties of the Clergy* 1.36–37, 175–77 (NPNF2 10:7, 30). Ambrose (d. 397), some fifty years after Constantine's death, already equates the church with the Roman Empire: "But the piety of justice is first directed toward God; secondly towards one's country; next, towards parents; lastly towards all" (1.127 [NPNF2 10:22]). Aquinas agrees with Ambrose, but places parents before country (ST 2.2.101.1).

106. *Didache* 1.1 (AF3 345).

form of the Christian life. And the other more humble, more human, permits men to join in pure nuptials and to produce children, to undertake government, to give orders to soldiers fighting for right . . . and other more secular interests . . . *and a kind of secondary grade of piety is attributed to them.*[107]

With vast numbers of "worldly" believers entering the church following Constantine's "Edict of Milan" (AD 314), Eusebius' new version of the "two ways" proved insufficient. Lay people also wanted to live a "perfect" life; as hordes of baptized pagans began to enter the church, the pressures upon serious lay people to pursue a new "way" of discipleship increased.[108]

As Harnack noted over a century ago, the monastics "fled not the world only, but worldliness in the church; yet they did not therefore flee *from* the church."[109] In short, the combination of infant baptism with imperial coercion (carrots and sticks) had a massive inflationary effect on baptism's social significance. The marriage of infant baptism to imperial coercion introduced a tidal wave of "worldliness" into the church. On the one hand, infant baptism made baptism as ordination to the royal priesthood different from any other ordination service of the ancient world, and the significance of baptismal ordination had to be reduced to match the capacities of an infant.[110] On the other hand, the requirement that all citizens of the Empire be baptized made the high level of ethical and priestly holiness described in the NT or by earlier theologians seem politically unrealistic.[111] The impact on the church within a single century was immediate and widespread.[112]

Similarly, monasticism's rise contributed to a reduction in discipleship—from being characteristic of the royal priesthood—to being the exclusive prerogative of the "spiritual," the "perfect," the "religious."[113] Before Constantine, the baptismal priesthood had already been demoted once, following the creation of Cyprian's "third priesthood"; after Constantine, the royal priesthood was again demoted by the "perfect" lay monastics. The

107. Eusebius, *Proof of the Gospel*, 48–50; emphasis added.

108. See Augustine's characterization of those seeking baptism in Hippo (*First Baptismal Instruction* 5.9).

109. von Harnack, *Monasticism*, 36; emphasis original.

110. Wright, *What Has Infant Baptism done to Baptism?*, 23, 33.

111. See Augustine's correspondence with the Roman patrician, Volusian (*Epistles* 136–37).

112. Compare Augustine (d. 430), who "appealed to unbaptized catechumens to be converted," and Bishop Caesarius (d. 542), who "urged conversion upon baptized Christians" (Kreider, "Changing Patterns of Conversion in the West," 38; 3–46).

113. See Daley's distinction between apostolic ministry (clergy) and discipleship (monastics) in " Ministry of Disciples," 605–29.

Syriac monk, Symeon the Stylite (d. 459), sitting between God and humanity, is a fitting symbol for the new class of Christians created by the monastic movement. For forty years Symeon sat high on a pillar as an ascetic discipline. As people gathered to look up at him, "he seemed poised halfway between earth and heaven, arms raised in prayer, a *mediator* between humankind and God."[114]

Pope Gregory the Great's (d. 604) words from his *Moralia in Job* summarized the tendencies of the previous two centuries and set the trajectory of western thought for the medieval period:

> Holy Church exits in three orders [*ordinibus*]: namely the married, the continent, and the leaders [*rectorum*]. For this reason, Ezekiel sees three men, namely, Noah, Daniel, and Job.[115]

Thus, between Gregory the Great and Luther, three primary distinctions were emphasized within the church: the clergy, the spiritual/religious laity (monastics), and the unspiritual/non-religious laity.[116] With the rise of monasticism the royal priesthood faced a further setback: baptized members were not only excluded from priestly ministry; they were also relegated to a second tier of discipleship. The next chapter describes how Luther's revolutionary ecclesiology rejects both of these reductions in favor of a renewed vision of the royal priesthood.[117]

Decommissioning of the Royal Priesthood's Baptismal Mission

Who gets to engage in priestly proclamation? By the sixth century the answer was almost entirely limited to those living on the edges of Christendom. Within a generation or two of Justinian's 529 decree requiring all citizens to baptize their infants, the priestly proclamation of the vast majority of members of the royal priesthood was effectively put to an end. To be born a Roman citizen was to be born a Christian.[118] The increasing absence of both theological reflection on mission and a commitment to the practice of missions in the new era which began with Constantine's conversion has

---

114. Harmless, "Monasticism," 497, emphasis added.

115. Gregory the Great, In *Ez.*, *Hom.* 7.3 (*PL* 76.967). Translation adapted from Osborne, *Ministry*, 297.

116. As noted above, some claim the emperor/king as a fourth class.

117. Yet the baby of missional orders must not be thrown out with the bathwater of monastic excess. See below on Luther and ecclesial sodalities.

118. Kreider, "Beyond Bosch," 63.

repeatedly and accurately been described by historians of mission as "the darkest hours," "the great recession," and the "Dark Age/s."[119]

Isaiah's eschatological priests were to share in the Servant's task of bearing light to the Gentiles (Isa 59:21—60:3; 61:6). Peter urged members of the royal priesthood to "proclaim the excellencies of him who called you out of darkness into his marvelous light" so that the Gentiles might "glorify God" (1 Pet 2:9, 12). So also Tertullian assumed that the royal priesthood's members had been given a mouth "for preaching the gospel of God" as "His priest and advocate before men."[120] In the age of the apostles and apologists, missional proclamation—in word and deed—was a central function of the royal priesthood.[121] Once all within the empire save a few pockets of Jews had been baptized ("saved"), the royal priesthood's missional posture atrophied.[122]

Where mission did take place in the post-Constantine era, it was primarily by imperial compulsion. Thus David Bosch famously assigned Luke 14:23, "compel them to come in," as *"the* missionary text" of the "period."[123] The logic seemed fairly straightforward. Baptism was believed to confer a *character indelibilius* marking the baptized for eternal salvation, even if the baptism had been forced. As Bosch explains, "to provide the individual with the opportunity to flee eternal damnation could not be wrong and certainly justified the use of pressure."[124] Beginning in AD 325 with the canons of Nicaea against Jews and Heretics, Christian mission was slowly changed by a strategy of coercive power.[125] Augustine was the first to make the argument

---

119. Latourette, *History of Christianity* 269–377; Neill, *History of Christian Missions*, 53–85; Bosch, *Transforming Mission*, 230.

120. Tertullian, *On the Resurrection*, 61 (ANF 3:592 [CCEL 3:1327]).

121. Pagans were converted by the "consistency they witness in their neighbors' lives" and by the "extraordinary forbearance" and "honesty" of Christian businessmen and women" (Justin, *1 Apol.* 16 [ANF 1:168; CCEL 1:440]; translation modified). Similarly, "the churches of God which have been taught by Christ [Isa 54:13], when compared with the assemblies of the people where they live, are 'as beacons in the world' [Phil 2:15]" (Origen, *Contra Celsum* 3.29 [ANF 4:476; CCEL 4:1077; translation modified).

122. Compare the number of Christian apologies written in the second and third centuries with the number written in the fifth and sixth centuries.

123. Bosch, *Transforming Mission*, 219; emphasis original. The use of force was so well established in Christendom that Bartholomé de Las Casas (d. 1566) had to vigorously defend his seemingly novel proposal of *conquista spiritual*—a gentle missionary approach based on preaching—against opponents who argued from Luke 14:23 that the sword/gun was the biblical and more effective evangelistic technique (236).

124. Ibid., 223.

125. Littell notes that a number of Jewish historians mark the "fall" of Jewish-Christian relations with Constantine's rise to power ("From 'Christendom,'" 322–23).

that Luke 14:23 meant that heretics could be forced to recant by imperial force as part of the church's disciplinary process. Gregory the Great went beyond Augustine, suggesting that those who would not listen to reason should be "chastised by beating and torture, whereby they might be brought to amendment."[126] He also was the first to propose that the Emperor should engage in an aggressive war for the sake of opening pagan lands for missionary activity.[127] The Crusades were the natural outcome of this line of missionary reasoning.

Peter Leithart has put forth a brilliant and long overdue defense of Constantine as a Christian Emperor. In my judgment, where he defends Constantine, he succeeds; where he denies a Constantinian shift—at least in the realm of ecclesiology—he is mistaken.[128] John Howard Yoder described Constantine's impact on the mission of the royal priesthood in a manner similar to the story told here.[129] Leithart disputes Yoder's claims, concluding that Yoder's portrayal is "false, and betrays either dishonesty or a quite breathtaking ignorance of medieval history."[130] Yet even if Yoder is wrong, Leithart should at least acknowledge that Yoder's view is a fairly standard narrative, shared by theologians such as Karl Barth, Lesslie Newbigin, Douglas John Hall, Stanley Hauerwas, Darrell Guder as well as mission historians such as Kenneth Scott Latourette, Stephen Neill, Ralph Winter, and David Bosch. Neither Yoder nor any of these others would claim that the missional vocation of the royal priesthood ceased completely in the 1,000 years between Constantine and Wycliffe (d. 1384). The challenge of missional witness to the unbaptized was a fact of daily life for the majority of pre-Constantinian believers,[131] but this missional challenge became irrelevant to all but the most elite monastic "shock troops" by the end of the sixth century.[132]

---

126. Bosch, *Transforming Mission*, 223.

127. Ibid., 224.

128. "There was no permanent, epochal 'Constantinian shift'" (Leithart, *Defending Constantine*, 287).

129. Yoder, "Constantinian Sources," 135–147; Yoder, "Disavowal of Constantine," 242–611.

130. Ibid., 290. Cf. Yoder's dissertation (not in Leithart's bibliography) published as *Anabaptism and Reformation in Switzerland*, 280.

131. See Celsius' complaint that ordinary Christians would not stop sharing their faith at home or work (Origen, *Against Celsus* 3.55 [SC 136:128–30; *ANF* 4:486; CCEL 4:1104]. See further Kreider, "They Alone," 169–86.

132. Faivre, *Emergence of the Laity*, 181.

Leithart refers positively to the members of the elite who maintained a missional identity within Christendom as "a crusading army."[133] This seems an unfortunate choice of words given the fact that Leithart's defense of Christendom's mission is silent on the medieval crusades; on Justinian's imperial decree requiring all citizens to have their infants baptized; on Gregory the Great's commendation of torture as a missionary method; on Torquemada's *auto da fé* and many other examples of imperial coercion providing the motivation for conversion.

Chapter Summary: The Royal Priesthood Moves from Actors to Audience

This chapter described the first major paradigm shift through which the apostolic doctrine of the royal priesthood passed on its journey to the present. It was a decline narrative. In short, the royal priesthood was gradually defrocked of its priestly privileges through a process of hierarchicalization, sacralization, and politicization. While members of the royal priesthood had once been players in the divine drama, their role was gradually reduced to passive audience. The names of Clement of Rome, Cyprian, and Constantine are each identified with a significant ecclesial first that eventually contributed to the larger decline narrated in this chapter. The royal priesthood was a major theme for the apostolic writers, and for a number of early church writers. But with exceptions that prove the rule, the doctrine moved steadily to the margins of the church's consciousness between the sixth and sixteenth centuries. The next chapter narrates a second paradigm shift in the doctrine's history: its rediscovery by Martin Luther.

---

133. Leithart, *Defending Constantine*, 290.

5

Reforming the Royal Priesthood: Luther and the Priesthood of All Believers

> Not only are we the freest of kings, we are also priests forever, which is far more excellent than being kings, for as priests we are worthy to appear before God to pray for others and to teach one another divine things. These are the functions of priests, and they cannot be granted to any unbeliever.
>
> —Martin Luther, *The Freedom of a Christian* (1520)

> This is the way to distinguish between the office of preaching, or the ministry, and the general priesthood of all baptized Christians. The preaching office is no more than a public service which happens to be conferred upon someone by the entire congregation, all the members of which are priests. But you may ask: "Wherein does this priesthood of Christians consist, and what are their priestly works?" The answer is as follows ... teaching, sacrificing, and praying.
>
> —Martin Luther, *Commentary on Psalm 110* (1535)

LUTHER IS *THE* THEOLOGIAN of the royal priesthood. No other in history has made a greater contribution to the doctrine's conceptual development or ecclesial use. The changes which took place during the paradigm shift identified in the last chapter required discussing a number of different theologians. In contrast, the changes which took place at the time of the Reformation are primarily associated with one man. This chapter explores the development of Luther's doctrine, provides a systematic account, and assesses positive and problematic aspects.

The vast scope of Luther's writings has contributed to a wide variety of opinions about his "priesthood of all believers." The only consensus is that it has repeatedly been misunderstood. Part of the problem is that Luther never wrote a systematic summary of his theology, so his thinking must be compiled from occasional pieces and then traced through stages of development. The priesthood of all believers is no exception; secondary sources find evidence of the doctrine in over fifty of Luther's writings, and Luther himself discusses it at length in some fifteen works.[1]

Luther's Doctrine of the "Priesthood of All Believers"

Luther's ecclesial world was divided into three estates: clerics, monastics, and laics.[2] After exploring this world, this section briefly outlines the development of Luther's doctrine, and concludes by proposing a concise definition.

Clergy, the Spiritual, and the Secular Laity: The Medieval Situation

Luther's doctrine must be understood within historical context. On July 2, 1505 Luther became a monk; two years later he became a priest. The significance of the two events is often confused. When Luther became a monk, he took vows that made him part of the *spiritual* or *religious* sector

---

1. Luther's fifteen most significant treatments of the doctrine are: *Treatise on the NT, that is, the Holy Mass* (1520); *To the Christian Nobility of the German Nation concerning the Reform of the Christian Estate* (1520); *The Babylonian Captivity of the Church* (1520); *The Freedom of the Christian* (1520); *Answer to the Hyperchristian, Hyperspiritual, and Hyperlearned Book by Goat Emser in Leipzig—Including some Thoughts Regarding His Companion, the Fool Murner* (1521); *Dr. Luther's Retractions of the Error Forced Upon Him by the Most Highly Learned Priest of God, Sir Jerome Esmer, Vicar in Meissen* (1521); *The Misuse of the Mass* (1522); *Sermons on the First Epistle of St. Peter* [2:5–9] (1522); *German NT* (1522)/ *OT Preface* (1523); *That a Christian Assembly or Congregation Has the Right and Power to Judge All Teaching and to Call, Appoint, and Dismiss Teachers, Established and Proven by Scripture* (1523); *Concerning the Ministry*, (1523); *The Private Mass and the Consecration of Priests* (1533); *Commentary on Psalm 110* [4] (1535); *Sermons on the Gospel of John 14–16* [15:8], (1537); *On the Councils and Churches* (1539).

2. Recall the three orders (*ordinibus*) celebrated by Gregory the Great discussed in Chapter 4 (*Ez., IIhom.* 7.3 [*PL* 76.967]).

of Christendom. This sector consisted of both lay and clergy, men and women, who had taken vows to follow the councils of perfection (poverty, chastity, obedience). The councils of perfection were reserved for those who wanted to follow Christ's perfect way of discipleship. In medieval "Europe" membership among the spiritual or religious was exclusively reserved for these vowed. Thus the first major ecclesial division in medieval society was between the spiritual and secular.[3]

The second major division was between laity and clergy. A clergyman could be spiritual or secular, but either way he was in a separate class from the layperson. The clergyman was a priest who offered sacrifices on behalf of the laity. He was a mediator between God and the layperson primarily through offering the Mass.[4] Luther's doctrine rejected both distinctions. All baptized believers are both spiritual and priestly by virtue of their union with Christ.[5]

Luther's rejection of these two divisions within the one "brotherhood" of Christ could be illustrated from numerous documents. Two of the clearest statements are found in *On Monastic Vows* (1521) and his vigorous 1521 debate with Jerome Esmer (d. 1527) over "priesthood" in 1 Pet 2:5-9. In *On Monastic Vows,* Luther argues that the concept of two classes of Christian based on two sets of commandments (the perfect and the permissible) is faulty. He firmly rejects the spiritual/secular division within the church, which had steadily been growing since Dionysian's hierarchical view of the cosmos received papal endorsement by Gregory the Great (ca. 600). Similarly, Luther rejected the concept that the vowed life was a greater guarantee of salvation than any other standing or estate (*Stand*).[6] Rather, our salvation is by faith; the vowed life is not necessarily more pleasing to God than others. There is only one spiritual estate in the body of Christ, and all believers share in it equally by faith.[7]

---

3. *LW* 44:243-400.

4. See Mass benefits in Kilmartin, *Eucharist in the West*, 112-15.

5. Thesis 37 in the 95 *Theses* (*LW* 35:28; cf. *LW* 31:189; *LW* 11:139, 333, 356).

6. The three primary medieval ecclesial estates were clergy, monastics, and laics. Some argued for a fourth, priest-king. The strongest Reformation defense of this fourth estate came from Henry the Eighth's *Assertio Septem Sacramentorum* written against Luther's *Babylonian Captivity* (Yarnell, *Royal Priesthood in the English Reformation*, Chapters 3 and 4).

7. "I shall also ignore all the useless talk you spew forth about consecration and priestly estate and the threefold meaning of 'spiritual'—*spirituale, ecclesiasticum, religiosum*—and that not all Christians are spiritual, *spirituales*. I call spiritual *spirituales*, devout Christians *ecclesiasticum*, and do not know *religiosum*" (*LW* 39:174); see also *LW* 44:127-34.

Besides rejecting the spiritual-secular divide, Luther also rejected the lay-clergy divide as it relates to priesthood. Luther denies the idea of a "churchy" (*kirchisch*) priesthood within the one royal priesthood.[8] "Yet all of us are in a common church; we are all spiritual and priests, *to the extent that we believe in Christ*. . . . Therefore, I think that goat Emser's dream of *two kinds of priesthood* lies in sand and mire."[9] There are not "two priesthoods" in the one common and spiritual priesthood all believers share in Christ. There is only one priesthood, but within that priesthood there are a variety of ministries. What Emser labeled the "churchly priesthood" is better a "ministry" or service in church office (*Amt*). Luther writes:

> Holy Scripture . . . writes of not more than one spiritual priesthood. . . . [it] makes all of us equal priests, as has been said, but the churchly priesthood which we now separate from laymen in the whole world, and which alone we call priesthood, is called "ministry" [*ministerium*], "servitude" [*servitus*], "dispensation" [*dispensatio*], "episcopate" [*episcopatus*], and "presbytery" [*presbyterium*] in Scripture. Nowhere is it called "priesthood" [*sacerdocium*] or "spiritual" [*spiritualis*].[10]

Luther's proposal of one spiritual estate—one priesthood—one brotherhood was revolutionary; it led to massive changes. Before describing them, it is helpful to explore the development of Luther's own thinking.

Development of Luther's Priesthood of All Believers

Luther's treatment can be divided into four periods: a Roman Catholic period (1505–17); a period of strong emphasis (1518–23); a transitional period (1524–25); and a period of weaker emphasis (1526–46). In Luther's first period, he held to a traditional Roman Catholic view of priesthood,[11] but there are hints of a changing attitude as Luther discovered justification by faith and the believer's share in Christ's benefits.[12] Most significant during this period are Luther's lectures on Hebrews, where his view of priesthood is permanently shaped by treatment of Jesus as the Priest-king of Ps 110:4. When Luther later begins to articulate his doctrine in earnest, it is

---

8. *LW* 39:152.
9. *LW* 39:159; emphasis added.
10. *LW* 39:154.
11. *LW* 35:234–35; Cf. *LW* 39:236–37.
12. *LW* 11:333, 356; 29:117; 35:28; cf. *LW* 31:189.

always based on the royal priesthood of Christ discovered while lecturing on Hebrews.

Luther's most productive writing on the doctrine was done between 1518 and 1523. He wrote eleven of his fifteen most important treatises during this period. Their significance is illustrated by Francisco Bravo, who has conducted the most extensive examination of Luther's doctrine (425 pp.), and ends his study in 1523.[13] After 1523 Luther's social situation changed significantly, and the years 1524-25 were transitional: Karlstadt (d. 1541), the teaching of the "enthusiasts" (*Schwärmer*), birth of the Anabaptists, and the Peasants' revolt all caused Luther to reexamine his euphoric commendation of the doctrine.[14]

In the final twenty years of Luther's life, the priesthood of all believers remains central to his ecclesiology but, due to fallout from the Peasants' War and Anabaptist teaching, it is no longer emphasized as before.[15] While the essence of Luther's doctrine remained constant,[16] his emphasis significantly decreased following 1524-25.[17] Decreased emphasis on the doctrine was also true for the emerging "Lutheran" church. Gerrish notes, "At the Diet of Augsburg in 1530 Philip Melanchthon advised against discussion of the priesthood of all believers, relegating it to the 'odious and unessential articles which are commonly debated in the schools.'"[18]

A Definition of Luther's Doctrine

Before discussing Luther's doctrine in depth, it is helpful to provide a short explanation of his terminology and a succinct definition. For Luther, all believers share in Christ's priesthood. Luther refers to this priesthood variously as "true priests consecrated to God," "a new and holy priesthood," the "general priesthood of all baptized believers," "the priesthood of Christians,"

---

13. Bravo, *El sacerdocio común*, 86-87. Other important studies include Brunotte, *Das geistliche Amt bei Luther*. Jeffcoat, "Martin Luther's Doctrine of Ministry"; Goertz, *Allgemeines Priestertum und ordiniertes Amt bei Luther*; Anizor, "*Royal Priesthood of Readers*," chap. 3; and Barth, *Einander Priester sein*, ch. 1. I am indebted to Anizor for use of additional unpublished research.

14. LW 40:47-59; LW 46:45-55.

15. Writing concerning Luther's *On the Councils and the Church* (1536), Barth notes, "geben zu erkennen, daß die These vom allgemeinen Priestertum durch Luther zwar prinzipiell nicht aufgegeben wurde, faktisch für ihn aber doch an Gewicht verloren hatte" (*Einander Priester sein*, 30n10).

16. Jeffcoat, "Martin Luther's Doctrine," 211.

17. Rogers, "Dangerous Idea?" 119-43; Gerrish, "Priesthood and Ministry," 404-22. Cf. Lohse, *Martin Luther's Theology*, 288.

18. Gerrish, "Priesthood and Ministry," 404.

"the one spiritual priesthood," "the one common priesthood," "our hereditary priesthood" [by virtue of new birth at baptism], and the "royal priesthood."[19] Hans Martin Barth points out that Luther never actually uses the exact phrase "Das allgemeine Priestertum aller Gläubigen," but that Luther does equate the priesthood with all Christians or all the faithful.[20] Thus Luther writes, "for priests, the baptized, and Christians are all one and the same"; or, on 1 Pet 2:9, "When St. Peter says here: 'You are a royal priesthood,' this is tantamount to saying: 'You are Christians.'"[21]

For Luther, to be a Christian is to be a priest. He refers to individual readers as priests hundreds of times, and one of his central priorities is to help Christians realize their priestly identity. In 1523 Luther published his *Preface to the First Five Books of Moses*. With reference to Hebrews and Rom 12:1, Luther advised readers to think about Christ when they read about the High Priest, but about themselves when they read about the High Priest's sons.[22] All of the Father's children, Christ's siblings, are members of a priestly family, although, unlike the OT, in this eschatological age those traditionally excluded from the priesthood—women, children, and the handicapped—can now be priests.[23]

As we will see below, there are tensions in Luther's thinking, especially his equation of "baptized" and "Christians" in a world that was coterminous with the church. Yet, despite these tensions, the traditional "*priesthood* of *all believers*" best describes Luther's understanding.[24] Each term ("priesthood," "all," "believers") is important. There is only one *priesthood*—Christ's, and *all* Christians (that is baptized "*believers*") share in it.[25] Not simply baptism made a "Christian priest," but rather baptism plus the Word and a response of faith.[26] Even though Roman Catholic priests had been baptized (and

19. *LW* 24:243; 13:296; 13:332); 13:332; "Eyn geystlich priesterthum" (*WA* 8:486; *LW* 35:101; cf. *LW* 39:154); "das eynige gemeyne priesterhum" (*WA* 8:254, 7; *LW* 39:237); *LW* 38:187; 29:117.

20. Barth, *Einander Priester*, 47n43.

21. *LW* 30:63, 64.

22. *LW* 35:247. In 1534 the preface was incorporated largely intact into Luther's complete German Bible.

23. But Luther does not permit them to be pastors except in emergency situations (*LW* 41:154).

24. *Contra* Wengert's claim that the "priesthood of all believers" is an "imaginary priesthood," a "pious myth" not found in Luther but invented by Jacob Spener (*Priesthood, Pastors, Bishops*, 6, 1).

25. "Believers" are repeatedly referred to in 1 Pet 2:4–9. Thus, Luther writes, "he who does not believe is no priest" (*LW* 30:62; also 31:354).

26. "We are all spiritual and priests, to the extent that we believe in Christ" (*LW* 39:159); "faith carries the priesthood along with it" (*WA* 10/III: 398, 24–29).

ordained), they were not actually *Christian* priests if they lacked faith.[27] Similarly, for Luther, the Roman Catholic Church was not actually a church because it lacked the preaching of the gospel.[28]

In sum, Luther's doctrine is the Christian's participation in the royal priesthood of Christ made possible through the new birth and baptism. Believers exercise their priesthood by preaching the word, praying, and offering spiritual sacrifices, thereby representing God to one another and each other to God.[29] This basic definition will be explored further in the systematic account below.

A Systematic Account of Luther's Priesthood of All Believers

This section explores in greater detail the two major components of Luther's understanding: 1) the single source of the priesthood of all believers is Christ's royal priesthood; 2) its functions are preaching, praying, and the offering of "spiritual sacrifices," functions directed toward God or neighbor.[30]

The Source of Luther's Spiritual Priesthood

A common misunderstanding assumes that the doctrine begins with 1 Pet 2:5–9,[31] but this passage is not the most foundational for Luther.[32] Like the NT authors, the source of Luther's doctrine is the identification of Jesus, the Anointed One (*Christos*), with the eschatological Melchizedekian Priest-king described in Ps 110:4. Luther's understanding grew from his exegesis

---

27. "That we are his brethren is true only because of the new birth" (*LW* 40:19).

28. "Just as the banner of an army is the sure sign by which one can know what kind of lord and army have taken to the field, so, too, the gospel is the sure sign by which one knows where Christ and his army are encamped" (*LW* 39:305).

29. Cf. Yarnell's "Reformation Development," 3.

30. For Luther, spiritual sacrifices are thanksgiving offerings offered by believers as members of the royal priesthood. All activities of daily life as well as activities of corporate worship can be offered as sacrifices of thanksgiving by members of the royal priesthood. Luther's understanding of "spiritual sacrifices" is thus consistent with both Heb 13:15–16 and Augustine (*City of God* 10.6 [FC 14:125]; *Trinity* 4.14 [FC 45:155]).

31. *Contra* Rogers, "Dangerous Idea?" 130.

32. Other texts Luther repeatedly references include: Exod 19:6; Isa 54:13; Ps 110:4; Rom 12:1 (*LW* 39:235), John 6:45; Rev 1:5; 5:10; 20:6. He also discusses the doctrine in sermons or commentary on Gen 12:3 (*LW* 13:308); Gen 14:17–20 (*LW* 13:309–15); Ps 51:17; Ps 82:4 (*LW* 13:59–63); Isa 61:6; 66:22 (*LW* 16:415); Mal 2:17 (*LW* 39:315); Luke 14; John 15:4; Galatians 3; Eph 4:11–12 (*LW* 13:295).

of Psalm 110 and its treatment in Hebrews.[33] A systematic understanding must begin by recognizing that the only foundation of the royal priesthood is its Priest-king.

A High Priest like Melchizedek: Psalm 110 and the Royal Priesthood of Jesus Christ

Luther followed the NT authors in giving greater attention to Psalm 110 than any other, and he lectured, wrote, or preached on the Psalm at three different points (1515, 1518, 1535).[34] The Psalm was of vital importance for Christology, the "very core and quintessence of the whole Scripture."[35] Anticipating discussions in contemporary biblical studies, Luther understood Hebrews to have "made a whole sermon" out of Ps 110:4.[36] Already in his 1517 lectures on Hebrews, Luther finds First Peter's royal priesthood to be founded upon the Melchizedekian priesthood of Christ.[37]

Luther was fifty-six when he worked through Psalm 110 for the final time. He found the core Christological insight in verse four, "The Lord has sworn and will not change his mind, 'You are a priest forever after the order of Melchizedek.'" Luther cannot overemphasize the verse's significance for the royal priesthood of Christ and of all believers: "It is a treasure, the source of all Christian doctrine, understanding, wisdom, and comfort. There is no single passage in Scripture which expresses this so richly or completely. . . . *It reveals all that our faith affirms and teaches.*"[38]

According to Luther, verse four unites "the kingly and priestly functions in one person."[39] It indicates that Christ's eschatological priesthood will be entirely different from the Levitical priesthood.[40] It finds its protol-

---

33. Hebrews cites or alludes to Psalm 110 a dozen times (Heb 1:3, 13; 5:6; 5:10; 6:20; 7:11, 15, 17, 21; 8:1; 10:12–13; 12:2).

34. His 1535 treatment runs 123 pages in ET (*LW* 13:225–348). Cf. Bornkamm, *Christus, König und Priester*.

35. *LW* 13:347; see also 227; 306.

36. Siggins, *Martin Luther's Doctrine*, 118. See also *LW* 36:306.

37. Commenting on Heb 1:8, Luther writes "Judah became a priesthood and Israel a dominion or kingdom, in order that He Himself might be King and Priest, and His people a priestly kingdom or a royal priesthood, as we read in 1 Peter 2:9: 'But you are a chosen race, a royal priesthood, a holy nation.' And Moses says in Ex. 19:5–6: 'All the earth is Mine, and you shall be to Me a priestly kingdom, a holy nation'" (*LW* 29:117); Goldingay, *Psalms: 90–150*, 299.

38. *LW* 13:323; emphasis added.

39. *LW* 13:305.

40. *LW* 13:306.

ogy in the Melchizedekian royal priesthood described in Genesis 14[41] and in the oath given by God to Abraham in Gen 12:3.[42] For Luther, the pope set up "his own priestcraft" (*Pfafferey*) in opposition to the Melchizedekian office of Christ.[43] In contrast to Rome's mass-priests (*Mess Pfaffen*), Luther expounds upon three functions of Christ's royal priesthood (addressed below).[44] He concludes with "some remarks about the way in which we Christians, too, are priests."[45] This 1535 sermon provides the clearest statement of Luther's doctrine. For Luther, *the only true priesthood is Christ's Melchizedekian priesthood,* in which disciples participate through the new birth and baptism.

Seed and Siblings of the Priest King: The Royal Priesthood of Believers

Luther's claim has two implications for baptized believers: 1) Believers are ordained to royal priesthood at their baptism; 2) All believers are called to priestly discipleship. First, Luther teaches that baptism represents a new birth whereby we enter the priestly family of Christ as his children and siblings.[46] God works through "the Gospel and Holy Baptism" to make those born of him "true children of a priest [*Priesters Kinder*]" who "inherit the same name from their father. Consequently every baptized Christian is a priest already."[47]

During the medieval period, the power and wonder of baptism had gradually been overshadowed by emphasis on penance and the Eucharist.[48] Luther recovered a sense of the awe felt by early Christians when they discussed their baptism.[49] Luther repeatedly emphasized that there is only one priesthood (Christ's) and only one priestly ordination (baptism).[50] All

---

41. *LW* 13:309–15.
42. *LW* 13:308. See also Wells, *God's Holy People*, ch. 3.
43. *LW* 13:315.
44. *LW* 13:315–29.
45. *LW* 13:29; see 29–34.
46. Bravo states that the NT does not clearly indicate the moment of origin for individual members of the royal priesthood, but he argues that according to Luther, the best explanation is at the new birth (*nacimiento nuevo*) signified at baptism. "El bautismo es el momento de la consagración sacerdotal de los creyentes" (*El sacerdocio común de los creyentes en la teología de Lutero*, 224; 188–234).
47. *LW* 13:329.
48. Tranvik, "Luther on Baptism," 24–30.
49. Luther, *Large Catechism*, Baptism 42 (*BC-T* 442).
50. "We are all consecrated priests through baptism" *LW* 44:127. See also *LW*

Christian priesthood finds its source in baptism, because that is where the believer is united with Christ's baptism.[51]

If baptism both unites believers with Christ and ordains them for service in the royal priesthood, this is because both actions are closely tied to justification by faith.[52] Faith makes a Christian a priest, not simply baptism.

> For faith must do everything. Faith alone is the true priestly office. It permits no one else to take its place. Therefore all Christian men are priests, all women priestesses, be they young or old, master or servant, mistress or maid, learned or unlearned. Here there is no difference unless faith be unequal.[53]

Luther is assuming that his readers are baptized. Faith makes baptism complete.[54] Without faith, the consecrations of bishops and tonsures avail nothing. Justification and ordination are combined in the believer's baptism. According to Tranvink, the logical order of this relationship for Luther has three dimensions: *God's Word* is spoken as a person is *baptized in water*, followed by an eventual *awakening of faith* in the baptized in response.[55] Tensions arose over this relationship with Luther's Anabaptist critics, and even among the Magisterial Reformers, the relationship between baptized pagans and baptized believers would remain unclear with a variety of solutions proposed.

Secondly, as noted above, the medieval church largely limited discipleship to those who had taken monastic vows or received the *character indelibilis* at ordination. The vowed and the ordained were true disciples; all other Christians were members of a lesser ecclesial estate (*Stand*).[56] Luther's former teacher, Jerome Emser, was representing the standard view when in his 1521 debate with Luther he claimed that the Sermon on the Mount applied only to the clergy:

> Tell him, holy Lord Jesus Christ, that you did not speak to the laymen but only to your apostles.... Tell him that *you did not*

30:63; 40:19.

51. WA 51:111.

52. For Tranvik, Luther's theology "centered on justification by faith and its corollary, the priesthood of all believers" ("Luther on Baptism," 37); see further Bravo, *El sacerdocio común*, 234–73.

53. LW 35:101; 12:289.

54. LW 40:246.

55. "Baptism is efficacious only in faith, which is awakened by God's word of promise.... Baptism is the earthly means by which the believer participates in justification" (Tranvik, "Luther on Baptism," 36–37).

56. LW 24:232.

speak to the common people but to them when you said, 'You are the salt of the earth.'[57]

Luther's doctrine democratized the monastic and clerical monopoly evident in Emser's words. It retrieved ontological equality before God for all believers, even if there remained a variety of offices (Ämter), functions, and gifts.[58] For Luther, the joyous exchange (*fröhliche Wechsel*), to which he repeatedly returns, means that all that belongs to Christ also belongs to the believer.[59] Whatever Christ possesses, especially as exemplified in privileges granted by Christ to his disciples, is shared with all believers.

Luther makes this point often, but especially in a 1537 sermon on John 15:8: "By this my Father is glorified, that you bear much fruit and so prove to be my disciple." Luther once remarked that the work in which this sermon is found (*Sermons on the Gospel of John 14–16*) was "the best book I have written."[60] In answer to the question, "Who is Christ's disciple? Who is the one who 'abides in Christ's Word?'" Luther paraphrases Christ:

> Call to mind what I have spent on you to make you righteous and to save you, to make you acceptable to the Father, to make you His priest and servant and My disciple. . . . You are priests and servants of God who offer holy and acceptable sacrifices to My Father without ceasing.[61]

Luther goes on to explain that the priestly sacrifices offered by disciples are the same ones described in Rom 12:1 and 1 Pet 2:5. Thus believers engage in priestly ministry, not only by keeping the first table of the Ten Commandments (vertically toward God), but also by keeping the second (horizontally toward neighbor). Whether our focus is on the first or second table: "Christ says: 'If you remain in Me, I will consecrate you to be holy priests—priests of My Father. Whatever you do will be not only proper and acceptable but also the precious service of God.'"[62]

---

57. Enders, *Luther und Emser*, 2:141. ET from *LW* 39:232; emphasis added.

58. *LW* 13:295; *LW* 40:36.

59. Luther often makes use of a marital analogy "Christ is the Groom and we are the bride, the bride has everything that the Groom has, even His own body. . . . Consequently, since He is the Priest and we are His brothers, all Christians have the authority, the command, and the obligation to preach, to come before God, to pray for one another, and to offer themselves as a sacrifice to God" (*LW* 30:53).

60. *LW* 24:240. Luther qualified by saying it was his best book after his German translation of the Bible.

61. *LW* 24:241, 242.

62. *LW* 24:242–43.

For Luther, the "precious service of God" is divine service—service previously limited to the spiritual or to the clergy. Now all God's people can perform priestly temple service. All "works are holy" and can be offered to God "as sacrifices acceptable to Him for His special honor and His highest service. How could a Christian life be extolled more?"[63] Luther defended the thesis that all believers have a holy *Beruf*, a spiritual calling or vocation in which they serve the Lord.[64]

To sum up, the central source of the royal priesthood is the Melchizedekian priesthood of Christ. All believers share equally in this priesthood, for to share in Christ's priesthood is to be both disciple and Christian. Through her baptism and new birth, each member of Christ's priesthood has a responsibility to exercise the priestly functions of Christ, even if the way in which these functions are exercised differs.

The Priestly Functions of Jesus Christ and His Royal Priesthood

Luther identifies three chief functions of Christ's priesthood: teaching, praying, and the offering of sacrifice. Believers share in the exercise of these priestly functions. They preach, pray, and offer spiritual sacrifices, thereby representing God to one another and each other to God. At times, Luther expands this list to seven priestly functions. Since believers share in Christ's priesthood, and exercise priestly functions, their priesthood is a real priesthood, not a metaphorical one.[65]

The Short List: Three Functions of Priesthood

As Luther begins his reforming activities in 1520, his initial discussions of the functions of Christ's priesthood vary. In *Freedom of a Christian*, he mentions only two, prayer and preaching.[66] These two functions are shared with believers through the *fröhliche Wechsel*, "thus we are worthy to appear

---

63. *LW* 24:243.

64. *LW* 36:78; 44:130; Froehlich, "Luther on Vocation," 121–33; Wingren, *Christian's Calling*.

65. Henri de Lubac rightly argues that "the 'kingly priesthood' attributed to all of us by St. Peter and St. John is not a kind of metaphor, and we have even less right to call it a 'priesthood, as it were'" (*Splendor of the Church*, 134; *contra* Wengert, *Priesthood, Pastors, Bishops*, 11).

66. *LW* 31:354.

before God to pray for others and to teach one another divine things."[67] Earlier that year, as Luther wrestled with the medieval concept of the Mass as sacrifice, he mentioned a third function of Christ's priesthood, namely, sacrifice.[68] Believers also share in this priestly function, yet in a way different from Christ. Already in *Lectures on Hebrews* (1517–18), Luther argued that Scripture describes only two kinds of sacrifices: sacrifices of thanksgiving and sacrifices of atonement.[69] Believers' spiritual sacrifices are always from the former category; Christ's once-for-all sacrifice was the latter. Luther retained this basic distinction throughout his career, and it defines an important dimension of his understanding of the priesthood of all believers.

In Luther's 1522 sermons on 1 Pet 2:4–9, he combines all three functions for the first time. True priesthood "embraces these three things: to offer spiritual sacrifices, to pray for the congregation, and to preach. He who can do this is a priest."[70] Thirteen years later, when Luther presents his most systematic outline, he repeats the same triad as the central responsibility of priests: "Hence the priestly office consists of three parts: to teach or preach God's Word, to sacrifice, and to pray. All three of these functions are abundantly referred to in the Scriptures."[71]

The Expanded List: Seven Functions of Believer Priests

Preaching, sacrifice, and prayer are the central functions of the priesthood of all believers, but on a number of occasions Luther speaks of four more (bearing the keys; judging doctrine; baptizing; celebrating communion). Only once does he list all seven together (*Concerning the Ministry*, 1523), although he often treats one of the seven on its own. Table 4 lists these seven functions:

67. *LW* 31:355.
68. *LW* 36:139, 148–49.
69. Jaroslav Pelikan, "Once for All the Sacrifice," 238–54.
70. *LW* 30:55.
71. *LW* 13:315. See also *LW* 31:355; 29:16; Anizor, "Royal Priesthood," chap. 3; Jeffcoat, "Martin Luther's Doctrine of Ministry," 17–41; Siggins, *Martin Luther's Doctrine*, 117–19.

Priestly Function	Representative Discussions by Luther
1) Proclaiming, Preaching, or Teaching the Word of God*	*LW* 40:21–23; 41:148–51; 52:139; 36:148–49, 152.
2) Baptizing*	*LW* 40:23–24; 41:151–44:128; 39:14.
3) Celebrating Holy Communion*	*LW* 40:24–25; 41:152; 36:116; 39:14.
4) Binding and Loosing Sins (Bearing the Keys)	*LW* 40:25–28; 41:153; 35:16, 12; 35:12–13, 16; 39:86; *WA* 10, III, 398, 24–29.
5) Offering Spiritual Sacrifices	*LW* 40:28–29; 39:235; 35:99, 248; cf. 41:164–65.
6) Prayer and Intercession	*LW* 40:29–31; 41:164; 36:139.
7) Judging Doctrine	*LW* 40:31–34; 44:135; 36:150; 39:305–14; cf. 154–64.

*Luther argues that any Christian could exercise these three functions in an emergency situation (*Not*) by virtue of their priestly office, but normally only those ordained by the congregation should do so (e.g., baptism, eucharist, and public preaching of the Word within the gathered congregation).

Table 4: Luther's Functions of the Priesthood of All Believers

While all priestly functions are ultimately aimed at divine service, some are directed exclusively toward God, and some are directed horizontally in a penultimate direction toward one's neighbor (*einander*). This basic idea can be seen in the famous opening lines of Luther's *Freedom of a Christian*: "A Christian is a perfectly free lord of all, subject to none. A Christian is a perfectly dutiful servant of all, subject to all."[72]

As a Christian relates to God, she is absolutely free. Thus she can pray directly to God and offer spiritual sacrifices of thanksgiving directly to God.[73] The priestly function of prayer meant two things for Luther. First that the believer had direct access to God; she did not need a mediator apart from Christ. Luther's commitment to the primacy of Scripture should be seen within this priestly function of prayer. Luther learned to read Scripture in the monastery, and there he learned that the only proper reading of Scripture is a prayerful or spiritual one (*Lectio Divina*). Luther considered

---

72. *LW* 31:343.

73. Scripture "makes prayer, access to God and teaching (all of which are fitting and proper to a priest) common to all" (*LW* 36:139). See further Anizor, *Royal Priesthood*, chap. 3.

all he did in God's Word to be a form of prayer:[74] it is "everything the soul does in God's word—hearing, speaking, composing, meditating, etc."[75] The priestly privilege of prayer meant that a believer could be taught directly by God (Isa 54:13, John 6:45) through the Word. Luther's commitment to Bible translation in vernacular language flows logically from his understanding of the priesthood of all believers.

Secondly, a believer's priestly service of prayer meant she had the responsibility and privilege of intercession for others. Here the second half of Luther's opening lines from *Freedom of a Christian* come into play: a Christian is a servant, "subject to all." Just as faith gives the believer freedom to go directly to God through Christ, so love compels the believer to use her access on behalf of neighbor. All of the remaining priestly functions can be seen in this twofold light. When a believer-priest offers his life as a spiritual sacrifice, he fulfills his calling on behalf of neighbor.[76] Luther's doctrine of vocation is intimately related to the priesthood of all believers. It is the believer's priestly standing which allows her to offer spiritual sacrifices in the midst of daily life (Rom 12:1).

Luther understood that all priestly ministry, if it was to be Christian service, must be done within the temple of the Holy Spirit, that is, within the one body or "loaf" of Christ. The priestly ministry of believers is especially a fraternal ministry between one priest and another (*einander*). The priestly ministry of preaching/teaching/proclamation, which Luther considered to be the first duty of a priest (Mal 2:7), is to be constantly exercised. While only those ordained should preach in the gathered congregation, all should daily preach to themselves, to their families at home, and to others.[77] Similarly, as members of the royal priesthood, "the keys are yours and mine."[78] Thus all believers had a priestly responsibility to pronounce forgiveness on Christ's behalf when a brother or sister confessed their sins before the Lord.[79] In addition to preaching and making use of the keys, Luther taught that believers had the responsibility to judge doctrine for themselves; to fail to exercise this function could place their souls in danger of eternal damnation. Initially, Luther stressed this function as a responsibility of all believers. After

---

74. Ebeling, "Beten als Wahrnehmen," 165.

75. *LW* 52:139.

76. Luther speaks of a "double vocation, a spiritual and an external." The former is shared by all baptized believers, the latter "contains a differentiation." The latter is just as divine of a service, but focuses on individual earthly concerns (*WA* 34/II: 300–06).

77. *LW* 52:139.

78. *LW* 35:16, cf. 12.

79. Thayer, *Penitence, Preaching, and the Coming*, 145–83.

the Peasants' War and conflicts with the *Schwärmer*, Luther tended to only emphasize the exercise of this function by the magistrates.⁸⁰

Luther placed the final two priestly functions (baptism and celebrating the Eucharist) in the same category as the public preaching of the Word within the congregation.⁸¹ All believers could baptize or lead a celebration of the Eucharist by virtue of the priestly ordination they received at baptism. However, for the sake of church order, these functions should only be exercised by a member who had been publicly called (originally Luther meant a public call from a congregation but, after the Peasants' War, Luther limited the right to call a pastor to the nobles and magistrates). No priestly disciple without a magisterially approved public calling could practice these three priestly functions unless in an emergency situation (*Not*). Examples include a baby just born and about to die—a midwife could baptize the infant by virtue of her own priestly consecration or a group of Christians taken captive by the Turks (Muslims). If no ordained pastor was among them, they could ordain a leader from their midst to preach, baptize, and lead the Lord's Supper. Such an appointment would be valid, for each of the baptized captives already received priestly consecration by virtue of union with Christ.

Assessing Luther's Doctrine of the Believer as Priest

This section concludes our study of Luther's priesthood of all believers by surveying its contributions and weaknesses. Before doing so, it is appropriate to briefly ascertain the doctrine's significance for Luther.

The Significance of Luther's Doctrine

For Luther, the priesthood of all believers was the "essence of the Church."⁸² Its importance is illustrated by an English opponent, Edward Powell (d. 1540), who thought the doctrine "indicative of his [Luther's] entire work."⁸³

---

80. *LW* 14:341.

81. Discussion of the seven ministerial functions largely follows Jeffcoat ("Martin Luther's Doctrine," 92–110).

82. Weimar's editors introduce *On the Councils and the Churches* by describing the doctrine's significance for Luther: "Während Luther in unserer Schrift alles auf die grundlegende Bedeutung der heiligen Schrift zurückführt, er dort von dem Wesen der Kirche, dem allgemeinen Priestertum der Gläubigen den Ausgang nimmt" (*WA* 50:489).

83. "opere quippe precium sibi omnino erat." Citation and translation in Yarnell, *Royal Priesthood in the English Reformation*, ch. 3.

Luther wrote extensively on the doctrine in some fifteen works, and makes reference to it in over fifty, thus, there is some validity in Powell's observation. Often a doctrine's significance can be discerned by how many other topics it addresses. Yarnell illustrates this principle by listing fourteen questions raised by various Reformation writers when relating the doctrine to Christology, the Christian life, and church order.[84] The priesthood of all believers is a productive mine; its resources deeply enriched the new ecclesiologies emerging at the Reformation. Yet, as Luther's career illustrates, its practical application proved difficult.

Positive Contributions of Luther's Doctrine

A comprehensive list of the positive contributions of Luther's doctrine to theology, ecclesial life, personal spirituality, and political order would be massive; the Reformation touched all of life. In this section, only four major contributions can be identified: 1) union with Christ gaining a central place in ecclesiology; 2) the royal priesthood retrieving its script; 3) the royal priesthood retrieving its ministry; 4) deep societal reforms.

Union with Christ as the Foundation of the Royal Priesthood

Medieval "ecclesiology" was clergy-centric; Luther's most significant contribution to ecclesiology was to make it Christocentric by returning to the foundational notion of Christ as the great Priest-king with whom believers are united at baptism.[85] Each baptized believer has priestly access to the Most Holy Place through her soul's union with Christ.[86] This theme of "union with Christ" was developed more fully by John Calvin, who saw believers as "colleagues in the Priesthood" with Christ.[87] Other reformers, such

---

84. Yarnell, "Reformation Development," 2. Wengert's contempt for the "priesthood of all believers" can be traced to confusion on this point. He reduces the doctrine to one sub-question, "pastoral authority," and then shows that Luther did not equate the royal priesthood with the teaching that every believer should have equal pastoral authority within the congregation. He successfully defends Luther against a heretical version, but does not recognize the doctrine's wider scope (see Wengert, *Priesthood, Pastors, Bishops*, 1–32).

85. On medieval "ecclesiology," see Pannenberg, *STh* 3:21–27.

86. This language reflects the medieval mysticism which had a significant impact on Luther's priesthood of all believers (*LW* 31:71). Philipp Spener discusses this influence on Luther and develops it further (*Pia Desideria*, 92–95, 110–11; Snyder, "Pietism, Moravianism, and Methodism, 166–71).

87. Calvin, *Catechism of the Church of Geneva* (1545), *TT* 96; see also *Institutes*

as Usinius, would follow Luther and Calvin's lead.[88] Indeed, four hundred years later, even the Roman Catholic Church endorsed a nuanced version of Luther's "priesthood of all believers."[89] In short, Luther's rediscovery of the soul's freedom in Christ through faith and the "great exchange" released the power of the priesthood of all believers for the first time in nearly a millennium. One example of this explosive power was retrieving the voice of God in the life of individual believers through Scripture "reading" (*Lectio Divina*).

The Royal Priesthood Retrieves its Script

One of Luther's favorite proof texts was Jesus' citation of Isa 54:13: "And they will all be taught by God" (John 6:45). In the prayerful "reading" of God's word, God himself speaks. For Luther, "reading" the word was often conceived orally as hearing God's Word—hence the primary function of the priesthood of all believers was proclamation.[90] In order to equip the German people for this task, Luther realized he needed to supply a translation of God's Word. Even Luther's opponents acknowledged that the priesthood of all believers required this step:

> For since all people, even the dregs of the vulgar, have been equally constituted priests by Luther.... unless the New and Old Testaments are translated into the barbaric languages, which the filthy common people will be able to understand, he will never be able to effectively make this happen.[91]

Luther's 1522 translation of the NT (1534 for the whole Bible) was immediately followed by translations into numerous other vernacular languages: Danish NT (1524 in Wittenberg), Swedish NT (1526), Italian NT/OT (1532), French NT/OT (1535),[92] English NT/OT (1535), Dutch NT/OT

2:7:1; 4:19:24, 26. For further discussion see Crawford, "Calvin and the Priesthood," 145–56.

88. Billings, *Union with Christ*, 160–65.

89. *Dogmatic Constitution on the Church* 2.10 (*DEC* 2:2857).

90. Smalcald Articles (1537), 3, 4 (*BC-T*, 310); *LW* 13:333. See esp. Anizor, "Royal Priesthood," ch. 3.

91. Edward Powell, cited in Yarnell, *Royal Priesthood in the English Reformation*, ch. 3.

92. Translated by Calvin's cousin. Calvin's *Institutes* was the first "theology" book published in French (Cf. 1447 translation of *Imitatio Christi*, not technically considered "theology").

(1536), Spanish NT (1543), OT (1559),[93] and Polish NT (1553, OT, 1561).[94] Luther's theological descendants, especially among the Pietists, continued to emphasize the relationship between every believer's reading of Scripture and the exercise of spiritual priesthood.[95] Of Anglicanism, Eastwood notes that "no single incident in our history has done more to implement the Reformation doctrine of the priesthood of all believers than the introduction of the English Bible."[96] Vernacular translations continue to be an important mark of the Protestant understanding, as they equip all believers to fulfill their priestly responsibilities to teach and proclaim God's word.

The Royal Priesthood Reforms its Priestly Ministry

Writers tend to stress either the vertical or the horizontal aspect of Luther's doctrine. Thus some solely emphasize a believer-priest's access to God, saying little about his horizontal ministry to neighbors. Others claim that Luther's doctrine is only about priestly ministry to neighbors, having nothing to do with personal access to God. Both extremes must be avoided. The two previous contributions have emphasized the free access of the believer to a speaking God through faith in Christ. Equally important to this vertical privilege was Luther's recognition that all believers have a horizontal ministry as well (Ten Commandment's second table). This realization had two implications: 1) every believer has a priestly responsibility to minister to other believers using his or her gifts; 2) all believers have received earthly vocations whereby they daily offer their lives to God as loving servants of their neighbors.

In 1 Peter, a corporate dimension of the priesthood of all believers is emphasized using temple language. All believer-priests serve in the same temple, the body of Christ. Luther is equally committed to this corporate dimension. A Christian priest is one who serves the body. One not serving as a member of a congregation where the gospel is preached may be a "priest," but he is not a Christian priest. Thus Luther continually emphasizes that all believers must use their gifts to serve one another. They must also exercise the priestly functions of blessing, preaching, pronouncing forgiveness, interceding, and judging doctrine together as members of Christ's body. These functions must be exercised in an orderly way; the biblical offices of

---

93. No vernacular Bibles were printed in Spain until 1793 or in Portugal until 1805.
94. Ellingworth, "From Martin Luther," 105–39.
95. Spener, *Pia desideria*, 92.
96. Eastwood, *Priesthood of All Believers*, 98.

leadership must be respected, but any believer failing to exercise his priestly functions must return anew to the elementary truths of baptism.

Luther also extended the Benedictine combination of prayer and work to all Christians. Now all believers are engaged in divine service, whether they are "the rustic laborer in the field," "a woman going about her household tasks," or "a cobbler, a smith, a peasant."[97] Luther has been accused of turning the whole world into his monastery. There is certainly truth in this accusation; Luther himself would agree with the charge. The central text in this regard was Rom 12:1, implying that all of life—at home or marketplace—was spiritual, an opportunity for priestly service.

Nowhere did this radical democratization of vocation have a more sweeping effect (for Luther personally as well as medieval society as a whole) than on the domestic front. Luther's revolutionary (or reformational) understanding of vocation led him to identify marriage as a new monasticism. Bernard Cooke observes that although "it took some decades to take effect completely, in Protestant regions of Europe 'family' replaced 'monastery' as the symbol for ideal Christian life."[98] The home was to be a center for priestly ministry. Fathers and mothers were to exercise their priestly responsibilities of teaching and preaching using the Scriptures, the Catechism, and the Lord's Prayer.[99] Even domestic chores were an opportunity for priestly service if done in faith for the glory of God.

A Political Doctrine: Luther and the Peasants' War

Walter Altmann is correct to claim that the priesthood of all believers is a political doctrine. He notes, "The discovery of the 'royal priesthood of all baptized believers' implied militant support for transformation of the church and the political reality."[100] Many Anabaptists, and Luther himself, would disagree with the adjective "militant," but the overall point is historically defensible.[101] Luther's doctrine led within five years to the continent's first popular declaration of universal human rights. This manifesto, called *The Twelve Articles*, built upon Luther's insights, applying them to both church order and political questions.[102] Even though Luther disavowed as-

---

97. *LW* 36:78; 44:130.

98. Cooke, *Distancing of God*, 206–07. Five hundred years later, Protestant churches struggle with the reciprocal issue: validating celibacy as an acceptable spiritual estate.

99. For a Roman Catholic perspective on the "priesthood of Fathers and Mothers of families" see Congar, *Theology of the Laity*, 202, 201–05.

100. Altmann, *Luther and Liberation*, 4; see also Montover, *Luther's Revolution*.

101. *LW* 46:17–43.

102. The *Twelve Articles* are reproduced in *LW* 46:8–16.

sociation with the peasants, his explanations were accepted neither by the peasants, who felt betrayed by Luther, nor by his Roman Catholic critics.[103]

Luther's priesthood of all believers, especially as articulated in writings such as *To the Christian Nobility* and *On Monastic Vows*, suggests an element that Cornel West might label "prophetic deliverance."[104] Luther's doctrine helped him identify concrete societal evils, leading to concrete reforms. While it cannot be explored here, Luther's doctrine was a significant contributor to the birth of modern democracy.[105] It contained both sociological leveling functions and one of the basic principles upon which to build a modern democracy—loving service to one's neighbor.

Problematic Dimensions of Luther's Doctrine

Luther's doctrine was not without problems; three are acknowledged here. First, within the state churches of the Reformation, political citizenship was never successfully distinguished from membership in the priesthood of all believers. Secondly, the Enlightenment's focus on "self" led to perversions of Luther's doctrine. Finally, the marriage of the office of proclamation with the civil government and the decommissioning of monastic sodalities left Magisterial churches without a mechanism for mission apart from colonial overtures.

A MAGISTERIAL TENSION: PRIESTHOOD OF THE BAPTIZED vs. PRIESTHOOD OF ALL BELIEVERS

Luther's doctrine left an ambiguity never fully resolved within the state churches of the magisterial Reformation.[106] The central issue can be seen in the two possible terms with which the doctrine is identified within confessional Lutheranism. Is the doctrine the "priesthood of all the baptized" or the "priesthood of all believers"? Luther never fully clarifies his position on this issue, and the topic has rarely been addressed by theologians working within confessional orthodoxy.[107] Already in Luther's day answers

---

103. *LW* 46:45–55; 46:57–84.

104. West, *Prophesy Deliverance!*. Cf. *LW* 49:59–68.

105. "In die Geschichte der Entstehung der modernen Demokratie gehört Luthers Auffassung vom allgemeinen Priestertum ganz gewiß hinein" (Barth, *Einander Priester sein*, 44; see also Strehle, *Egalitarian Spirit of Christianity*, 1–40).

106. Barth, *Einander Priester sein*, 46–47.

107. "This complex of questions. . . . has seldom been a theme of discussion in dogmatics or even fundamental theology" (Pannenberg, *STh* 3:122n80).

were being proposed. For Anabaptists, the key term was "believers," and membership within the royal priesthood was defined by those who believed and made their own baptismal vows. For Bucer, the solution was not credobaptism, but a careful fence around the Lord's Supper, whereby baptized believers "endowed with the Holy Spirit"—and thus members of the royal priesthood—could be distinguished from baptized pagans.[108] Neither the Anabaptist proposal nor Bucer's won much magisterial support, and the result was that the priesthood of all believers received little more than lip service outside of Pietist and Anabaptist circles in continental Europe.

Enlightenment, Individualism, and the Priesthood of All Believers

The Enlightenment brought exaltation of human reason, but it also "regarded people as *emancipated, autonomous individuals*."[109] Luther's doctrine did have an element of what E. Y. Mullins later called "soul competency."[110] Each person would one day stand before God alone. Each person must be baptized for himself, and believe for himself. Yet Luther's doctrine was more than this; it was irreducibly relational. The individual was always a priest in relation to both God and neighbor. For Luther, to be a member of the royal priesthood meant to "give myself as a Christ to my neighbor, just as Christ offered himself to me."[111] Later theologians often ran into difficulties when they allowed reason or the autonomous experience of the individual to be the measure of the royal priesthood (e.g., Schleiermacher).[112] Luther was too much the biblical theologian to reduce the NT doctrine to an autonomous priesthood separated from Christ's body. "Atomistic" priests might claim priesthood, but Luther would deny that they were *Christian* priests. Later theologians would not always be so discerning.

Protestant Mission and the Decommissioning

---

108. Van't Spijker, *Ecclesiastical Offices*, 71–80.
109. Bosch, *Transforming Mission*, 267; emphasis original.
110. See George, " Priesthood of All Believers," 85–86.
111. *LW* 31:367.
112. Yarnell suggests that Luther's contemporary, William Tyndale (d. 1536), was one of the first to propose "atomistic individualism" when describing the priesthood of all believers (*Royal Priesthood in the English Reformation*), ch. 3.

OF ECCLESIAL SODALITIES

Luther's entire world was baptized.[113] While he knew of Turks and Jews, they were largely alien to his experience of German society.[114] Yoder may be overstating the case when he writes, "for the Reformers, there is no such thing as the 'world,'" but he does make an important point.[115] Luther's world was largely synonymous with his church. Magistrates could correct doctrine and appoint pastors because they were baptized just like everyone else. Thus in Luther's Wittenberg, the "educational task of the church dissolves its missionary task."[116] This social context also influenced Luther's doctrine. When he speaks about priestly ministry to the neighbor, he almost always assumes that the neighbor is at least baptized, but usually that he is a believing Christian.[117] Thus, while Luther's doctrine included a proclamatory dimension, it usually was directed toward a fellow baptized priest.[118] The ambiguity identified above between "baptized" and "believer" within Luther's Christendom meant that the concept of evangelism received little attention in Lutheran and Reformed orthodoxy, and it was eventually completely subsumed under the *Amt* of the magisterially appointed pastor.[119]

A further change in Luther's attitude toward the missional implications of the priesthood of all believers can be discerned following the Peasants' War of 1525 and his conflicts with the *Schwärmer*. Against the practices of the more missionary-minded Anabaptists, Luther emphasized that all public offices of proclamation must be tied to a geographic parish. He denied that any believer could "preach the gospel to all creation"; one now needed the permission of the magistrate.[120] This principle was reified by Melanchthon who taught *cuius regio, eius religio*. Melanchthon believed it

---

113. Luther met fewer than two dozen unbaptized adults in his entire life (Ingemar Öberg, *Luther and World Mission*, 2007], vii).

114. While he does speak of them from time to time, "it all amounts to exceedingly little" (Neill, *History of Christian Missions*, 189).

115. Yoder, *Anabaptism and Reformation*, 281.

116. Ibid.

117. "Luther pictures a mutual priesthood within the Church rather than a priestly mission of the Church to the 'nations'" (Gerrish, "Priesthood and Ministry," 420). Cf. *LW* 13:295.

118. Brunotte summarizes Luther's doctrine in four points, the last of which is the believer's duty to pass on the gospel (*Das geistliche Amt bei Luther*, 133).

119. Bosch, *Transforming Mission*, 245–46; Williams, *Radical Reformation*, 271.

120. *LW* 13:64; cf. "For to be a pastor one must be not only a Christian and a priest but must have an office and a field of work committed to him" (*LW* 13:65). Öberg identifies a parallel transition in Luther's thinking toward the Jews (*Luther and World Mission*, 426–28).

was the duty of the kings and princes to decide the religion of the land over which they ruled. This doctrine placed responsibility for mission almost entirely upon political leaders.[121]

By and large, the attitude advocated by the Magisterial churches was simple: heretics could flee, be burned or drowned; Jews and other infidels should be pressured to convert.[122] Mission was the responsibility of the state, not the church. In 1652 the theological faculty at Wittenberg released their "Opinion" on the missionary question, denying that "the Lutheran church had any missionary calling; this responsibility rested solely with the state."[123] If other means failed, the state should convert infidels using *jure belli* (military force).[124] Öberg's masterful study concludes:

> Concerning the missiology of Lutheran orthodoxy, one must sadly certify that during the seventeenth century it came to be encapsulated and paralyzed by the theory that all people on the earth *de facto* had already been introduced to the Gospel. . . . There was no longer any duty to spread God's reign, except the duty resting on the princes who ruled over non-Christian areas (compare with the Sami in Scandinavia) and their colonies.[125]

Other reformers, like Calvin, followed a similar trajectory, arguing that the offices of apostle, prophet, and evangelist were not "perpetual," lasting "only for a time."[126] He suggests that the "Great Commission" (Matt 28:19-20) applied primarily to the twelve, and secondarily in a limited way to ordained teachers.[127] Karl Barth would later label this Reformation tendency toward ecclesiocentrism, "Holy Egotism."[128]

A strength of Luther's doctrine is its clarion call for believers to return to the deep truths of their baptism. His primary objection to monastic

---

121. Ibid., 6n3, 499.

122. The actual history is of course more complicated. This paragraph marks a transition from Luther to Lutheranism. Luther himself was opposed to crusades (ibid., 489), never denying the importance of the church's mission to the nations (7, 11, 491, 495-96).

123. Bosch, *Transforming Mission*, 251.

124. Ibid.

125. Öberg, *Luther and World Mission*, 501.

126. Calvin, *CNTC* 11:180. Calvin did suggest that it was theoretically possible for the office of evangelist to be raised up *extra ordinem* outside of Christendom, but this possibility received little reflection among his heirs.

127. Calvin, *CNTC* 3:251-52; see discussion of this passage in: Warneck, *Outline of a History of Protestant Missions*, 20n1; Friesen, *Erasmus*, 76-136; McGrath, *Christianity's Dangerous Idea*, 175-78.

128. *CD* IV/3.2, 568-71, 767.

orders was that the required vows resulted in "baptismal-forgetfulness" (*Taufvergessenheit*); monastic vows often became more important than baptismal vows.[129] Luther called for the abolition of most "brotherhoods" and monastic orders.[130] Within Protestant territories, monastic orders nearly disappeared within a decade. Luther understood that democratizing monasticism meant a new educational system was needed, and he repeatedly challenged magistrates and pastors to establish schools. However, he failed to recognize that by decommissioning monastic sodalities, he was also decommissioning the voluntary societies which were the primary means by which mission had been conducted since apostolic times.[131]

Luther's Roman Catholic critics recognized that the Reformers' absence of mission to the unbaptized was a major flaw. Cardinal Bellarmine (d. 1621) argued that this proved the Reformation Churches were not the true church:

> Heretics are never said to have converted either pagans or Jews to the faith, but only to have perverted Christians. But in this one century the Catholics have converted many thousands of heathens in the new world. . . . the Lutherans compare themselves to the apostles and the evangelists; yet though they have among them a very large number of Jews, and in Poland and Hungary have the Turks as their near neighbors, they have hardly converted even so much as a handful.[132]

Luther began decommissioning voluntary ecclesial sodalities in the 1520s; Protestants in Europe would have to wait a full two hundred years before a missionary sodality would be formed.[133] Intense persecution led the surviving Anabaptists to redirect much of their initial missionary zeal inward. It was not until Spener's godson, Count Nicholas Zinzendorf (1700–60), rose to leadership that continental Protestants began to respond

---

129. They "despise the baptismal vow. . . . this is to blaspheme baptism, which is everything to all Christians" (*LW* 44:356).

130. *LW* 35:67-71; 44:243-44.

131. Bosch, *Transforming Mission*, 245; Winter, "Two Structures," 220-30.

132. Cited in Neill, *History of Christian Missions*, 188-89.

133. A careful reading of *On Monastic Vows* reveals that Luther is not opposed to a task-oriented sodality *per se*; he is against the taking of vows beyond our baptismal vows if they are understood as contributing to justification. While some monastic sodalities did survive the Reformation (Bloesch, *Church*, 211-18), the first "Protestant" mission sodality/society mentioned in Neill's work is *The Anglican Society for the Propagation of the Gospel in Foreign Parts,* founded in 1701 (*History of Christian Missions*, 192). Previously, missionary work had been conducted in the Americas by John Eliot (d. 1690). Cf. David Brainerd (d. 1747).

to Cardinall Bellarmine's challenge. Zinzendorf led Moravian believers to send missionaries to twenty-eight territories in their first thirty years under his leadership.[134] Mission to the unbaptized remained largely exclusive to pietist circles, until thrust into the light by Baptist cobbler William Carey with his 1792 tract, *An Enquiry into the Obligations of Christians to Use Means for the Conversion of the Heathen*. Carey provided a simple defense for why the "Great Commission" applied to all believers, and the text has remained a central passage for Protestant missions.[135]

Chapter Summary

Luther's priesthood of all believers was the right doctrine for the right time. As Protestant churches came into existence, the doctrine provided a firm foundation upon which to build. It was a basic pillar of the emerging ecclesiologies of the Magisterial, Anabaptist, and Anglican churches in the sixteenth century. Luther's doctrine is fundamentally the Christian's participation in the royal priesthood of Christ made possible through the new birth and baptism. Believers exercise their priesthood by preaching the word, praying, and offering spiritual sacrifices, thereby representing God to one another and each other to God. Luther's doctrine was not without problematic dimensions; especially significant was its failure to develop implications for mission. That realization was championed some four hundred years later by Karl Barth, and its story is the topic of our next chapter.

---

134. See Atwood, *Community of the Cross*.

135. Prior to Carey, the Anabaptists were the only ecclesial group to consider the Great Commission binding on every believer. There is no text to which they more often appeal (Bosch, *Transforming Mission*, 246, 340).

6

Sending the Royal Priesthood: Karl Barth, Lesslie Newbigin, and Missional Theology

> There is no participation in Christ without participation in His mission to the world. That by which the Church receives its existence is that by which it is also given its world-mission. "As the Father hath sent Me, even so send I you."
>
> —Lesslie Newbigin, Willingen, 1953

> Again, each individual is responsible for its actually being a missionary community.... We have to remember that every Christian is to be a missionary, a recruiting officer for new witnesses. If our congregations do not recognize this and act accordingly, they cannot be missionary congregations, and therefore they cannot be truly Christian.
>
> —Karl Barth, *CD* III/4, 505

KARL BARTH'S DOCTRINE OF the priesthood of all believers, like his missionary ecclesiology, has suffered from neglect in academic theology.[1] Barth's three explicit references to the priesthood of all believers are made largely in passing, and it is not surprising that his contribution to the doctrine has

---

1. Bender's monograph was the first book-length treatment of Barth's ecclesiology in thirty years (*Karl Barth's Christological Ecclesiology*. Stout describes a similar gap in Barth scholarship on ecclesiology (*Fellowship of Baptism*, 1). Flett has identified an equally serious omission in the treatment of Barth's understanding of mission, especially as it relates to God and the church (*The Witness of God*). None give substantial attention to Barth's doctrine of the priesthood of all believers.

received little attention.[2] Yet Barth's contribution represents the doctrine's third major paradigm shift. As the first major post-Christendom theologian, Barth viewed the doctrine of the royal priesthood from a different perspective, and this perspective revealed a major blindspot of Christendom versions. Barth's emphasis on the church as a witnessing community expands the focus from an upward and inward direction to include an outward one. Like Luther, Barth makes a significant contribution, his work providing a new paradigm.

The chapter examines three paragraphs in the *CD* where Barth explicitly discusses the priesthood of all believers (§§67, 69, 72), and then surveys the most significant of Barth's twenty-five uses of 1 Pet 2:9. This careful reading lays the groundwork for a discussion of the three most important elements of Barth's doctrine: election, baptism as ordination, and witness as the royal priesthood's vocation. The chapter concludes with Lesslie Newbigin's "priesthood in the world," a version of the priesthood of all believers illustrative of the paradigmatic changes suggested by Barth's Christological and missionary ecclesiology.

Karl Barth and the Priesthood of All Believers

We begin with two architectural observations. Barth only explicitly treats the priesthood of all believers in the final two chapters of the *CD* (IV/2, IV/3),[3] chapters focused upon Christology. Barth's first discussion takes place in §67 and his final two in §69 and §72.

---

[2]. Karl Barth does not appear in Hans Barth's *Einander Priester sein*. As the title suggests, the emphasis (like Luther's) falls on the priestly ministry of believers to one another. Barth's contribution is not discussed in Muthiah's, *The Priesthood of All Believers in the Twenty-First Century*.

[3]. There are indicators of Barth's doctrine of the priesthood of all believers related to 1 Pet 2:9 as early as §35 (*CD* II/2).

	Ch. 14: Lord as Servant (IV.1)	Ch. 15: Servant as Lord (IV.2)	Ch. 16: The True Witness (IV.3.1–2)
Traditional Categories Addressed by Barth	Christ as God; Christ as Priest	Christ as Man; Christ as King	Christ as God-Man; Christ as Prophet
Barth's Category	Obedience of the Son of God, §59	Exaltation of the Son of Man, §64	**The Glory of the Mediator, §69**
Knowledge of Sin	Pride, §60	Sloth, §65	Falsehood, §70
Knowledge of Reconciliation	Justification, §61	Sanctification, §66	Vocation, §71
The Holy Spirit	Gathers the Community, §62	**Builds up the Community, §67**	**Sends the Community, §72**
The Holy Spirit Works in the Individual Christian	To Awaken Faith, §63	To Quicken Love, §68	To Enlighten with Hope, §73

Table 5: Architecture of Barth's Christological Ecclesiology

As Table 5 illustrates, Barth's first contribution is a structural one. His three formal discussions are interwoven into larger Christological chapters, a structural feature which guards against many historical abuses. For example it warns against those arguing for a "priesthood of *the* believer," a natural priesthood exercised in independence of Christ's "earthly-historical form of existence," i.e., the church.[4] Secondly, two of his three discussions take place in a chapter focusing on Christ's *witness* to the world. Thus, from the table of contents alone, we are able to identify what may be Barth's most significant contribution to a contemporary articulation of the priesthood of all believers, namely, the royal priesthood's vocation as witness. With these structural clues in mind, we turn to the three relevant paragraphs.

§67, The Priesthood of All Believers in "The Holy Spirit and the Upbuilding of the Christian Community"

Barth's first explicit mention takes place in paragraph sixty-seven, the second of three paragraphs discussing the work of the Holy Spirit in the *Gemeinde* ("community," cf. §62, §72).[5] He writes: "Law and order in the community are never the particular priesthood of a few, but the universal priesthood of all believers."[6] His first reference to the priesthood of all be-

---

4. *CD* IV/3.2, 681–84. See Yarnell, "Changing Baptist Concepts," 236–52.

5. Barth's use of *"Gemeinde"* over *"Kirche"* carries theological freight lost in English translation. John Howard Yoder calls it "a theological battle cry" with significant implications for Free Church ecclesiology ("Basis of Barth's Social Ethics," 8).

6. *CD* IV/2, 694. "Ordnung und Recht in der Gemeinde ist nie und nimmer das besondere Priestertum einiger, sondern das allgemeine Priestertum aller Gläubigen"

lievers is significant. The casual way in which the term is affirmed implies comfortable familiarity, fitting well with the larger ideas in this section. Barth is attempting to describe the form of the *communio sanctorum*; he is in conversation, but not complete agreement, with Brunner and Sohm on the order of the church.[7] Like Luther, Barth recognizes that there is a place for commissioned leaders within the body, not least those commissioned to preach.[8] But he sees the heart of church order as every member sharing equally and actively in divine service.[9] Thus, church order must "avoid the fatal word "office" and replace it by "service," which can be applied to all Christians. Or, if it does use it, it can do so only on the understanding that in the Christian community either all are office-bearers or none; and if all, then only as servants."[10]

Barth is concerned about even "practical clericalism," which would permit some members of the royal priesthood to be passive, while others are active.[11] "All Christians do not have to serve equally, i.e., in the same function. But they all have to serve, and to do so in one place with the same eminence and responsibility as others do at other places."[12] As seen below, Barth is not afraid to speak of "chosen vessels" who offer exemplary service within the royal priesthood—in this he differs from Sohm and Brunner, but he does see every member engaged in divine service ordered by the Word of God, baptism, the Lord's Supper, and prayer.[13]

§69, The Priesthood of All Believers in "The Glory of the Mediator"

Barth's second use of the term takes place in the first paragraph of the final chapter of the *CD*.[14] Barth is introducing his larger treatment of "Jesus Christ, the True Witness," an exposition which will ultimately run some 942 pages (ET). This exposition of Christ's work as witness adds "no further

---

(KD IV/2, 786).

7. CD IV/2, 676, 679, 683–86.

8. Barth, *Knowledge of God*, 213.

9. Barth's earlier discussion of Rom 12:1 in this paragraph offers important warrant for this claim: CD IV/2, 639–40.

10. CD IV/2, 695.

11. CD IV/2, 695.

12. CD IV/2, 693.

13. CD IV/2, 699–706.

14. CD, IV/3.1, 33. KD, IV/3.1, 34.

development of our material knowledge of the event of reconciliation."[15] The "material content of the doctrine of reconciliation is in fact exhausted" by the discussion of Jesus Christ as the Priest-king in the previous two chapters (chs. 14, 15).[16] Barth has here arrived independently at the same major insight Luther identified (Psalm 110); the role of Jesus as Priest-king (*munus duplex*) is the center of the Christian faith, not "an arbitrarily invented theologoumenon, but a necessity grounded in the thing itself."[17]

The third problem of the doctrine of reconciliation—its necessary declaration—is thus a *"formal* problem" as "distinct from the first two *material* problems. Its concern is with the How of the event in its inalienable distinction from the What."[18] There is an important implication for ecclesiology here. If Jesus Christ is *materially* the Priest-King, and *formally* a witness, then his siblings (ἀδελφοί) can *materially* be understood as the royal priesthood, and *formally* as witnesses.[19] Thus the third problem does not reveal "anything different, higher, or deeper, any independent truth" about the Priest-King or the royal priesthood; it rather reveals how they relate to the world, that is, their vocation.[20] The formal vocation of the Priest-king and the royal priesthood is joyful and prophetic witness.

This insight into vocation reveals a blind spot in Calvin's doctrine of the *munus propheticum*. Barth begins with a twenty-eight page (ET) small print historical introduction to Jesus Christ as witness, and related implications of the church's witness in history. Barth notes that Jesus Christ, the one mediator, is also the witness (τὸ μαρτύριον; 1 Tim 2:6). He then identifies five sets of questions about the office of Christ as prophet or witness as it has developed dogmatically since Calvin's formulation in his final edition of the *Institutes*.[21] Barth observes that Calvin's doctrine is in danger of ending in "a blind alley,"[22] for Calvin primarily defines the prophetic office as the teaching office of Christ, only exercised in relation to the elect—for Calvin, these are primarily those already within the church. "Holy egotism" blinded the church to its vocation of witness in the world.

---

15. *CD* IV/3.1, 7.

16. *CD* IV/3.1, 6.

17. *CD* IV/3.1, 6; "nicht um ein willkürlich ersonnenes Theologumenon, sondern um eine in der Sache begründete Notwendigkeit handelt" (*KD* IV/3.1, 5).

18. *CD* IV/3.1, 8, emphasis added.

19. Luther's emphasis on Christ as Priest-king made a similar point. He understood more clearly than Barth the importance of Psalm 110.

20. *CD* IV/3.1, 8. Cf. §71.

21. *CD* IV/3.1, 14–18.

22. *CD* IV/3.1, 19.

Barth continues with an insightful description of the relation between ecclesial mission and modernity. Despite the unfortunate direction in which Calvin's doctrine developed, it is no accident that the prophetic office was rediscovered as a *diastasis* (rupture) was taking place between the church and the world.[23] In other words, as the western church moved to the margins in the modern era, it also rediscovered its vocation of witness (μάρτυς). "In these centuries when an unprofitable union with the world has been broken a materially profitable encounter with the world has been achieved."[24] Barth then illustrates the profitable gains made during the past 450 years with six examples. The church has: 1) again become "a Church of the Word";[25] 2) entered "an age of Christian mission unparalleled since the days of the apostles and the time of the christianisation of Europe"; [26] 3) awakened to the dangers of its "internal paganism";[27] 4) become epistemologically aware of its hermeneutical tendency to "project itself" and thereby distort the Word of God;[28] 5) begun to accept the priesthood of all believers with its critique of an internal distinction within the people of God between clergy and laity;[29] and, finally, 6) become ecumenically sensitive to the fact that the church's witness to the world requires serious attention to Jesus' prayer for unity in John 17:21.[30]

Barth's historical analysis reveals a critical insight: the priesthood of all believers is closely linked to the church's witness to the world.[31] When Luther identified the pope with the world/antichrist, he was well-positioned in 1520 to trumpet three loud blasts in support of the priesthood of all believers. After the political realities of the Peasants' revolt forced him to

---

23. *CD* IV/3.1, 20–21, 38.

24. *CD* IV/3.1, 21.

25. *CD* IV/3.1, 21.

26. *CD* IV/3.1, 22. Leithart's *Defending Constantine* is helpful; it falls short, however, in its critique of Yoder on this point (287–90). With Constantine's conversion, church-world distinctions became increasingly difficult to discern within Christendom. As distinctions disappeared, the church's commitment to both the doctrine of the royal priesthood and to its missional vocation went into exponential decline. The crusades epitomize the relative inability of the medieval Roman Catholic Church to imagine mission apart from Christendom (the occasional Franciscan and Dominican excepted). Apart from the Anabaptists and Pietists, the situation was the same in the Reformation churches for nearly 200 years (Bosch, *Transforming Mission*, 220–26, 239–61).

27. *CD* IV/3.1, 26.

28. *CD* IV/3.1, 31–32.

29. *CD* IV/3.1, 33–35.

30. *CD* IV/3.1, 35–38.

31. See further Barth, "The Christian as a Witness," 94–143.

emphasize a union of sorts between the world and the church, the doctrine faded from his theology.[32] Thus it was not in the Magisterial Reformation churches, but among the Pietists and Anabaptists, who tended to maintain a sharp church-world distinction, that the priesthood of all believers most freely developed.[33] The fruit of this development was a flowering of mission, both with regard to foreign missions (Zinzendorf)[34] and "Inner Mission" (J. H. Wichern).[35]

In summary, Barth gives the doctrine a prominent place when introducing the vocation of Christ and his body. While there are dangers to the practical exercise of the priesthood of all believers, Barth emphasizes the centrality of personal and communal witness. The breakdown of the barrier between a "priestly" clergy and a "non-priestly" laity is essential for faithful witness in the world.[36]

§72, *The Ministry of the Priesthood of All Believers*, in *"The Holy Spirit and the Sending of the Christian Community"*

Barth's final explicit reference to the doctrine comes in §72. This paragraph is Barth's third and longest treatment of ecclesiology and is divided into four sub-sections: 1) "The People of God in World-Occurrence," 2) "The Community for the World," 3) "The Task of the Community," and 4) "The Ministry of the Community." The reference comes in the final sub-section. Before discussing it, however, we make three observations about its context.

First, the church's vocation as witness is the locus of Barth's primary explication of the doctrine. Barth wants his readers to understand that the Old and New Testament communities are a people in "World-Occurrence." The community "should understand itself" as 1 Pet 2:9's "royal priesthood" called to be a light to the world (Matt 5:14).[37]

Secondly, the city on the hill does not shine its light for itself, but for the world. Its existence is first for God, then for the world, and only subsequently for itself. It is *"per definitionem* summoned and impelled to exist for God and therefore for the world and [humanity]. In this way but only in this way, as the human creature thus orientated, can it and will it also exist

---

32. *CD* IV/3.1, 28–29, 33. Cf. Avis, *Church in the Theology*, 95–108.

33. *CD* IV/3.1, 25–28. Cf. Spener, *Pia desideria*; Snyder, 'Pietism, Moravianism, and Methodism; Barth, *Einander Priester sein*, 54–78.

34. *CD* IV/3.1, 25.

35. *CD* IV/3.1, 27. See Barth, *Einander Priester sein*, 79–103.

36. *CD* IV/3.1, 35. This is also emphasized in Newbigin's work.

37. *CD* IV/3.2, 733. Barth often links 1 Pet 2:9 and Matt 5:14.

for itself."[38] The fruit of the Holy Spirit is not meant simply to fatten the community itself; rather it is to be served to the world. Barth describes Reformation and post-Reformation ecclesiology as failing to mind the "gap," often ignoring its responsibility to engage in mission to the world.[39] In a memorable phrase, Barth describes these centuries of failure as *sacro egoismo* ("holy egoism"), a danger the church continues to wrestle with today.[40]

Finally, Barth argues that the "very definite task" of the community is to proclaim joyfully the gospel.[41] Every member of the community has freedom in the *hic et nunc* to proclaim the gospel according to "the differences in their vocation to the community," differences which prevent the individual proclamation of members of the royal priesthood from ever becoming "the monotonous function of a collective."[42] Barth is aware of the difficulties of pure proclamation of the gospel, but he is clear that the task of proclamation is itself essential to the royal priesthood.[43]

Moving from context to content, we turn to Barth's final reference to the priesthood of all believers in §72's fourth sub-section, "The Ministry of the Community."[44] After discussing the definiteness and limitations of the community's ministry,[45] Barth examines what remains constant.[46] In every form of ministry, three things remain the same: the proclamation, explication, and application of the gospel to the world. In other words, every form

---

38. *CD* IV/3.2, 763.

39. Barth refers to this "gap" four times in this small-print portion (*CD* IV/3.2, 764–67).

40. *CD* IV/3.2, 767. Cf. Barth's fullest discussion (568–71).

41. *CD* IV/3.2, 795.

42. *CD* IV/3.2, 801.

43. *CD* IV/3.2, 813–30. Newbigin's doctrine of the priesthood of all believers is fundamentally shaped by these issues (*Gospel in a Pluralistic Society*, 229–32).

44. Barth intentionally uses ecclesiologically freighted terms in order to emphasize the priestly office of the whole community, *die Heiligen* (*KD* IV/2, 578). Flett, like his mentor Darrell Guder, has concerns about translating *Dienst* as "ministry" instead of "service" (*Witness of God*, x–xi). He also expresses concerns about Bromiley's translation of *Bestimmung* as "ordination" and of *Berufung* as "vocation." Bromiley may be working from a clerical paradigm, but it is also clear that he can understand the English word "ministry" as something that belongs to all Christians: "as Christians, we are necessarily ministers" (Bromiley, *Christian Ministry*, 111). In my view, the English terms "ministry," "ordination," and "vocation," can render Barth accurately, and need to be redeemed and recognized as belonging to the whole people of God rather than retired and removed from use (although in some ecclesial contexts these nouns may be less helpful than others).

45. *CD* IV/3.2, 830–43, esp. 836.

46. *CD* IV/3.2, 843–54.

of ministry is actually a form of witness. The "concept of witness" is the "sum of what the Christian community has to offer."[47]

With this base, Barth then describes twelve forms of missional ministry;[48] reference to the priesthood of all believers is found in his ninth example. He describes the ministry of "'chosen vessels' (Acts 9:15)," those who have received particular graces to serve the community. Barth is careful not to limit these chosen vessels to ordained church leaders, and elsewhere identifies a division of grace within the priestly people of God as damaging to the community.[49] All members of the royal priesthood have received grace and a vocation to the ministry of witness; nevertheless:

> It does not in any way contradict the priesthood of all believers . . . that the community always needs and may point to the existence of specific individuals who . . . stand out as models or examples in their special calling and endowment, its witness being more clear and comprehensible and impressive in their persons and activity than in those of others.[50]

Again, Barth's casual affirmation of the priesthood of all believers implies a great deal, namely, that the doctrine functions as a basic presupposition, upholding his view of the ministry (and thus witness) of the community.

In sum, Barth's explicit uses of "priesthood of all believers" emphasize the doctrine's divine service or ministry. This priestly ministry is shared by every member of Christ's body and is not the exclusive prerogative of ordained leaders. It is first and foremost a ministry of proclamation, and the vocation of the royal priesthood is thus a vocation of witness.

Barth's Use of 1 Peter 2:9 and "Royal Priesthood"

Barth refers to 1 Pet 2:9 twenty-five times, making it one of the most frequently cited verses in the *CD*.[51] Barth's "basic rule of all church dogmatics" is that theology must be grounded in the "self-revelation of God attested

---

47. *CD* IV/3.2, 843.

48. *CD* IV/3.2, 854–901.

49. Barth speaks of "the system of fatal preferences" in a division of grace where clergy receive a different kind of grace than that of the rest of the body of Christ (*CD* IV/1, 88). Cf. Coffey, "Common and the Ordained Priesthood," 209–36.

50. *CD* IV/3.2, 888–89.

51. Including two citations from *CL*. Citations must be weighed, not simply counted. Still, 1 Pet 2:9 may be the second most quoted verse in the *CD*. By my count, the only verse cited more frequently is Gal 2:20.

in Holy Scripture."[52] Thus, in attempting to understand his doctrine of the priesthood of all believers, it is appropriate to attend to his treatment of 1 Pet 2:9:[53]

> Ihr aber seid das auserwählte Geschlecht, die königliche Priesterschaft, das heilige Volk, das Volk des Eigentums, damit ihr die herrlichen Taten dessen verkündigt, der euch aus der Finsternis zu seinem wunderbaren Licht berufen hat.[54]

The importance of this verse for Barth's doctrine is well illustrated by a sub-section of §55 on "The Active Life," found within Barth's ethics of creation. For Barth, the active life commanded by God is to be identified with the ministry (*Dienst*) of the Christian community.[55] Barth assumes that all members are called to engage in its priestly ministry. Thus, a proper understanding of the ministry requires that the distinction between an active clergy and a passive laity be "abolished." "All are mere 'laity' in relation to their Lord, and therefore in truth, yet all are 'clergy' in the same relation and therefore in truth. . . . All can and should and may serve; none is ever 'off duty.'"[56] The importance of 1 Pet 2:9 then becomes apparent when Barth cites it alone and claims that "the Protestant conception of the Church" would have been much more happily worked out along these lines.[57]

Barth suggests that "an overdue and far more comprehensive reformation of the Church than that of the sixteenth century" is needed, and his development of the line of thought summarized by 1 Pet 2:9 extends twenty-six pages.[58] This second reformation will begin with taking baptism seriously. Baptism represents an ordination to priestly ministry, a starting place.[59] It requires every member's commitment to the "inner history" of

---

52. *CD* II/2, 35.

53. 1 Pet 2:9 cites Exod 19:6; Barth's only significant discussion of the latter describes Israel's royal priesthood as possessing a "mediatorial ministry" to the nations (*CD* IV/1, 424).

54. *KD* III/4, 561. Barth uses "Priesterschaft" rather than Luther's "Priestertum." On the significance of one term over the other see Elliott, *Elect and the Holy*, 68–69.

55. *CD* III/4, 488.

56. *CD* III/4, 489–90.

57. Barth also cites Question 32 of the Heidelberg Catechism which includes the cultic idea of "offering myself as a living sacrifice" (*CD* III/4, 490). *Contra* Herbert, *Kenosis and Priesthood*, 187n304.

58. *CD* III/4, 490–516. See further Torrance, "A New Reformation?," 259–83.

59. *CD* III/4, 490–95. Baptism is "a consecration or ordination to take part in the mission which is committed to the whole church. . . . all those baptized as Christians are *eo ipso* consecrated, ordained, or dedicated to the ministry of the church" *CD* IV/4, 201.

the community, to building up the body,⁶⁰ and it requires every member to engage in witness, proclaiming the gospel.⁶¹ "Remember that every Christian is to be a missionary, a recruiting officer for new witnesses."⁶² First Peter 2:9 states that the function of every member of the royal priesthood is to proclaim the virtues of him who called them out of darkness into his glorious light. For Barth, this principle is the only starting place for Christian ethics.⁶³ The importance of 1 Pet 2:9 for Barth's theology of the priesthood of all believers could be illustrated from many more texts.⁶⁴ While we cannot explore them all, several more will be examined in discussions below.

Barth's Three Contributions to a Protestant Priesthood of All Believers

The previous two sections have shown that the priesthood of all believers plays an important role in Barth's ecclesiology. In this section, we describe three ways Barth's doctrine can inform a contemporary theological account.

Election and Priestly Access to the Father for the Holy Ones

Barth's supralapsarian doctrine of election is both creative and problematic; a full treatment is beyond this chapter's scope. Yet Barth's doctrine, like the biblical doctrine, cannot be understood without reference to election. All three of Barth's explicit discussions of the priesthood of all believers take place within his larger treatment of Christology. In those passages there is an implicit relationship between election and the royal priesthood. Below we overview three paragraphs (§§ 35, 64, and 66) where Barth's use of 1 Pet 2:9 makes this relationship explicit.⁶⁵

Barth first makes the connection between election and the royal priesthood in paragraph thirty-five ("The Election of the Individual"). Three times he describes all believers as priests.

60. *CD* III/4, 495–97.
61. *CD* III/4, 497–515.
62. *CD* III/4, 505. See Chapter epigraph.
63. *CD* III/4, 516.
64. For example, Barth's exposition of the four Nicene marks begins with a small-print discussion referencing 1 Pet 2:9 and two other texts (*CD* IV/1, 668). Cf. *CD* III/2, 505, etc.
65. I do not have space to discuss Barth's three uses of 1 Pet 2:9 in §68, but the results would be similar to that discussed below (*CD* IV/2, 733, 769, 806).

> There is no longer any need of special men of God. . . . Just as Christians have their being as *a whole elected race of priests* and kings, a holy and peculiar people (1 Pet 2:9), similarly *every one* of them has his being on the basis of his personal election.[66]
>
> They have "the unction (χρῖσμα) from him who is holy" (1 John 2:20. cf. 2:27). They are themselves prophets, *priests* and kings (1 Pet 2:9) because He is this, and has made them His own.[67]
>
> They are this as those whom Jesus has won for Himself by giving Himself for them. It is in virtue of His priestly office and ministry that *they are priests*.[68]

There is now only one office of Priest-king, an office filled by Jesus Christ the elect one. Because believers share in Christ's election, they share in his royal priesthood, but this sharing applies "to all believers in the same way, with no basic difference."[69] All of the elect now share in the apostolate, a "sharing in Jesus' own mission."[70] Sharing in Christ's royal priesthood is most clearly seen in the historical example of the twelve apostles. "It is in them that each individual member of the Church can and should recognize the meaning and purpose of his own election."[71] Like the apostles, the believer's election is for the sake of going out into the world and "baptizing it. . . . If God elects a man, it is that he may be a witness to Jesus Christ, and therefore a proclaimer of His own glory."[72] Barth's emphasis on election for witness makes a significant contribution to Luther's version of the priesthood of all believers.

A second paragraph relating election and the royal priesthood, "The Exaltation of the Son of Man" (§64), develops further implications of the believer's election in Christ due to her present ontological unity with Jesus in heaven.[73] For Barth, "to be a Christian is *per definitionem* to be in Christ (ἐν χριστῷ)," and to be in Christ is to be ontologically connected to him.[74] This ontological union with Christ has two implications for believers. First, as we

---

66. *CD* II/2, 342; emphasis added.
67. *CD* II/2, 432; emphasis added.
68. *CD* II/2, 442; emphasis added.
69. *CD* II/2, 428.
70. *CD* II/2, 432. Barth's position is consistent with Matthew's portrayal of the disciples (ch. 3 above) and with Luther's understanding of all believers as priestly disciples (ch. 5 above).
71. *CD* II/2, 449.
72. *CD* II/2, 449.
73. *CD* IV/2, 278.
74. *CD* IV/2, 277, 275. See also Newbigin, "One Body," 22.

saw in §35, the ontological union with Christ is the basis of the Christian community's "missionary character."[75] Secondly, the believer's ontological union with Christ implies access to the Father: "What is really meant is that they are already with Him in heaven, that they have already taken this *sedes*, that they live already in the πολίτευμα ἐν οὐρανοῖς of Phil 3:20."[76] All members of Christ's body have priestly access to the Father through their union with the Son (Heb 10:19–25).[77] "This understanding of their being is the lever which gives a basis and power to the warnings and encouragements addressed to them."[78] For Barth, the ontological union of believers with Christ has already *made* each member a sharer in Christ's priesthood.[79]

Barth's discussions of election and the royal priesthood guard against individualistic perversions. While every member of the royal priesthood is a priest, each member's priesthood is only valid through his or her participation in Christ. Thus, no saint can claim to exercise the privleges and responsibilities of priesthood independently from Christ's body—the church. A believer's status as an elect saint, as a royal priest, is not an independent ontological status, but solely a feature of participation in the Elect One, the Anointed (Χριστός), the eschatological Priest-king (Psalm 110).

Baptism as Ordination to the Ministry of the Royal Priesthood

Careful readers will have noted several references to baptism in the preceding discussion.[80] Barth's second contribution to a contemporary doctrine of the priesthood of all believers is his retrieval of the relationship between baptism and priestly ministry. Like Barth's doctrine of election, we cannot fully explore the implications of his view. Nevertheless, a few comments are appropriate.

Barth's lengthiest discussion of baptism takes place in the final paragraph of *CD* published during his lifetime: "The Foundation of the Christian Life" (§75). It is a fragment in what would have been Volume IV's ethics chapter. Baptism is a twofold act consisting of God's action toward us,

75. *CD* IV/2, 275.

76. *CD* IV/2, 277.

77. Leithart, *Priesthood of the Plebs*, 96–102; Scholer, *Proleptic Priests*, 125–31. *Contra* Garrett, *Systematic Theology*, 562.

78. *CD* IV/2, 365.

79. The eschatological reality of heaven is also the reality on earth. Thus, the "harassed flock is the kingdom of God and its members are *His elect priests*" (*CD* III/3, 473).

80. See discussion of §§ 67, 69, and 55 above.

"Baptism with the Spirit," and our obedient response to him, "Baptism with Water."[81] The "true basis" of baptism is not Jesus' command in Matt 28:19, but his example of baptism.[82] Jesus' baptism models the obedient response to the Father which is fundamental to all later baptisms. For this reason, believer's baptism is the appropriate form since it is the first step in a life of obedient response to God.[83]

But Jesus' baptism not only illustrates his obedience to the Father; it also marks his ordination to public ministry. Baptism launched his history of a twofold ministry to God and humanity.[84] Baptism is teleological, leading to a life of obedience in the name of Jesus.[85] To be baptized is to live in obedient hope. It is "to be commissioned to declare the great acts of God."[86] As the believer takes his place in the "missionary church," as he "takes part in this mission, the Christian is on his way from his baptism into his further future."[87] Barth sums up by pointing readers to Isa 42:6, stating that she who is baptized has become "an active member" among those called to serve as "a *mediator* of the covenant among the nations."[88]

Leithart's recent work provides further warrant for Barth's claim.[89] Leithart disagrees with Barth at a number of important points, but his overall thesis that baptism represents an ordination to priesthood resonates with Barth's theology of baptism.[90] For Barth, baptism leads to a liturgical life of prayer.[91] In the posthumously published fragments of Volume IV's ethics, we learn this liturgical life's threefold form. It begins in baptism, is lived in prayer (especially the Lord's Prayer), and renewed at the Lord's Supper.[92]

---

81. On the former see *CD* IV/4, 3–40, on the latter 41–213.

82. *CD* IV/4, 50–68.

83. *CD* IV/3.2, 517–18; *CD* IV/4, 102–52, 165–94.

84. *CD* IV/4, 60–61.

85. *CD* IV/4, 68–100.

86. *CD* IV/4, 199.

87. *CD* IV/4, 200.

88. *CD* IV/4, 201. Emphasis added.

89. Leithart, *Priesthood of the Plebs*, 21–24. Stout's linking of infant baptism with Constantinianism raises a significant issue for Leithart (*A Fellowship of Baptism*, 116–46).

90. For example, Leithart argues for a nuanced type of baptismal regeneration (*Priesthood of the Plebs*, 165–74). For Leithart, the primary vocation of the royal priesthood is to serve in Yahweh's house as temple servants (48–86), and stress on witness is largely absent.

91. *CD* IV/4, 209.

92. For Barth, the entirety of Christian life consists of divine service. Complete devotion to divine service is an ideal of priesthood (Exod 28:35–36, Rom 12:1–2, etc.). See *CL*.

Thus, like the baptism of Jesus, the believer's baptism is an ordination to priestly ministry. More specifically, for Barth, the priestly ordination received at baptism is ordination to the ministry of witness.[93]

Witness: Every Member of the Royal Priesthood is a Missionary

The passages surveyed above argue that all believers have an active role to play within the royal priesthood; most also emphasized the missionary nature of the doctrine. Royal priests are those whose vocation is to mediate the light of Christ to those in darkness.[94] In the "event of vocation" the believer has received illumination, and this light has created a missional member of the royal priesthood.[95] The vocation of missional ministry or witness is shared equally by all the κλητός. "It is not that some of them who are specially endowed or commissioned for special service in the community are given this latter title, but all of them without difference or exception."[96] Flett has convincingly demonstrated this basic principle of Barth's Christological ecclesiology: God is a missionary God, and the church must reflect this essential truth by itself becoming a missionary community.[97]

John Webster makes an important qualification here. While baptism represents a believer's ordination to a priestly ministry of witness in the world, this ministry does not replace Christ's "perfect" and "complete" ministry as the Mediator.[98] Christ himself is directly active in the world through the Holy Spirit, and he has not "resigned his office and transferred it to the missionary community."[99] If Christ himself is active in the world as mediator, what place is left for the missionary ministry of the royal priesthood? Webster raises the question, but Paul Nimmo provides a solution via the *concursus Dei*.[100] The *concursus Dei* is Barth's explanation for how God's Lordship in a given activity does not negate human freedom in that activity.

---

93. CD IV/4, 201, 211. See Stout's final chapter, 'Baptism and the Witnessing Community'; it could be strengthened by interaction with the *concursus Dei* (*A Fellowship of Baptism*, 147–81).

94. Barth engages in a mini-theology of light-bearing in his doctrine of creation (CD III/1, 220, cf. 227). He cites 1 Pet 2:9 to show that light-bearing is a central concern of the royal priesthood, who share the apostolic privlidge of bearing the light.

95. *CD*, IV 3.2, 510.

96. *CD*, IV 3.2, 525.

97. Flett, *Witness of God*. See my review of Flett in *TJ*.

98. Webster, "'Eloquent and Radiant,'" 148.

99. Ibid.

100. Nimmo, *Being in Action*, 118–35.

Nimmo uses believer's baptism as an illustrative case study, but the doctrine applies equally to the life of priestly witness commenced at baptism.[101] Keith Johnson summarizes well the implications of the *concursus Dei* for the missional witness of the royal priesthood. For Barth, "human action in the church counts. It does not count for our own benefit, however; it counts for the benefit of those who have yet to hear."[102] Baptism is not about my own salvation; it is about my public commissioning to carry the light to others.

To sum up, Barth's Christological ecclesiology is a missionary ecclesiology, and his doctrine of the royal priesthood is thus both Christological and missionary. It especially emphasizes election, baptism, and witness. Barth's pleas for a missionary version of the royal priesthood did not fall on deaf ears. As the first great post-Christendom theologian, Barth's theology represents a paradigm shift in the relation of the church to the world and thus a new perspective on the priesthood of all believers. He significantly widens the doctrine's scope from Reformation versions to include a missionary vocation of witness.

Lesslie Newbigin and a Missionary Priesthood of All Believers

One who took Barth's Trinitarian, Christological and missionary emphases seriously was Bishop Lesslie Newbigin. Newbigin was a missionary in India for forty years where he served as a church planter, Bishop of Madras overseeing one thousand churches, and an ecumenical leader. After he "retired" to England, he served as a college professor, inner-city pastor, author, and speaker. This section reviews Newbigin's relationship to Barth, then examines Newbigin's missional version of the priesthood of all believers, and finally explores a few contemporary examples of a missional view of the royal priesthood.

Newbigin, Barth, and Missionary Ecclesiology

Geoffrey Wainwright characterized Newbigin as comparable to the "Fathers of the Church."[103] Newbigin's agenda during the final quarter of his life (1974–98) can be summarized as an attempt to see the West repent of its advanced state of syncretism and be reconverted to the gospel of

---

101. Nimmo, *Being in Action*, 126–30.
102. Johnson, "Being and Act of the Church," 226.
103. Wainwright, *Lesslie Newbigin*, v.

Jesus Christ. This agenda was informed by Barth's missional view of the royal priesthood and its vocation of witness. Newbigin was exposed to Barth during his theological studies through one of his mentors, Archie Craig (1933–36), although he found Barth's commentary on Romans a bit "incomprehensible."[104] He first met Barth in 1948, but did not get to spend extended time with him until 1951, when both participated in a week-long gathering of theologians commissioned by the WCC Central Committee to prepare a study paper on the topic, "Christ the Hope of the World." Newbigin and Barth worked closely together in one of the drafting groups, and a clue to their shared view of the missional nature of the royal priesthood can be found in Newbigin's description of what happened when he presented his paper on "the Apostolate of the Church" to the twenty-five theologians present. The paper "was strongly attacked from all quarters and I was almost sunk until Barth came to my rescue with all guns firing."[105]

We no longer have access to Newbigin's 1951 study commission paper, but we do have a good idea of the kinds of things it might have said from two documents written the following year. In 1952, Newbigin drafted the final statement of the theological commission of the International Missionary Commission gathered in Willingen, Germany. The Willingen conference was an event of historic importance for a number of reasons: 1) it placed ecclesial mission within a trinitarian framework for the first time; 2) it placed the missionary calling of the church as an item of central dogmatic importance; 3) it introduced the language of *missio Dei* into missiological and theological discourse.[106] The redeemed are to be "committed to full participation" in Christ's mission.[107]

At Willingen, Newbigin clearly states that the church is a missionary church because it participates in the mission of Christ. In a second document from 1952, "The Christian Layman in the World and in the Church," Newbigin begins with 1 Pet 2:9, and the identity of the laity as members of the royal priesthood. He argues that the church needs to practically rediscover Christ's body as "witnesses and soldiers in the secular world" in order

---

104. Newbigin, *Unfinished Agenda*, 19–20, 29.

105. Ibid., 124. Newbigin is being characteristically self-deprecating when he goes on to say, "—not I think, because he agreed, but because everyone else was against me!"

106. Flett describes Willingen as a "Copernican turn for mission theology"; despite its problems, it was the closest the ecumenical community has come to "a complete definition of *missio Dei*" (*Witness of God*, 157, 61; cf. 150–61). Flett overstates the facts when he writes, "Newbigin, as the drafter of the Willingen statement, had no experience with Barth's work" (161). On Barth's influence on Newbigin, note Goheen, *Newbigin's Missionary Ecclesiology*, 14n1.

107. See chapter epigraph (Goodall, *Missions Under the Cross*, 190).

that "divine service" can become "the true centre and interpretation of all daily work."[108]

Newbigin continued to develop these themes of the missionary nature of the royal priesthood and the local congregation. After his "retirement" in 1974, Newbigin "became deeply indebted to the mature Barth of the *Church Dogmatics*."[109] Whatever Newbigin's exact relationship to Barth before retiring at age sixty-five, there can be little doubt that afterward he found deep resonance with Barth's emphasis on the missionary responsibilities of believers.[110] After reading Barth's dogmatics, Newbigin wrote fifteen books and over one hundred and sixty shorter pieces. The missionary nature of the priesthood of all believers is often a theme, explored further below.

Newbigin's "Priesthood in the World"

Michael Goheen has conducted the most extensive study of Newbigin's ecclesiology, demonstrating that it passes through two developmental stages. Newbigin's first major shift was from a Christendom to a missionary ecclesiology (1909–59); his second major shift was from a Christocentric to a trinitarian-missionary ecclesiology (1959–98).[111] Goheen helpfully describes Newbigin's mature position as "Christocentric-Trinitarian" in contrast to the "Cosmocentric-Trinitarian" viewpoint championed by theologians such as Hans Hoekendijk.[112] Newbigin's priesthood of all believers must be understood within the context of his Christocentric-Trinitarian and missionary ecclesiology. In the next chapter, we return to the Christocentric-Trinitarian nature of Newbigin's priesthood of all believers; here we focus on its missionary nature.

In contrast with the upward (access to God) and inward (priests-to-one-another) emphases of Luther's doctrine, Newbigin's royal priesthood is almost entirely focused on the world. His discussions take place in the context of the believer's responsibility to witness in the world. He describes how one evening in 1957 he "spent the entire night on the plane from Bombay to Rome reading right through the New Testament and noting every reference to 'the world.'"[113] This set his mind thinking in a new direction and he began to emphasize that, within Christendom, the "priestly ministry of the

---

108. Newbigin, "Christian Layman," 188, 189.
109. Wainwright, *Newbigin*, 31.
110. Newbigin did not uncritically endorse Barth (e.g., *Household of God*, 50).
111. Goheen, *Newbigin's Missionary Ecclesiology*, 12–59; 60–114.
112. Ibid., 116–21; Newbigin, *Unfinished Agenda*, 130, 144.
113. Newbigin, *Unfinished Agenda*, 144.

whole body on behalf of the world has been tragically lost."[114] Practically, this meant that Newbigin began to place strong emphasis on the church's responsibility to equip believers for their priestly ministry in the world. Goheen correctly notes that this missional calling of believers in the world "is a stress in Newbigin's work that has been neglected, even eclipsed, in the writings of many in North America."[115]

In what may be his most important book, *The Gospel in a Pluralistic Society*, Newbigin describes six marks of a gospel-centered congregation. The fourth mark is "a community where men and women are prepared for and sustained in *the exercise of the priesthood in the world.*"[116] Newbigin is explicit about the nature of this priesthood:

> I hope I have made clear my belief that it is the whole Church which is called to be—in Christ—a royal priesthood, that every member of the body is called to the exercise of this priesthood, and that *this priesthood is to be exercised in the daily life and work of Christians in the secular business of the world.*[117]

> The office of a priest is to stand before God on behalf of people and to stand before people on behalf of God. . . . The church gathers every Sunday, the day of the resurrection and of Pentecost, to renew its participation in Christ's priesthood. But *the exercise of this priesthood is not within the walls of the Church but in the daily business of the world.*[118]

In a series of eleven articles he called "his closest approach to a dogmatics," Newbigin wrote the final article on 1 Pet 2:5–9 and the mission of the royal priesthood in the world.[119] There he made a similar claim:

> This *priesthood of all believers is exercised in the working days of the week*. On the Lord's Day we gather to renew our membership in the body of Christ, the one great High Priest. Those who are called to leadership in our gathering, though in our tradition we do not call them priests, *are called to help us in renewing our priesthood.*[120]

---

114. Newbigin, "Ministry and Laity," 480.

115. Goheen, "Missional Calling," 40. Goheen does not follow Newbigin in relating the believer's missional calling to the priesthood of all believers.

116. Newbigin, *Gospel in a Pluralistic Society*, 229; emphasis added.

117. Ibid., 35; emphasis added.

118. Ibid., 230; emphasis added.

119. Goheen, *Newbigin's Missionary Ecclesiology*, 458–59.

120. Newbigin, "X-Ray to Make God Visible," 7; emphasis added. Similarly, see *Catechism of the Catholic Church*, 386, §1547.

The strong emphasis on ministry to the world in Newbigin's doctrine is distinct from "Constantinian" versions. Newbigin's recognition of the *diatasias* between church and world equips him to emphasize the believer's priestly responsibility to mediate God's light to the world.

Two additional comments need to be made. First, the believer's priestly and missional responsibility to the world is not limited to humanity (Rom 8:18–25; Mark 16:15). Newbigin believed that the church also had a priestly ministry to all of creation.

> In other words, our calling, if you like to put it so, is to be the priests of nature, priests in the double sense of priesthood—to represent God to the creation and to represent the creation to God. We are to be the agency through which God fulfills his purpose for creation (which let us again say is not to be an untamed wilderness), the agents through whom God is to fulfill His purpose for creation, but also the agents through whom the creation is to offer up its glory to the Creator in its beauty and riches.[121]

Newbigin's reflections on ecological dimensions of the royal priesthood's ministry recall humanity's original creation mandate in Eden. They also provide interesting opportunities for dialogue with more recent discussions on creation care.[122]

Secondly, while Newbigin's insight on the ecological dimension represents an expansion and more holistic understanding of the missional component of the doctrine, he also displays some reductionist tendencies. Newbigin's doctrine overemphasizes the missional dimension to the neglect of other components. He is not ignorant of a believer's priestly access to God, and the importance of daily exercise of priestly offerings.[123] He also endorses Yves Congar and Hendrik Kraemer's emphasis on the responsibility of all God's people to do priestly ministry.[124]

However, when Newbigin speaks of the priesthood of all believers, he limits its exercise within the assembly to officers.[125] This represents an un-

---

121. Newbigin, *Come Holy Spirit*, 6.

122. Wright, *Mission of God*, 415; Bordeianu, "Priesthood Natural, Universal, and Ordained," 405–33.

123. "If we are to be in truth a holy priesthood, we need a secret altar, a place in our innermost life where, day by day, we offer to God through Jesus Christ every bit of our lives, our most secret thoughts and our most public actions, and where we receive afresh through Christ God's ever-new gift of grace and mercy" (Newbigin, "X-Ray to Make God Visible," 7).

124. Newbigin, "Ministry and Laity," 480.

125. "The exercise of this [lay] priesthood is not within the walls of the Church but

necessary conflation of office with *charisma*. Given that the Christendom church neglected the missional dimension for over a thousand years, it could be that Newbigin overemphasizes witness in order to restore a more balanced version.[126] In sum, Newbigin embraces Barth's emphasis on the missionary nature of the church, and the result is one of the first articulations of the missionary nature of the priesthood of all believers since Constantine.

The Missional Nature of the Priesthood of All Believers in Context

This chapter's discussion of the missional nature of Barth and Newbigin's doctrine is illustrative of a larger paradigm shift within ecclesiology as a whole. Barth and Newbigin, with their heavy involvement in the WCC, are representative of a major shift from a Christendom to missionary ecclesiology—a shift evident across the ecumenical spectrum. The IMC's 1952 endorsement of the missionary nature of the church at Willingen was followed by similar statements in Roman Catholic, evangelical, and mainline Protestant gatherings. In 1963-65 Vatican II embraced as central the idea that the "pilgrim church is of its very nature missionary."[127]

Similarly, the 1974 Lausanne Congress, which gathered 2,700 delegates from 150 nations, endorsed a missional ecclesiology close to Willingen's: "We affirm that Christ sends his redeemed people into the world as the Father sent him, and that this calls for a similar deep and costly penetration of the world."[128] John Stott, primary author of the Lausanne Covenant, would tirelessly argue that "the living God is a Missionary God."[129] Barth, Newbigin, and Stott have influenced a whole generation of evangelicals so that the slogan "a missionary church worships a missionary God" is "relatively common."[130] Many evangelicals find God's missionary nature revealed in his canonical story, and see God's people called to participate in God's mission.[131]

---

in the daily business of the world" (Newbigin, *Gospel in a Pluralistic Society*, 230).

126. Cf. Newbigin, "Lay Presidency at the Eucharist," 178. Newbigin is not always entirely consistent, yet he consistently demonstrates an unusual ability to accurately assess the big picture (Goheen, "Missional Calling," 42).

127. *Ad Gentes*, 2 (*DEC* 2:1011). See Bevans and Gros, *Evangelization and Religious Freedom*, 3-148.

128. Lausanne Covenant, 6; Stott, *MCN*, 28.

129. Stott, "Living God," 3-9. Originally a lecture given at the 1976 Urbana missions conference. Stott, *Christian Mission*, 22.

130. See Holmes, "Trinitarian Missiology," 72.

131. "World mission is thus the first and most obvious feature of early Christian

In North America, the 1998 monograph *Missional Church: A Vision for the Sending of the Church in North America*, represents a major milestone. It seems to be largely responsible for introducing the terms "missional" and *missio Dei* to a wider ecclesial audience.[132] Darrell Guder, the organizing editor, argues that one of the first resources to be mined for a missional ecclesiology is "Luther's vision of the priesthood of all believers."[133] A number of the contributors discuss the priesthood of all believers as foundational to a missional ecclesiology, but none give it extended reflection.[134] Missional church discussions of the royal priesthood assume it is a missionary doctrine, yet need further reflection on how it relates to more traditional versions, which emphasize the believer's priestly access to God and her responsibility to serve as a priest to other members of Christ's body.[135]

Chapter Summary: Barth and Newbigin's Call to Priestly Witness

Barth's emphasis on the missionary nature of the priesthood of all believers represents a paradigmatic shift. As the western church moves from Christendom to a post-Christendom setting, her holy egotism has been revealed. The need for fresh understanding of the priesthood of all believers has become evident. In this chapter, the focus has been on Karl Barth and Lesslie Newbigin, but other students of Barth could also have been discussed. Thomas Torrance built upon Barth's Christological ecclesiology to emphasize that the royal priesthood participates in Christ's ministry and that this ministry must lead to mission in the world (from *soma* to *pleroma*).[136] Similarly, John Howard Yoder's criticism of Christendom's deleterious effects on the witness of the church bears many resemblances to Barth's critiques; like Barth he also placed great emphasis on believers' ministry to one another through their union with Christ.[137]

Even though the chapter has been limited primarily to Barth and Newbigin, we have discovered an important insight: the royal priesthood

---

praxis" (Wright, *New Testament*, 362). See also Wright, *Mission of God*, 224–25, 239, 250–51, 255–57, 329–33, 369–75.

132. Guder, "Church as Missional Community," 114.

133. Ibid., 122.

134. Guder, *Missional Church*, 190–91, 195, 210, 212. See also discussions of 1 Pet 2:9 on 114, 117–19, 135–37, 248.

135. Cf. Muthiah, *Priesthood of All Believers*, 177.

136. Torrance, *Royal Priesthood*, 25; Colyer, *How to Read T. F. Torrance*, 272–82.

137. See Yoder, *Fullness of Christ*. Cf. Nikolajsen, "Distinctive Identity," 2010).

participates in Christ's vocation (John 20:21) through the power of the Spirit. Barth's Christological and missionary ecclesiology reveals that a dogmatic account of the priesthood of all believers: 1) must be closely related to a believer's sharing of Christ's election as the Priest-king; 2) is rooted in a theology which sees baptism as ordination to priestly ministry; 3) identifies a central vocation of the royal priesthood as witness to the world. Newbigin further developed this third aspect of Barth's doctrine: believers must be a "priesthood in the world." The missionary nature of the royal priesthood has found affirmation in Orthodox, Roman Catholic, Evangelical, and mainline Protestant discussions. Yet there remains a need for a systematic explanation of how the members of this royal priesthood relate to God, the world, and each other. The following two chapters make a systematic proposal for these three relationships and proposes seven practices for the royal priesthood.

Part III

The Royal Priesthood in Today's World

7
The Priesthood of All Believers in Trinitarian Perspective

> Our first task, therefore, must be to consider how to teach trinitarian religion, how to initiate our congregations into the trinitarian way of life.... It is better that we should enrich our spiritual life by exploring to the full the possibilities of our threefold relationship to Him than that for fear of Tritheism we should impoverish it and never enter fully into the heritage of our Christian revelation.
>
> —Leonard Hodgson[1]

> The goal of all Christian watchfulness and all Christian progress is a pious and sober understanding of the Trinity.
>
> —Augustine, *De libero arbitrio* 3.21.60

THE CHURCH BELONGS TO God (ἐκκλησία θεοῦ).[2] It is God who makes the church distinctive from all other human assemblies. The citizens of the Greek city were called to assemble by the town clerk; the citizens of the divine city are called to assemble by God. But the God who calls the church is not the God of Greek philosophy or the Muslim Qur'an. This point should not be taken for granted. The modern western theological tradition is far more influenced by these two streams than is often recognized.[3] This chap-

---

1. Hodgson, *Doctrine of the Trinity*, 177, 180.
2. 1 Tim 3:15; Acts 20:28; 1 Cor 1:2; cf. 1 Cor 11:16.
3. Newbigin, *Open Secret*, 28.

ter wrestles with the question, "What difference does it make that the royal priesthood serves the triune God revealed by Jesus?"

To explore this question further, we begin with the assumption that the God served by a "priesthood of all believers" will determine the nature and functions of that priesthood. Perspective can thus be gained by carefully considering the nature of the God worshipped in Nicene communities. For example, there are many versions of the "priesthood of all believers," including examples from non-orthodox Christian traditions. Islam has a version of the "priesthood of all believers," but its God is a supreme monad, not a triune deity.[4] Another tradition, The Church of Jesus Christ of Latter Day Saints, places greater emphasis on "the priesthood of all believers" than most Nicene branches of Christianity; all of its adult members wear white priestly undergarments purchased from regional temples. But because its concept of God is different, its royal priesthood differs significantly from a Nicene version.[5]

A systematic definition seeking to be faithful to the God revealed in the Christian Scriptures must take seriously the creedal confession that God is triune. Just as the Gospels' authors could only answer the question, "Who is Jesus?" by making reference to the Father who sent him and the Spirit who empowered him (Mark 1:1–12), so a trinitarian framework is necessary to adequately answer the question, "What is the Christian doctrine of the priesthood of all believers?"[6]

This chapter proposes an explicitly trinitarian account. The first section moves beyond Luther's Christocentric-only doctrine to a Christocentric-Trinitarian version, especially emphasizing the *missio Dei*. The chapter's second section describes how it is possible for members of the royal priesthood to relate in especially appropriate ways to the Father (*latreia*), the Son (*diakonia*), and the Holy Spirit (*martyria*). Since not only Muslims and Mormons have proposed alternative doctrines of the priesthood of all

---

4. Loimeier does not emphasize the theological aspects of Islam's "priesthood of all believers" but does summarize sociological evidence for forms of Islam displaying characteristics similar to Luther's doctrine ("Is There Something," 216–54). Cf. Eastwood, *Royal Priesthood*, 109–20.

5. Mormonism's sophisticated doctrine is based on Levitical and Melchizedekian typology. One way its doctrine of God affects its priesthood of all believers is that priesthood is limited to teenage and adult males. Women only experience priesthood through their fathers, husbands, sons, and other male relatives. "While the sisters do not hold the priesthood, they share in the fullness of its blessings in the celestial kingdom with their husbands" (Joseph Smith, *Doctrines of Salvation*, 3:132; Davies, *Introduction to Mormonism*, 175).

6. Newbigin, *Open Secret*, 28.

believers, the chapter's final section addresses three inadequate Protestant forms.

Christocentric-Only or Christocentric-Trinitarian?

For Luther, the Melchizedekian priesthood of Christ, found in Ps 110:4, "is a treasure, the source of all Christian doctrine, understanding, wisdom, and comfort."[7] Luther was correct to identify the Melchizedekian priesthood of Christ as the starting point for the priesthood of all believers. No other entry point compares for a Christian understanding of the doctrine. Baptized believers have priestly access to the Father in the Holy of Holies through their soul's union with the Priest-king by the Spirit. As Luther argued, this application of Christ's priesthood results in a priestly ministry for all believers.

But in light of the renewed interest in trinitarian doctrine during the last fifty years, it is now necessary to critique Luther's version as reductionist—its Christocentricity is insufficiently trinitarian.[8] The recent retrieval of trinitarian theology paves the way for a deeper understanding of the priesthood of all believers. Fred Sanders writes, "Progress has been made in trinitarian theology in our time. . . . the advance is real, and the doctrine of the Trinity is so important that even a modest clarification in this field will be rewarded across the entire range of Christian theology."[9] The progress to which he refers is a deeper understanding of the Trinity through increased attention to the divine economy.[10]

In critiquing Luther's doctrine, I am not suggesting that his Christocentricity was wrong—more so that it did not go far enough. To be specific, Luther's doctrine is Christocentric-only in emphasis (cf. Ps 110).[11] Luther correctly emphasizes the place of all believers *in Christ*, and thus as members of the royal priesthood. He identifies prayer as one of the royal

---

7. *LW* 13:323.

8. See also Barth's concerns about the "holy egoism" of Luther's theological descendants discussed in Chapter 6.

9. Sanders, *Image of the Immanent Trinity*, viii.

10. Ibid., 188–89.

11. Luther's doctrine does have a pneumatic dimension related to believers' use of the Spirit's gifts. See especially Luther's discussion of Ps 110:3 and 1 Pet 4:10 (*LW* 13: 294–95; 30:123–24). Snyder sees Calvin as especially responsible for the eclipse of the Spirit in the Reformed tradition and Hinlicky places the blame for Lutheranism's "binitarian" trends on Melanchthon (Snyder, *Community of the King*, 113; Hinlicky, *Paths Not Taken*, 127–28, 170–76).

priesthood's three central functions, and thus consistently emphasizes that one of the privileges is access to the Father through the Son. Yet, as seen in Chapter 5, a weakness of Luther's doctrine was its failure to emphasize the responsibility of believers to bear witness in the world. When viewed within a trinitarian framework, this weakness can be aligned with the inadequate attention given to the Spirit's role in leading the royal priesthood to witness in the world.[12]

In proposing a shift from Luther's Christocentric-only doctrine to a Christocentric-trinitarian version, it is important to keep in mind Sanders' trinitarian axiom: "*The more Trinity-centered we become, the more Christ centered we become, and vice-versa.*"[13] The recent history of the ecumenical movement reminds us that a call to be "more trinitarian" can lead to neglecting Christ's centrality with a concurrent rejection of the church's centrality as sign and foretaste of the kingdom in the world.[14] In order to move beyond Luther's Christocentric-only version of the priesthood of all believers, much can be learned from Lesslie Newbigin's Christocentric-Trinitarian ecclesiology.[15] Newbigin's ecclesiology provides the foundation for the Christocentric-Trinitarian doctrine proposed in this chapter.

Lesslie Newbigin's Shift to a Christocentric-Trinitarian Ecclesiology

In suggesting that the priesthood of all believers must become more attuned to the trinitarian economy, I am following a similar shift made by Lesslie Newbigin. Newbigin was heavily involved in ecumenical discussions about the *missio Dei*. Through those discussions, he realized that his ecclesiology was insufficiently trinitarian.[16] Goheen documents this shift relating the

---

12. Luther's quenching of the pneumatological emphasis is especially associated with the events of 1524–25, including his opposition to the "enthusiasts" (*Schwärmer*), the birth of the Anabaptists, and the Peasants' revolt. Luther's later "Christocentric-only" emphasis became a norm in Lutheranism.

13. Sanders, *The Deep Things of God*, 168; emphasis added.

14. Illustrated by Hoekendijk, *Church Inside Out*; and Raiser, *Ecumenism in Transition*. See Newbigin's review of the WCC General Secretary's agenda in "Ecumenical Amnesia," 2–5; and Raiser's reply, "Is Ecumenical Apologetics Sufficient?" 50–51.

15. I owe the term "Christocentric-Trinitarian" to Michael Goheen's nuanced description of Newbigin's ecclesiology, which developed as an alternative to Hoekendijk and Raiser's "cosmoscentric-Trinitarian" ecclesiology (*Lesslie Newbigin's Missionary Ecclesiology*, 64n1; 160).

16. Newbigin, "Ecumenical Amnesia," 2.

Holy Spirit and mission.[17] He identifies three stages in Newbigin's understanding. In the first stage, the Holy Spirit has no connection to the mission of the church, simply bringing benefits to believers. This was Newbigin's position before missionary work woke him to the holy egotism that characterizes this line of thinking. In the second stage, Newbigin recognized that the Spirit equips the church for mission, but mission remained primarily a human-centered activity of the church. In his final and most mature stage, Newbigin recognized that mission is God's work and thus the Spirit is the primary witness: "In sober truth the Spirit is himself the witness who goes before the church in its missionary journey. The church's witness is *secondary and derivative*. The church is witness insofar as it follows obediently where the Spirit leads."[18]

Newbigin's understanding of the Spirit at work in the world was an important component of his "priesthood in the world." How might this broader understanding of the trinitarian economy affect Luther's doctrine? With Luther, we agree that the royal priesthood shares in the mission of its Priest-king. We also affirm that participation in this Melchizedekian mission means that the royal priesthood must be in constant communion with the Father. The lives of royal priests are to be characterized by communion with their heavenly *Abba* as they approach his throne in prayer through the mediation of Christ in the Spirit (Rom 8:15, 29, 34). Beyond Luther, however, we suggest that the royal priesthood is continually being led by the Spirit to bear witness in the world (Mark 1:12)—to proclaim the excellencies of the one who called them out of darkness and into the light (1 Pet 2:9). It was especially the work of the Spirit which was truncated in scholastic Lutheranism. As a result, the royal priesthood's participation in the Spirit's witness to the world was not emphasized in most Protestant versions. What might a more pneumatically sensitive doctrine look like?

The Royal Priesthood and the Triune missio Dei

A Christocentric-Trinitarian priesthood of all believers continues to understand its vocation to participate in the *missio Dei* through the lens of the Priest-king. The royal priesthood understands itself to be sent by the Father to participate in the mission of the Son by the power of the Holy Spirit (Figure 3). As the royal priesthood relates to the Father, they join in the Son's prayer and praises (Worship). As the royal priesthood relates to itself (those "in Christ"), they embrace the Son's identity as a Servant (Work of service).

17. Goheen, *Lesslie Newbigin's Missionary Ecclesiology*, 155.
18. Newbigin, *Open Secret*, 61; emphasis added.

As the royal priesthood relates to the Spirit, they humbly follow his lead into the world proclaiming the Son (Witness).

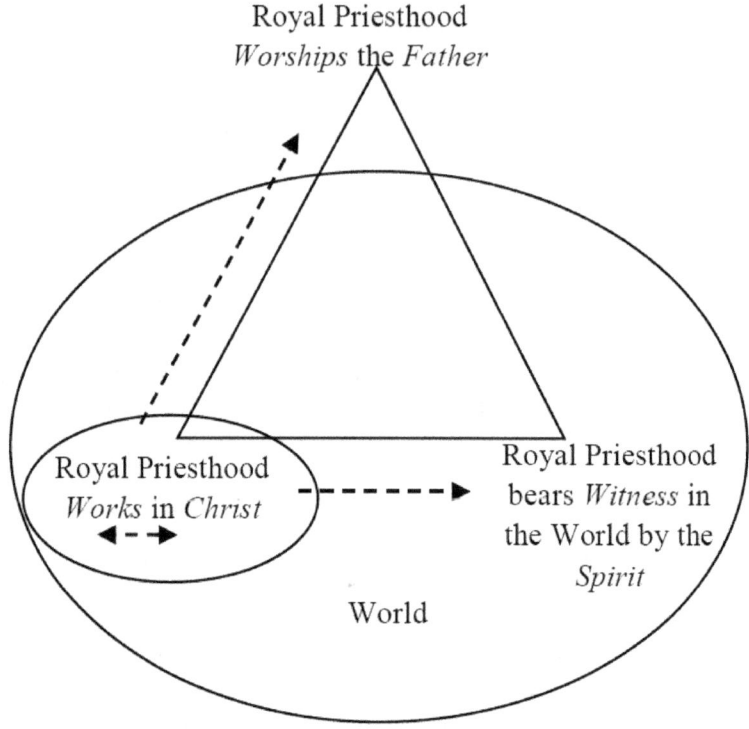

Figure 3: The Royal Priesthood in Trinitarian Perspective

Any portrayal of the Trinity, the royal priesthood, and the world will have its limitations. For example, Figure 3 above fails to illustrate the significance of Christ's ascension and coming Parousia; in actuality, the Son is now in heaven and the royal priesthood is "in him" only through the Spirit. It also fails to show that the cosmos is replete with the Spirit; there is no corner where he is not present (Acts 17:28; Psalm 139).[19] Yet Figure 3 helps us think about the mission of God in relation to Godself, God's people and God's world. The royal priesthood participates in God's mission in the world "in a secondary, derivative, but nonetheless real sense."[20] Exploring the dynamics

19. Blocher, "Immanence and Transcendence," 110; Hodge, *Systematic Theology*, 1:383.

20. Newbigin, *Open Secret*, 53.

of the royal priesthood's relationship to the Father, Son, and Holy Spirit is the focus of the next section.

Responding to the Triune God

How can the priesthood of all believers be shaped by a Christological-Trinitarianism? More broadly, is it possible and desirable for recent trinitarian insights to norm ecclesial concepts?[21] This section suggests that the doctrine of appropriation provides a way by which ecclesial responses to the triune God can be normed.[22] It suggests that the concept of appropriation, not *perichoresis*,[23] is needed to bridge the gap between ecclesiology and trinitarian theology, thereby opening the door to a Christological-Trinitarian doctrine of the priesthood of all believers.

More specifically, this section explores the question: "What is appropriate trinitarian appropriation, and what significance does the concept have for ordering the ecclesial economy?" Or stated differently, "How do royal priests ministering in God's house (the eschatological temple) appropriately respond to their triune God and his mission in the world?"[24] We begin with a definition:

> Appropriation is a way of speaking about God in which an attribute, action, or effect of an action is assigned to a particular divine person. This appropriation is founded on the distinctive *properties* of each person and its explicit goal is to better manifest the divine persons to the mind of believers.[25]

As Augustine noted, trinitarian investigations are not to be taken lightly: "Nowhere else is the error more dangerous, the search more laborious,

---

21. Gunton claims that from a historical perspective, for the most part, "the conception of God as a triune community made no substantive contribution to the doctrine of the Church" ("Community," 61).

22. From the Latin *ad* and *proprium*, "toward the proper." Barth calls it both a "concept" and a "doctrine" (*CD* I.1, 373).

23. In contrast to Volf ("Trinity and the Church," 153–74) and Muthiah's application of Volf to the royal priesthood (*Priesthood of All Believers*, 47–68).

24. 1 Pet 2:9; Rev 1:6; Rom 12:1. "Since the church is the new temple of the Spirit (1 Cor 6:19), and since baptism inducts into ministry in the body (1 Cor 12:12–31), baptism ordains housekeepers" (Leithart, *Priesthood of the Plebs*, 93).

25. By "properties" I refer to the triune relations of origin, namely: 1) paternity, innascibility or "not begotten"; 2) filiation, begotten; 3) procession. My definition of appropriation is adapted from: Emery, *Trinity*, 165–66; Barth, *CD I.1*, 373–74; Aquinas, *ST* 1.39.7.

and the results more rewarding."²⁶ Conscious of the dangers, this exploration of trinitarian theology pursues Augustine's promised reward in three steps. First, the doctrine of appropriation is introduced. Second, the central thesis is presented: just as it is appropriate to associate particular works (creation, redemption, sanctification) with particular persons of the Trinity (Father, Son, Spirit), so it is appropriate to speak of a particular response by the royal priesthood to the divine person (or "mode of being") associated with that work.²⁷ Finally, the thesis is tested by showing how prayer and spiritual sacrifices are an especially appropriate response by members of the royal priesthood to God the Father (Worship); how service to *one another* is an especially appropriate response to the Son (Work); and how Witness is an especially appropriate response to the Holy Spirit.

The Use of Appropriation in Christian Theology

Although the concept of appropriation as a doctrinal tool can be traced to Hilary of Poitiers (d. 367), it is not commonly used in contemporary discussions of the triune God.²⁸ Many recent monographs do not mention appropriation, nor is it discussed in the majority of systematic theologies.²⁹ In contrast, appropriation was a vital tool for Barth's trinitarian reflection. It provided an important "guarantee of the unity of God which would be endangered" if we were not "guided by this apparently—but only apparently—very speculative intratrinitarian insight."³⁰ Barth's attempts to embrace a trinitarian understanding of God were made with two doctrinal arms: his right arm was the doctrine of appropriation and his left was *perichoresis*.³¹ The latter has received extended discussion in recent trinitarian discourse, the former very little.

Appropriation finds biblical warrant in a number of NT texts. Hilary of Poitiers uses appropriation when reflecting on the significance of the

---

26. Augustine, *Trinity* 1.3.5 (FC 45:8).

27. See discussion of John Owen and Leonard Hodgson below.

28. Exceptions include: Blocher, "Immanence and Transcendence," 121–23; Emery, *Trinity*, 161–75; Vanhoozer, "Triune Discourse," 58–63.

29. Bavinck is an exception (Bavinck, *Reformed Dogmatics*, 318).

30. Barth, *CD* I.1, 395.

31. Barth saw both as necessary for understanding triunity (ibid., 375). *Perichoresis* (Latin *circumincessio*) is the divine dance whereby the three triune persons mutually indwell one another in a reciprocal manner. The concept is first discussed at length by John of Damascus (d. 749) in *The Orthodox Faith* 8 (FC 37:186–87), although originally coined for fifth-century Christological conversations. Cf. Volf, *After Our Likeness*, 208–13.

triune name with which we are commanded to baptize (Matt 28:19–20).[32] Basil's discussion of spiritual gifts leads him into trinitarian appropriation (1 Cor 12:11); the Father is the source of the gift, the Son the sender of the gift, and the Spirit the messenger who brings the gift.[33] Aquinas and Barth both cite 1 Cor 1:24 as an example of biblical appropriation, where the "wisdom" of God is attributed to Jesus.[34] Luther made use of appropriation to explain the threefold divine blessing proclaimed by the Aaronic priesthood (Num 6:24–26).[35] The very names Father, Son, and Holy Spirit, often associated with particular attributes and actions, lead to reflection on how each can refer to a single God;[36] so also do the divine actions on Good Friday, Easter, and Pentecost.[37]

Thomas Aquinas gives what Barth calls the "clearest and most complete definition:"[38]

> To appropriate is nothing else, than to apply that which is common to one in particular . . . not . . . because it is the case that it belongs more to one person than to another . . . but because that which is common has a greater likeness to that which is proper to one person than to what is proper to another.[39]

In the patristic and medieval church (e.g., Hilary, Augustine, Aquinas), appropriation seems to have primarily been used to explain how essential divine attributes could be attributed to a particular person of the Trinity.[40] Beginning with Hugh of St. Victor (d. 1141), however, we find a new use of appropriation relating not only to divine attributes, but also to the divine economy.[41] Hugh suggested that each of the divine persons could be as-

32. Hilary of Poitiers, *Trinity* 2.1 (FC 25:35).

33. Basil the Great, *On the Holy Spirit* 16.35 (PP 42:61).

34. Other biblical texts discussed with reference to appropriation include John 14:6 (Aquinas); Rom 11:36 (Chemnitz) 1 Cor 8:6 (Vanhoozer); and Eph 4:6 (Bavinck).

35. "Der Segen, so man nach der Messe spricht über das Volk, aus dem vierten Buche Mosi am 6. Capitel" (*WA* 30 III, 581–82). See discussion of this passage in MacDonald, "Trinitarian Palimpsest," 310.

36. See "whether appropriation of essential names to the persons is permissible" (Aquinas, *ST* 1.39.7).

37. Barth, *CD* I.1, 375.

38. Ibid., 373.

39. Aquinas, *De verit.* 7.3. Cited by Barth, *CD* I.1, 374.

40. Augustine writing about Hilary, "A certain writer, wishing to explain the proper *attributes* of each person of the Trinity as briefly as possible . . ." (*Trinity* 4.10 [FC 45:212]; emphasis mine). Aquinas writes, "Appropriation [*appropriatio*] means the making known of the divine persons by means of essential attributes" (*ST* 1.39.7).

41. Hilary is the first post-canonical theologian discussed by Aquinas to use

sociated with a particular work in salvation history; thus it was especially appropriate to associate creation with the Father, redemption with the Son, and sanctification with the Holy Spirit.

For centuries theologians have used appropriation and *perichoresis* in their pursuit of a deeper understanding of God's Triunity.[42] On the one hand, appropriation was developed in the West, and primarily refers to how the attributes and works of God relate to the economy of salvation. Its focus is on the work of God *ad extra*. *Perichoresis*, in contrast, was developed in the East and primarily refers to the way the three persons mutually indwell one another ontologically; the focus is on triune life *in se*. Both terms speak to the Triunity of God, *perichoresis* focusing more on ontology and appropriation more on either the divine economy or on how particular attributes are manifested in one of the divine persons. Since appropriation focuses especially on the triune economy, it provides a better foundation for ordering the ecclesial household than *perichoresis*.[43] In suggesting that it has relevance for the ordering of the royal priesthood we are consciously rejecting a dogmatic tradition (Kant and Schleiermacher) that deems the Trinity as largely irrelevant to the fellowship between the triune God and his people.[44]

Triune Appropriation and the Ordering of the Royal Priesthood

Paul's exhortation to "be imitators of God" (Eph 5:1) provides broad biblical incentive for exploring how the ecclesial household economy might relate to the trinitarian God served by the royal priesthood.[45] Why might appropriation provide a better starting place than *perichoresis* for ordering the royal priesthood's service in God's house? In recent years, where trinitarian reflection has informed ecclesiology, it has usually centered on the concept of *perichoresis*. Miroslav Volf is a well-known example. He is aware that "hu-

---

appropriation (*ST* 1.39.8); Augustine uses the Latin term (*congruenter*) in passing (*The Trinity* 2.5.9). The technical term *appropriation* was coined by Hugh of St. Victor (Vanhoozer, "Triune Discourse," 60; cf. Emery, *The Trinity*, 165).

42. "Triunity" is Barth's term for the combination of "unity in trinity and trinity in unity" (*CD I.1*, 368).

43. The move to appropriation helps address concerns raised by John Flett, Kathryn Tanner and Bruce Marshall below.

44. Schleiermacher, *Christian Faith*, 741; Kant, *Religion and Rational Theology*, 264.

45. Cf. Eph 4:24. For incipit trinitarianism in Ephesians, see Letham, *Holy Trinity*, 73–85; Volf, "Trinity is Our Social Program," 404.

man beings have no perfect equivalent to the interpenetration of the divine persons," but "the perichoresis of divine persons *does* possess inter-ecclesial relevance."[46] Similarly, for Colin Gunton, speaking about the being of the church "necessitates a move from the economic to the immanent trinity."[47] Yet the argument that the divine ontology implied by *perichoresis* is normative for ecclesiology faces significant challenges.

Appropriation helps us see that the economic Trinity is epistemologically prior to the ontological Trinity. According to Flett, the central problem with Volf and Gunton's use of *perichoresis* is that "an absolute account of [God's] being occurs without reference to his economy."[48] Kathryn Tanner states a similar concern about attempts to model our ecclesial life on the immanent Trinity without adequate attention to the economy.[49] She argues that the "basic insight" of the economic Trinity lies in its showing us how the Trinity relates to human life. For Tanner, it is from the economy, especially as revealed in Jesus Christ, that we learn the appropriate way in which the people of God are to relate to the triune God. Once having recognized the importance of the economy, we also discover that "Jesus' way of life . . . *is* the trinitarian form of human social relations."[50] From the economic Trinity we learn about appropriate relationships with Godself, one another, and the world.

Since the economy has been relatively slighted by those emphasizing *perichoresis* and Cappadocian ontology, cannot a better model for the life of the church be found in the concept of appropriation?[51] Like Volf and Gunton, we are not beginning with a "being anterior to that of the persons,"[52] but with Barth and the Augustinian tradition we are emphasizing the triune economy via appropriation instead of considering the being of God independently.[53] With the social trinitarians (and others) we are asking the more *personal* question, "How do the people of God relate differently to the triune God than they would to a monolithic God?" Rather than starting with imitation of divine *perichoresis*, we are seeking an appropriate response

---

46. Volf, "The Trinity and the Church," 165, 167; emphasis mine.
47. Gunton, "Community," 71.
48. Flett, *Witness of God*, 43.
49. Tanner, "Trinity," 328–31.
50. Ibid., 329; emphasis original.
51. Gunton provides examples of the "misuse of appropriation" in the work of Kenneth Kirk and Henri de Lubac. I agree with his concerns however, he makes no attempt to use the concept constructively (Gunton, "Community," 73).
52. Ibid., 74.
53. Cf. ibid.

from the royal priesthood based upon each person's distinctive role in the economy.[54]

Thus, just as it is appropriate to associate particular works with particular persons of the Trinity (Creation, Redemption, Sanctification), so it is appropriate to speak of a particular response by God's people to the divine person associated with each work. While not fully settled, Bruce Marshall indicates that the idea of a particular response to each person is becoming more widely accepted:

> Father, Son, and Spirit are irreducibly distinct personal agents in their interaction not only with one another, but with us. The divine actions of creation and salvation therefore establish a relationship with creatures unique to each of the divine persons.[55]

Stated more radically, *the Trinitarian economy norms the ecclesial economy.*

A number of theologians have pointed in a similar direction. John Owen (d. 1683), who was more influenced by eastern thought than many in the western tradition, was particularly concerned that saints exercise "distinct communion with each person of the Trinity."[56] At one point when summarizing the proper work of the saints, he notes, "There is no . . . duty or obedience performed, but they are distinctly directed unto Father, Son, and Spirit."[57] Owen's view of the royal priesthood's communion with the trinitarian persons is explicitly grounded in his understanding of appropriation.[58] Three hundred years later, a similar point was made by Leonard Hodgson (d. 1969). Hodgson taught that fundamental to trinitarian theology is a trinitarian way of life which he calls "trinitarian religion." It is marked by a continuous effort to grow in "*consciously* realizing our distinct relationship to each Person of the Blessed Trinity."[59] More recently, Ajith Fernando has provided another example of this line of thought.[60]

---

54. For a more detailed critique of Volf's proposal for ecclesial "perichoretic personhood" see Husbands, "Trinity Is Not Our Social Program," 124.

55. It is not clear that Marshall himself agrees with this statement, but he is stating a general consensus ("Trinity," 188). Cf. Emery, *Trinity,* 164–65.

56. Owen, *Communion with the Triune God,* 95. See further: Vanhoozer, "Triune Discourse," 60–61; Gunton, "Community," 75–77; Packer, "Puritan Perspective," 91–108.

57. Owen, *Communion,* 101.

58. Ibid., 105–06.

59. Hodgson, *Doctrine of the Trinity,* 179; emphasis added.

60. Fernando, "Grounding Our Reflections," 191–256.

We earlier identified the explicit goal of the doctrine of appropriation as "better manifesting the divine persons to the mind of believers." This manifestation demands a particular response from the royal priesthood. Just as appropriation may not be arbitrary, neither should be the ecclesial response. There is a grain in God—a direction in which all God's works flow.[61] For more than fifteen hundred years theologians have agreed with Athanasius that "the Father does all things through the Word in the Holy Spirit."[62] The responses of the royal priesthood to their triune God are most appropriate when they work with this grain.

At this point an example may be helpful. Consider the Trinity's act of adoption as presented by Thomas Aquinas. "Adoption, while it is common to the whole Trinity, is appropriated to the Father as its author; to the Son as its model [*examplari*], to the Holy Spirit as the person who imprints on us the likeness of this model."[63] The one effect of adoption is brought about by the single action of the whole Trinity but, as we reflect upon the Father as the source, the Son—the begotten—as the model of our adoption, and the Spirit as the applier or imprinter of the gift of adoption, we find that the eternal properties of each person are made manifest.[64] In this example, an ecclesial response to each of the persons must also be consistent with each person's properties. An appropriate response might be thanks to the Father as the source of the adoption, imitation of the Son as the model or exemplar of adoption, and openness or invitation to the Spirit as the one who imprints adoption upon believers.[65]

In sum, the manifestation of particular attributes and actions in particular divine persons leads the royal priesthood to especially associate particular human responses with each of the divine persons. Spatial restraints prevent thorough exploration of the full implications of this claim, but a pattern of appropriation is examined below (Creator, Servant, Witness) together with parallel responses from the royal priesthood (prayer, service, witness).

---

61. See the helpful discussion of this analogy in Sanders, *Deep Things of God*, 212–14.

62. Athanasius, *Letters to Serapion*, 1.28.3 (PP 43:97).

63. Aquinas, *ST* 3.23.2.3.

64. Emery's axiom proves correct, "As one is, so one acts" (*The Trinity*, 163). For a more extended discussion of appropriation and adoption, see 167–68.

65. The doctrine of the *concursis Dei* is helpful here. God forms us into the image of his Son, and we pursue maturity into the Son's likeness (Eph 4:13).

Praying to our Father in Heaven: Worship in the Temple

"We believe in one God, the Father Almighty, maker of heaven and earth . . ." (Nicene Creed). The church and her theologians have consistently used the doctrine of appropriation to attribute the work of creation to the Father Almighty. Barth explains:

> There is an affinity between the relation of the Father to the Son on the one hand and the relation of the Creator to the creature on the other. . . . In respect of this affinity it is not merely permitted but commanded that we ascribe creation as a *proprium* [thing proper] to the Father and that we regard God the Father *peculiariter* [particularly] and specifically as the Creator. . . . it would be just as improper to say that God the Father died as to say that Jesus of Nazareth or the Spirit of Pentecost created heaven and earth.[66]

Transcendence and omnipotence are attributes especially associated with the act of creation and thus can be appropriated to the Father.[67] "*Te aeternum Patrem omnis terra venerator*" (*Te Deum*).

What is the royal priesthood's appropriate response to the Father as the almighty, transcendent Creator? Two of Luther's three functions of the royal priesthood are relevant: prayer and the offering of spiritual sacrifices.[68] These two functions are an especially fitting response to the omnipotence and transcendence displayed by the Father as the source of creation.[69] This claim receives biblical warrant from Revelation's prologue, Jesus Christ has made believers "priests *to* his God and Father" through his blood.[70] According to Beale, the "*to*" indicates "clearly to whom our priestly service is directed."[71] Similarly, in 1 Pet 2:5 the royal priesthood is called "to offer spiritual sacrifices acceptable to God through Jesus Christ." In the context of 1 Peter, God is associated with the Father.[72] Thus the offering of spiritual sacrifices, like the offering of prayers and praise, is especially directed toward the Father.

---

66. Barth, *CD* I.1, 397.

67. Blocher's attribution of transcendence to the Father is especially related to his work as Creator ("Immanence and Transcendence," 122).

68. *LW* 30:55.

69. See Hodgson, *Doctrine of the Trinity*, 231.

70. Rev 1:6, emphasis added. See also John 4:20–24; Heb 13:15.

71. *Revelation*, 194. He identifies the "to" as a dative of reference. Later, the twenty-four elders proclaim that because the Lamb was slain, people from "every tribe and language and people and nation" have been made priests *to* God (Rev 5:9–10).

72. 1 Pet 1:2, 3, 21; 2:4; 3:18; 3:22; 4:11; 5:10.

The divine action (creation), attributes (omniscience, transcendence), and the ecclesial response (prayer, offering of spiritual sacrifices) are rooted in the same unique property (incommunicable characteristic) of the Father. The Father has the unique property of paternity and is the source of all things (Heb 2:10–11). He is not begotten like the Son; nor does he proceed like the Spirit (John 15:26). As the source of all, it is especially appropriate for him to receive prayer and praise. The dominical command and example also support this ecclesial claim. Jesus taught his disciples to direct their prayer to "our Father."[73] When the Gospels portray Jesus in prayer, he consistently addresses God as Father.[74] Paul too agrees; the Spirit leads the believer to cry, "Abba, Father" (Rom 8:15–17).

Both the Son and the Spirit are *autotheos*. We must not deny that prayer or sacrifices of thanksgiving can be offered to the Son and Spirit—the work of the triune God cannot be divided.[75] Yet the doctrine of appropriations leads us to conclude that prayer and the offering of spiritual sacrifices are an especially appropriate response to the Father as the almighty, transcendent Creator. Making this point requires pastoral responsibility, and Barth is helpful. Because there is a single triune subject acting in creation, it is "improper" to attribute creation to the Father. Similarly, it is "improper" to attribute prayer or the offering of spiritual sacrifices as the especially appropriate response of the royal priesthood to the Father, but as Barth notes:

> "Improper" here can only mean that it is not an exhaustive understanding, that it is one-sided, that it needs to be supplemented, that we cannot and should not adopt it exclusively, that we cannot and should not proclaim its exclusive validity.[76]

Appropriate appropriation leads the members of the royal priesthood to especially respond to the Father as Creator with prayer and the offering of spiritual sacrifices, but this response does not exclude the Son and Spirit

---

73. Matt 6:9; Luke 11:2. For distinction between the essential and personal dimensions of "Father" see Chemnitz, *Loci Theologici*, 76.

74. Jesus, as the incarnate Son, calls God his Father sixty-five times in the synoptic Gospels and over one hundred times in John. In eight places Scripture records words spoken by Jesus to the Father. Seven of his eight prayers begin with "Father" (Luke 10:21; John 11:41; 12:27–28; 17:1–26; Matt 26:39, 42 // Mark 14:36 // Luke 22:42; Luke 23:34; Matt 27:46 =Ps 22:1 [Jesus' only prayer without explicit reference to his Father]; and Luke 23:46).

75. In Rev 5:13 the Lamb also receives worship. Cf. Hodgson's observation that, "there is extant no instance of hymns or prayers to the Holy Spirit that is certainly earlier than the tenth century" (*Doctrine of the Trinity*, 231).

76. *CD* I.1, 395.

from these actions (1 Pet 2:5; Jude 20).⁷⁷ This work of prayer and the offering of spiritual sacrifices can be summarized as Worship or *latreia* (Rom 12:1).⁷⁸

Serving One Another in Christ: Work in the Temple

The divine economy especially appropriates service to the Son. In the Incarnation, the Son took on the form of a servant. Jesus is among his disciples as one who serves (Luke 22:27). He came to serve, not to be served (Mark 10:45). After performing the work of a servant, Jesus tells his disciples, "I have given you an example (ὑπόδειγμα), that you also should do just as I have done to you" (John 13:15). As was shown in Chapter Two, Jesus identified himself with the royal and priestly Servant of Isaiah 53. This Servant was promised an eschatological reward—a seed, the servants (*'ebedîm*), who would exercise his royal and priestly functions in the eschatological age and participate in his mission of bringing light to the Gentiles.⁷⁹

In light of the Son's suffering service (Phil 2:5–7), it is especially appropriate for his siblings to respond to his example with humble service (*diakonia*) toward one another (*allēlōn*).⁸⁰ Christ's body is the eschatological temple upon which the Holy Spirit has been poured out. Those who now serve in this temple are royal priests by virtue of their union with the Priest-king. Every member of this royal priesthood has a particular ministry of edification, directed toward other members of Christ's body (1 Pet 4:10). Ephesians 4:12 calls this their "work of service" (ἔργον διακονίας). When capitalized in this book, Work refers to this specialized sense of service within Christ's temple-body.⁸¹ As royal priests serve one another, especially the least of these (ἐλάχιστος, μικρός), they are serving Christ himself (Matt 25:40; 10:40–42).⁸² It is thus especially appropriate to associate the royal priesthood's ecclesial temple-service with the Son, the great Priest-king.

Following the Spirit:

---

77. See Sanders, *Deep Things of God*, 193–210; Redding, *Prayer and the Priesthood*, 281–99 193–210.

78. Torrance, *Royal Priesthood*, 10, 14–22.

79. See discussion of Phil 2:14–18 above, 54–55, 91–92.

80. Eph 4:12; 1 Cor 12:4–6; John 13:12–20; Heb 10:24; James 5:16; 1 Pet 4:9–10; 1 John 4:11–12.

81. On the term's wider significance see definition in Volf, *Work in the Spirit*, 10–14.

82. See Kupp, *Matthew's Emmanuel*, 196–98, 230–33.

Temple Witness in the World

Returning to the divine economy, we see that witness (*martyria*) can be appropriated to the Spirit. While it is true that both the Father and the Son bear witness (John 5:37; 18:37; Rev 1:5), after Jesus' glorification "the Spirit is the one who bears witness [μαρτυροῦν]" in the world (1 John 5:6 cf. John 7:39). In his farewell message, Jesus appropriated this work of ongoing witness to the Spirit: "But when the Helper comes, whom I will send to you from the Father, the Spirit of truth, who proceeds from the Father, he will bear witness about me. And you also will bear witness . . ." (John 15:26–27a). Witness is from the Father and about Christ. It is not an arbitrary appropriation for the Spirit; it is an eternal property. From before to beyond time, the Spirit bears witness to the love between Father and Son.

The Spirit bears the Father's witness to the Son in the church and world. Vanhoozer provides an illustration of the Spirit witnessing in the church. When a member of the royal priesthood approaches Holy Scripture to hear God's voice it will be the Holy Spirit whom she hears speaking. Vanhoozer notes, "The voice or logos the church hears in and through the human words is the voice of the third person of the Trinity speaking from the Father through and about the Son."[83] The Spirit speaking to the children of God through the Word of God is one reason that sanctification has traditionally been appropriated to the Spirit.[84]

The Spirit also bears witness outside the church, in all creation: "Where shall I go from your Spirit? Or where shall I flee from your presence?" (Ps 139:7). The prevenience of the Spirit means that he is witnessing everywhere in creation; he is the Witness. How then should the royal priesthood respond? The answer can be found in the divine economy; we are to respond in the same way Jesus did.[85] The Spirit led Jesus into the world (Mark 1:12; Luke 4:1), into a ministry of proclamation and healing presence (Luke 4:18–21). Lesslie Newbigin applies this example to the Witness of the church. The appropriate response to the Spirit's prevenience or "previousness" is an obedient movement of Witness into the world while proclaiming the kingdom of the Father and practicing the healing presence of the Son.[86]

---

83. Vanhoozer, "Triune Discourse," 67.

84. Didymus the Blind was an early proponent of appropriating sanctification to the Spirit (*On the Holy Spirit* 11 [PP 43:146]).

85. Köstenberger and Swain write, "*The role the Spirit plays in relation to the disciples is analogous to the role he played in relation to Jesus during his earthly ministry*" (*Father, Son, and Spirit*, 146; emphasis original). See also Issler, "Jesus' Example," 189–225.

86. Newbigin, *Open Secret*, 56.

The attentive reader may have questions on two of the terms used in the previous paragraph, namely, "witness" (with its relation to mission/*missio*) and "world" (*kosmos*). "Witness" draws attention to the fact that the subject matter (*res*) to which the Holy Spirit witnesses is the same in the Word (Scripture) as in the world. The single witness of the Spirit is that Jesus, the Son of the Father, is Lord. The relation of the Spirit's Witness (*martyria*) to the *missio Dei* is that the former is subordinate to the latter. The Spirit bears witness to the mission of Christ, and Christ testifies to his Father as the almighty Creator of all. The Spirit's witness is thus a Christocentric-Trinitarian witness. It points to Christ, the Savior of the world (redemption), and through Christ it points to the Father who is source and sustainer of all (creation, providence). The next chapter returns more specifically to the royal priesthood's Witness in relation to the larger *missio Dei*.[87]

Second, when the Spirit leads the royal priesthood to witness in the *world*, we recognize that the English word "world" refers to multiple concepts in Scripture. Christopher Wright identifies some nine Hebrew and Greek words or phrases used to refer to the English concept "world."[88] Wright further divides the biblical use of "world" into five categories, amidst which the categories of creation and humanity are especially relevant.[89] A Christocentric-Trinitarian understanding of the priesthood of all believers avoids a reductionist understanding of Witness. From the beginning, the royal priesthood has been called to mediate God's presence to all of creation.[90] This priestly responsibility must not be reduced to the care of souls alone.[91]

To sum up, if prayer and the offering of spiritual sacrifices are an especially appropriate ecclesial response to the Father, and ministry to one another an especially appropriate response to the Son, then an especially appropriate response of the royal priesthood to the work of the Spirit is Witness (*martyria*).[92] As the Spirit bears eternal witness to the Father's love

---

87. See Guder, *Continuing Conversion of the Church*, 49–70.

88. Wright, "World in the Bible," 208–09.

89. The five categories are 1) World of creation; 2) World of humanity; 3) World of sin and judgment; 4) World of God's salvation; 5) World to come (ibid., 209–18).

90. This was the responsibility of the protological priest-king (Adam, Gen 1:26–27); the first recorded priest-king of Jerusalem (Melchizedek, Gen 14:19); and it is the mission of those who continue the work of the eschatological Priest-king (Mark 16:15). See further Beale, *Temple and the Church's Mission*, 81; Wright, *Mission of God*, 314.

91. Newbigin, *Come Holy Spirit*, 6.

92. Luke 24:48–49; John 15:26–27; Acts 1:8; cf. 1 Pet 2:9.

within the Trinity, so the Spirit leads the church into the world to bear Witness (*martyria*) to the Son.[93]

Protestant Perils and the Priesthood of All Believers

Nicene Christians neglect a Christocentric-Trinitarian doctrine of the royal priesthood to their peril. This section illustrates this claim by looking at three inadequate Protestant versions.[94] Contemporary examples are used because it is more helpful to address the errors of one's own generation than those whose chronological context is far removed.[95] Similarly, the focus is on inadequate Protestant forms for two reasons. First, Roman Catholic and Orthodox traditions have already given significant attention to the doctrine during the last fifty years. Secondly, as Reinhold Neibuhr once reminded his Detroit parishioners, confronting Protestant sin is important "because it happens to be our sin and there is no use repenting for other people's sins. Let us repent of our own."[96]

The three inadequate Protestant doctrines of the royal priesthood discussed below are inversely related to the trinitarian appropriations identified in the previous section. The first, related to the royal priesthood's access and service to the *Father*, is fundamentally an eschatological error. The second, often rooted in spiritual pride, addresses two common inadequate uses of the *Son's* royal priesthood: those who on the one hand pursue an individualistic priestly ministry and, on the other, those who overreact to this danger by denying any priestly ministry to individuals, only recognizing a collective priesthood. The final inadequate version of the royal priesthood is *Spirit*-ignoring, one that fails to adequately follow the Spirit's leading toward missional witness in the world.

Protestant Monopolies on Priestly Access and Service to the Father

The book's first three chapters identified the importance of inaugurated eschatology. The NT authors believed that the eschaton had begun in Jesus.

---

93. Matthew 28:20; John 20:21–23. For further discussion of the essential and personal relationships between the Holy Spirit, mission, and the church see Augustine, *The Trinity* 2–4 (FC 45:51–173); Holmes, "Trinitarian Missiology," 72–90; Newbigin, *Open Secret*, 56–65.

94. Cf. Barth, *CD* I.2.630–31; Rea, *Common Priesthood*.

95. Ellul, *False Presence*, 4.

96. Fox, *Reinhold Niebuhr*, 91.

He is the eschatological Priest-king, and those united to him share in his royal priesthood. All who have believed and been baptized are united with the Melchizedekian Priest-king, sharing in his royal and priestly mission. Isaiah's vision of a unified and democratized priesthood has been proleptically realized. The torn temple veil reveals the beginning of a new age and the birth of a new priesthood. Divine service and priestly access, previously available only to the high priest and the Levitical priesthood are now accessible to all who have been united to Jesus.

Luther's triumphant great exchange means that all that is Christ's is now mine. While Protestant churches have tended to emphasize the believer's resulting access to the Father, they have often failed to emphasize the privilege of temple service now required of all believer priests. Too often priestly service, "ministry," has been limited to ordained leadership. This monopoly on ministry is a legacy of a medieval and reductionist version of sacerdotal priesthood, one firmly renounced by the Roman Catholic Church at Vatican II.[97]

In the twentieth century, it was actually a Roman Catholic theologian, Yves Congar, who more than any other single voice called all Nicene churches to recognize that priestly ministry belongs to every member. Congar's study is not properly a work in biblical theology, but it does represent one of the most thorough engagements with a biblical theology of the people (*laos*) of God ever produced. Congar spends one hundred pages discussing the function of the royal priesthood.[98] His most significant contribution is recognizing the multiplicity of "ministries" within the royal priesthood. Not just the clergy are called to serve in these ministries. In a 1972 essay, Congar is explicit about this contribution. He points out that historically the "ministries" of God's people have *not* been viewed as priestly service within the church. For Congar,

> The plural noun [ministries] is essential. It signifies that the church of God is not built up solely by the actions of the official presbyterial ministry but by a multitude of diverse modes of service, more or less stable or occasional, more or less spontaneous or recognized and when the occasion arises consecrated, while falling short of sacramental ordination.[99]

These forms of priestly service include "mothers at home catechizing the children of the neighborhood"; "the woman visiting the sick or prisoners"; "the organizer of a biblical circle"; it could even be "someone who

---

97. *Dogmatic Constitution on the Church* 2.10 (*DEC* 2:857).
98. Congar, *Lay People in the Church*, 112–221.
99. Congar, "My Path-Findings," 176.

initiates help to the unemployed, arrange[s] hospitality for migrant workers or someone responsible for the family hearth or for a course in basic literacy."[100]

All these ministries relate to the *diakonia* of the church, being "*charisms*" given to build up Christ's body for the common good (Eph 4:12, 1 Cor 12:7, 11).[101] Congar notes that these ministries of the whole priestly people of God "do actually exist but up to now were not called by their true name, ministries, nor were their place and status in ecclesiology recognized."[102] Thus the whole people of God, and every one of its members, has a priestly ministry—a work of service, to which each and all have been called.

Michael Horton, a leading Protestant theologian, provides an example of an eschatologically inadequate version of the priesthood of all believers. Horton is rightly concerned about his North American context in which churches are enmeshed in a syncretic blend of egalitarianism, individualism, and narcissism.[103] Horton's concerns have deep roots in western culture. The biblical understanding of individualism—limited by a creaturely anthropology and the law of love—was twisted during the Renaissance into the idea of the "autonomous" individual.[104]

Yet while Horton is correct to be concerned about how the "autonomous individual" has been blended into Protestant versions of the priesthood of all believers, he is incorrect to promote a clerical monopoly on ministry. Horton provides a contemporary illustration of Calvin's *sacro egoismo*.[105] While nodding to the concerns of the missional church, he continues to describe the church's mission exclusively in terms of the preaching, offering of sacraments, and pastoral care of church *officers*. "*The mission of the church is to execute the marks of the church, which are the same as the keys of the kingdom.*"[106] He defines keys as preaching, sacraments, and discipline, functions which he limits to church officers. Both Barth and Newbigin would protest strongly against this definition of the church's mission which seems to exclude lay Work and Witness.

In Horton's writings, "ministry" and the title "ministers" are not only denied to the "laity" they are even denied to any *presbyterion* unordained as

100. Ibid.
101. Congar, *Lay People in the Church*, 309–32.
102. Congar, "My Path-Findings," 176.
103. Horton, *Christian Faith*, 897.
104. Niebuhr, *Nature and Destiny of Man*, 60–61.
105. Barth, *CD* IV/3.2, 568–71; 765–66.
106. Horton, *Christian Faith*, 897; emphasis added.

teacher. He writes, "all ministers are elders but not all elders are ministers."[107] Horton denies the term "ministry" to any work beside the preaching of the Word and the administering of sacraments by ordained preachers.[108] His larger concerns are admirable. He wants to raise the dignity of office holders (1 Tim 5:17; Heb 13:7, 17). But this worthy aim cannot be pursued by denying a priestly ministry to all believers. To do so fails to recognize the eschatological age in which we now live, where all believers are living stones in a temple that God is building (1 Pet 2:4–9). By virtue of union with Christ, as part of God's temple-people, each believer has a priestly ministry, a place to serve in God's house.[109]

---

107. Ibid., 856.

108. "We even refuse the label 'ministry,' reserving that hallowed noun for the church" ("Church after the Parachurch," 53). Horton here makes "church" synonymous with "clergy."

109. First Peter 4:10–11; Eph 4:11–16; Leithart, *Priesthood of the Plebs*, 48–86, 152, 213.

Individualistic and Collective Priesthoods: Two Inadequate Appropriations of Christ's Priesthood

There exists a "natural priesthood" or a "priesthood of all human beings" which must be distinguished from the Christian doctrine of the royal priesthood. The two are often confused, with catastrophic results for the ecclesial household. The idea of a "natural priesthood" can be related to the "soul competency" proposed by Baptist theologian E. Y. Mullins.[110] The essence of soul competency is found in creedal affirmations; we believe that Jesus "will come again in glory to judge the living and the dead" (Nicene Creed). As Timothy George notes, "Soul competency means that every individual is accountable to God. . . . There are no sponsors or proxies in the relation of the individual to God."[111] Natural priesthood, or soul competency, is thus a component of the doctrine of creation. In contrast to this, as Martin Luther and Karl Barth have illustrated, the royal priesthood finds its proper doctrinal locus within redemption. Believers are made royal priests only as united to the Priest-king through faith and baptism.

One of the idols of contemporary western culture is individualism.[112] When this idol is brought into the church, it produces a perversion of the royal priesthood as destructive in our age as the clerical-sacerdotal version was during the lowest points of medieval Roman Catholicism. The hierarchical version critiqued in the previous sub-section is a leftover Protestant remnant from that inadequate medieval understanding, a "Protestant sacerdotalism."[113] Far more prevalent today, at least in western culture, is the "atomistic priesthood," a version which its proponents claim can be exercised in independence of the church.[114]

George Barna, an influential church practitioner in North America, illustrates an inadequate "atomistic" priesthood of all believers.[115] He argues that millions of believers in North America have profitably moved beyond

---

110. Mullins, *Axioms of Religion*.

111. George, "Priesthood of All Believers," 86.

112. Lesslie Newbigin, the "scandalous prophet," makes this claim explicit in "Speaking the Truth to Caesar" (373). Helpful in unmasking the idolatry of individualism in its North American context are: Bellah et al., *Habits of the Heart*, esp. 27–51, 142–63, 219–49; Putnam, *Bowling Alone*, esp. 65–79, 408–10; Bauman, *Individualized Society*, esp. 153–60, 238–50. Muthiah helpfully summarizes the relation of Bellah, Putnam, and Bauman to the priesthood of all believers (*Priesthood of All Believers*, 103–20).

113. Torrance, *Theology in Reconstruction*, 167–68.

114. For critique of both the "hierarchical priesthood" and "atomistic priesthood" see Yarnell, "Congregational Priesthood," 128.

115. See his autobiographical claims in Barna, *Revolution*, 143. His book sold over 100,000 copies by 2012.

church. He writes that "these people are devout followers of Jesus Christ who are serious about their faith" but often "grow in their relationship with God outside the ministry of a local church."[116] Barna opens his apology for a new kind of church with the story of two believers who meet for "Church on the Green," that is, to talk about life and God on the golf course Sunday morning rather than with a local congregation.[117]

Barna's potential strength is in cultural analysis. Missionary theologians such as Lesslie Newbigin and Craig Van Gelder have raised many of the same concerns regarding the western church's cultural captivity.[118] But, while sharing many of Barna's concerns, Newbigin and Van Gelder refuse to bow to the idol of individualism in their pursuit of faithful ecclesial practices. The problem with the atomistic priesthood is failing to recognize that membership in Christ's royal priesthood is impossible without participating in Christ's body. It unknowingly confuses natural priesthood with royal priesthood, producing a gnostic priesthood—one which does not recognize the humanity of the body of Christ.[119] Luther's priesthood of all believers was not gnostic, and had an essential horizontal dimension.[120] Believers cannot fully exercise their priestly ministry if living independently from Christ's body.

A second danger of the atomistic priesthood is its vulnerability to spiritual pride and the powers. It is instructive that there is no mention of baptism in Barna's book. Baptist theologian Thomas Grantham (d. 1692) has a relevant warning about versions of the royal priesthood lacking roots in ecclesial practices such as baptism, the Lord's Supper, and the laying on of hands:

> Religion will in a little time either vanish, or become an unknown conceit, every man being at liberty to follow what he supposes to be the motions of the Spirit of God, in which there is so great a probability of being mistaken, as in nothing more; for man's ignorance being very great, and Satan very subtle, and the way of the Lord neglected, men lie open to every fancy which pleaseth best.[121]

---

116. Barna, *Revolution*, 8, 131.

117. Ibid., 3. The 2012 edition begins differently, but its narrative remains problematic.

118. See Goheen, *Lesslie Newbigin's Missionary Ecclesiology*, 97–99; Van Gelder, *Essence of the Church*, 27–44.

119. On gnostic dangers see Newman, "Priesthood of All Believers," 93–94; Leithart, *Priesthood of the Plebs*, 3–4.

120. *LW* 13:315.

121. Cited in Freeman, et al., *Baptist Roots*, 89.

An atomistic priesthood is in grave danger of kindling fire on God's altar in vain (Mal 1:10). Blindness to personal and corporate sin can make a priest's approach to the presence of God an abomination. The current pre-Parousia eschatological reality of the proleptic priesthood cuts two ways: not only has the Spirit been poured out upon those united with the Son, but they also continue to live in a world tainted by sin and tormented by the devil. Reinhold Niebuhr catalogs four forms of pride; the worst is spiritual pride where God is made "the exclusive ally of our contingent self."[122] He goes on to write, "The Protestant doctrine of the priesthood of all believers may result in an individual self-deification against which the Catholic doctrine has more adequate checks."[123]

We must condemn the atomistic priesthood as the greatest of the contemporary Protestant perversions. Yet in their zeal to condemn atomistic versions of the priesthood of all believers, many have embraced a reciprocally inadequate version, denying that "the priesthood has to do with individuals."[124] In so doing they deny an important truth. A collective version is just as inadequate as an individualistic version. Collective versions argue that the priesthood of all believers only applies to the church as a whole, not to individual believers.

It is a reductionist reading to claim that the first-century Syrian Christian hymn-writer who wrote, "I am a priest of the Lord, and to him I serve as a priest," was wrong when he identified himself as a "priest of the Lord." Recent work on Paul's use of cultic vocabulary related to the temple has shown that members of Christ's body are related both to each other and to Christ.[125] Neither bond can be denied in a biblical understanding of temple access or priesthood. As Adewuya notes, "believers are no longer separate 'monads,' but part of the people of God," yet "the individual does not disappear into the corporate mass within Christianity."[126] Believers are ordained as royal priests at their baptisms; to deny them the privilege of exercising their priesthood in the church and world is no longer an adequate option for Protestant theologians. Schleiermacher was correct to insist that the

---

122. Niebuhr, *Nature and Destiny of Man*, 201.

123. Ibid., 202.

124. Newman, "Priesthood of All Believers," 60; "The expression 'priesthood of all believers' is an unfortunate one as it carries with it a ruinous individualism" (Torrance, *Royal Priesthood*, 35). See also commentators on 1 Pet 2:4–9 discussed in Chapter 1 (e.g., Elliott).

125. Gupta, "Which 'Body.'"

126. Adewuya, *Holiness and Community*, 189–90.

believer is first united with Christ, and then through Christ united to the church.[127]

To sum up, the priesthood of all believers is a Christocentric-Trinitarian doctrine. Versions claiming access to the Father—usually by means of the Spirit, yet which deny the necessity of membership in the body of Christ—must be rejected as deficient. The overreaction to these atomistic versions has resulted in an equally inadequate version—a collective priesthood denying priesthood to individual believers. Both versions must be rejected by Protestants as unsatisfactory.

A Spirit-Ignoring Priesthood: Holy Egotism and Priestly Witness

This chapter began with a case for a Christocentric-Trinitarian doctrine of the priesthood of all believers rather than Christocentric-only. These arguments need not be repeated, but it should be emphasized that "Christendom" versions tended to be "Spirit-ignoring."[128] In ecclesiologies where the church-world distinction begins to break down, it becomes more difficult to discern the Spirit's call to bear Witness. Yet the Spirit continually bears witness to Christ, and invites the royal priesthood to share in the task. Too often the members of the royal priesthood have forgotten that they are "bearers not exclusive beneficiaries" of the blessings of the Spirit (e.g., Jonah).[129]

Luther's Christocentric-only doctrine resulted in a binitarian view of priestly ministry. For Luther, the royal priesthood's ministry was primarily directed toward the Father or other believers. Peter Leithart provides a contemporary example of both Luther's strengths and weakness. Leithart's monograph, *The Priesthood of the Plebs*, is the most important book to be written on the priesthood of all believers in the last twenty years. It recovers many riches missing from contemporary ecclesiology. Yet as helpful as his work is, it is guilty of the same holy egotism that has characterized most Protestant versions since Luther.

Unlike Barth and Newbigin's doctrine, Leithart's priesthood of the baptized does not emphasize (or mention) the believer's priestly responsibility to join in the Spirit's witness to the world. Leithart emphasizes the ministry of the royal priesthood as household or temple service, thus focusing on the baptized believer's ministry to the Father and to one another. For

---

127. Vanhoozer, "Voice and the Actor," 86.
128. See Sanders, *Deep Things of God*, 168–71.
129. Newbigin, *Open Secret*, 32.

Leithart, the nature of the ministry of the royal priesthood is summed up in Heb 12:28—13:17. This passage

> spells out the nature of New Testament "housekeeping" as love for brothers, hospitality, sexual purity, generosity, offering praise, and eating the Eucharistic flesh denied Aaronic priests ... these facets of ecclesial life have a priestly character.[130]

Leithart correctly identifies that the royal priestly ministry includes vertical and horizontal dimensions. What he fails to make explicit is that the horizontal dimension of priestly ministry is primarily directed toward the world. All priests, not only the High Priest, are "appointed to act on behalf of men in relation to God" (Heb 5:1).[131] Leithart is aware of the centrifugal force implicit in Heb 13:13's exhortation for believers to move outside the camp.[132] But he does not build on this insight to articulate the calling of the royal priesthood as proclaiming the excellencies of the one who has called them out of darkness into the light (1 Pet 2:9). Leithart recognizes that for baptized priests all labor "becomes a sphere for the exercise of *virtus* and a form of λειτουργία," but he does not indicate that this λειτουργία is μαρτυρία when directed toward the world.[133]

To use Fred Sanders' helpful terminology, Leithart's Christocentric doctrine is not "Father forgetful" but it is "Spirit ignoring."[134] As illustrated by Barth and Newbigin, the Spirit leads the royal priesthood to participate in mission. The gathering and upbuilding of the royal priesthood are always for the sake of witness. When there is a failure to recognize the prevenience of the Spirit's work in the world, church mission all too often becomes propaganda—the preaching of the gospel plus our own contextualized ecclesial culture.[135] Christendom ecclesiologies have all too often been guilty of such propaganda. Leithart's doctrine of the royal priesthood is inadequate without including this essential emphasis on the royal priesthood's mission in the world.

---

130. Leithart, *Priesthood of the Plebs*, 196.
131. See Laansma, "Hebrews and the Mission," 341–43.
132. Leithart, *Priesthood of the Plebs*, 212–13.
133. Ibid., 213.
134. Sanders, *Deep Things of God*, 168.
135. See Martin Kähler's distinction between mission and propaganda in Flett, *Witness of God*, 63–64.

Chapter Summary

This chapter proposed an explicitly trinitarian doctrine of the priesthood of all believers. It identified the need to move beyond Luther's Christocentric-only doctrine to a Christocentric-Trinitarian version, one which especially emphasizes the *missio Dei*. The second section described the appropriate response of members of the royal priesthood to each of the three divine persons: the Father, the Son, and the Holy Spirit. It is especially appropriate even if, as Barth notes, it is also technically "improper," to associate a response of *latreia* (Worship) with the Father, *diakonia* (Work) with the Son, and *martyria* (Witness) with the Holy Spirit. In the chapter's final section, three inadequate Protestant forms of the doctrine were rejected as unsatisfactory. The next chapter concludes our larger study by examining the royal priesthood's seven "Central Practices."

8

The Practices of a Priestly People: Baptismal Ordination and the Offering of Spiritual Sacrifices

> Baptism, in short, announces the formation of a polis that offers priesthood to the plebs. Destruction of the archaic system of graded priesthood is central to the gospel of the broken wall, the rent veil, the open sanctuary, the accessible altar.
>
> —Peter Leithart[1]

> You yourselves like living stones are being built up as a spiritual house, to be a holy priesthood, to offer spiritual sacrifices acceptable to God through Jesus Christ.... that you may proclaim the excellencies of him who called you out of darkness into his marvelous light.
>
> —1 Pet 2:5, 9b

THE ROYAL PRIESTHOOD RESPONDS to Father, Son and Holy Spirit with Worship (*latreia*), Work (*diakonia*), and Witness (*martyria*). This priestly responsibility is fulfilled through seven "Central Practices." Each practice is rooted in the apostolic doctrine of the royal priesthood (Chapters 1–3), and each has played an important role in the doctrine's history (Chapters 4–6). This chapter explores these practices in four steps. First, the royal priesthood's seven "Central Practices" are related to larger discussions about ecclesial "practices," and the concepts of "Constitutive" and "Core Practices" are introduced. Second, the chapter returns to Matt 3:13—4:1 and 1 Pet 2:4–

---

1. Leithart, *Priesthood of the Plebs*, xxii.

9, and examines baptism as the ordination practice of the royal priesthood, a Constitutive Practice. The third section explores the royal priesthood's spiritual sacrifices, which are categorized as Worship, Work, and Witness. Within this threefold division, the royal priesthood's five Core Practices are outlined: 1) "Prayer"; 2) *Lectio Divina* (Divine Reading); 3) "Ministry"; 4) "Church Discipline"; and 5) "Proclamation." Finally, the chapter describes the Lord's Supper as the royal priesthood's consummative Constitutive Practice, the seventh of the Central Practices.[2] A brief summary concludes this outline of the royal priesthood's ethics.

The Royal Priesthood's Practices

What are the practices of the royal priesthood? This section first describes the mutually informing nature of beliefs and practices. It then defines "practices" with reference to Alasdair MacIntyre's definition, and divides ecclesial practices into two major categories: Constitutive and Core Practices. Finally, it describes the perichoretic, or mutually indwelling, nature of the royal priesthood's seven Central Practices; they can be differentiated but not divided.

Lex Orandi and Lex Credendi

In one of his most cited passages, MacIntyre concludes that "the new dark ages are ... already upon us."[3] If this is so, there is no better time to heed the Apostle Paul's exhortation to "shine like stars in the universe as you hold out the word of life" (Phil 2:15b–16a [NIV1]). Yet how is the royal priesthood to respond? This chapter addresses the implications of the priesthood of all believers for Worship, Work, and Witness. What Miroslav Volf has said of theology in general is true for the royal priesthood in particular: "*At the heart of every good theology lies not simply a plausible intellectual vision but more importantly a compelling account of a way of life, and that theology is therefore best done from within the pursuit of this way of life.*"[4]

What is the way of life to which the priesthood of all believers beckons? It is a way of life marked by particular practices, practices that lead ever deeper into the doctrine itself. Practice shapes belief, just as belief shapes practice; worship (*lex orandi*) informs belief (*lex credendi*) and vice

---

2. This structure generally follows the outline in Barth's fragmentary ethics of reconciliation (*CD* IV.4.1 and *CL* 45).

3. MacIntyre, *After Virtue*, 263.

4. Volf, "Theology for a Way of Life," 247; emphasis original.

versa. Exploring the doctrine of the royal priesthood through its practices is helpful for at least four reasons. First, contemporary theology has taken a cultural turn, and attention to practices helps us attend to how particular cultures influence beliefs. Today, responsible theologians must take seriously Newbigin's Gauntlet: the triad of Gospel, Church, and Culture.[5] Second, contemporary theologians have turned to the concept of "practices" during the last twenty years as they have begun to recognize and repent of the church's holy egotism and the closely related "clerical paradigm" which has dominated so much ecclesial action.[6] Theories of practice are more conducive to exploring the priesthood of all believers than the comparable field of ritual studies.[7] Third, attention to practices helps break "a way of life down into parts that are small enough to be amenable to analysis."[8] Practices help us think more specifically about the way of life to which the doctrine of the royal priesthood leads, better grasping how we offer our bodies as living sacrifices, holy and pleasing to the Lord (Rom 12:1). Finally, the language of practices permits us to bypass some questions which—while historically interesting and theologically significant—are not directly relevant. Peter Leithart provides a helpful metaphor by contrasting a camera's zoom lens with a wide-angle lens.[9] For centuries the church has viewed the Lord's Supper through a zoom lens—resulting in a myopic focus; in contrast, when using a wide-angle lens, we begin to discover how royal priests are attending to one another, to God, and to the world. We discover that the priesthood of all believers empowers us to affirm together more than we might have previously realized, not only across various Protestant traditions, but also in wider ecumenical settings.

Identifying Seven Central Practices of the Royal Priesthood

Before proceeding further, it is helpful to define the word "practices." Theologians using the language of practices have especially relied upon frameworks provided by Alasdair MacIntyre and Pierre Bourdieu.[10] MacIntyre's

---

5. Hunsberger, "Newbigin Gauntlet," 3–25.

6. For a classic discussion of the "clerical paradigm" see Farley, *Theologia*, 127–35. Cf. Conner, *Practicing Witness*, 76–77.

7. Cf. Leithart who prefers ritual theory as a tool for sociological analysis (*Blessed are the Hungry*, 156–69).

8. Bass and Dykstra, "Theological Understanding," 18.

9. Leithart, *Blessed are the Hungry*, 153–61.

10. See Bourdieu, *Outline of a Theory of Practice*. For summary and critique see

definition has received the most attention, not only in theology, but across dozens of academic disciplines. Because MacIntyre is describing human practices in general, most theologians have found it necessary to adapt his definition when reflecting upon ecclesial practices. Theologians who have organized significant work around a concept of ecclesial practices similar to that of MacIntyre include James Wm. McClendon, John Howard Yoder, Stanley Hauerwas, Nancey Murphy, Jonathan R. Wilson, Dorothy Bass, and Craig Dykstra. Of this group, Dorothy Bass and Craig Dykstra's work has served as the basis of dozens of recent theological studies.[11] Robert Muthiah is the first to apply the practices conversation to the royal priesthood.[12]

Defining Practice

MacIntyre's definition of practices is rooted in the Aristotelian tradition. Theologians have further nuanced his definition by recognizing that ecclesial practices are human responses to divine initiative (Eph 2:9–10). This book defines practices as (1) complex and (2) communal responses to God's grace with (3) internal goods (virtues) and (4) standards of excellence which embody a (5) particular concept of the good (*telos*).[13] One of MacIntyre's examples illustrates the general concept of practice, and each of the five components of the definition is briefly explained below.

Imagine David, who is learning to play chess from his grandfather, a former World Chess Champion. Chess is (1) *complex*, made up of a series of smaller activities—there are six pieces which can be diversely deployed. It is (2) *communal*, usually played with someone else. Yet even if played on a computer, it is still part of a larger communal tradition dating back centuries. Perhaps David's grandfather offers David a piece of candy to learn to play chess. The candy would be an external good not necessarily tied to the game of chess, one David might receive in other ways. On the other hand, David may eventually come to love the game for itself. He might begin to treasure the game's mental stimulation—especially as he plays against his grandfather. Love of the game and mental stimulation are examples of (3) *internal goods*. Chess has its own (4) *standards of excellence*. While David could initially win by cheating—gaining the external good of candy—he

---

Smith, "Theories of Practice," 244–54.

11. Bass, *Practicing Our Faith*; Volf and Bass, *Practicing Theology*; Bass and Dykstra, *For Life Abundant*. See esp. Mikoski, *Baptism and Christian Identity*.

12. My proposal of Central, Constitutive, and Core Practices builds on his work (Muthiah, *Priesthood of All Believers*, 134–73).

13. MacIntyre, *After Virtue*, 187.

would miss out on the game's internal goods. Finally, chess embodies a (5) particular conception of the good. In chess, this conception of the good, the *telos*, might be friendships formed and critical-thinking skills developed.

Returning to our definition, we briefly define each of its five components. Practices are (1) *complex* involving multiple activities. Baptismal vows are one activity within the larger practice of baptism; they are not a practice by themselves. Practices are (2) *communal responses* to God's grace. The word communal implies that practices are always part of a tradition and a wider community. The practices of prayer and *Lectio Divina* (a prayerful reading of Scripture) are often done alone, but they can still count as practices when seen as part of the Christian tradition's "shared spirituality."[14] The emphasis on God's grace distinguishes our definition from MacIntyre's Aristotelian tradition which emphasizes human achievements—achievements often possible only for an elite few. In contrast, Christian practices are open to all (Gal 3:28) and are better understood as participatory actions than as human achievements. Wilson explains that this distinction does not mean "activity in Aristotle versus passivity *in Christ*. Rather the contrast is between the activity of achievement and the activity of participation."[15]

Practices (3) possess their own *internal goods* (virtues), which for the royal priesthood are especially faith, hope, and love.[16] Practices (4) maintain their own *standards of excellence*. For example, baptism has often been offered as an alternative to death by conquering crusader armies. In this case, the practice's internal standard of excellence is violated. As MacIntyre notes, the standards themselves can be debated by practitioners, but "to enter a practice is to accept the authority of those standards and the inadequacy of my own performance as judged by them."[17]

Finally, practices (5) embody a *particular conception of the good*. They are best understood in relation to the *telos* of a particular community. *Telos* not only refers to the goal or objective of the community, but more deeply to the purpose for which the community was created. Wilson uses the example of a hammer to illustrate.[18] A hammer's purpose is not sawing boards, but driving nails. It can be used for other purposes, but it was created for the *telos* of nail driving. The *telos* of the people of God is to serve as a royal

---

14. Davis, *Sacred Roots*, 49–58.

15. Wilson, *Why Church Matters*, 20; emphasis added. See further Owens, *Shape of Participation*, 2010).

16. Karl Barth would include freedom and gratitude (*CL* 37, 39–44). See further Wilson, *Gospel Virtues*; and "Three Virtues, Nine Varieties of Fruit, and One Body," in Wright, *After You Believe*, 181–218.

17. MacIntyre, *After Virtue*, 190.

18. Wilson, *Why Church Matters*, 12.

priesthood. In Christ, the royal priesthood already participates in this *telos* through the power of the Spirit. This *telos* is explicitly mentioned five times in Revelation, including 5:9–10, "They sang a new song . . . 'by your blood you ransomed people for God from every tribe and language and people and nation, and you have made them a kingdom and priests to our God, and they shall reign on the earth.'" [19]

All the royal priesthood's practices must be viewed in light of this *telos*, and it especially informs the NT's language of spiritual sacrifices. All the royal priesthood's practices are offered to God as spiritual sacrifices (Rom 12:1). This *telos* can be described with other language as well, most significantly the language of discipleship.[20] Chapter Three showed that both Matthew and John can equate the language of discipleship with that of royal priesthood. Chapter Six showed that this theological judgment equating discipleship with royal priesthood was one of Luther's core insights.[21] The disciples of the Priest-king are a royal priesthood called to embody a particular conception of the good; this *telos* is to "serve our God and rule the world."[22]

Central, Constitutive, and Core Practices

Before discussing the royal priesthood's Central Practices, it is important to distinguish between Constitutive and Core Practices. The *Constitutive Practices* are baptism and Eucharist.[23] They uniquely portray the contours of the resurrection life, a life made new by the believer's union with Christ. They uniquely encapsulate all other practices in "liturgical summation," identifying them as Christian practices.[24] These two practices are unique within

---

19. Rev 1:5–6; 3:21; 5:9–10; 7:15; 20:4–6. See Chapter 3 above; Beale, *Revelation*; Wright, *After You Believe*, 78–79.

20. Wilson names disciplemaking as the chief *telos* of God's people (*Why Church Matters*, 17–18). Elsewhere he equates this with participation in the royal priesthood (Wilson, *God so Loved the World*, 167–68).

21. *LW* 24:241, 242.

22. Yoder, "To Serve our God," 127–40. N. T. Wright makes a similar claim, arguing that the *telos* of God's people is to "be the renewed world's rulers and priests" (*After You Believe*, 67). Beale's *The Temple and the Church's Mission* also describes the *telos* of God's people as royal and priestly service (368, 395–402).

23. Cf. Nancey Murphy, who, in conversation with Yoder, argues that Discernment, Discipling (including "binding and loosing"), Worship, Works of Mercy, and Witness are "the practices constitutive of the church's mission and identity" (Murphy, et al., *Virtues & Practices in the Christian Tradition*, 37, see also 132).

24. Bass and Dykstra, "Theological Understanding," 30. On the Eucharist see Hauerwas and Wells, *Blackwell Companion*, 3–50. Cf. Volf, "Theology for a Way," 248.

the Great Tradition. Baptism is the public ordination ceremony of the royal priesthood, and the Lord's Supper is the ongoing renewal of the believer priest's union with the great Priest-king. They are constitutive because they uniquely identify the royal priesthood's location *in Christ*.

The royal priesthood's five *Core Practices* are canonical and catholic, consisting of Prayer, *Lectio Divina*, Ministry, Church Discipline, and Proclamation. They are canonical because they receive apostolic witness in the NT. John Howard Yoder proposes five practices, all of which overlap with our list.[25] He argues that all are dominical ordinances on equal plane with baptism and the Lord's Supper. This is an overstatement, yet Yoder is correct to give priority to the practices commanded by the NT. The five Core Practices are not exhaustive, but history confirms their importance. They are catholic—practiced across cultures and centuries.

Together with the two Constitutive Practices, the five Core Practices form the seven *Central Practices* of the royal priesthood.[26] They are central for several reasons. As noted above, all are canonical and catholic. Each has dominical and apostolic warrant, and has proven essential to the health of the royal priesthood across centuries and cultures.[27] For example, Luther once proposed a very similar list of seven "practices." Table Seven lists the seven Central Practices alongside parallel lists from Luther (1523, 1539), Yoder, and Barth. [28]

---

25. Yoder, *Body Politics*.

26. Muthiah's discussion of the royal priesthood's five practices (Witness; Lord's Supper, Discernment; Friendship; and Confession) seems somewhat arbitrary and neglects baptism (*Priesthood of All Believers*, 134–73).

27. This is true across traditions, e.g., pietism (Snyder), monasticism (Boff), and Latin America's base communities (Barth). See Snyder, "Pietism, Moravianism, and Methodism," 166–71; Boff, *Francis of Assisi*; Barth, *Einander Priester sein*, 134–60.

28. Cf. the traditional *seven* sacraments: Baptism, Confirmation (Chrismation), Eucharist, Penance, Anointing of the Sick, Holy Orders, and Matrimony (Aquinas, *ST* 3.65.1).

Seven Central Practices	Luther's Seven Practices (1523)	Luther's Seven Practices (1539)	Yoder's Five Practices	Barth's Fourteen Practices
Baptism	(2) Baptism	(2) Baptism	(3) Baptism	(14) Baptism
Prayer	(6) Prayer and Intercession	(6) Prayer	--	(7) Prayer; (1) Praising God
Lectio Divina	(7) Judging of Doctrine	--	(5) Rule of Paul = Discernment	(3a) Biblical Studies
Ministry	5) Offering Spiritual Sacrifices	(5) Ordination/ Office	(4) Fullness of Christ = Ministry of Whole Body	(2) Preaching; (3) Teaching; (6) Ministry of Theology; (10) Diaconate Ministry
Church Discipline	(4) Binding and Loosing Sins (Bearing the Keys)	(4) Office of Keys	(1) Binding and Loosing = Rule of Christ	(7) Cure of Souls
Proclamation	(1) Preaching the Pure Gospel.	(1) Proclamation (7) Suffering	--	(4) Evangelization; (5) Mission to the Nations; (9) Personal Example (11) Prophetic Witness
Lord's Supper	(3) Lord's Supper	(3) Lord's Supper	(2) Lord's Supper	(13) Lord's Supper (12) Fellowship

Table 6: Parallel Lists of Church Practices[29]

As noted above, the royal priesthood's seven practices find their closest parallel in Martin Luther's 1523 essay, *Concerning the Ministry*. This is not surprising since he wrote this list during his most productive period on the royal priesthood, and his emphasis later shifted following the events of 1525.[30] Yoder's five "ordinances" or practices also line up with the seven Central Practices although his list is missing prayer and a specific practice of proclamation.[31] Luther's "discerning of doctrine," Yoder's "discernment," and Barth's "biblical studies" have been placed in parallel with *Lectio Divina*.[32] This should give some initial perspective on the breadth of this prac-

---

29. Numbers refer to order in original source. See *Concerning the Ministry* (LW 40:21–34); *On the Councils and the Church* (LW 41:143–78; WA 50: 509–653); Yoder, *Body Politics*; Barth, CD IV.3.2, 830–901, esp. 901. Barth's list places baptism and the Lord's Supper within fellowship, but I have separated them. Based on *CL*'s structure, he would have placed Baptism, Prayer, and the Lord's Supper in the same order proposed here.

30. Hütter bases his discussion of church practices on Luther's 1539 *On the Councils and the Church* (*Suffering Divine Things*, 128–34). Daniel Treier is thus correct to critique Hütter's overly clerical understanding of *theologia* (*Virtue and the Voice of God*, 84–8). At least part of the blame for Hütter's clericalism lies with the later Luther.

31. As his subtitle suggests, he sees all ecclesial practices as participating in proclamation—but the neglect of a specific practice of proclamation is problematic (Yoder, *Body Politics*). Cf. his discussion of the "missionary dimension of being a Christian" (Yoder, *For the Nations*, 8) and of 1 Pet 2:9 (ibid., 40–41).

32. See Murphy on the relationship between Yoder's practice of discernment and Scriptural interpretation (*Virtues and Practices*, 133).

tice. The two Constitutive Practices serve as bookends below, and the five Core Practices are treated within the larger categories of Worship, Work, and Witness.

In addition to the seven central practices, the doctrine of the royal priesthood invites us to consider every action of the believer-priest as holy, set apart unto God. Her entire life is to be offered as a spiritual sacrifice (Rom 12:1); this holistic view leads to recognition of a third type of practice. *Creational Practices* are those "things people do together over time to address fundamental human needs in response to and in the light of God's active presence for the life of the world [in Jesus Christ]."[33] They are the wider set of practices in which the seven Central Practices are located. While the term "Creational Practices" is mine, the definition comes from Dorothy Bass and Craig Dykstra (including practices such as friendship, marriage, parenting, and celibacy).[34] Creational Practices provide the context for the seven Central Practices, but they do not receive substantial attention in this work.

The Royal Priesthood's Perichoretic Practices—Worship, Work, Witness

Baptism and Eucharist are set off from the other Central Practices, and the remaining five are divided into categories of Worship, Work, and Witness. To create this distinction may invite the question of which is closer to the essence of the church. Recently a debate has raged about whether worship or witness should receive priority. Reflecting on ecclesial practices through the lens of the royal priesthood provides a way past this false dilemma. Baptism is ordination to the ministry and mission of the royal priesthood. This mission is defined by the Priest-king in whose ministry the royal priesthood participates. Participation in all of the practices of the royal priesthood then becomes participation in the *missio Dei* itself.

For members of the royal priesthood, witness is worship and worship is witness.[35] The body's work of upbuilding is for the purpose of faithful worship and witness. Darrell Guder correctly affirms that the first priority of witness is worship, and that "the public worship of the mission community always leads to the pivotal act of sending."[36] If we follow the lead of the Great Commandment and the Ten Commandments, then the upward direction

---

33. Bass and Dykstra, "Theological Understanding," 18.

34. Bass, *Practicing Our Faith*; Muthiah, *Priesthood of All Believers*, 159–62; Jones, *Transformed Judgement*, 75–86.

35. Conner, *Practicing Witness*, 99–102.

36. Guder, "Missional Structures," 243.

takes precedence over the horizontal. Yet the Great Commandment's two halves and the Ten Commandments' two tables cannot be separated without the royal priesthood falling into the false worship condemned in Isaiah 58.[37] There the eschatological royal and priestly seed of the Servant is warned not to separate what God himself has joined in the mission of the Servant.

Karl Barth points out that the royal priesthood's vocation of witness must not be separated from our justification and sanctification. In the same way, the members of the royal priesthood cannot separate worship from witness; we might say they are perichoretically woven together. To use "perichoresis" adjectively is not to make a trinitarian claim, but to recognize that our human finitude makes it fitting to look at particular practices from multiple perspectives. In the 1989 film *Romero* there is a powerful illustration of the perichoretic nature of the royal priesthood's practices. In one scene, Raúl Juliá, playing the part of Salvadorian Archbishop Óscar Romero (d. 1980), is kicked out of a church where he had attempted to celebrate the Eucharist. The building had been confiscated by a group of heavily armed government soldiers who had been terrorizing the local population. After being kicked out, Romero turns and leads the faithful back into the church even with soldiers threatening to shoot.

How do we categorize the act portrayed in the movie? Is the celebration of the Eucharist an act of Worship, or Witness, or the Work of edification? Clearly they are interwoven. All of the royal priesthood's spiritual sacrifices are Worship: ultimately directed to the Father, through the Son, by the Spirit. All are Witness: done in the power of the Holy Spirit before the eyes of a watching world. All are Work: edifying the other members of Christ's body.[38] In sum, the royal priesthood's practices are perichoretic—they mutually indwell each other and, though distinct, are one. While they can be distinguished, they must not be divided.

Baptism: The Royal Priesthood's Practice of Ordination

This section explores baptism as an ecclesial practice that publicly ordains believers to share in Christ's royal and priestly ministry. It only examines the practice as it relates to the royal priesthood.[39] Baptism as ordination to the

---

37. Cf. Wright and Hanson's contrasting priorities for the people of God (Hanson, *People Called*, 75–78; Wright, *Mission of God*, 56, cf. 316–23).

38. See Conner, *Practicing Witness*, 99–102; Senn, *Witness of the Worshiping Community*.

39. On baptismal literature see Kavanagh, *Shape of Baptism*, ix.

royal priesthood is not a new claim, but it is rarely emphasized in Protestant discussions of baptism or royal priesthood.[40] The situation is different in Orthodox and Roman Catholic communions, where baptism is unanimously understood as ordination to the royal priesthood. Susan Wood is representative of both Orthodox and Roman Catholic positions when she writes that the "priesthood of all believers is constituted by baptism."[41] Since Vatican II, the Roman Catholic Church has returned emphasis to this early Christian consensus.[42]

The ecumenical consensus is correct. The first and last words spoken by Jesus in the Gospel of Matthew are about baptism. At his baptism Jesus is ordained to his royal and priestly ministry, and his baptism serves as the model for his disciples. Tertullian, writing in the second century, knew no other practice. After believers were baptized, they were anointed with oil like Levitical ordinations.[43] Augustine and Luther understood baptism as ordination to the royal priesthood, and Barth emphasized the resultant vocation of priestly ministry and witness.[44] The section below synthesizes insights from previous chapters by returning to Matt 3:12–4:1 and 1 Pet 2:4–9.

Baptism in the Name of the Father, Son, and Holy Spirit: Matthew 3:13–4:1

If evangelical Protestants wish to reengage with the Great Tradition's emphasis on baptism as ordination to the royal priesthood, then there are at least four lessons to glean from Matthew's narrative of Jesus' baptism. Baptism must be understood in Christocentric-Trinitarian perspective. Beginning with Christ's paradigmatic baptism, it there attends to the activity of the Father, the Son, and the Spirit.

First, there is only one priesthood and one priestly ordination recognized by the NT. This is the eschatological and royal priesthood of the Son of David, Jesus the Christ (*Christos*). Understanding baptism as the royal priesthood's ordination begins with an understanding of Jesus' baptism as ordination to his ministry as Israel's Priest-king. Luther explains that the

---

40. See Muthiah, Yarnell, Garrett, and most contemporary Protestant systematic theologies. Barth and Leithart are exceptions.

41. Wood, *One Baptism*, 12; Wood, *Ordering the Baptismal Priesthood*.

42. Orr, *Gift of the Priesthood*, 220–57.

43. Tertullian, *On Baptism* 7 (*ANF* 3:672 [CCEL 3:1496]).

44. See Dabin's coverage of 348 theologians, including twenty-six pages on Augustine (*Le Sacerdoce Royal des Fidèles*).

two must remain together: "You must not separate your baptism from the baptism of Christ; but you must enter the baptism of Christ with your baptism, so that Christ's baptism becomes your baptism and your baptism becomes Christ's baptism and there is only one baptism."[45] If Protestants can agree that the baptism of Jesus provides the basis and norm for baptism, then significant progress toward recognizing the relationship between baptism and the priesthood of all believers will be made.[46]

Second, at the baptism, the *Father* ordains Jesus to his public ministry as Israel's eschatological Priest-king. Attention to this Trinitarian activity is important. Jesus was about thirty when he was baptized, the age when priests were ordained for public ministry, the age when Joseph and David were publicly "ordained" as typological Priest-kings. Chapter Three reviewed the two OT passages quoted by the Father at the baptism, one from the ordination song of the Davidic Priest-king (Psalm 2), and one from the ordination song of the Davidic Servant (Isaiah 42). In relation to the world and to his followers, Jesus' baptism marks a turning point, the beginning of his public ministry. What was true for Jesus is also true for his disciples. Baptism places each believer in a new relationship to other believers and to the world.[47] It publicly unites believers with the Son's baptismal ordination to royal and priestly ministry.

Third, the *Son's* action at the baptism provides a key to the relationship between the Son's ordination to ministry and the royal priesthood's ordination to a share in that eschatological ministry. The first words Matthew's readers hear Jesus speaking are of great significance for the royal priesthood: *"Let it be so now, for thus it is fitting for us to fulfill all righteousness"* (Matt 3:15; emphasis added). With these words, Jesus states his commitment to obey the Father's will.[48] The Father called the Son to a particular office and task: serving as the Anointed One, as Israel's eschatological priest-king, as the Suffering Servant, the faithful Son Israel failed to be. Jesus is introduced to Matthew's readers as the obedient Son who says "I do" to the Father's requirement of a righteous covenant partner.

Baptism is thus about covenant, about a volitional commitment between the Father and the Son in which the Son publicly agrees to faithfully fulfill the Father's calling. In the ecclesial practice of baptism, believers take

---

45. WA 51:111. ET in Pelikan, "Once for All the Sacrifice," 251.

46. Karl Barth, *CD* IV.4, 50–68.

47. It also places them in a new position in relation to themselves, as their personal identity shifts following baptism. In Chapter 3, I made this claim for Jesus as well.

48. Karl Barth, *CD* IV.4, 15. Barth, however, does not make a connection to baptismal vows.

baptismal vows.⁴⁹ These vows reflect their identification with the Son's obedience. At the baptism, Jesus accepted his vocation to royal and priestly ministry. In a similar way, at their baptism, each member of the royal priesthood takes vows to participate in the Son's obedience to the Father by the Spirit. Just as Jesus' "I do" to John's question indicated the direction of Christ's life, so the "I dos" at believers' baptisms indicate their acceptance of their public commissioning to a vocation of royal priesthood. Jesus' baptism is "a call narrative, a story of vocation and responsive obedience which is paradigmatic for the first great act of Christian obedience."⁵⁰

Fourth, at Jesus' baptism the Spirit is at work. The Father ordains, the Son covenants obedience, and the *Spirit* anoints with power for royal and priestly ministry. In the OT the Spirit would especially come upon kings and priests to empower them for royal and priestly ministry, but this elite arrangement was promised to change in the eschaton.⁵¹ With Christ's baptism, a new eschatological age begins. Jesus is the first of many siblings who will walk in a new way with the Holy Spirit. This "pentecostal" empowerment means that the least of Jesus' brothers and sisters will be greater than the greatest of those who lived in the age before Pentecost (Matt 11:11). Jesus' anointing at the baptism cannot be understood as a "new birth"; it must rather be understood as an empowering for ministry—a coming of the Spirit with the gifts described in Isa 11:1–4, the original "spiritual gifts" proof text.⁵² It is best to think of Jesus' anointing at the baptism in a small "p" pentecostal way.⁵³ The coming of the Spirit brings a new empowerment for mission and ministry as Israel's eschatological Priest-king.

Similarly, baptism is a moment of pentecostal empowerment for the royal priesthood.⁵⁴ Debate will continue as to the exact nature of the em-

---

49. As early as the third century Tertullian referenced this activity and compared it to the oath (*sacramentum*) taken by soldiers when joining the Roman army. See *On Idolatry* 19 (ANF 3:73 [CCEL 3:148]).

50. This is Webster's summary of Barth's understanding (*Barth's Ethics of Reconciliation*, 151).

51. See Irenaeus, *Against Heresies*, 3.17.1 (ANF 1:444 [CCEL 1:1121]; Habets, *Anointed Son*, 131–44.

52. See "Baptism: Commissioning of the Royal Priest (Matthew 3:13–17 and the Royal Priesthood (Matthew 28:16–20)" in Chapter Three above.

53. Newbigin, *Household of God*, 95; Smith, *Thinking in Tongues*, xvii. On the priesthood of all believers and the Pentecostal "baptism of the Spirit" see Macchia, "Baptized in the Spirit," 19. Cf. Francis of Riez's (d. 495) influential view of a second empowering by the Holy Spirit at confirmation (Orr, *Gift of the Priesthood*, 194–95).

54. The relationship between Spirit baptism (regeneration—divine action) and water baptism (human action) is beyond the book's scope. See Barth's *concursus Dei* discussed by Nimmo (*Being in Action*, 118–35).

powerment at baptism, but nearly all traditions should be able to agree that a believer's baptism is a significant moment of empowerment for witness to the world.[55] This empowerment is for a particular vocation. As the Spirit publicly came upon Christ to empower him for service, so the royal priesthood is publicly empowered at baptism for participation in Christ's royal and priestly service. Because Christ's ministry must ultimately be understood Trinitarianly, it is best understood as participation in the *missio Dei*. Baptismal ordination today, therefore, leads through Christ to participation in the trinitarian *missio Dei*.

If baptism is understood as ordination by the Father, to participation in the Son's royal and priestly ministry, in the power of the Holy Spirit, then a major turn will be made for Protestant ecclesiology and the priesthood of all believers. The turn does not require neglecting the truths related to the objective accomplishment of Christ on the cross to which baptism testifies, but rather a parallel emphasis on the new life in which the baptized believer walks. This new life is one with a particular royal and priestly vocation, a vocation best understood in terms of Worship, Work, and Witness. First, however, we relate our earlier conversation about practices to baptism in particular.

Exploring baptism as a practice widens our perspective. The ecumenical consensus treats the baptism of believers ("adults") as the norm. For example, Susan Wood speaks about candidates old enough to make their own baptismal vows as "normative." It is the *Rite of Christian Initiation of Adults* which provides "the form that determines the meaning of baptism."[56] This norm implies that candidates for baptism are usually old enough to profess their faith, and it holds even for Christian communions such as the Roman Catholic in which the vast majority of baptisms are infant baptisms. Attending to the tradition or social nature of baptism calls our attention to the complex actions associated with early baptismal practice. For many of the early Christian theologians, baptismal practice took place in four stages. L. Gregory Jones, focusing especially on Augustine's practice, identifies four stages: 1) a season of preparation often lasting two to three years; 2) a penultimate period of intense preparation often associated with Lent; 3) the baptismal act (vows, immersion, priestly robes); and 4) a "homecoming" celebration culminating in the newly baptized's first communion.[57]

Considering baptism as a practice also invites us to consider its eschatological nature, its *telos*. Baptism not only requires a backward look, but

---

55. Johnson, "Being and Act of the Church," 226.
56. Wood, "Baptism as a Mark," 26.
57. Jones, "Baptism," 153.

also an understanding that the baptized is entering a new way of life, Christ's life, leading ultimately to royal and priestly service before God's throne (Rev 5:10).[58] Yet, because the eschaton has broken into time through Christ, the baptized already experiences some measure of this royal and priestly ministry in the present.[59]

In sum, baptism is the foundation of the priesthood of all believers. It is the public ordination of believers to their missional ministry as part of Christ's royal priesthood. At baptism, believers are publicly identified with Christ's obedient response to his Father and empowerment by the Holy Spirit. For believers, baptism is the public commissioning to a share in the *missio Dei*.

The Baptized Life as Participation in Christ's Ongoing Royal-priestly Ministry: Returning to 1 Peter 2:4–9

Baptism points to a new life in Christ and a sharing in his royal and priestly vocation. "Baptism, however, is not over when it is done"; our bodies never dry off.[60] Often Protestants neglect this point. Baptism is reduced to a testimony about "an already completed inward working of God"; its focus is almost entirely in the past tense.[61] It is worth stating again that the objective element of baptism, the believer's union with the royal and priestly work of Jesus on the cross, must not be minimized. Yet the present and future tenses of baptismal practice must also be parsed, and the priesthood of all believers helps with this task. The last section looked at the present tense. At her baptism, a believer is publicly ordained to the ministry of the royal priesthood through participation in Christ's baptismal ordination. But baptism also has a future tense; it is eschatological, pointing the newly baptized toward a life of ministry as a royal priest. As suggested by 1 Pet 2:4–9's cultic triad, the *priests* who serve in the eschatological *temple* are primarily occupied with the offering of *spiritual sacrifices*.[62]

The royal priesthood offers "spiritual sacrifices acceptable to God through Jesus Christ" (1 Pet 2:5).[63] These spiritual sacrifices are best

---

58. See also Rev 7:15; 20:6; Barth, *CD* IV.4, 68–100.

59. Kärkkäinen, "Calling of the Whole People," 144–62; Kärkkäinen, *Spiritus Ubi Vult Spirat*, 332–58.

60. Torrance, *Royal Priesthood*, 34.

61. Grenz, "Baptism and the Lord's Supper, 83.

62. If 1 Peter 2 is understood as part of a baptismal homily, then connections between baptism and royal priesthood receive further support.

63. For Garrett spiritual sacrifice is the central function of the royal priesthood

understood as the entire lives of the royal priesthood's members—every thought, word, and action. Augustine put it this way: "There is, then, a true sacrifice in every work which unites us in a holy communion with God, that is, in every work that is aimed at that final Good in which alone we can be truly blessed."[64] The life into which baptism directs the members of the royal priesthood is a liturgical life, continually offering spiritual sacrifices.[65] Baptism publicly ordains believers to share in Christ's royal and priestly ministry. This priestly ministry primarily consists of the offering of spiritual sacrifices as part of the eschatological temple. The next section considers the spiritual sacrifices of the royal priesthood in the categories derived from Chapter Seven's trinitarian reflection: Worship, Work, and Witness. Within these three categories, the five Core Practices of the royal priesthood are outlined.

Spiritual Sacrifices as Practices: Romans 12:1–2 and the Royal Priesthood's Worship, Work, and Witness

An ancient Rabbi describing the eschatological age wrote, "In the future all sacrifices will cease, but the sacrifice of thanksgiving will not cease to all eternity."[66] A similar hope for the messianic age was shared by Paul. For Paul the eschaton had already dawned, and the age of atoning sacrifice was complete. For those who have repented, believed, and been baptized (Romans 1–6), the only sacrifices left are sacrifices of praise and thanksgiving for God's mercy (Rom 12:1). As the second question of the Heidelberg Catechism suggests, the Christian life is lived from gratitude. All members of the royal priesthood share the responsibility and privilege of offering thanksgiving (spiritual) sacrifices.

Since the second century, there has been a continual danger of reducing this responsibility and privilege to an elite few, a group John Howard Yoder identifies as the "religious professional."[67] Major breakthroughs for the priesthood of all believers have come when this reductionist tendency is reversed. Luther's understanding of the priestly nature of all believers' callings (*Berufe*) and Barth's rediscovery of the missionary vocation of every member of the royal priesthood are examples. Similarly, Congar's emphasis

---

(Garrett, "Biblical Doctrine," 148).

64. Augustine, *City of God* 10.6 (FC 14:125); Augustine, *Trinity* 4.14 (FC 45:155).

65. Corriveau, *Liturgy of Life*.

66. *Pesikta (de Rab. Kahana)* 79a, cited in Behm, "θύω, θυσία, θυσιαστήριον," 3:187.

67. See Chapter 4.

on the ministries of the whole people of God has brought renewal to more than a billion Catholics through Vatican II.[68]

The royal priesthood's five Core Practices must be understood theologically as spiritual sacrifices. It is not possible to defend or even suggest a comprehensive definition of each of the five Core Practices below. This leaves the option of either ignoring them completely, or providing a provisional outline for future dialogue and reflection. This study does the latter, and its chief contribution is its selectivity. If a constructive dialogue about why these particular practices are especially appropriate to the royal priesthood, and a discussion about their complexities, communal nature, internal goods (virtues), embodied standards of excellence, and eschatological *telos* is launched, then the section will have been successful. The doctrine of the royal priesthood leads believers to view all of human life as thanksgiving sacrifices of Worship, Work, and Witness offered to the Father through the Son by the Holy Spirit. The five Core Practices (Prayer, *Lectio Divina*, Ministry, Church Discipline, and Proclamation) are discussed in the three categories of Worship, Work, and Witness below.

Worship: The Practices of Prayer and Lectio Divina

In the category of Worship, we consider the two Core Practices in which royal priests relate directly to God. These are the practices of prayer and *Lectio Divina,* practices that overlap, yet maintain different emphases (speaking, hearing). Together they emphasize the royal priesthood's "communicative praxis" with God.[69] While once controversial, an ecumenical consensus now agrees that both practices belong to all members of the royal priesthood.

Prayer as a Practice of the Royal Priesthood

Prayer is especially the royal priesthood's practice of speaking to God. It begins with the Melchizedekian Priest-king who is now at the right hand of the Father interceding.[70] Because this great Priest-king has shed his blood for his siblings, believers can now draw near through the rent veil into the

---

68. Congar wrote over 1,600 books and articles, the most relevant being *Lay People in the Church* (ET 1957). Richard J. Beauchesne records Congar's description of the paragraphs he wrote for *Lumen Gentium,* including 2.9 where the people of God are described as a royal priesthood ("Worship as Life," 85n18).

69. Treier, *Virtue and the Voice of God,* 84.

70. Both Rom 8:34 and Heb 7:25 (cf. 9:24) speak of Christ's role as priestly intercessor with reference to Ps 110:1–4. Cf. Exod 28:29–30.

Most Holy Place. Through Christ the members of the royal priesthood come with joy and reverence before the throne of God (Heb 10:19–24; cf. Rev 7:15).[71] The members of the royal priesthood pray with hope and faith in the name of Jesus because in so doing they join in the priestly intercession of Christ, and his Spirit intercedes in and through them (Rom 8:26).[72] The foundation of the royal priesthood's prayer is thus its union with Christ's royal and priestly intercessory ministry, to which believers are ordained at their baptisms. The royal priesthood prays "through Christ, in Christ, and with Christ."[73]

The royal priesthood's practice of prayer is rooted in the High Priestly ministry of Jesus. Its first virtue is humility, and its first prayer is the "Our Father."[74] It is deepened and developed as the royal priesthood learns to pray the Psalms.[75] In joining with Christ's prayer, the Spirit leads the members of the royal priesthood deeper into the *missio Dei*, for the royal priesthood's prayer, like its mission, is for the glory of God and the sake of the world. In one sense, all seven Central Practices of the royal priesthood can be understood as forms of prayer. Thus, a case could be made that prayer is also a Constitutive Practice; it is of first importance.[76]

Lectio Divina as a Practice of the Royal Priesthood

Lectio Divina, or "divine reading," refers to the royal priesthood's practice of listening to God's voice in Scripture. It is a special term for a special book, a term reminding us that the church's practice of reading Scripture possesses a rich tradition. [77] The *"Divina"* in *Lectio Divina* reminds us that Scripture is a book different from all other books, and the royal priesthood approaches it with distinctive reading practices. For thousands of years God's people have practiced hearing God's voice in Scripture: "Open my eyes that I may see wonderful things in your law . . . whoever has ears, let them hear what the Spirit says to the churches" (Ps 119:18, Rev 2:29). In the OT, one of the priests' original responsibilities was to serve as oracular spokespersons. They were to inquire of the Lord, and to speak his Word to the people. The

71. Barth, *CD* IV/2, 277. See Chapter Six.
72. Calvin, *Institutes* 3.20.17–20 (LCC 21:874–78).
73. Redding, *Prayer and the Priesthood of Christ*, 286.
74. Calvin, *Institutes* 3.20 (LCC 21:850–920).
75. See de Lubac, *Medieval Exegesis*, vol. 3, 626n305; 658n184, cf. 658n182; 724n182.
76. Cf. Calvin, *Institutes* 3.20.28 (LCC 21:888).

77. The practice of *Lectio Divina* is to be distinguished from contemporary "devotional" reading and from the "academic" reading of scholarly guilds. See further Studzinski, *Reading to Live*, 1–19, 177–222; Robertson, *Lectio Divina*, xi–37.

only time God speaks directly to Aaron in Leviticus is to describe Aaron's priestly responsibility to teach and to judge (Lev 10:10). The responsibility to judge was originally symbolized in "the breastpiece of judgment" worn on the chest of the high priest containing the Urim and the Thummim (Exod 28:30; cf. Num 27:21).

The importance of the priests' responsibility to know the Word of God so as to be ready to teach remained throughout Israel's history: "For the lips of a priest should guard knowledge, and people should seek instruction from his mouth, for he is a messenger of the Lord of hosts" (Mal 2:7; cf. Ezra 7:10; Col 3:16). In the division of labor proposed here, teaching properly falls under the Core Practice of ministry. But, as Barth reminds us, to teach the Word of God first requires hearing it, and hearing God's voice in Scripture is *Lectio Divina*'s aim. Barth is correct; to know Scripture "and to have a part with all one's powers in the attempt to understand it, is not merely the affair of a few specialists but fundamentally the affair of the whole community."[78] All of God's people are "taught by the Lord" (Isa 54:13).[79]

Attending to *Lectio Divina* as a reading practice of the royal priesthood encourages us to explore its performance throughout the Christian tradition. In the medieval period, the reading of Scripture was largely reduced to a monastic practice. Monks approached Scripture in community through prayerful reading, memorization, meditation, and contemplation. This practice is evidenced in *The Rule of St. Benedict*, where the community prays the Psalter weekly.[80] The Carthusian monk Guigo II (d. 1188) divided the reading of Scripture into four parts (*lectio, meditatio, oratio, contemplatio*), a practice which became known as *Lectio Divina*.

Luther set *Lectio Divina* free from its Babylonian captivity and returned it to the royal priesthood. His most important contribution to the priesthood of all believers was his insistence that the Scriptures are the place where God speaks to all believers.[81] Luther learned from the monastic tradition that "everything the soul does in God's word—hearing, speaking, composing, meditating, etc." is prayer.[82] His radically "new" claim was that the monastery's practice of *Lectio Divina* should also be the practice of every ordained (baptized) member of the royal priesthood. Each had the right and responsibility to judge doctrine—reading Scripture to hear God's voice. This

---

78. CD IV.3.2, 870, see also 871; Irenaeus, *Against Heresies* 4:33:1 (*ANF* 1:506 [*CCEL* 1:1259]).

79. See 87–88 above.

80. For example, Benedict, *Rule of St. Benedict* 4.55–56; 8.3; 9:1–10; 38:1–12; 48:14–23 (pgs. 28, 38–39, 60, 70).

81. Pelikan, "Bible and the Word of God," 50.

82. *LW* 52:139.

privilege was to be practiced in community, and was why Luther believed so strongly in vernacular translations. Luther's contemporaries understood that the priesthood of all believers could not be practiced "unless the New and Old Testaments are translated into the barbaric languages, which the filthy common people will be able to understand."[83] They were correct. As the Scriptures are translated into the vernacular, and the royal priesthood begins to hear God's voice in Scripture, the power of the gospel is unleashed.[84]

Luther had many reasons for believing that a local community of royal priests was competent through the power of the Holy Spirit to recognize the voice of their Shepherd in contrast to the siren songs of false teachers.[85] Recently, Uche Anizor has built on Luther's thought, developing a biblical theology of the ideal reader of Scripture as a Priest-king.[86] He correctly identifies Jesus as the ideal reader of Scripture. Through baptism, with its joyous exchange, God's people have now been ordained to share in Christ's privileged status as ideal readers of Scripture. The people of God are now royal and priestly readers who can approach Scripture with confidence expecting to hear the God who speaks.[87]

Issues related to *Lectio Divina*'s standards of excellence and internal goods (virtues) have been addressed by recent scholarship on the theological interpretation of Scripture.[88] As with all the royal priesthood's practices, these standards and their internal goods can be debated. Yet an ecumenical consensus now agrees that all members of the royal priesthood should have access to the Word through which the Holy Spirit speaks.[89] Before moving to the next set of priestly practices it is worthwhile to recall the "atomistic priesthood." While all members of the royal priesthood share in Christ's status as ideal reader of Scripture, none are *the* Christ. On this side of the Parousia all readings will be read through a veil stained by the flesh, the

---

83. Edward Powell, cited in Yarnell, *Royal Priesthood in the English Reformation*, ch. 3. See 206–08 above.

84. Sanneh, *Translating the Message*.

85. See Luther's exegesis of John 6:45; 10:4; Matt 7:15; 24:4–5; 1 Thess 5:21 in *LW* 39:305–314.

86. Anizor, "Royal Priesthood of Readers."

87. See Fred Sanders' discussion of "The Tacit Trinitarianism of Evangelical Bible Reading" (*The Deep Things of God*, 193–209).

88. Treier, *Introducing Theological Interpretation of Scripture*; For my own position see Voss, "From 'Grammatical-historical Exegesis,'" 140–52.

89. Not all members of the royal priesthood are literate, and orality plays an important role in *Lectio Divina*. See Anizor, "Royal Priesthood of Readers," 303–311.

world, and the Devil. Discernment (Yoder) is necessary as the royal priesthood reads Scripture in pursuit of wisdom.

Work in the Temple: The Practices of Ministry and Church Discipline

This book defines "Work" as the service (*diakonia*) of one royal priest to another. The royal priesthood is the eschatological temple in which God's Spirit dwells, and each member is called to particular temple-service. Largely for heuristic reasons, "Work" is used for those practices directed between members of the royal priesthood. Yet, there is also good NT precedent for calling the saints service to one another "Work" (*ergon*).

Ministry (*diakonia*) as a Practice of the Royal Priesthood

Ephesians teaches that God has prepared good works ("ἔργοις ἀγαθοῖς") for believers to walk in (2:10), works explicated further in Eph 4:11–12. There, God's gift of leaders are those who use God's word to equip the saints to do the "work of ministry" ("ἔργον διακονίας").[90] The NT describes great diversity in these ministries (Romans 12, 1 Corinthians 12), and each is a gift (χάρισμα) given to serve Christ's body (1 Pet 4:10–11; 1 Cor 12:7). Ministry is not an exclusive function of ecclesial office holders; it is rather the Work of every member of the royal priesthood. To serve in the royal priesthood is to use one's gifts to build up the eschatological temple.

Protestants have not yet universally acknowledged Ministry as belonging to the whole people of God.[91] Miroslav Volf suggests that recognizing the diversity of the Spirit's ministry leads to an understanding of the church as a "polycentric community. . . . Thus the Spirit does not constitute the church exclusively through its office holders, but also through every member serving others with his or her gifts."[92] What then is the role of church officers within the royal priesthood? If they do not exclusively do the ministry, what is their unique function? To answer this question fully is impossible here.[93] Leadership within the church could easily be understood as its own

---

90. Equip, or καταρτισμὸν, is only used as a noun in the NT in Eph 4:12. Its verbal cognate is used in 2 Tim 3:17 and Heb 13:21, both uses support an equipping understanding of Eph 4:12. See Arnold, *Ephesians*, 262–64.

91. Yoder, *Body Politics*, 47–60; Yoder, *Fullness of Christ*.

92. Volf, *After Our Likeness*, 224, 226–27.

93. Resources for the development of a theology of ordination compatible with the doctrine of the royal priesthood proposed here can be found in Afanasiev, *Church of the*

sub-practice within the larger practice of Ministry.[94] Here we can only make a few initial observations.[95]

First, note the question's dogmatic location. It takes place within the larger category of the royal priesthood's Ministry.[96] Gifts of leadership and ecclesial officers are gifts from the Spirit in the same way that those who give liberally are gifts to the church (Rom 12:8). Ecclesial leadership, even if the first among equals, is still only one activity among many together making up the royal priesthood's practice of Ministry. Second, ecclesial office in the NT is especially concerned with oversight ("ἐπίσκοπος"; Acts 20:28; Phil 1:1) and character. Twenty-two of the twenty-four characteristics of the "ἐπίσκοπος" listed in Titus 1:5–9 and 1 Tim 3:1–7 are related to character. Finally, word-gifts, especially teaching and preaching, are especially important for office holders (1 Tim 3:2). This observation leads back to Eph 4:11–12's list of word-gifts (apostle, prophet, evangelist, pastor-teacher).[97] Those members of the royal priesthood who have these gifts are to use them to equip the saints so the saints can do their Work of service (Eph 4:12).[98] As each saint does his or her Work, the body of Christ is built up toward maturity—the fullness of Christ (Eph 4:13).[99] As the body grows toward maturity, it is better equipped to proclaim God's excellencies (1 Pet 2:9).

The most important responsibility of ecclesial office holders is to ensure that the gospel is continually heard and understood within the community. The first task of the royal priesthood is to preach the gospel. Where the royal priesthood has ceased to teach, preach, guard, and proclaim the gospel, there the royal priesthood has ceased to exist, and there the officers of the royal priesthood have failed in their unique function of oversight.[100]

The royal priesthood's larger practice of ministry is broader than ecclesial office and each member's exercise of particular *charisms* in service to the

---

Holy Spirit; Küng, *Church*; Volf, *After Our Likeness*; Kärkkäinen, *Spiritus Ubi Vult Spirat*; and Holmes, "Towards a Baptist Theology," 247–62.

94. Owens, *Shape of Participation*, 90, 65–94.

95. See also Barth, *CD* IV/3.2, 888–89; III/4, 489–90, 495–97; IV/2, 695 (discussed in Chapter Six).

96. For a similar remark, see Root, "Freedom, Authority," 104.

97. On gifts vs. office see Hoehner, *Ephesians*, 539. Cf. *LW* 39:314.

98. There is a revisionist interpretation of this verse which denies "ministry" to all except ordained ecclesial officers. It is especially associated with the "Gordon-Conwell school" (T. David Gordon, Andrew T. Lincoln, and John Jefferson Davis). See my discussion of thirty-two modern and ancient translations in "Who Are (Or Were) the Revisionists? A History of the Interpretation of Ephesians 4:12" in Voss, "Exalted Clergy," 57–75.

99. For exegetical defense see esp. ibid., 76–108; Hoehner, *Ephesians*, 538–79.

100. Webster, "Ethics of Reconciliation," 123.

body. Each member is also called to "speak the truth in love" (Eph 4:15).[101] Every member of Christ's body is "to instruct" (Rom 15:14), to "teach and admonish" (Col 3:16), and to "exhort one another" (Heb 3:13). Treier notes that the eschatological age has brought a new "diffusion of the Holy Spirit, who previously was connected to special task or office, upon every member of the church."[102] The practice of the royal priesthood's ministry includes use of gifts as well as all members exhorting one another. This second activity of ministry—speaking the truth in love—is closely related to church discipline, a practice we now explore.

Church Discipline: Binding and Loosing

Church Discipline, otherwise known as binding and loosing, the rule of Christ, or the ministry of the keys, is the royal priesthood's fourth Core Practice.[103] Luther could consider it a third sacrament.[104] Similarly, Balthasar Hubmaier (d. 1528), writing a few months before being burned at the stake, wrote, "Where this [fraternal admonition] is lacking, there is certainly also no church, even if Water Baptism and the Supper of Christ are practiced."[105] Church Discipline is closely tied to the royal priesthood's holiness, and holiness is a central mark of both OT and NT priesthoods (1 Pet 2:5).[106]

Church Discipline has little to do with church officers. For many centuries "church" meant "clergy" to the exclusion of other members of the royal priesthood.[107] Yet, the officers' portion of the practice is only a tiny fraction of its larger activity. The practice of Church Discipline is complex, consisting of activities such as confrontation, confession, forgiveness, and restoration.[108] It finds particular biblical warrant in Matt 18:15–20. Jesus' instructions for conflict resolution within the royal priesthood is personal, always remaining on the lowest possible social level (Matthew 18). The vast

---

101. On speaking the truth as a practice see Pohl's *Living into Community*, 111–55.

102. Treier, *Virtue and the Voice of God*, 86.

103. Kidder provides an ecumenically balanced overview (*Making Confession, Hearing Confession*). Yoder made "binding and loosing" the royal priesthood's first practice (*Body Politics*, 1–13). See also Küng, *Church*, 330–44.

104. *LW* 36:81–90; cf. 124; and Pelikan, *Spirit Versus Structure*, 28–30; 126–30.

105. Hubmaier, *Balthasar Hubmaier*, 387.

106. Nelson, *Raising up a Faithful Priest*, 26; Webster, *Holiness*, 57, 78; Wells, *God's Holy People*, 216–31, 245–46.

107. Wycliffe, *De Ecclesia* (WLW, iv). On the *ecclesia clericorum*, see Congar (*Lay People*, 48); cf. Osborne, *Ministry*, 473–80, esp. 474.

108. Jones, *Embodying Forgiveness*; Oden, *Corrective Love*, 205–11; Stott, *Confess Your Sins*; Tutu, *No Future Without Forgiveness*.

majority of sin is to be addressed by the member most directly affected. Not only office holders but all members of the royal priesthood have the privilege and responsibility of standing *in persona Christi*. Bonhoeffer explains:

> Now our brother stands in Christ's stead. . . . Christ became our brother in order to help us. Through him our brother has become Christ for us in the power and authority of the commission Christ has given to him [John 20:23]. . . . He hears the confession of our sins in Christ's stead and he forgives our sins in Christ's name. He keeps the secret of our confession as God keeps it. When I go to my brother to confess, I am going to God. [109]

This priestly responsibility and privilege is shared by all members of the royal priesthood.

Luther's rediscovery that "the keys are yours and mine" was one of the Reformation's most revolutionary aspects.[110] The Roman penitential system has a long and fascinating history, but most agree that by Luther's day it needed major reforms. In Yoder's view, part of this need for reform stems from the failure of the medieval church to recognize that the royal priesthood must be a voluntary community.[111] Anabaptism finds a connection between baptismal vows and a willingness to submit to church discipline.[112] When church discipline is imposed by civil authorities on unbelievers (baptized or not), it quickly becomes oppression, as illustrated by Hawthorne's *Scarlet Letter* or the infamous Salem Witch Trials.[113]

The practice of church discipline has historically been of great importance to movements emphasizing the priesthood of all believers. This is true for Luther's original Reformation doctrine, the Anabaptist movement, Pietism's attempt to retrieve Luther's doctrine, Moravian choirs, Wesleyan classes, and sectors of contemporary evangelicalism.[114] To sum up, the Work of the royal priesthood consists especially of ministry and church discipline. The next section explores the royal priesthood's Witness.

---

109. Bonhoeffer, *Life Together*, 111–12. Of course his words apply equally to "sisters."

110. *LW* 35:16, cf. 12.

111. Yoder, *Body Politics*, 5.

112. See Hubmaier's sixth question in "A Form for Water Baptism," *Balthasar Hubmaier*, 389.

113. Bloom, *Nathaniel Hawthorne's the Scarlet Letter*.

114. Kidder, *Making Confession*, 103–38; Yoder, *Body Politics*, 7; Cole, *Organic Church*.

Witness in the World: The Practice of Proclamation

First, we again emphasize that *Witness* is primarily the activity of the Holy Spirit in the world. The Holy Spirit bears witness to Christ for the glory of the Father. Thus the royal priesthood's witness participates in the life and activity of Godself, in the *missio Dei*. The royal priesthood's appropriate response to the Spirit's prevenience is an obedient movement of witness into the world, proclaiming the kingdom of the Father and practicing the healing presence of the Son. The witness of the royal priesthood is a Christocentric-Trinitarian witness.

Secondly, the royal priesthood bears witness in the *world*. The biblical concept of "world" is complex, but some type of distinction (*diastasis*) between church and world must be made.[115] The church cannot exist for the world if the church and the world are synonymous. The magisterial Reformers' failure to adequately address the church-world relationship has become increasingly evident as Christendom's monuments crumble.[116] The royal priesthood's primary function in relation to the world is to testify to Christ and to Christ's way, to be a "sign, foretaste, and instrument of the kingdom."[117]

Witness is any activity of the royal priesthood within the world, but especially that activity directed toward the world.[118] In world context, all of the royal priesthood's practices are ultimately related to Witness, just as all could be related to Worship as spiritual sacrifices.[119] The Constitutive and Core Practices can all be related to Witness. Yet while all bear some relationship to Witness as a function of both the royal priesthood's location in the world and their participation in the witness of the Spirit, it is particularly appropriate to consider the royal priesthood's practice of Proclamation here.

The royal priesthood's calling to *Proclamation* is announced in 1 Pet 2:9, "But you are a chosen race, a royal priesthood . . . that you may proclaim ["ἐξαγγείλητε"] the excellencies of him who called you out of darkness into his marvelous light." Luther explains that "A priest must be God's messenger . . . the first and foremost duty we Christians should perform [as priests] is to proclaim the wonderful deeds of God."[120] He exhorts the royal priesthood

---

115. Barth, *CD* IV.3.1, 11–38.

116. Yoder, *Anabaptism and Reformation*, 281.

117. This was Lesslie Newbigin's preferred way of speaking about the church (Goheen, *Lesslie Newbigin's Missionary Ecclesiology*, 172).

118. See further Philibert's five dimensions of the royal priesthood's witness (*Priesthood of the Faithful*, 89–90).

119. Barth, *CD* IV/3.2, 843–54; see Chapter Six.

120. *LW* 30:64–66. It is not clear that Luther would have made this statement after

that proclamation is "your chief function as a priest... your chief work."[121] The royal priesthood's anointing with the Holy Spirit is for the purpose of participating in witness (Acts 1:8). Their mission is to shine as lights while holding forth the word of life (Phil 2:15–16).[122] Understanding Proclamation as a practice can account for a wide variety of activities. Wisdom can be gained from careful reflection on the practice's tradition. For example, its location within the larger category of witness (*martyria*) reminds us that Proclamation is associated with suffering (Heb 12:2) as testify the church's one million martyrs from the last decade (2000–2010).[123]

The literature on Proclamation is immense, and our chief objective must simply be to identify its significance for the royal priesthood. But first some clarifications: Proclamation, as understood here, is not primarily the speaking of truth in love to other brothers and sisters, nor the preaching and teaching of God's Word for ecclesial edification. These activities are better understood within the practice of Ministry. Rather, Proclamation is the announcement of the good news of Jesus Christ to the poor, the sick, the hungry—to those oppressed by darkness (Matt 11:2–6; Luke 4:16–44; Phil 2:14–18). The last fifty years have seen an important, but often sterile debate between advocates for two of Proclamation's activities: word and deed.[124] Sixty years ago, evangelical Protestants had an uneasy conscience due to their neglect of deeds;[125] today they are uneasy about their verbal testimony.[126] Both are necessary Proclamation in word and deed is the royal priesthood's chief responsibility to the world.[127]

Two additional comments need to be made about the royal priesthood's proclamation. First, it is especially proclamation to the poor. The triune God of Scripture has revealed himself to be especially concerned

---

1525. Following the Peasants' War he limits the proclamation of non-magisterially appointed believers to domestic proclamation (e.g., parents to children). Luther assumes a baptized world, and his proclamation is primarily one "brother" to "another." His "proclamation" is better understood as an activity within the practice of Ministry (speaking the truth in love).

121. Ibid., 66.

122. Ware, *Mission of the Church*, 256–84.

123. The best data indicate approximately 1.6 million Christian martyrs between 1990 and 2000, and approximately one million between 2000 and 2010 (Barrett, et al., "Christianity 2011," 28–29).

124. See the Lausanne Study Group's essays (Nicholls, *In Word and Deed*).

125. Henry, *Uneasy Conscience*, 35–46.

126. Newbigin, *Unfinished Agenda*, 230.

127. See Davis and Cornett, "Empowering People for Freedom," 4:310–39.

with the lowly, the humble, the poor (Isaiah 58; Isa 66:2; Matt 5:3).[128] In the OT God's people were to show particular care for the poor as a mark of holiness. In particular, the poor were to be a special concern for the priests who represented Yahweh.[129] The Temple was supposed to be a center for justice and provision for the poor and oppressed.[130] Isaiah prophesied that the priestly seed of the Servant could be distinguished from false priests by their care for the poor (Isaiah 58).[131]

Secondly, numerous other activities of proclamation could be discussed: missionary congregations, missional sodalities, missional orders, go structures, mission organizations, and parachurch agencies. Similarly, terms related to proclamation could be explored: preaching, evangelism, personal evangelism, incarnational evangelism, evangelization, integral evangelism, centripetal mission, social justice, spiritual warfare, and creation care (cf. Mark 16:15).[132] Each of these terms represents important debates taking place about proclamation. Especially important for the royal priesthood's proclamation are the proposals for *integral mission* put forth by Latin American teachers.[133] A healthy Protestant doctrine of the priesthood of all believers will welcome these discussions. It will rejoice in the growing awareness of the centrality of the practice of proclamation to every member of the royal priesthood.

Finally, as noted above, all of the royal priesthood's activities can be perichoretically related to Proclamation. Their everyday service to the wider world motivated by love of God and neighbor can be offered as a spiritual sacrifice to God as part of their priestly vocation (*Beruf*). Here service to God offered as a doctor, lawyer, plumber, tax accountant, manager, therapist, banker, or computer programmer can be understood as priestly work,

---

128. "Lausanne Occasional Paper 22: Christian Witness to the Urban Poor;" Davis, *Foundations for Christian Mission*, 175–226, 251–56.

129. Every third year Israel was to bring the priests a third tithe especially for the poor (Deut 14:28–15:18; Tob 1:6–7; Josephus, *Antiquities* 4.8.22 [*Josephus the Complete Works*, CCEL 238]).

130. Perrin, *Jesus the Temple*, 114–48.

131. See Blomberg, *Neither Poverty nor Riches*; Longenecker, *Remember the Poor*. Longenecker has no interaction with Blomberg.

132. Many of these issues are discussed in a seminal collection of thirty essays: Chilcote and Warner, *Study of Evangelism*. Important issues unaddressed include missional sodalities, missional orders, and go structures, for which see Winter, "Two Structures," 220–30; Goheen, *Lesslie Newbigin's Missionary Ecclesiology*. Also absent are "integral mission" and the relationship between evangelism and spiritual warfare.

133. See esp. Roldán, "Priesthood of All Believers;" Rodas, "La misión integral," 25–38; Segura, "La misión como liberación integral," 23–40.

divine service bearing witness to Christ (Eph 6:6–7; Col 3:23–24).[134] The past two sections have discussed baptism and the royal priesthood's five Core Practices (Prayer, *Lectio Divina*, Ministry, Church Discipline, and Proclamation). We now turn to the royal priesthood's seventh and final Central Practice—the Lord's Supper.

The Lord's Supper as Consummation of the Royal Priesthood's Spiritual Practices

Peter Leithart is a Protestant who has rightly embraced weekly congregational practice of the Lord's Supper. Despite clear NT evidence, and the unified witness of the Great Tradition, the Lord's Supper is not celebrated weekly in a majority of Protestant churches.[135] Reflecting on his congregation's practice, Leithart claims:

> The Lord's Supper is the world in miniature; it has cosmic significance. Within it we find clues to the meaning of all creation and all history, to the nature of God and the nature of man, to the mystery of the world, which is Christ. It is not confined to the first day for its power fills seven. Though the table stands at the center, its effects stretch out to the four corners of the earth.[136]

Leithart is not alone in his high view of the Lord's Supper; Thomas Aquinas taught that it is the "greatest of all the sacraments . . . all the other sacraments are ordered to this one as to their end."[137] While not agreeing with Aquinas on the sacramental nature of the Lord's Supper, Karl Barth still viewed it as having a uniquely formative role in the life of the royal priesthood. His unfinished *Ethics of Reconciliation* was to have culminated in a "paragraph" on the Lord's Supper as "the thanksgiving—*eucharistia*—which renews the Christian life."[138]

---

134. While there is one primary call (Eph 4:1–4) to Worship, Work, and Witness, each believer also has specific activities—a secondary call—to individually walk in (Eph 2:10). All of these secondary activities can be offered by members of the royal priesthood to God as spiritual sacrifices. This perichoretic understanding of Worship, Work, and Witness has been modeled historically by the lay Benedictine communities. See further Volf, *Work in the Spirit*, 123–54; Stevens, *Other Six Days*, 106–30.

135. "Both theologically and sociologically, the Lord's Supper was the central act of the weekly assemblies of the early church" (Ferguson, *Church of Christ*, 249).

136. Leithart, *Blessed are the Hungry*, 11.

137. Aquinas, *ST* 3.65.3.

138. Barth, *CL*, ix.

Baptism and the Lord's Supper are uniquely formative practices. Together they are the royal priesthood's two Constitutive Practices, the "prologue and epilogue" of the Christian life.[139] They provide the key to all of creation, life, history, and the royal priesthood's practices. Baptism and Eucharist are not necessarily more important than the royal priesthood's Core Practices (e.g., Prayer or Proclamation), but they are uniquely constitutive of the identity of the royal priesthood as those humans who have been united to Jesus Christ.

For many centuries the Lord's Supper has been known as the Eucharist, a wonderful reminder that the Lord's Supper is the royal priesthood's first thanksgiving sacrifice.[140] Chapter Four identified a problematic turn in the royal priesthood's Eucharistic practice when Cyprian claimed exclusive rights to the offering of this sacrifice for the bishop.[141] Luther recovered the practice as a festal meal of the whole church, and the parched throats of God's people were once again wetted with the first fruits of heaven's vine.[142] The Lord's Supper is thus the paradigmatic spiritual sacrifice, providing the model for all spiritual sacrifices. It constantly renews the royal priesthood's vocation to a liturgy of life rooted in the cruciform model of its great Priest-king.[143]

How does the royal priesthood practice the Lord's Supper? The answer's complexities are as deep and beautiful as the peoples of every tongue and tribe and nation who will gather at the wedding feast of the Lamb (Rev 5:9–10; 19:7; 22:17). Here we simply offer a brief parsing of the practice's past, present, and future significance in light of seven words: remembrance, forgiveness, Eucharist, covenant, communion, nourishment, and anticipation.[144]

First, the Lord's Supper recalls the *past*, calling the royal priesthood to remembrance of forgiveness, Eucharist, and covenant. Jesus commands the royal priesthood to "do [ποιεῖτε] this in remembrance of me" (1 Cor 11:24). The Lord's Supper, like baptism, points to the forgiveness of sins purchased

---

139. Ibid., 45.

140. On the Lord's Supper as sacrifice, see Smith, *A Holy Meal*, 61–65.

141. Some Roman Catholic theologians tell this story differently. Many argue that Cyprian's turn represents the Holy Spirit's binding pattern on the church for all time. See Daly, *Sacrifice Unveiled*; Levering, *Sacrifice and Community*; O'Connor, *Hidden Manna*; Kilmartin, *Eucharist in the West*.

142. Pelikan, *Luther the Expositor*, 136–254. Vatican II's liturgical reforms restored at least the option of the laity's sharing in the cup.

143. Corriveau, "Temple, Holiness, and the Liturgy."

144. Smith treats each of these words in its own chapter. I have rearranged them to correspond with a past, present, and future schema (*A Holy Meal*, cf. 82).

by Christ on the cross (Matt 26:28; 1 Pet 2:24).[145] The finished work of Christ calls us to joyful thanksgiving, a Eucharistic life.[146] The cup of blessing is not meant to be drunk with sorrow (1 Cor 11:16), for Jesus drank the cup of sorrow on our behalf. Like the Israelites rejoicing after their deliverance at the Red Sea, the royal priesthood rejoices with thanksgiving at God's table.[147] The table also reminds us of the new covenant (Luke 22:20; 1 Cor 11:25), and of our baptismal oath to participate in this covenant (Matt 3:13; 2 Cor 3:6). As especially the Puritan theologians have emphasized (e.g., Jonathan Edwards), the Lord's Supper invites us to remember and renew our baptismal covenant every time we come to the table.[148]

Second, the royal priesthood's practice of the Lord's Supper calls for particular activities in the present. This includes forgiveness, Eucharist, covenant, communion, and the receiving of nourishment. These have already been hinted at above. The forgiveness we remember at the Lord's Supper, like the forgiveness we pray for in the Lord's Prayer, is basic to the Christian life. To eat with Jesus at table is to eat with forgiven sinners. Jesus' company at meals often caused surprise among religious people (Matt 9:9–13), and to miss the power of his forgiveness is to miss the essence of his message (Matt 6:14–15; 18:21–35).[149] At the Lord's Supper, we "rejoice with joy that is inexpressible"; although we do not yet see Jesus, we taste his goodness in the present (1 Pet 1:7).

At the Lord's Supper we renew our baptismal vows. This renewal is a public sign of our commitment to live the prayer, "may your kingdom come, may your will be done on earth as it is in heaven" (Matt 6:10). The Lord's Supper, like baptism and the Lord's Prayer, is a reminder that all of life is to be offered as a thanksgiving sacrifice. John's theological exegesis of the Lord's Supper is the story of Jesus washing his disciples' feet (John 13). In the same way, participation in the Lord's Supper calls the royal priesthood to humble service and faithful proclamation of the good news to the poor.[150]

The royal priesthood's practice of the Lord's Supper also calls its members to enjoy fellowship (*koinonia*) and to receive nourishment in the present.[151] At the Lord's Supper, the royal priesthood fellowships with Christ

---

145. Jones, *Transformed Judgement*, 147; Smith, *A Holy Meal*, 57–66.

146. The opposite of an evil life is a life of thanksgiving (Eph 5:4). The Greek word for thanksgiving (*eucharistia*) shares a root with the Greek word for grace (*charis*) and joy (*chairō*).

147. Smith, *A Holy Meal*, 99–108.

148. Ibid., 67–79.

149. Wainwright, *Eucharist and Eschatology*, 33–34.

150. Gutiérrez, *Theology of Liberation*, 148–50.

151. Smith, *Holy Meal*, 45–56, 81–90.

(Rev 1:12–20), with one another, and proleptically with the communion of saints (1 Cor 10:16).[152] This fellowship illustrates again how the Lord's Supper is paradigmatic. The *koinonia* of the Spirit is deepened through the royal priesthood's obedient practice of any of the seven Central Practices. Like manna, the Lord's Supper provides nourishment (John 6:35), and the royal priesthood is renewed for obedient service and witness.

Finally, the royal priesthood's practice of the Lord's Supper points toward the future with anticipation and hope.[153] It is a proleptic participation in the wedding feast of the Lamb and his bride. It is ultimately a consummative practice, summing up all other practices and eschatologizing them. The Lord's Supper reminds the royal priesthood that all of its practices are leading to a particular *telos*. At Pentecost, the music of the wedding feast began to be heard on earth, and in the Lord's Supper the royal priesthood proleptically raises its glass in a joyous toast to her groom.

In sum, the royal priesthood's practice of the Lord's Supper has past, present, and future significance especially captured in the words remembrance, forgiveness, Eucharist, covenant, communion, nourishment, and anticipation. In the Lord's Supper, the foundation of the royal priesthood's vocation is recalled and baptismal vows are renewed. The royal priesthood's Practices are circumscribed by the spiritual sacrifice of thanksgiving offered at the Lord's Table.

Chapter Summary

This chapter provides the royal priesthood's "Ethics in Outline." Each of the royal priesthood's seven Central Practices (Baptism, Prayer, *Lectio Divina*, Ministry, Church Discipline, Proclamation, and the Lord's Supper) could be treated in much greater depth. This chapter's primary contribution is not a comprehensive treatment of each practice, but rather its discussion of the relationship between each practice and the priesthood of all believers. A second contribution relates to the theological judgments required for the selection of the practices. By distinguishing between Constitutive, Core, and Creation practices the chapter places particular dogmatic weight on seven Central Practices, which are essential to the health of the royal priesthood. My prayer is that the royal priesthood will put them into practice to the glory of the Father through the Son in the power of the Holy Spirit.

---

152. "οὐχὶ κοινωνία ἐστὶν τοῦ αἵματος τοῦ Χριστοῦ; τὸν ἄρτον ὃν κλῶμεν, οὐχὶ κοινωνία τοῦ σώματος τοῦ Χριστοῦ ἐστιν;"

153. Luke 22:16, 18; Matt 25:1–13; Rev 19:7. See Smith, *A Holy Meal*, 91–98.

Conclusion

THE PRIESTHOOD OF ALL believers is a pillar undergirding Protestant ecclesiology. The book has examined this pillar's canonical, catholic, and contextual dimensions. We sum up by identifying eight theses on the priesthood of all believers, each offering a point of departure for future study. Finally, we conclude with a brief statement of the book's contribution to missional theology, Protestant ecclesiologies, and contemporary discussions of the royal priesthood.

Chapter Theses

Thesis One

The royal priesthood is a significant theme in biblical theology, and its scope is far greater than the four texts to which it is often limited (1 Pet 2:5–9; Rev. 1:6; 5:10; 20:6). The doctrine must be understood with reference to the eschatological temple and spiritual sacrifices.

Thesis Two

Isaiah's eschatology played a foundational role in forming the first Christian theologians' doctrine of the royal priesthood; Jesus was understood as Isaiah's Suffering Servant (*'ebed Yahweh*), the Davidic Priest-king whose climatic self-offering ushered in an eschatological age of democratized priesthood for those identified as the Servant's seed, the *'ebedîm*.

Thesis Three

At the heart of the NT's understanding of the royal priesthood is Jesus, the anointed Melchizedekian Priest-king (Psalm 110), who has brought a new eschatological reality in which the OT's promise of royal priesthood has been realized by his disciples through union with Christ.

Thesis Four

The royal priesthood was gradually defrocked of its priestly privileges through hierarchicalization, sacralization, and politicization in the third through sixteenth centuries.

Thesis Five

Luther's priesthood of all believers centers on the Christian's participation in the royal priesthood of Christ made possible through the new birth and baptismal ordination. It is exercised by believers as they preach the Word, pray, and offer spiritual sacrifices, thereby representing God to one another and each other to God.

Thesis Six

Karl Barth's post-Christendom perspective opened a new paradigm for the priesthood of all believers in which their vocation of witness in the world receives proper emphasis.

Thesis Seven

A Christian doctrine of the priesthood of all believers should be developed with a Christocentric-Trinitarian understanding of the *missio Dei*. There are especially appropriate ways for the royal priesthood to relate to the Father (*latreia*), the Son (*diakonia*), and the Holy Spirit (*martyria*).

Thesis Eight

A canonically and catholically informed priesthood of all believers leads contextually to particular ecclesial practices. The seven Central Practices are 1) Baptism as public ordination to the royal priesthood; 2) Prayer; 3) *Lectio Divina*; 4) Ministry; 5) Church Discipline; 6) Proclamation; and 7) the Lord's Supper.

Contributions

What contribution does this book make to missional theology, Protestant ecclesiologies, and a contemporary doctrine of the priesthood of all believers? Beyond simply addressing a neglected theological topic, this book has brought together a number of natural conversation partners.

First, missional theology, in service to church and world, is theology's future. Protestant discussions of missional theology assume the priesthood of all believers, but the doctrine is often a wax nose, bent variously, and looking a bit different after each use. By providing a Christocentric-Trinitarian version of the doctrine, and sketching seven Central Practices, this book provides a concrete proposal for future discourse. It also guards against missional theology inadvertently contributing to a reductionist version of the priesthood of all believers. For example, Newbigin's contribution was his clarity on the royal priesthood's priestly responsibilities in the world; however, his claim that "the exercise of this priesthood is not within the walls of the Church but in the daily business of the world" is unbalanced.[1] The royal priesthood exercises its priestly ministry when gathered and scattered. Luther's twin emphases on the royal priesthood's access to the Father and their ministry to one another must be combined with Newbigin's emphasis on priestly ministry to the world. If missional ecclesiologies only emphasize the royal priesthood's priestly witness in the world, then the doctrine faces dangers similar to Raiser's "cosmocentric-Trinitarian" ecclesiology.[2]

Historically, inadequate versions of the doctrine were the result of similar reductions. On the one hand, some suggested that the priesthood of all believers is primarily an anthropological doctrine. Thus, it only has to do with believers' responsibilities to one another, not with believers' access to God. On the other hand, some traditions used the doctrine to focus on an individual believer's relationship with God, neglecting neighbors, often resulting in a gnostic priesthood. In contrast to reductionist tendencies, the royal priesthood's Worship, Work, and Witness must be held together by those seeking to faithfully perform the doctrine. The seven Central Practices (Chapter 8) provide standards of excellence for this dialogue. In sum, Protestant missional ecclesiologies need to be attentive to the Christocentric-Trinitarian nature of the priesthood of all believers in order to avoid reductionism.

Second, the priesthood of all believers is a pillar of Protestant ecclesiology. As western believers walk deeper into a post-Christendom culture,

---

1. Newbigin, *Gospel in a Pluralistic Society*, 230.
2. See 257–58 above.

"reshapings of ecclesial thought and practice greater than those of the Reformation and comparable, perhaps, to the fourth century may well be unavoidable."[3] An ecclesiological *ressourcement* is needed. This book attempts such a retrieval through its canonical, catholic, and contextual examination of the priesthood of all believers. The doctrine provides a foundational resource for both western and non-western believers in search of faithful ecclesiologies. If this book aids in this project, then it will have accomplished a central aim.

Finally, as far as making a specific contribution to contemporary conversations on the priesthood of all believers, four aspects can be highlighted. First, the book has brought recent discoveries in biblical studies and biblical theology into conversation with missional theologians and those writing on the priesthood of all believers. The study emphasizes the relationships between royal priesthood, eschatological temple, and spiritual sacrifice. While some theologians (e.g., Congar), have reflected deeply on this triad, many Protestants treat one without referencing the others. The book's attentiveness to all three in 1 Pet 2:4-9 draws attention to the concepts' intricate relationships. The book also names the significance of Isaiah 56-66 for the NT's description of disciples as an eschatological royal priesthood. While at least one writer has noted the larger "Kultmotiv in Tritojesaja," this book is the first to give significant theological reflection to this exegetical insight.[4] It also widens the canonical discussion of the royal priesthood beyond its traditional four NT texts, especially retrieving Luther's emphasis on Psalm 110.

The second aspect is properly theological; the book is the first to treat the doctrine from an explicitly Christocentric-trinitarian framework. It builds on the rich ecumenical recovery of trinitarian doctrine during the last century, especially as it relates to the ecclesial household.[5] It makes a third contribution by being the first major study to critically examine Christendom's effect on the priesthood of all believers, particularly on witness. As heated debates about Christendom continue, increased clarity on how previous versions have affected the royal priesthood add light. Finally, the book proposes seven Central Practices. Protestants too believe in the one, holy, catholic, and apostolic church. Yet there is much diversity in understanding the meaning of these marks.[6] Concentrating attention on the royal priesthood's seven Central Practices gives them a particular dogmatic weight in

---

3. Lindbeck, "Scripture, Consensus, and Community," 90.
4. Schüssler Fiorenza, *Priester für Gott*, 162-64.
5. Cf. Muthiah, *Priesthood of All Believers*, 47-86.
6. See esp. Barth, *CD* IV/1, 686; Berkouwer, *Church*; cf. Dever's summary of twenty Protestant "marks" lists from the 1990s (*Nine Marks*, 234-42).

these conversations. As grace is given for wise participation in these practices, the royal priesthood's Worship, Work, and Witness will increase to the glory of the triune God.

APPENDIX

Significant Figures and Events for the Royal Priesthood:

First through Twenty-First Centuries

GIVEN THE DEARTH OF recent works on the priesthood of all believers, this appendix serves as a type of annotated bibliography. It is selective, not exhaustive, and is meant to aid future research. The appendix identifies persons, documents, and historical events especially significant to the doctrine. It also provides access to the thirty most important theologians identified in Paul Dabin's monograph (1950), a work inaccessible to many. Where an item is discussed in this text, readers are usually simply referred to the relevant chapter. In this appendix, RP refers to Royal Priesthood, MP to Ministerial Priesthood, and PoAB to Priesthood of All Believers.

First Century

Date and Author	Emphasis/Event	Further Discussion in:
Jerusalem (AD 30 or 33)	Jesus Crucified, Temple Veil Torn, Pentecost, Ascension	Voss, Ch. 3; esp. Gurtner (2007).
Paul's *Epistles* (ca. 57–65?)	Believers offering spiritual sacrifices and engaging in priestly ministry.	Voss, Chs. 1, 3.
1 Peter (ca. 62–63), Rome	Believers called a "royal priesthood."	Voss, Ch. 1, 3.
Hebrews (ca. 60s), Rome	Believers engage in a priestly ministry.	Voss, Ch. 1, 3.
Gospel of Matthew (ca. 70), Antioch	Disciples engaged in a priestly ministry.	Voss, Ch. 1, 3.

Date and Author	Emphasis/Event	Further Discussion in:
Jewish Temple Destroyed (70), Jerusalem	Radical implications for cultic activities and understandings of temple, priest, and sacrifice.	Chilton/Neusner (1995).
Christians excluded from Synagogues, Palestine (ca. 85)	Pushed Christians to further reflect on their understanding of priest, temple, and sacrifice.	Chilton/Neusner (1995).
Revelation (ca. 95), Asia Minor (Turkey)	Jesus portrayed as a Priest-king, and believers called priests.	Voss, Ch. 3.
Clement of Rome, *1 Clement* (ca. 96)	First to refer to those not serving in ecclesial office as λαϊκὸς (lay persons), although he emphasized that all baptized believers had a priestly ministry.	Voss (2013), Chs. 3–4; Stewart (2006), 242–44; Hellerman (2001), 133–39; Bulley (2000), 51–54, 141–43, 227–36; Noll (1993), 57–86; Faivre (1990), 15–24; Daly (1978), 313–17; Eastwood (1963), 56–59.
The Didache (ca. 100), Syria/Palestine	Refers to leaders as high priests, but does not deny that all Christians are priests.	Stewart (2006), 240–42; Bulley (2000), 54–57, 143–44; 227–36; Noll (1993), 257–312; Eastwood (1963), 59.

Patristic: Ante-Nicene Fathers (100–325)

Date and Author	Emphasis/Event	Further Discussion in:
Odes of Solomon (ca. 95–125), Antioch	First outside of NT to explicitly mention a believer as a priest offering sacrifices.	Voss (2013), Chs. 1, 3; Bulley (2000), 65, 159, 219–20; *contra* 153; Hanson (1985), 85.
Ignatius, (d. ca. 107), Antioch	High view of both the ministry of the bishop and of the unity of the church.	Bulley (2000), 57–59, 145–46, 227–36; Noll (1993), 87–134; Eastwood (1963), 67.
Epistle of Barnabas (ca. 130), Alexandria	All Christians are exhorted to offer sacrifices and to be temples.	Bulley (2000), 148–50, 227–36; Noll (1993), 157–86.
Bar Kochba Revolt (135), Palestine	Major breaking point between Jews and Christians with implications for how Christian priesthood is viewed in relation to Jewish priesthood.	Stewart (2006), 27, 260–61; Yoder (1987) 20.

SIGNIFICANT FIGURES AND EVENTS FOR THE ROYAL PRIESTHOOD   249

Date and Author	Emphasis/Event	Further Discussion in:
Shepherd of Hermes (ca. 140), Rome	A non-presbyter has authority to teach and provide ecclesial direction for the church.	Bulley (2000), 146–48, 227–36; Noll (1993), 187–256 cf. Hellholm (2010), 219–28.
Polycarp (ca. 135, d. ca. 155), Smyrna, Asia-Minor	Widows described with cultic language as those who offer sacrifices.	Bulley (2000), 148, 227–36; Noll (1993), 135–56; Eastwood (1963), 59–61.
Justin Martyr, (d. 165), Rome	Second outside of NT to explicitly mention general "priesthood of all believers." He describes believers as a "high priestly race" all of whom offer sacrifices.	Voss (2013), Chs. 3, 4; Bulley (2000), 59–62, 150–53; 237–40; Faivre (1990), 25–35; Daly (1978), 323–37; Eastwood (1963), 61–66; Pelikan (1971), 25.
Melito of Sardis (d. ca. 180), Sardis, Asia-Minor	Believers are described as a "new priesthood and an eternal people."	Voss (2013), Ch. 4; Bulley (2000), 159, 219.
Irenaeus (d. ca. 200), Smyrna (Turkey) and Lyons (France)	Jesus, the disciples, and the church share in priesthood.	Voss (2013), Ch. 3; Faivre (1990), 35–40; Daly (1978), 339–59; Eastwood (1963), 66–70.
First Christian Public Spaces (ca. 200–250)	The church begins to transition from exclusively meeting in the homes of believers to meeting in buildings set aside for public worship.	Stewart (2006); 82–96.
Clement of Alexandria (d. 216)	All mature believers have priestly privileges and responsibilities.	Osborne (1993), 132–34; Faivre (1990), 53–59; Daly (1978), 440–87; Eastwood (1963), 71–73; de Lubac (1950), 138; Dabin (1950), 512–16.
Tertullian (d. 220), Carthage, Africa, Married	Believers are "priests of the spiritual temple." They are ordained as priests at their baptism.	Voss (2013), Ch. 4; Stewart (2007), 35–54; Leithart 2003 (87); Osborne (1993), 139–43; Orr (1991), 21–39; Faivre (1990), 45–51; Eastwood (1963), 73–75; de Lubac (1950), 136–39; Dabin (1950), 69–72; Rea (1947), 2–12.
Apostolic Tradition (ca. 215–250?), Rome	Describes the baptismal rite as an ordination to priestly ministry.	Stewart (2007), 55–98; Osborne (1993), 127–31; Faivre (1990), 74–85; Afanasiev (1997 ET/1971 Russian), 26–27; cf. Bradshaw (2002), 1–17.

Date and Author	Emphasis/Event	Further Discussion in:
Didascalia Apostolorum, (ca. 230), Syria/Palestine	Refers to the whole church as a royal priesthood, and to the bishop as the high priest. Refers to laymen as "brothers." Associates baptism with the anointing received by OT priests.	Stewart (2007), 99–105; Leithart (2002), 136; Faivre (1990), 85–104; Osborne (1993), 145–49.
Origen, (d. 254), Alexandria	All the faithful can serve as High Priests by their sharing in Christ's priesthood. Last important "lay" teacher for more than 1,000 years (his clerical ordination came late in life).	Voss (2013), Ch. 4; O'Collins/Jones (2010), 72–76; Stewart (2007), 136–75; Faivre (1990), 59–71; Osborne (1993), 143–39; Eastwood (1963), 77–80; de Lubac (1950), 137–38; Dabin (1950), 517–24.
Cyprian (d. 258), Carthage, Africa	First to argue consistently that bishops hold a special priesthood due to their presiding at the Eucharist where they offer a unique sacrifice. Cyprian is thus the innovator of a "third" Christian priesthood.	Voss (2013), Ch. 4; O'Collins/Jones (2010), 76–79; Brent (2010), idem, (2009), 260–76; Stewart (2007), 176–211; Siniscalco and Mattei (2006), 65–88; Hellerman (2001), 182–212; Osborne (1993), 143–45; Cooke (1990), 69–70; Garrett (1988), 22–25; Laurance (1984), 149–230; Eastwood (1963), 80–90.
Acts of the Martyrs (ca. 100–339)	Lay martyrs were often given a special spiritual status in the church.	Osborne (1993), 145, 150–53, 157.

Patristic: Nicene and Post Nicene (325–600)

Date and Author	Emphasis	Further Discussion in:
Canons of Nicea (325)	Lay ministry clearly differentiated from clerical ministry. New relationship of church to the socio-political world.	Osborne (1993), 149–50; Faivre (1990), 150–57.
Constantine the Great (d. 337)	First Christian Emperor, he assumed high ecclesial responsibilities and set the stage for later issues of *Regnum et Sacerdotium*.	Voss (2013), Ch. 4; Osborne (1993), 163–232; 312–25.
Eusebius of Caesarea (d. 339)	Discusses priestly offerings of the nations and describes the church as "priests of God."	Voss (2013), Ch. 4; Stewart (2007), 212–32; Dabin (1950), 529–32.

SIGNIFICANT FIGURES AND EVENTS FOR THE ROYAL PRIESTHOOD 251

Date and Author	Emphasis	Further Discussion in:
Ephrem the Syrian (d. 373)	Jesus became priest at his baptism, and this is the model for believers.	Voss (2013), h. 3; Brock (1987), 15; Dabin (1950), 533.
Emperor Gratian (d. 383)	Removed state support for pagan temples and gave up the title *Pontifex Maximus*	Voss (2013), Ch. 4; Drobner (2007).
Emperor Theodosius (d.390)	In 380 proscribed all religions except Christianity (380).	Drobner (2007).
Ambrose (d. 397)	Wrote on "spiritual priesthood"; had significant influence on Emperors Gratian and Theodosius. Opposed any church vs. Christian Empire ("state") dichotomy, although he saw each realm having different competencies.	Voss (2013), Ch. 4; Drobner (2007), 309–11; Orr (1991) 52–66); de Lubac (1950), 136.
John Chrysostom (d. 407), Antioch (Syria)	All believers are priests who can offer spiritual sacrifices, although the priesthood excels the laity as the soul the body.	Voss (2013), Ch. 4; O'Collins/Jones (2010), 79–86; Bagchi (1989), 158; Hinson (1989), 9–10; Garrett (1988); Dabin (1950), 547–52.
Jerome (d. ca. 420), Rome, Bethlehem	Emphasizes Melchizedekian priesthood of Christ in which believers share. First to describe baptism as making *sacerdotium laici* ("the priesthood of the layman"). Provides vernacular translation of Scripture. Encouraged a two-class view of lay discipleship.	Orr (1991), 40–51; Faivre (1990), 197–205; Ryan (1962), 37, 44; Dabin (1950), 82–87.
Augustine (d. 430), Hippo (Africa)	Believers are priests by virtue of their sharing in Christ's priesthood through baptism. Provided theological rationale for infant baptism.	Voss (2013), Ch. 4; O'Collins/Jones (2010), 46–47; 86–97; Wright (2007), 68–88; Leithart (2003), 223–27; Hinson (1989), 11–12; Eastwood (1963), 91–101; Ryan (1962), 35–37; de Lubac (1950), 134–39; Dabin (1950), 89–115; Rea (1947), 144–70.
Cyril of Alexandria (d. 444)	The Royal Priesthood of the church comes up frequently in his writings.	Ryan (1962), 31; Dabin (1950), 557–62.
Leo the Great (d. 461), Rome	Architect of the doctrine of Petrine supremacy, but held a high view of RP.	Orr (1993), 61–62; Orr (1991) 67–78; de Lubac (1950), 134–35, 141; Palmer (1947), 584.

Date and Author	Emphasis	Further Discussion in:
Faustus of Riez (ca. 410–95), France	Faustus argues that baptism is the work of Christ while confirmation is the work of the Spirit.	Orr (1991) 194–95; cf. de Lubac (1950), 134–35.
Odovacer (d. 493), Rome	First Barbarian King of Italy, raises issue of language and education for doctrine of royal priesthood as the Roman Catholic church uses Ecclesiastical Latin until Vatican II in liturgical services.	Hinson (1989), 8–13; Osborne (1993), 291–97.
Pseudo-Dionysius (d. ca. 485–528)	First to use term "hierarchy" of church leaders. Priestly hierarchy on earth mirrors hierarchy in heaven and God can only be accessed through intermediaries.	Voss (2013), Ch. 4; Levering (2010), 251–72; Power (2003), 102; Osborne, (2003), 221–25; Cooke (1990), 90–94; Bagchi (1989), 160–63; Gould (1989), 29–40; Lewis (1964) 70–75; de Lubac (1950), 138–39.
Procopius of Gaza (d. 528 A.D.), Palestine	Argued that the "servants" of Isa 65:15 are in fact the royal priesthood of 1 Pet 2:9.	Ryan (1962), 31–32; Dabin (1950), 568–72.
Emperor Justinian, (529), Constantinople (Turkey)	In 529 he made infant baptism compulsory for all Roman citizens and he closed the Neoplatonic Academy at Athens.	Voss (2013), Ch. 4; Humfress (2009), 377–78, 385–87; Kreider (2005), 60; Kreider (1996), 355; Osborne (2003), 188, 202, 217–21.
St. Benedict of Nursia (d. ca. 547), Italy	Preserved a high view of the ministry of the royal priesthood as including the "lay" brothers in monastic orders.	Voss (2013), Ch. 4; Eastwood (1963), 179–86.
Primasius of Hadrumetum (d. ca. 560), Africa	Authored an important commentary on Revelation and builds on Augustine's thought about the church as a royal priesthood.	Dabin (1950), 135–139.
Gregory of Tours (d. 594)	Last to record testimony of layman taking a "leading or even articulate" part of theological conversation in the West.	Southern (1963), 103.
Gregory the Great (d. 604), Rome	Tripartite view of the world (laymen, monks, clergy) dominates church until Gratian. Eliminates the position of senior lay leaders in Africa.	Voss (2013), Ch. 4; Osborne (1993), 221–23; 254–58; 297–98; Faivre (1990), 153; Hinson (1989), 10; Eastwood (1963), 105–109.

Medieval (600–1500)

Date and Author	Emphasis	Further Discussion in:
Muhammad (d. 632), Arabia	Launched a rival religion to Christianity where there is no priestly hierarchy.	Voss (2013), Ch. 7; Eastwood (1963), 109–120.
Isidore of Seville (d. 636), Spain	Relates the Levitical anointing to baptism and thus to the royal priesthood, "we are a royal and priestly race." Moved understanding of the Eucharist to emphasis on passive receptivity by laity.	Power (2003), 103–04; de Lubac (1999), 134–36; Cooke (1990), 123–24, 135–36; Congar (1969), 57–58; de Lubac (1950), 135; Dabin (1950), 145–48.
Venerable Bede (d. 735), England	Commentaries on Revelation and 1 Peter discuss royal priesthood (first extant Latin commentary on 1 Peter).	Yarnel (2013), ch. 3; Orr (1991) 80–89; Dabin (1950), 150–57.
Veronese Sacramentary (ca. 700–800)	A collection from the Roman tradition of *libelli missarum*, it refers over sixty times to both RP and MP as *plebs*.	Orr (1991) 96–132.
Gelasian Sacramentary (ca. 750)	RP still emphasized using language of 1 Pet 2:9, but development of material culture is reducing emphasis on RP and increasing emphasis on MP.	Orr (1991) 133–69.
Gregorian Sacramentary (785/86)	The priestly nature of the people receives less emphasis than the *Veronese* or *Gelasian* Sacramentaries. People are becoming increasingly spectators rather than participants in the priesthood.	Orr (1991) 170–192.
Alcuin of York (d. 804), England, Holy Roman Empire	Urged Charlemagne to stop baptisms on pain of death. Identified priesthood of the church more with christening than with baptism.	Orr (1993), 64; Orr (1991), 262–63; Dabin (1950), 163–67.
Amalarius of Metz (d. ca. 850)	Writings continue to centralize spiritual sacrifice in the MP.	Orr (1991), 198–99.
Rabanus Maurus (d. 856), France/Germany	In his *De Clericorum Institutione* he built on Faustus of Riez's claims in order to suggest a second outpouring of the Holy Spirit at the ordination of the clergy.	Orr (1991), 195–98.

Date and Author	Emphasis	Further Discussion in:
Florus of Lyon (d. ca. 860)	Placed emphasis on the RP in his writings.	Orr (1991), 200–01.
Paschasius Radbertus (d. 865), France	First to argue that hierarchical priests had power to change bread and wine into historic body of Christ.	Voss (2013), Ch. 4; Dabin (1950), 190–92; Eastwood (1963), 128–120.
Peter Damien (d. 1072), Italy	Involved with reforms of Gregory VII, a number of his sermons discuss the royal priesthood and contrast with clerical priesthood.	Brooke (1989), 67–71; de Lubac (1950), 135, 142; Dabin (1950), 203–208.
Investiture Controversy (1077)	Henry IV and Gregory VII famous standoff was one of the key turning points in this long contest between clergy and laity.	Leithart 2003 (223–48).
Pope Gregory VII (d. 1085), Rome	Removed most remaining priestly dignity from laity and increased distinction between lay and clergy.	Voss (2013), Ch. 4; Leithart 2003 (223–48); Osborne (1993), 333–90; Congar (1977), 351; idem (1969) 61–62.
Rupert of Deutz (d. 1129), Belgium	Discusses the different ways in which the royal priesthood and the hierarchical priesthood participate in the mass.	Dabin (1950), 222–32.
Peter Abelard (d. 1142), French, Married	First to use the term "extreme unction." He related it to the anointings of the royal priesthood received at baptism and confirmation.	Dabin (1950), 236–41.
Honorius of Autun (d. 1154), Europe	Reflected upon Mary as a member of the royal priesthood.	Dabin (1950), 247–53; cf. Pelikan (1978), 166.
Peter Lombard (d. 1164), Italy and France	Included ordination as one of the seven sacraments. He limited ordination to priests and deacons, excluding minor orders, bishops, and laity.	Osborne (2003), 212–14; 217–20; Colish (1994), 516–32, 614–28; Dabin (1950), 259–61.
Gottfried of Admont (d. 1165), Austria	Emphasized the role of the Holy Spirit in the anointing of the Royal Priesthood.	Dabin (1950), 262–65.
Gratian, (d. 1179), Rome	Institutionalized Gregory's reform; his *Decretum* (1142) centralized hierarchical authority, and governed Canon Law until 1917.	Voss (2013), Ch. 4; Eastwood (1963), 133; Congar (1953, ET 1985), 7–8; Dabin (1950), 270–71.

SIGNIFICANT FIGURES AND EVENTS FOR THE ROYAL PRIESTHOOD   255

Date and Author	Emphasis	Further Discussion in:
Martin of Leon (d. 1203), Spain	Discusses relationship of the royal priesthood to the Eucharist.	Dabin (1950), 274–78.
Pope Innocent III (d. 1216)	Claimed that the rights of royal priesthood were primarily located in the papacy. Required confession of all at least once a year and called the Fourth Lateran Council in 1215.	Yarnell (2013), ch. 3; de Lubac (1950), 142–43.
Peter Waldo (d. ca. 1218), Lyons (France)	Argued for lay rights to priestly ministry, and organized first vernacular translation of Scripture into western Europe.	Voss (2013), Ch. 5; Audisio (2007), 63–65, 203; Rea (1947), 12–38.
Mendicant Orders (1206–56), Europe	In a fifty-year period five lay orders were recognized by the pope, all engaged in "priestly" ministry.	Voss (2013), Ch. 4; Eastwood (1963), 186–94.
Saint Francis of Assisi (d. 1226)	Influential lay preacher and missionary.	Voss (2013), Ch. 4; Eastwood (1963), 186–94.
Thomas Aquinas (d. 1274), Italy	All Christians share in priesthood of Christ, but "auxiliaries" are needed to access the "satisfaction" achieved by Christ's priestly offering.	Voss (2013), Ch. 4; O'Collins/Jones (2010), 105–27; Levering (2010); Eastwood (1963), 138–148; Dabin (1950), 294–302; Rea (1947), 177–211.
John Duns Scotus (d. 1308), Scotland, France	Systematically explains how the sacrifice of the mass is mediated to the laity by the priests, but also recognizes that God is free in how he relates to creation.	Kilmartin (1998), 160–61, 165–68; Lang (1998), 249–53; Osborne (1993), 374–76.
Master Eckhart (d. ca. 1327)	Associated with the *Friends of God* movement, the *Theologia Germanica,* and an emphasis on the soul's direct access to God without the need of clerical mediation.	Eastwood (1963), 195–224.
Marsiglio of Padua (d. 1328)	Argued for a high view of dignity and authority for all members of the church.	Osborne (1993), 382–88; Eastwood (1963), 163–71.
Gerard Groote (d. 1384), Dutch	A deacon and gifted preacher, he founded the Brethren of the Common Life, a movement that influenced both Erasmus and Luther and emphasized a high level of lay spirituality.	Hadsburg (2011), 31–48.

Date and Author	Emphasis	Further Discussion in:
John Wycliffe (d. 1384), England	All the faithful are priests and deserve access to God's Word. First vernacular English translation of the Bible.	Yarnell (2013), ch.1; Mikolaski (1988), 6–8; Eastwood (1963), 171–78; Rea (1947), 39–83.
Walter Brut (d. ca. 1405), England, Lollard	His view of the PoAB included the possibility of confessing sins directly to God, and women both preaching and celebrating the Eucharist.	Yarnell (2013), ch. 2.
John Purvey (d. 1415), England, Lollard	His view of PoAB included the possibility of women preaching and celebrating the Eucharist.	Yarnell (2013), ch. 2; Hornbeck (2010), 166–67.
John Hus (d. 1415), Prague	The church consists not only of the hierarchy, but the whole body of the laity.	Wycliffe, *De Ecclesia* (WLW, iv).
Jacob of Mies (d. 1429), Prauge	First to argue for a return of early church practice where laity have right to both elements at the Eucharist (*Utraquism*)	
Jean Gerson (d. 1429)	Defended Brethren of the Common Life at the Council of Constance. Argued that laity could directly access God and were called to pursue perfection just as those in monastic orders.	Hadsburg (2011), 81–84.
Thomas á Kempis (d. 1471)	Probable author of the *Imitatio Christi*.	Habsburg (2011), 31–48.
Gabriel Biel (d. 1495)	Develops Scotus' teaching on the priest's power to distribute the "fruit" of the mass to whom he desires.	Habsburg (2011), 82; Kilmartin (1998), 161–63; Lang (1998), 249–53.

Reformation and Post-reformation (1500–1700)

Date and Author	Emphasis	Further Discussion in:
John Colet (d. 1519), England, Roman Catholic	All believers are priests, but laity are a passive and submissive wife while clergy are the active husband.	Yarnell (2013), ch. 3.
Luther Posts 95 Theses (1519)		

Significant Figures and Events for the Royal Priesthood   257

Date and Author	Emphasis	Further Discussion in:
Peasants' War (1525)	Following the Peasants' War Luther's emphasis on the priesthood of all believers dramatically decreased.	Voss (2013)
Sebastian Lotzer (d. 1525?)	Co-author of the *The Twelve Articles*, a document which called for human rights based on the PoAB.	Yarnell (1996), 108–10.
Thomas Muntzer (d. 1525), German, Protestant	Sought a radically egalitarian and pneumatic priesthood, and encouraged violent revolution to achieve it.	Yarnell (1996), 103–08.
Conrad Grebel (d. 1526), Swiss, Anabaptist	Brought a focus on the "believers" in the PoAB; first Reformation Anabaptist.	Yarnell (1996), 110–114.
Hieronymus Emser (d. 1527), German, Roman Catholic	A fierce opponent of Luther, argued for two priesthoods; a "spiritual" and a "physical."	Voss (2013), Ch. 5; Bagchi (1989), 156–59; Luther (1521), *LW* 39:105–238.
Michael Sattler (d. 1527), German, Anabaptist	Authored *The Schleitheim Articles* which applied the evangelical counsels of perfection to all believers. Priestly discipleship was no longer limited to the clergy and spiritual, but available to all believers.	Yarnell (1996), 133–41.
Balthasar Hubmaier (1528)	Anabaptist theologian emphasized practices of royal priesthood such as vernacular Bible reading and the rule of Christ (keys).	Voss (2013), Ch. 8; Pipkin and Yoder (1984), 32–34; 372–85.
Diet of Speyers 1529, Holy Roman Empire	Protestantism receives its name, and Anabaptists are condemned to death by both Roman Catholic and "Protestant" electors.	
Diet of Augsburg	Philip Melanchthon advised against further discussion or emphasis on the priesthood of all believers	Voss (2013); Gerrish (1965).
Johannes Oecolampadius (d. 1531)	One of the first to offer communion in both kinds to the people.	Yarnell (1996), 54–55. Pelikan (1984), 268.

Date and Author	Emphasis	Further Discussion in:
Huldrych Zwingli (d. 1531)	Held to a limited PoAB but especially emphasized the kinship relationship of all believers.	Yarnell (1996), 39–55.
Cardinal Thomas Cajetan (d. 1534), Italy, Roman Catholic	Opposed Luther at the Diet of Augsburg in 1518. His commentary on 1 Peter argues that "royal priesthood" is merely metaphorical.	Kilmartin (1998), 163–165; Dabin (1950), 332–36.
Cardinal John Fisher (England), Roman Catholic	Opposed Luther's understanding of the PoAB and instead argued that the laity were priests only "for themselves" with no mediatorial responsibilities.	Yarnell (2013), ch. 3.
William Tyndale (d. 1536), England, Protestant	Christ is the only priestly mediator, and believers share it. No other human mediation is necessary to access God.	Yarnell (2013), ch. 3.
Desiderius Erasmus (d. 1536)	By virtue of their baptism, all believers are priests and have the right to access God through Scripture and to be "theologians."	Yarnell (2013), ch. 3; Gerrish (1965), 404–405.
Anneken Jansdochter (d. 1539), Netherlands	Anneken was martyred for her non-trinitarian beliefs, but saw herself as one of many royal priests.	Yarnell (1996), 118–20.
Edward Powell (d. 1540), England, Roman Catholic	Saw the priesthood of all believers as "indicative of his [Luther's] entire work," and opposed vernacular Bible translation because it supported the doctrine.	Voss (2013), Ch. 5; Yarnell (2013), ch. 3.
Andreas Rudolf-Bodenstein von Karlstadt (d. 1541), Germany, Protestant	He celebrated the first "Protestant" Eucharist, and continued to work against sacerdotalism.	Voss (2013), Ch. 5; Yarnell (1996), 96–103.
Sebastian Franck (d. 1543), Germany	A rationalist who saw the spiritual priesthood as excluding external forms in most situations.	Yarnell (1996), 120–22.

Significant Figures and Events for the Royal Priesthood 259

Date and Author	Emphasis	Further Discussion in:
Martin Luther (d. 1546), Germany, Protestant,	Most important Protestant teacher on the PoAB. He touches on aspects of the doctrine in over fifty extant documents, although his primary exposition takes place in fifteen.	Voss (2013), Ch. 5; Anizor (2012), 182–217; O'Collins/Jones (2010), 128–48; Rogers (2010), 120–34; Wengert (2008) 1–32; Lohse (1999), 289–291; Yarnell (1996), 7–38; Barth (1990), 29–53; Eastwood (1960), 1–65; Rea (1947), 84–124; Spener (1675; ET [1964], 92–95).
Henry VIII (d. 1547), England, Anglican	Wrote *Fidei Defensor* defending the seven sacraments and explicitly denied Luther's PoAB.	Yarnell (2013), ch. 3; Bagchi (1989), 159–63.
Martin Bucer (d. 1551), France, Germany, England, Protestant	Was especially concerned with the relation between church discipline and the PoAB.	Voss (2013), Ch. 5; Van 'T Spijker (1996) 39–112; Yarnell (1996), 55–62; Bravo (1963) 92–95.
Pilgrim Marpeck (d. 1556), Austria, Anabaptist	Recognized both a fulfilled and future dimension to the royal priesthood. Emphasized the necessity of all believers to offer their lives as a spiritual sacrifice.	Yarnell (1996), 123–124; 130–33.
Thomas Cranmer (d. 1556), England, Anglican	Returned the cup to the laity in England; his emphasis on congregational worship returned an active role to the congregation alongside church officers.	Yarnell (2013). Chs 2–10; Eastwood (1960), 95–107.
Menno Simons	Believers are priests who offer their own bodies as living sacrifices. They offer their bodies as sacrifices daily using the "knife of the divine Word."	Yarnell (1996) 132–33.
Peter Martyr Vermigli (d. 1562), Italy, England, Protestant	Made an important contribution in examining the relationship between the Eucharist, spiritual sacrifices, and the royal priesthood.	Yarnell (1996), 62–67.
Calvin (d. 1564), French/Swiss, Protestant	Calvin emphasized the believer's priestly union with Christ and the resultant priestly access to the Father in prayer and Bible study. He also related the PoAB to vocation.	Voss (2013), Ch. 5; O'Collins/Jones (2010), 148–62; Yarnell (1996), 68–90; George (1991) 92–93; Hinson (1989), 19–20; Crawford (1968), 145–56; Eastwood (1960), 66–90.

260   APPENDIX

Date and Author	Emphasis	Further Discussion in:
Catechism of the Council of Trent (1566)		O'Collins/Jones (2010), 165–82; Dabin (1950), 355–61.
Roman Missal, Pope Pius V (1570)	Pope Pius V required use by almost all churches. Vernacular translation was prohibited, and the *Missal* further reduced RP's participation in liturgical worship.	Orr (1991), 220–35.
Zacharias Ursinus (d. 1583)	Primary author of the Heidelberg Catechism which relates PoAB directly to the priesthood of Christ (q. 31–32).	Billings (2012), 160–65.
Alfonso Salmeron (1585), Europe, Roman Catholic	His commentaries on 1 Peter and Revelation discuss royal priesthood which he sees applying primarily to the Pope.	Dabin (1950), 367–73.
Thomas Cartwright (d. 1603), England, Anglican	Contributed to discussions on the spiritual priesthood in writings against the Rhemists' translation of the Bible (1582).	Strehle (2009), 10–14; Eastwood (1960), 132–42.
John Smyth (d. 1612), England, Holland, Baptist	High view of PoAB and relates Matt 18:20 to the high dignity of the RP.	Yarnell (2002), 236–43; Eastwood (1960), 155–63; Volf (1998), 130–37.
Cardinal Robert Bellarmine (d. 1621), Italy, Roman Catholic	Argued against Luther's understanding of PoAB and for the secular nature of the laity.	Voss (2013), Ch. 5; Bosch (1995), 242–43; Dabin (1950), 386–90.
Francis de Sales (d. 1622), France, Roman Catholic	Wrote against Protestant PoAB, but upheld a high vision for lay spirituality.	Dabin (1950), 391–94.
Robert Browne (d. 1633), England,	Father of Congregationalism, emphasized the priestly responsibility of the whole assembly to appoint officers.	Strehle (2009), 2–7; Eastwood (1960), 142–45.
Cornelius Cornelii a Lapide (d. 1637), Belgium/France, Roman Catholic	Extensive discussion of the royal priesthood in his commentary on 1 Peter 2:4–9. He calls the laity "mystical priests."	Dabin (1950), 401–07.

SIGNIFICANT FIGURES AND EVENTS FOR THE ROYAL PRIESTHOOD 261

Date and Author	Emphasis	Further Discussion in:
First London Confession (1646)	Articles 36–47 make PoAB important component of Baptist ecclesiology.	Dever (1998), 88, 112.
Thomas Hooker (d. 1647), England, American Colonies	Rejected sacerdotal priesthood, but embraced a MP focused on the gospel.	Eastwood (1960), 108–11.
Jean-Jacques Olier (d. 1657), France, Roman Catholic	Emphasis on RP through their participation in Christ's priesthood by baptism. Half of Vatican II's bishops were trained in schools influenced by his view.	O'Collins/Jones (2010), 192–201, 203–5.
John Owen (d. 1683), England	Emphasized that the MP operated from within the RP.	Voss (2013), Ch. 7; Eastwood (1960), 145–50.
George Fox (d. 1691), England, Quaker	Strong emphasis on the spiritual priesthood, and every believer's access to the Father through Jesus.	Eastwood (1960), 171–82.

Modern (1700–1918)

Date and Author	Emphasis	Further Discussion in:
Miguel de Molinos (d. 1697), Spain, Roman Catholic	Father of Quietism, taught that ultimately neither church nor Jesus were necessary mediators for communion with God.	Molinos (2010).
Jacques-Bénigne Bossuet (d. 1704), France, Roman Catholic	Discusses RP in response to Protestant teaching and against mystical interpreters (e.g. Molinos, Fenelon [d.1715], Madame Guyon [d. 1717]).	Dabin (1950), 424–32.
Louis Bourdaloue (d. 1704), France, Roman Catholic	Provided theological "qualifications" on the doctrine of the royal priesthood in light of Protestant and quietist teaching.	Dabin (1950), 432–40.
Philip Jacob Spener (d. 1705), Protestant	Accused Lutheranism of failing to follow through with Luther's "spiritual priesthood"; first to use phrase "Priesthood of all Believers."	Wengert (2008), 1–4; Barth (1990), 54–78; Snyder (1989), 166–74.

Date and Author	Emphasis	Further Discussion in:
American (1775–1783) and French (1789–1799) Revolutions	United States and France's civil governments challenge hierarchical and political assumptions related to the PoAB.	Osborne (1993), 464–517; Strehle (2009).
John Wesley (d. 1791), England, Anglican	Wesley emphasized faith, prayer, and ministry as privileges of the RP. His "bands" and "societies" opened new doors for priestly ministry.	Eastwood (1960), 183–237.
Joseph Milner (d. 1797) and Isaac Milner (d. 1820)	Emphasized the importance of faith (belief) for the PoAB.	Eastwood (1960), 116–21.
Isaac Backus (d. 1806)	Argued that priesthood of all believers implied a necessary separation between church and state.	Pitts (1988), 34.
William Carey (d. 1834), England, India	His 1792 tract, *An Enquiry into the Obligations of Christians to Use Means for the Conversion of the Heathen*, directly addressed the "holy egotism" of the Magisterial Reformers and was heavily dependent upon the doctrine of the PoAB.	Voss (2013), Ch. 7; Newbigin (1987), 32.
Charles Simeon (d. 1836), England	Emphasized that the whole RP had a responsibility to proclaim the gospel, especially to those who had not yet heard.	Eastwood (1960), 122–29.
Johann Adam Möhler (d. 1838), German	Argued that Luther had "horribly disfigured" the doctrine of the RP, but that its proper form should be a regular part of the faithful's doctrinal instruction.	Dabin (1950), 457–64.
Johann Hinrich Wichern, (d. 1861), Germany, Protestant	Founded Germany's Inner Mission (Home Mission) to the poor, sick, and prisoners based on PoAB.	Hans Barth (1990), 79–103.
Matthias Joseph Scheeben (d. 1888), Germany	Tried to expand Aquinas' definition of priesthood, and explored the biblical warrant for a division between lay and hierarchical priesthoods.	Dabin (1950), 468–73.

Date and Author	Emphasis	Further Discussion in:
Cardinal John Henry Newman (d. 1890), England, Roman Catholic	Emphasizes Christ as Prophet, Priest, and King; this plays an important role in development of later Roman Catholic ecclesiology.	O'Collins/Jones (2010), 208–222; Dabin (1950), 473–76.
Charles Gay (d. 1892), France, Roman Catholic	Emphasized a high view of the privileges and responsibilities of the laity as a "divine race" consecrated as royal priesthood by baptism.	Dabin (1950), 476–80.
P. T. Forsyth (d. 1921), England, Protestant, Congregationalist	Emphasized that RP met a responsibility to priestly ministry as salt and light in the world.	Mikolaski (1988), 14.
Maurice de la Taille (d. 1933), French, Roman Catholic	Liturgical Theologian who focused on the Eucharist and the royal priesthood's participation.	Dabin (1950), 488–91.

Contemporary (1919–2013)

Date and Author	Emphasis	Further Discussion in:
Edgar Young Mullins (d. 1928), U.S.A., Baptist	Proposed "priesthood of *the* believer" and soul competency.	Rogers (2010), 119–20, 127–34; Yarnell (2002), 236–43; George (1991), 85–86.
James Rae (1947), American, Roman Catholic	Argued against four Protestant "heretical" versions of the PoAB.	Michalski (1996), 226; Rae (1947).
Paul Dabin (d. 1950), French, Roman Catholic	Authored the two most comprehensive studies of the RP. His biblical theology of the RP (483 pages) and historical study (643 pages) have not received adequate attention.	Dabin (1939, 1941, 1950).
Vatican II (1962–65)	The whole people of God share in the priesthood of Christ through their baptismal consecration. The "common priesthood of the faithful . . . differ in essence and not just degree" from the MP.	O'Collins/Jones (2010), 234–38; Kärkkäinen (1999), 144–62; Michalski (1996), 11–65; Tanner (1990), 856–57; Hans Barth (1990), 104–33; Osborne (1988), 315–324.

APPENDIX

Date and Author	Emphasis	Further Discussion in:
Nikolay Afanasiev (d. 1966), Russia/France, Orthodox	His Eucharistic theology radically challenged clericalism in the Orthodox church and argues for the royal priesthood of the baptized as a foundational concept for ecclesiology.	Afanasiev (2007), 1–80. Demacopoulos (2011), 456–58; Levering (2010), 187–98. Bordeianu (2010), 415–21.
1967 Believers' Church Conference	Important gathering of Baptist and Anabaptist communions in North America. Affirmed that "every believer participates in the full ministry of Christ. Every believer is a priest . . . ."	Garrett (1969), 317.
Missale Romanum, 1970.	This Missal reflects the concerns of Vatican II and Pope VI and was the first in the Roman tradition to regularly make reference to 1 Pet 2:9's RP.	Orr (1991), 236–57.
Watchman Nee	Strong advocate for pneumatically informed version of the PoAB.	Dever (1998), 90–91; Ng (1986).
Lausanne Covenant (1974)	Protestant statement emphasizing missional vocation of RP.	Voss (2013), Ch. 7.
Baptism, Eucharist, and Ministry (WCC), 1982	Eccumenical document that recognizes the importance of the ministry of the whole people of God. MP flows out of the RP, both rooted in Christ's priesthood.	Muthiah (2009), 28–30; Bulley (2000), 5–17; 316–26; Kärkkäinen (1999), 144–62; Mikolaski (1988), 10–11.
Anglican-Roman Catholic International Commission (ARCIC), 1982	Priesthood of laity and clergy are "two different realities which relate each in its own way to the high priesthood of Christ"; they do not participate in each other but relate by way of analogy.	Bulley (2000), 5–17; Newbigin (1996), 178.
Letter to the Bishops of the Catholic Church on Certain Questions Concerning the Minister of the Eucharist (1983).	Explains Vatican II's statement about the RP differing from the MP in *essential et non gradu tantum different* as the MP's unique power to "confect the Eucharistic Mystery."	Michalski (1996), 84–83.
Henri de Lubac (d. 1991)	Argues that all the baptized possess a "spiritual" or "internal" priesthood which is not metaphorical, but is distinct from the "external" MP.	Michalski (1996), 126; de Lubac (ET 1986 [1956]), 134–44.

Significant Figures and Events for the Royal Priesthood

Date and Author	Emphasis	Further Discussion in:
Thomas O'Meara (d. 1992), U.S.A., Roman Catholic	Explores the RP and MP's relationship with evangelization, pastoral guidance, and spiritual direction.	Michalski (1996), 175–93.
Dumitru Staniloae (d. 1993), Romanian, Orthodox	Suggests that "natural priesthood," or "priesthood to creation," is an important component of universal priesthood.	Bordeianu (2010), 405–33.
Edward Kilmartin (d. 1994), U.S.A., Roman Catholic	Reflected on the RPs relationship to Trinity and Eucharist.	Hahnenberg (2005), 262–67; Michalski (1996), 151–63.
Yves Congar (d. 1995), French, Roman Catholic	Emphasized the plurality of ministries, and the necessity of returning priestly ministry to the whole body of Christ.	O'Collins/Jones (2010), 230–34; Fox (2003), 121–151.
"Some Questions Regarding Collaboraton of Nonordained Faithful in Priests' Sacred Ministry," (1997), Roman Catholic	Argue that all ministry is priestly, but specifies a variety of ministries that are not options for non-ordained members of the royal priesthood.	Philbert (2005), 144–145.
"Apostolic Exhortation, *Pastores Gregis*," (2003), Roman Catholic	Vatican document referring to relationship between the MP and PoAB as a kind of "*perichoresis*."	Philbert (2005), 148–151.
Heinz Schütte (d. 2007), German, Roman Catholic	Primary difference between RP and MP is functional. Vatican II's *essentia* is not an intensification of the mission given at baptism, but a new mission and power. There are not two classes.	Michalski (1996), 84–83.
George Tavard (d. 2007), U.S.A., Roman Catholic	Continued to develop Congar's emphasis on ministry of the RP.	Michalski (1996), 193–205.
Thomas Torrance (d. 2007), Presbyterian, Scotland	Roots RP in union with Christ; emphasizes significance of Christ's Ascension and vocation for RP.	O'Collins/Jones (2010), 224–229; Torrance (1993).
John Howard Yoder (d. 2007), U.S.A., Anabaptist	Emphasized the RP as a central pillar of his ecclesial writings.	Muthiah (2009), 35–41.

Date and Author	Emphasis	Further Discussion in:
Jean Galot (d. 2008), Belgium, Roman Catholic	Clergy are shepherds and laity are passive sheep. There is a radical difference between the mission of the clerical priests and the royal priesthood.	Michalski (1996), 127–35; Osborne (1988), 30–39.
Edward Schillebeeckx (d. 2009), Belgium/ Netherlands, Roman Catholic	Emphasizes a pneumatological understanding of church office which leads him to see clergy and laity with functional but not ontological distinctions.	Michalski (1996), 93–110.
Frans van Beeck (d. 2011), Netherlands/ U.S.A., Roman Catholic	Further developed Congar's reflections on the ministry of the RP.	Michalski (1996), 205–19.

Living Writers on the Royal Priesthood (2013)

Date and Author	Emphasis	Further Discussion in:
Hans Küng (b. 1938), Swiss, Roman Catholic	Made the PoAB a central theme of his ecclesiology.	Küng (ET 1967), 363–480.
Gisbert Greshake (b. 1933), Austria, Roman Catholic	Clergy as priests participate uniquely in Christ's office and their representation of Christ to the community gives them their *character indelibilis* vis-à-vis the royal priesthood.	Michalski (1996), 110–20.
Paul Wess (b. 1936), Austria, Roman Catholic	European advocate of Base Ecclesial Ministries who sees general and ministerial priesthoods equal but the ordained priest provides a necessary sign of unity between the local *Gemeinde* and the universal *Kirche*.	Michalski (1996), 121–26; Wess (1983), 101.
Bernard Cooke (b. 1923), U.S.A., Roman Catholic	His understanding of church office has significant implications for PoAB.	Michalski (1996), 137–50; Cooke (1990).
David Power (b. 1932), U.S.A., Roman Catholic	Sees MP as those with charism of leadership within the RP.	Michalski (1996), 163–74.

Significant Figures and Events for the Royal Priesthood 267

Date and Author	Emphasis	Further Discussion in:
Elizabeth Schüssler Fiorenza, German/ U.S.A., Roman Catholic	Conducted major study on PoAB in Revelation and argues for a radically egalitarian understanding of the doctrine.	Michalski (1996), 205.
Gustavo Gutiérrez (b. 1928), Roman Catholic	A key theologian bridging the European Catholic Action movement to Latin American Liberation Theologies.	Cf. Osborne (2003), 199.
Leonardo Boff (b. 1938), Brazil, Roman Catholic	Provided theological explication of the more than 1,000,000 Latin American Base Ecclesial Communities whose theological roots lie in the PoAB.	Hans Barth (1990), 134–60. Cf. Osborne (2003), 199.
Hans-Martin Barth (b. 1939), German, Protestant	Emphasizes that the PoAB has a social component of ministry to others.	Voss (2013).
Howard Snyder, U.S.A./Brazil, Protestant	Refers to the PoAB as pillar of Protestant ecclesiology.	Dever (1998), 98–99; Snyder (2004), 113.
James Leo Garrett, U.S.A., Protestant	Leading Baptist theologian on the PoAB. Emphasizes offering of spiritual sacrifices as chief function of the RP.	Voss (2013). Tie (2010)
David Orr, Australia, Roman Catholic	Argues that a chief function of the MP is to equip the RP for priestly ministry.	Voss (2013), Ch.4.
Timothy Wengert, U.S.A., Protestant	Argues against appeals to Luther by those advocating for a purely egalitarian version of the PoAB.	Voss (2013), Ch. 5.
Peter Leithart, U.S.A., Protestant	Argues for a version of the RP intimately related to baptismal ordination.	Voss (2013).
Miroslav Volf (b. 1956), Eastern Europe/ U.S.A., Protestant	Appeals to John Smyth's understanding of the PoAB in order to suggest a more pneumatically informed doctrine of the ministry of the RP.	Voss (2013), Chs. 7–8; Muthiah (2009), 42–45, 47–86; Kärkkäinen (1999), 144–62.
Malcolm Yarnell, U.S.A., Protestant	Has conducted two major historical studies of the PoAB and builds on Garrett's proposals in his constructive work.	Voss (2013).

Bibliography

Achtemeier, Paul. *1 Peter: A Commentary on First Peter*. Hermeneia. Minneapolis: Fortress, 1996.

Adewuya, J. Ayodeji. *Holiness and Community in 2 Cor 6:14—7:1: Paul's View of Communal Holiness in the Corinthian Correspondence*. New York: Peter Lang, 2003.

Ådna, Jostein. "Isaiah 52:13—53:12 in the Targum of Isaiah with Special Attention to the Concept of the Messiah." In *The Suffering Servant: Isaiah 53 in Jewish and Christian Sources*, edited by Bernd Janowski and Peter Stuhlmacher, translated by Daniel Bailey, 189–224. Grand Rapids: Eerdmans, 2004.

Afanasiev, Nicholas. *The Church of the Holy Spirit*. Edited by Michael Plekon. Translated by Vitaly Permiakov. Russian Orig. 1971. Reprint, Notre Dame, IN: University of Notre Dame Press, 2007.

Altmann, Walter. *Luther and Liberation: A Latin American Perspective*. Eugene, OR: Wipf & Stock, 2000.

Ambrose. *Some of the Principal Works of St. Ambrose*. Translated by H. de Romestin, E. de Romestin, and H. T. F. Duckworth. NPNF2 Vol. 10. Buffalo, 1885–1896. Electronic ed.

Anizor, Uche. "A Royal Priesthood of Readers." PhD diss., Wheaton College, 2012.

Aquinas, Thomas. *Summa Theologiae*. 61 vols. New York: McGraw-Hill, 1964–1981.

Arnold, Clinton E. "Early Church Catechesis and New Christians' Classes in Contemporary Evangelicalism." *JETS* 47 (2004) 39–54.

———. *Ephesians*. ECNT. Grand Rapids: Zondervan, 2010.

Athanasius. *Works on the Spirit: Athanasius's Letters to Serapion on the Holy Spirit, and, Didymus's on the Holy Spirit*. Translated by Mark DelCogliano, Andrew Radde-Gallwitz, and Lewis Ayres. Vol. 43. PP. Yonkers, NY: St. Vladimir's Seminary Press, 2011.

Attridge, Harold. *The Epistle to the Hebrews: A Commentary on the Epistle to the Hebrews*. Edited by Helmut Koester. Philadelphia: Fortress, 1989.

———. "How Priestly is the 'High Priestly Prayer' of John 17." *CBQ* 75 (2013) 1–14.

Atwood, Craig. *Community of the Cross: Moravian Piety in Colonial Bethlehem*. University Park, PA: Pennsylvania State University Press, 2000.

Audisio, Gabriel. *Preachers by Night: The Waldensian Barbes (15th-16th Centuries)*. New York: Brill, 2007.

Aufhauser, Joh. "Die Sakrale Kaiseridee in Byzanz." In *The Sacral Kingship: Contributions to the Central Theme of the Fifth International Congress for the History of Religions*, 531–42. Leiden: Brill, 1959.

Augustine. *The City of God Against the Pagans*. Translated by Eva Sanford and William Greene. Vol. 415. LCL. Cambridge, MA: Harvard University Press, 1960.

———. *De doctrina Christiana*. Translated by R. P. H. Green. OECT. New York: Clarendon, 1995.

———. *The Trinity*. Translated by Stephen McKenna. Vol. 45. FC. New York: Fathers of the Church, 1962.

———. *Works of Saint Augustine*. Edited by John E. Rotelle and Boniface Ramsey. Hyde Park, NY: New City, 1990.

Ausín, Santiago. "El Espíritu Santo en la Comunidad Escatológica (Is 61:1–11)." *EstBib* 57 (1999) 97–124.

Avis, P. D. L. *The Church in the Theology of the Reformers*. Louisville: John Knox, 1981.

Bagchi, David. "'eyn Mercklich Underscheyd': Catholic Reactions to Luther's Doctrine of the Priesthood of All Believers, 1520–25." In *The Ministry: Clerical and Lay*, edited by W. J. Sheils and Diana Wood, 155–65. SCH 26. Oxford: Blackwell, 1989.

Bailey, Daniel. "Our Suffering and Crucified Messiah" (Dial. 111.2): Justin Martyr's Allusions to Isaiah 53 in His Dialogue with Trypho with Special Reference to the New Edition of M. Marcovich." In *The Suffering Servant: Isaiah 53 in Jewish and Christian Sources*, edited by Bernd Janowski and Peter Stuhlmacher, translated by Daniel Bailey, 324–417. Grand Rapids: Eerdmans, 2004.

Baptism, Eucharist, Ministry. Faith and Order Paper #111. Geneva: WCC, 1982.

Bardill, Jonathan. *Constantine, Divine Emperor of the Christian Golden Age*. New York: Cambridge University Press, 2012.

Barker, Margaret. *The Great High Priest: The Temple Roots of Christian Liturgy*. New York: T. & T. Clark, 2003.

Barna, George. *Revolution: Finding Vibrant Faith Beyond the Walls of the Sanctuary*. Wheaton, IL: Tyndale, 2005.

Barrett, David B., Todd M. Johnson, and Peter F. Crossing. "Christianity 2011: Martyrs and Resurgence of Religion." *IBMR* 35.1 (2011) 28–29.

Barth, Hans Martin. *Einander Priester sein: Allgemeines Priestertum in ökumenischer Perspektive*. KKVK. Göttingen: Vandenhoeck & Ruprecht, 1990.

Barth, Karl. "The Christian as a Witness." In *God in Action: Theological Addresses*, translated by E. G. Homrighausen and Karl J. Ernst, 94–143. New York: Round Table, 1936.

———. *The Christian Life: Church Dogmatics IV, 4: Lecture Fragments*. Translated by Geoffrey W. Bromiley. Grand Rapids: Eerdmans, 1981.

———. *Church Dogmatics*. Edited by G. W. Bromiley and T. F. Torrance. 4 Vols. In 14 parts. 1956–75. Reprint, Peabody, MA: Hendrickson, 2010.

———. *The Epistle to the Romans*. Translated by Edwyn Hoskyns. New York: Oxford University Press, 1960.

———. *Die Kirchliche Dogmatics*. 4 Vols. In 13 parts. 1932 Reprint, Zürich: TVZ, 1938–65.

———. *The Knowledge of God and the Service of God*. Translated by J. L. M. Haire and Ian Henderson. London: Hodder and Stoughton, 1938.

———. "Die Theologie und die Mission in der Gegenwart." *Zwischen den Zeiten* 10 (1932) 189–215.

Basil the Great. *On the Holy Spirit*. Translated by David Anderson. Vol. 42. PP. Crestwood, NY: St. Vladimir's Seminary Press, 1980.

Bass, Dorothy C., ed. *Practicing Our Faith: A Way of Life for a Searching People*. San Francisco: Jossey-Bass, 1997.

Bass, Dorothy C., and Craig R. Dykstra. *For Life Abundant: Practical Theology, Theological Education, and Christian Ministry*. Grand Rapids: Eerdmans, 2008.

———. "A Theological Understanding of Christian Practices." In *Practicing Theology: Beliefs and Practices in Christian Life*, edited by Miroslav Volf and Dorothy C. Bass, 13–32. Grand Rapids: Eerdmans, 2002.

Bass, Dorothy C., and Miroslav Volf, eds. *Practicing Theology: Beliefs and Practices in Christian Life*. Grand Rapids: Eerdmans, 2002.

Bauckham, Richard. "God Crucified." In *Jesus and the God of Israel: God Crucified and Other Studies on the New Testament's Christology of Divine Identity*, 1–59. Grand Rapids: Eerdmans, 2009.

———. "James, 1 Peter, Jude and 2 Peter." In *A Vision for the Church: Studies in Early Christian Ecclesiology in Honour of J. P. M. Sweet*, edited by Markus Bockmuehl, 153–66. Edinburgh: T. & T. Clark, 1997.

———. *Jude, 2 Peter*. WBC. Waco, TX: Word, 1983.

Bauman, Zygmunt. *The Individualized Society*. Malden, MA: Blackwell, 2001.

Bavinck, Herman. Reformed Dogmatics. Edited by John Bolt. Translated by John Vriend. 4 Vols. Grand Rapids: Baker Academic, 2003–08.

Beale, G. K. *The Temple and the Church's Mission: A Biblical Theology of the Dwelling Place of God*. NSBT. Downers Grove, IL: InterVarsity, 2004.

———. *We Become What We Worship: A Biblical Theology of Idolatry*. Downers Grove, IL: InterVarsity Academic, 2008.

Beale, Gregory. *The Book of Revelation*. NIGTC. Grand Rapids: Eerdmans, 1999.

Beasley-Murray, George. *Baptism in the New Testament*. New York: Macmillan, 1962.

Beaton, Richard. "Isaiah in Matthew's Gospel." In *Isaiah is the New Testament*, edited by Steve Moyise and Maarten Menken, 63–78. New York: T. & T. Clark, 2005.

———. *Isaiah's Christ in Matthew's Gospel*. Cambridge: Cambridge University Press, 2002.

Beauchesne, Richard J. "Worship as Life, Priesthood and Sacrifice in Yves Congar." *Église et théologie* 21 (1990) 79–100.

Bellah, Robert N., et al. *Habits of the Heart: Individualism and Commitment in American Life*. Berkeley: University of California Press, 1985.

Bender, Kimlyn. *Karl Barth's Christological Ecclesiology*. Barth Studies. Burlington, VT: Ashgate, 2005.

Benedict. *The Rule of St. Benedict in English*. Edited by Timothy Fry. Collegeville, MN: Liturgical, 1981.

Berkouwer, G. C. *The Church*. Translated by James E. Davidson. Grand Rapids: Eerdmans, 1976.

Best, Ernest. "I Peter 2:4–10: A Reconsideration." *NovT* 11 (1969) 270–93.

———. "Spiritual Sacrifice: General Priesthood in the New Testament." *Interpretation* 14 (1960) 273–99.

Betz, Otto. "Jesus and Isaiah 53." In *Jesus and the Suffering Servant: Isaiah 53 and Christian Origins*, edited by W. H. Bellinger and William Reuben Farmer, 70–87. Harrisburg, PA: Trinity, 1998.

Beuken, W. A. M. "The Main Theme of Trito-Isaiah, 'The Servants of Yhwh.'" *JSOT* 47 (1990) 67–87.

Bevans, Stephen B., and Jeffrey Gros. *Evangelization and Religious Freedom: Ad Gentes, Dignitatis Humanae*. New York: Paulist, 2009.

BéVenot, Maurice. "'Sacerdos' as Understood by Cyprian." *JTS* 30 (1979) 413–29.

Billings, J. Todd. *Union with Christ: Reframing Theology and Ministry for the Church*. Grand Rapids: Baker Academic, 2011.

Blenkinsopp, Joseph. *Isaiah 56–66. A New Translation with Introduction and Commentary*: AB. New York: Doubleday, 2003.

———. *Opening the Sealed Book: Interpretations of the Book of Isaiah in Late Antiquity*. Grand Rapids: Eerdmans, 2006.

Blocher, Henri. "Immanence and Transcendence in Trinitarian Theology." In *The Trinity in a Pluralistic Age: Theological Essays on Culture and Religion*, edited by Kevin Vanhoozer, 104–23. Grand Rapids: Eerdmans, 1997.

———. *Songs of the Servant: Isaiah's Good News*. Vancouver: Regent College, 2005.

Block, Daniel. "Bringing Back David: Ezekiel's Messianic Hope." In *The Lord's Anointed: Interpretation of Old Testament Messianic Texts*, edited by Philip Satterthwaite and Gordon Wenham, 167–88. Grand Rapids: Baker, 1995.

———. "My Servant David: Ancient Israel's Vision of the Messiah." In *Israel's Messiah in the Bible and the Dead Sea Scrolls*, 17–56. Grand Rapids: Baker, 2003.

Bloesch, Donald G. *The Church: Sacraments, Worship, Ministry, Mission*. Christian Foundations. Grand Rapids: InterVarsity, 2002.

Blomberg, Craig. *Neither Poverty nor Riches: A Biblical Theology of Material Possessions*. NSBT. Grand Rapids: Eerdmans, 1999.

Bloom, Harold, ed. *Nathaniel Hawthorne's the Scarlet Letter*. New York: Bloom's Literary Criticism, 2011.

Blount, Brian. *Revelation: A Commentary*. Louisville: Westminster John Knox, 2009.

Boff, Leonardo. *Francis of Assisi: A Model for Human Liberation*. Translated by John W. Diercksmeier. Maryknoll, NY: Orbis, 2006.

Bonhoeffer, Dietrich. *Life Together: Prayerbook of the Bible*. Edited by Geffrey Kelly. Translated by Daniel Bloesch and James Burtness. Minneapolis: Fortress, 2006.

Bordeianu, Radu. "Priesthood Natural, Universal, and Ordained: Dumitru Staniloae's Communion Ecclesiology." *Pro Ecclesia* 19.4 (2010) 405–33.

Boring, M. Eugene. *1 Peter*. Nashville: Abingdon, 1999.

———. "Narrative Dynamics in First Peter: The Function of Narrative World." In *Reading First Peter with New Eyes: Methodological Reassessments of the Letter of First Peter*, edited by Robert Webb and Betsy Bauman-Martin, 7–40. LNTS 364. New York: T. & T. Clark, 2007.

Bornkamm, Karin. *Christus, König und Priester: das Amt Christi bei Luther im Verhältnis zur Vor- und Nachgeschichte*. Beiträge zur historischen Theologie. Tubingen: J. C. B. Mohr, 1998.

Bosch, David J. *Transforming Mission: Paradigm Shifts in Theology of Mission*. Maryknoll, NY: Orbis, 1995.

Bourdieu, Pierre. *Outline of a Theory of Practice*. Translated by Richard Nice. New York: Cambridge University Press, 1977.

Bradshaw, Paul, Maxwell Johnson, and L. Edward Phillips, eds. *The Apostolic Tradition: A Commentary*. Hermenia. Minneapolis, MN: Fortress, 2002.

Bravo, Francisco. *El sacerdocio común de los creyentes en la teología de Lutero*. Vitoria: ESET, 1963.

Brent, Allen. *Cyprian and Roman Carthage*. New York: Cambridge University Press, 2010.
———. *A Political History of Early Christianity*. London: T. & T. Clark, 2009.
Bright, Pamela. "Priesthood." In *The Westminster Handbook to Origen*, edited by John McGuckin, 179–81. Louisville: Westminster John Knox, 2004.
Broadhead, Edwin K. "Jesus and the Priests of Israel." In *Jesus from Judaism to Christianity: Continuum Approaches to the Historical Jesus*, edited by Tom Holmén, 125–44. LNTS 352. London: T. & T. Clark, 2007.
———. *Naming Jesus: Titular Christology in the Gospel of Mark*. Sheffield: Sheffield Academic, 1999.
Brock, Sebastian. "The Priesthood of the Baptised: Some Syriac Perspectives." *Sobornost* 9 (1987) 14–22.
Bromiley, Geoffrey William. *Christian Ministry*. Grand Rapids: Eerdmans, 1960.
Brooke, Christopher. "Priest, Deacon and Layman, from St. Peter Damian to St. Francis." In *The Ministry: Clerical and Lay*, edited by Diana Wood and Christopher Brooke, 65–85. Studies in Church History. Oxford: Blackwell, 1989.
Brown, Jeannine. *The Disciples in Narrative Perspective: The Portrayal and Function of the Matthean Disciples*. Atlanta, GA: SBL, 2002.
Brown, Raymond, and John Meier. *Antioch and Rome: New Testament Cradles of Catholic Christianity*. New York: Paulist, 1983.
Brueggemann, Walter. *Isaiah*. Louisville: Westminster John Knox, 1998.
Bruner, Frederick. *The Christbook: A Historical Theological Commentary: Matthew 1–12*. Waco, TX: Word, 1987.
Brunotte, Wilhelm. *Das geistliche Amt bei Luther*. Berlin: Lutherisches Verlagshaus, 1959.
Bryan, Steven. *Jesus and Israel's Traditions of Judgement and Restoration*. New York: Cambridge University Press, 2002.
Büchsel, Friedrich. "ἀλλογενής." In vol. 1 of *TDNT*, 267.
Bulley, Colin. *The Priesthood of Some Believers: Developments from the General to the Special Priesthood in the Christian Literature of the First Three Centuries*. Waynesboro, GA: Paternoster, 2000.
Bultmann, Rudolf Karl. *Theology of the New Testament*. New York: Scribner, 1965.
Calvin, John. *Calvin's Commentaries*. 44 vols. Edinburgh: Calvin Translation Society, 1844–1856. Reprinted in 22 vols. Grand Rapids: Baker, 1981.
———. *Calvin's New Testament Commentaries*. Edited by David W. Torrance and Thomas F. Torrance. 12 vols. Grand Rapids: Eerdmans, 1959–1972.
———. *Institutes of the Christian Religion*. Edited by John Thomas McNeill. Translated by Ford Lewis Battles. 2 vols. LCC. Philadelphia: Westminster, 1960.
Campbell, Douglas. "'The Priesthood of All Believers'—A Pauline Perspective." *JCBRF* 129 (1992) 14–24.
Carr, David McLain. "Reading Isaiah from Beginning (Isaiah 1) to End (Isaiah 65–66): Multiple Modern Possibilities." In *New Visions of Isaiah*, edited by Marvin Sweeney and Roy Melugin, 188–218. Sheffield: Sheffield Academic, 1996.
———. *Writing on the Tablet of the Heart: Origins of Scripture and Literature*. New York: Oxford University Press, 2005.
Carroll Rodas, M. Daniel. "La misión integral: ser bendición: un aporte desde el Antiguo Testamento." *Kairós* 36 (2005) 25–38.
Catechism of the Catholic Church. San Francisco: Ignatius, 1994.

Cazelles, Henri. "Sacral Kingship." In vol. 5 of *ABD*, 863–66.
Charles, Robert, ed. *The Book of Jubilees: Or the Little Genesis*. London: Black, 1902.
Charlesworth, James, ed. "Odes of Solomon." In *The Old Testament Pseudepigrapha*, translated by James Charlesworth, 2:725–71. Garden City, NY: Doubleday, 1985.
Chemnitz, Martin. *Loci Theologici*. Translated by Jacob A. O. Preus. St. Louis: Concordia, 1989.
Chilcote, Paul W., and Laceye C. Warner, eds. *The Study of Evangelism: Exploring a Missional Practice of the Church*. Grand Rapids: Eerdmans, 2008.
Childs, Brevard. *Isaiah*. OTL. Louisville: Westminster John Knox, 2001.
Chilton, Bruce, *The Temple of Jesus: His Sacrificial Program Within a Cultural History of Sacrifice*. University Park, PA: Pennsylvania State University Press, 1992.
———, ed. *The Isaiah Targum: Introduction, Translation, Apparatus and Notes*. Collegeville, MN: Liturgical, 1990.
Chilton, Bruce, and Jacob Neusner. *Judaism in the New Testament: Practices and Beliefs*. New York: Routledge, 1995.
Chrupcała, Lesław Daniel. *The Kingdom of God: A Bibliography of 20th Century Research*. Jerusalem: Franciscan, 2010.
Clarke, Andrew. *A Pauline Theology of Church Leadership*. LNTS. London: T. & T. Clark, 2008.
———. *Serve the Community: Christians as Leaders and Ministers*. Grand Rapids: Eerdmans, 2000.
Clement of Alexandria. *Christ the Educator*. Translated by Simon Wood. Vol. 23. FC. New York: Fathers of the Church, 1954.
Clement of Rome. "1 Clement." In *The Apostolic Fathers: Greek Texts and English Translations*, edited by Michael Holmes. 3rd ed. Grand Rapids: Baker Academic, 2007.
Clowney, Edmund. *The Message of 1 Peter: The Way of the Cross*. Downers Grove, IL: InterVarsity, 1988.
Coffey, David. "The Common and the Ordained Priesthood." *Theological Studies* 58.2 (1997) 209–36.
Cole, Neil. *Organic Church: Growing Faith Where Life Happens*. San Francisco: Jossey-Bass, 2005.
Colish, Marcia. *Peter Lombard*. New York: Brill, 1994.
Collins, John. *Diakonia: Re-interpreting the Ancient Sources*. Oxford: Oxford University Press, 1990.
Colyer, Elmer M. *How to Read T. F. Torrance: Understanding His Trinitarian and Scientific Theology*. Downers Grove, IL: InterVarsity, 2001.
Congar, Yves. "The Different Priesthoods: Christian, Jewish, and Pagan." In *A Gospel Priesthood*, translated by P. F. Hepburne-Scott, 74–89. New York: Herder and Herder, 1967.
———. *Lay People in the Church: A Study for a Theology of Laity*. Translated by Donald Attwater. Rev. ed. Westminster, MD: Newman, 1967.
———. "Ministry in the Early Church and Subsequent Historical Evolution." In *Asian Colloquium on Ministries in the Church*, 348–54. Manila, Philippines: Federation of Asian Bishop's Conferences, 1977.
———. "My Path-Findings in the Theology of Laity and Ministries." *The Jurist* 32 (1972) 168–88.

———. *The Mystery of the Temple: Or the Manner of God's Presence to His Creatures from Genesis to the Apocalypse.* Westminster, MD: Newman, 1962.

———. "The Sacralization of Western Society in the Middle Ages." In *Sacralization and Secularization*, edited by Roger Aubert, 55–71. New York: Paulist, 1969.

Conner, Benjamin T. *Practicing Witness: A Missional Vision of Christian Practices.* Grand Rapids: Eerdmans, 2011.

Cooke, Bernard. *The Distancing of God: The Ambiguity of Symbol in History and Theology.* Minneapolis: Fortress, 1990.

Corriveau, Raymond. *The Liturgy of Life: A Study of the Ethical Thought of St. Paul in His Letters to the Early Christian Communities.* Montreal: Desclée De Brouwer, 1970.

———. "Temple, Holiness, and the Liturgy of Life in Corinthians." *Letter and Spirit* 4 (2008) 145–66.

Cramer, Peter. *Baptism and Change in the Early Middle Ages, C. 200-C. 1150.* New York: Cambridge University Press, 1993.

Crawford, John Richard. "Calvin and the Priesthood of All Believers." *SJT* 21 (1968) 145–56.

Cullmann, Oscar. *The Christology of the New Testament.* Translated by S. C. Guthrie and C. A. M. Hall. Philadelphia: Westminster, 1963.

Cyprian. *The Letters of St. Cyprian.* Translated by Clarke Graeme. 4 Vols. ACW. New York: Newman, 1984–88.

———. *On the Church: Select Treatises.* Translated by Allen Brent. Crestwood, NY: St. Vladimir's Seminary Press, 2006.

———. *Saint Cyprian: The Lapsed, The Unity of the Catholic Church.* Translated by Maurice BéVenot. Vol. 25. New York: FC, 1958.

Dabin, Paul. *El Sacerdocio Real de los Laicos y la Accion Catolica.* Translated by Juan Carlos Zuretti and Luis Aned. 2 Vols. Buenos Aires: Editorial Difusion, 1939.

———. *Le Sacerdoce Royal des Fidéles dans les Livres Saints.* Paris: Bloud and Gay, 1941.

———. *Le Sacerdoce Royal des Fidèles dans la Tradicion Ancienne et Moderne.* Paris: L'Edition Universelle, 1950.

Daley, Brian. "The Ministry of Disciples: Historical Reflections on the Role of Religious Priests." *TS* 48 (1987) 605–29.

Daly, Robert. *Christian Sacrifice: The Judaeo-Christian Background before Origen.* Washington, DC: Catholic University of America, 1978.

———. *Sacrifice Unveiled: The Origins of Early Christian Sacrifice.* New York: T. & T. Clark, 2009.

Davies, Douglas James. *An Introduction to Mormonism.* New York: Cambridge University Press, 2003.

Davies, John. *A Royal Priesthood: Literary and Intertextual Perspectives on an Image of Israel in Exodus 19.6.* JSOTSup 395. New York: T. & T. Clark, 2004.

Davies, W. D., and Dale Allison. *The Gospel According to Matthew.* 3 Vols. ICC. Edinburgh: T. & T. Clark, 1988.

Davis, Don, and Terry Cornett. "Empowering People for Freedom, Wholeness, and Justice." In *Foundations for Christian Mission*, edited by Don Davis, 4:310–39. 16 vols. Capstone Curriculum. Wichita, KS: Urban Ministry Institute, 2005.

Davis, Don. *Evangelism and Spiritual Warfare.* Vol. 8. 16 vols. Capstone Curriculum. Wichita, KS: The Urban Ministry Institute, 2005.

———. *Foundations for Christian Mission.* Vol. 4. 16 vols. Capstone Curriculum. Wichita, KS: Urban Ministry Institute, 2005.

———. *Sacred Roots: A Primer on Retrieving the Great Tradition*. Wichita, KS: Urban Ministry Institute, 2010.

Demacopoulos, George. "Priesthood." In *Encyclopedia of Eastern Orthodox Christianity*, edited by John McGuckin, 456–58. Vol. 2 Malden, MA: Wiley-Blackwell, 2011.

Demarest, Bruce. *A History of Interpretation of Hebrews 7:1–10 from the Reformation to the Present*. BGBE. Tübingen: Mohr, 1976.

Dempster, Stephen G. *Dominion and Dynasty: A Biblical Theology of the Hebrew Bible*. Downers Grove, IL: InterVarsity, 2003.

DeSilva, David. "The Invention and Argumentative Function of Priestly Discourse in the Epistle to the Hebrews." *BBR* 16.2 (2006) 295–323.

Dever, Mark. *Nine Marks of a Healthy Church*. Wheaton, IL: Crossway, 2000.

———. "The Priesthood of All Believers: Reconsidering Every Member Ministry." In *The Compromised Church: The Present Evangelical Crisis*, edited by John H. Armstrong, 85–116. Wheaton, IL: Crossway, 1998.

Didymus the Blind. *Works on the Spirit: Athanasius's Letters to Serapion on the Holy Spirit, and, Didymus's on the Holy Spirit*. Translated by Mark DelCogliano, Andrew Radde-Gallwitz, and Lewis Ayres. Vol. 43. PP. Yonkers, NY: St. Vladimir's Seminary Press, 2011.

Dodd, C. H. *According to the Scriptures: The Sub-Structure of New Testament Theology*. 1950. London: Nisbet, 1952.

Drake, H. A. "The Church, Society, and Political Power." In *The Cambridge History of Christianity: Constantine to c. 600*, edited by Augustine Casiday and Frederick Norris, 2:403–28. New York: Cambridge University Press, 2007.

Drobner, Hubertus. "Christian Philosophy." In *The Oxford Handbook of Early Christian Studies*, edited by Susan Ashbrook Harvey and David G. Hunter, 672–90. New York: Oxford University Press, 2008.

———. *The Fathers of the Church: A Comprehensive Introduction*. Translated by Siegfried Schatzmann. Peabody, MA: Hendrickson, 2007.

Dunn, James. *The Theology of Paul the Apostle*. Grand Rapids: Eerdmans, 1998.

Eastwood, Cyril. *The Priesthood of All Believers: An Examination of the Doctrine from the Reformation to the Present Day*. 1960. Reprint, Eugene, OR: Wipf & Stock, 2009.

———. *The Royal Priesthood of the Faithful: An Investigation of the Doctrine from Biblical Times to the Reformation*. 1963. Reprint, Eugene, OR: Wipf & Stock, 2009.

Ebeling, Gerhard. "Beten als Wahrnehmen der Wirklichkeit des Menschen, wie Luther es Lehrte und lebte." *Luther-Jahrbuch* 66 (1999).

Ellingworth, Paul. "From Martin Luther to the Revised English Version." In *A History of Bible Translation*, edited by Phil Noss, 105–39. Rome: Edizioni de storia e letteratura, 2007.

Elliott, John. *1 Peter*. AB. New York: Doubleday, 2000.

———. "Death of a Slogan: From Royal Priests to Celebrating Community." *Una sancta* 25 (1968) 18–31.

———. *Elect and the Holy: An Exegetical Examination of 1 Peter 2:4–10 and the Phrase basileion hierateuma*. NovTSup. Leiden: Brill, 1966.

———. "Ministry and Church Order in the Mt: An Exegetical Examination of 1 Peter 2:4–10 and the Phrase 'basileion Hierateuma.'" *Catholic Biblical Quarterly* 32 (1970) 367–91.

Ellul, Jacques. *False Presence of the Kingdom*. New York: Seabury, 1972.

Emery, Gilles. *The Trinity: An Introduction to Catholic Doctrine on the Triune God.* Translated by Matthew Levering. Washington, DC: Catholic University of America Press, 2011.
Enders, Ludwig. *Luther und Emser: Ihre Streitschriften aus dam Jahre 1521.* Halle, 1889.
Eusebius. *The Ecclesiastical History.* Translated by J. E. L. Oulton. Vol. 265. LCL. New York: Harvard University Press, 1932.
———. *The Proof of the Gospel.* Translated by William John Ferrar. 1920. Reprint, Eugene, OR: Wipf and Stock, 2001.
Evans, Craig. "Context, Family, and Formation." In *The Cambridge Companion to Jesus*, edited by Markus Bockmuehl, 11–24. Cambridge: Cambridge University Press, 2001.
Faivre, Alexandre. *The Emergence of the Laity in the Early Church.* Translated by David Smith. New York: Paulist, 1990.
Farley, Edward. *Theologia: The Fragmentation and Unity of Theological Education.* Philadelphia: Fortress, 1983.
Farrow, Douglas. *Ascension and Ecclesia: On the Significance of the Doctrine of the Ascension for Ecclesiology and Christian Cosmology.* Grand Rapids: Eerdmans, 1999.
———. "Melchizedek and Modernity." In *The Epistle to the Hebrews and Christian Theology*, edited by Richard Bauckham, Daniel Driver, Trevor Hart, and Nathan MacDonald, 281–301. Grand Rapids: Eerdmans, 2009.
Fee, Gordon. *The First Epistle to the Corinthians.* NICNT. Grand Rapids: Eerdmans, 1987.
———. "Laos and Leadership under the New Covenant." *Crux* 25.4 (1989) 3–13.
Ferguson, Everett. *Baptism in the Ancient Church: History, Theology, and Liturgy in the First Five Centuries.* Grand Rapids: Eerdmans, 2009.
———. *The Church of Christ: A Biblical Ecclesiology for Today.* Grand Rapids: Eerdmans, 1996.
———. "Spiritual Sacrifice in Early Christianity and Its Environment." In *vorkonstantinisches Christentum: Vchaeltnis zu roemischem Staat und heidischer Religion*, edited by Haase Wolfgang, 1151–89. New York: de Gruyter, 1980.
Fernando, Ajith. "Grounding Our Reflections in Scripture: Biblical Trinitarianism and Mission." In *Global Missiology for the 21st Century: The Iguassu Dialogue*, edited by William David Taylor, 191–256. Grand Rapids: Baker Academic, 2000.
Fletcher-Louis, C. H. T. "The High Priest as Divine Mediator in the Hebrew Bible: Dan 7:13 as a Test Case." *SBLSP* 4 (1997) 161–93.
———. "Jesus as the High Priestly Messiah: Part 1." *Journal for the Study of the Historical Jesus* 4.2 (2006) 155–175.
———. "Jesus as the High Priestly Messiah: Part 2." *Journal for the Study of the Historical Jesus* 5.1 (2007) 57–79.
Flett, John G. *The Witness of God: The Trinity, Missio Dei, Karl Barth, and the Nature of Christian Community.* Grand Rapids: Eerdmans, 2010.
Floor, Lambertus. "The General Priesthood of Believers in the Epistle to the Hebrews." In *Ad Hebraeos*, 72–82. Pretoria: Die Nuwe-Testamentiese Werkgemeenskap, 1971.
Flusser, David. "The Eschatological Temple." In *Judaism of the Second Temple Period*, 207–13. Grand Rapids: Eerdmans, 2007.
Fox, Richard Wightman. *Reinhold Niebuhr: A Biography.* New York: Pantheon, 1985.

Fox, Zeni. "Laity, Ministry, and Secular Character." In *Ordering the Baptismal Priesthood: Theologies of Lay and Ordained Ministry*, edited by Susan Wood, 121–51. Collegeville, MN: Liturgical, 2003.

———. *Lay Ecclesial Ministry*. Lanham, MD: Rowman and Littlefield, 2010.

France, R. T. *Jesus and the Old Testament: His Application of Old Testament Passages to Himself and His Mission*. Downers Grove, IL: InterVarsity, 1971.

Freeman, Curtis W., James William McClendon, and C. Rosalee Velloso da Silva. *Baptist Roots: A Reader in the Theology of a Christian People*. Valley Forge: Judson, 1999.

Freyne, Sean. "Jesus and the 'Servant Community' in Zion: Continuity in Context." In *Jesus from Judaism to Christianity: Continuum Approaches to the Historical Jesus*, edited by Tom Holmén, 109–23. LNTS 352. London: T. & T. Clark, 2007.

Friesen, Abraham. *Erasmus, the Anabaptists, and the Great Commission*. Grand Rapids: Eerdmans, 1998.

Froehlich, Karlfried. "Luther on Vocation." In *Harvesting Martin Luther's Reflections on Theology, Ethics, and the Church*, edited by Timothy J. Wengert, 121–33. Grand Rapids: Eerdmans, 2004.

Garrett, James Leo. "The Biblical Doctrine of the Priesthood of the People of God." In *New Testament Studies: Essays in Honor of Ray Summers in His 65th year*, edited by Huber Drumwright and Curtis Vauchan, 137–49. Waco, TX: Baylor University Press, 1975.

———. "The Pre-Cyprianic Doctrine of the Priesthood of All Christians." In *Continuity and Discontinuity in Church History*, edited by F. Forrester Church and Timothy George, 45–62. Leiden: Brill, 1979.

———. "The Priesthood of All Christians: From Cyprian to John Chrysostom." *SwJT* 30 (1988) 22–33.

———. *Systematic Theology: Biblical, Historical, and Evangelical*. Grand Rapids: Eerdmans, 1995.

———, ed. *The Concept of the Believers' Church: Addresses from the 1967 Louisville Conference*. Scottdale, PA: Herald, 1969.

Gärtner, Bertil. *The Temple and the Community in Qumran and the New Testament: a Comparative Study in the Temple Symbolism of the Qumran Texts and the New Testament*. Cambridge: Cambridge University Press, 1965.

Gelder, Craig, Van. *The Essence of the Church*. Grand Rapids: Baker, 2000.

George, Timothy. "The Priesthood of All Believers." In *Essays on the Believer's Church*, edited by Paul Basden and David Dockery, 85–95. Nashville, TN: Broadman, 1991.

Gerrish, Brian A. "Priesthood and Ministry in the Theology of Luther." *Church History* 34.4 (1965) 404–22.

Gignilliat, Mark. *Paul and Isaiah's Servants: Paul's Theological Reading of Isaiah 40-66 in 2 Corinthians 5:14–6:10*. LNTS 330. New York: T. & T. Clark, 2007.

———. "Who Is Isaiah's Servant? Narrative Identity and Theological Potentiality." *SJT* 61.2 (2008) 125–36.

Gillespie, Thomas. "The Laity in Biblical Perspective." *ThTo* 36 (1979) 315–27.

Goertz, Harald. *Allgemeines Priestertum und ordiniertes Amt bei Luther*. Marburg: Elwert, 1997.

Goetzmann, Jürgen. "House." In vol. 2 of *NIDNTT*, 247–53.

Goheen, Michael. *"As the Father has Sent Me, I am Sending You": Lesslie Newbigin's Missionary Ecclesiology*. Zoetermeer: Boekencentrum, 2000.

———. *A Light to the Nations: The Missional Church and the Biblical Story.* Grand Rapids: Baker Academic, 2011.

———. "The Missional Calling of Believers in the World: The Contribution of Lesslie Newbigin." In *A Scandalous Prophet: the Way of Mission After Newbigin*, edited by Thomas F. Foust, George R. Hunsberger, and J. Andrew Kirk, 37–54. Grand Rapids: Eerdmans, 2001.

Goldingay, John. *Psalms: 90–150.* Grand Rapids: Baker Academic, 2006.

Good, Deirdre. *Jesus the Meek King.* Harrisburg, PA: Trinity, 1999.

Goodall, Norman, ed. *Missions Under the Cross: Addresses Delivered at the Enlarged Meeting of the Committee of the International Missionary Council at Willingen, in Germany, 1952; with Statements Issued by the Meeting.* London: Edinburgh, 1953.

Gould, Graham. "Ecclesiastical Hierarchy in the Thought of Pseudo-Dionysius." In The *Ministry: Clerical and Lay*, edited by Diana Wood and C. Brooke, 29–40. Studies in Church History. Oxford: Blackwell, 1989.

Goulder, M. D., and M. L. Sanderson. "St. Luke's Genesis." *JTS* 8 (1957) 12–30.

Gourgues, Michel. *A la droite de Dieu: résurrection de Jésus et actualisation du Psaume 110:1 dans le Nouveau Testament.* Paris: Gabalda, 1978.

Green, Gene. *1 Pedro Y 2 Pedro.* CBH. Miami: Editorial Caribe, 1993.

Green, Joel. *I Peter.* THNTC. Grand Rapids: Eerdmans, 2007.

Greenfield, Jonas, Michael Stone, and Esther Eshel, eds. *The Aramaic Levi Document: Edition, Translation, Commentary.* Boston: Brill, 2004.

Grenz, Stanley. "Baptism and the Lord's Supper as Community Acts: Toward a Sacramental Understanding of the Ordinances." In *Baptist Sacramentalism*, edited by Anthony Cross and Philip E. Thompson, 76–95. Waynesboro, GA: Paternoster, 2003.

Grudem, Wayne. *The First Epistle of Peter: An Introduction and Commentary.* TNTC 17. Downers Grove, IL: InterVarsity, 1988.

Grundmann,, Walter. "χρίω, χριστός, ἀντίχριστος, χρῖσμα, χριστιανός." In vol. 9 of *TDNT*, 492–579.

Guder, Darrell L. "The Church as Missional Community." In *The Community of the Word: Toward an Evangelical Ecclesiology*, edited by Mark Husbands and Daniel J. Treier, 114–28. Downers Grove, IL: InterVarsity, 2005.

———. *The Continuing Conversion of the Church.* Gospel and Culture. Grand Rapids: Eerdmans, 2000.

———. "Missional Structures: The Particular Community." In *Missional Church: A Vision for the Sending of the Church in North America*, 221–47. Gospel and Culture. Grand Rapids: Eerdmans, 1998.

Guder, Darrell L., and Lois Barrett, eds. *Missional Church: A Vision for the Sending of the Church in North America.* Grand Rapids: Eerdmans, 1998.

Gunton, Colin E. "The Community. The Trinity and the Being of the Church." In *The Promise of Trinitarian Theology*, 58–85. Edinburgh: T. & T. Clark, 1991.

Gupta, Nijay. "A Spiritual House of Royal Priests, Chosen and Honored: The Presence and Function of Cultic Imagery in 1 Peter." *PRSt* 36 (2009) 61–76.

———. "Which 'Body' Is a Temple (1 Corinthians 6:19)? Paul beyond the Individual/Communal Divide." *CBQ* 72 (2010) 518–36.

Gurtner, Daniel. *The Torn Veil: Matthew's Exposition of the Death of Jesus.* Cambridge, U.K.: Cambridge University Press, 2007.

Gutiérrez, Gustavo. *A Theology of Liberation.* Maryknoll, NY: Orbis, 1988.

Habets, Myk. *The Anointed Son: A Trinitarian Spirit Christology*. Eugene, OR: Pickwick, 2010.

Hagner, Donald Alfred. *Matthew 14–28*. 33B. Dallas, TX: Word, 1995.

———. *The Use of the Old and New Testaments in Clement of Rome*. NovTSup 34. Leiden: Brill, 1973.

Hahn, Scott. *Kinship by Covenant: A Canonical Approach to the Fulfillment of God's Saving Promises*. New Haven: Yale University Press, 2009.

Hahnenberg, Edward P. "The Ministerial Priesthood and Liturgical Anamnesis in the Thought of Edward J. Kilmartin, SJ." *Theological Studies* 66.2 (2005) 253–78.

Hanson, Paul. *The People Called: The Growth of Community in the Bible*. Louisville: Westminster John Knox, 2001.

Hanson, R. P. C. *Studies in Christian Antiquity*. Edinburgh: T. & T. Clark, 1985.

Harink, Douglas. *1 & 2 Peter*. BTCB. Grand Rapids: Brazos, 2009.

Harmless, J. William. "Monasticism." In *The Oxford Handbook of Early Christian Studies*, edited by Susan Ashbrook Harvey and David G. Hunter, 494–517. New York: Oxford University Press, 2008.

Harnack, Adolf von. *Monasticism: Its Ideals and History, and the Confessions of St. Augustine*. Translated by E. E. Kellett. London: Williams & Norgate, 1913.

Harper, Brad, and Paul Louis Metzger. *Exploring Ecclesiology: An Evangelical and Ecumenical Introduction*. Grand Rapids: Brazos, 2009.

Hauerwas, Stanley, and Samuel Wells, eds. *The Blackwell Companion to Christian Ethics*. Malden, MA: Blackwell, 2004.

Hay, David. *Glory at the Right Hand: Psalm 110 in Early Christianity*. Nashville: Abingdon, 1973.

Hays, Richard B. *Echoes of Scripture in the Letters of Paul*. New Haven: Yale University Press, 1989.

———. *The Moral Vision of the New Testament: Community, Cross, New Creation: A Contemporary Introduction to New Testament Ethics*. San Francisco: HarperCollins, 1996.

Hellholm, David. "The Shepherd of Hermas." In *The Apostolic Fathers: An Introduction*, edited by Wilhelm Pratscher, 215–42. Waco, TX: Baylor University Press, 2010.

Hellerman, Joseph. *The Ancient Church As Family*. Minneapolis: Fortress, 2001.

Henry, Carl F. H. *The Uneasy Conscience of Modern Fundamentalism*. Grand Rapids: Eerdmans, 1947.

Herbert, T. D. *Kenosis and Priesthood: Towards a Protestant Re-Evaluation of the Ordained Ministry*. Colorado Springs, CO: Paternoster, 2008.

Hess, Klaus. "Serve, Deacon, Worship." In vol. 3 of *NIDNTT*, 544–53.

Hilary of Poitiers. *The Trinity*. Translated by Stephen McKenna. Vol. 25. FC. New York: Fathers of the Church, 1954.

Hill, David. "'To Offer Spiritual Sacrifices . . .' (I Peter 2:5): Liturgical Formulations and Christian Paraenesis in I Peter." *JSNT* 16 (1982) 45–63.

Himmelfarb, Martha. *A Kingdom of Priests: Ancestry and Merit in Ancient Judaism*. Philadelphia: University of Pennsylvania Press, 2006.

Hinlicky, Paul R. *Paths Not Taken: Fates of Theology from Luther Through Leibniz*. Grand Rapids: Eerdmans, 2009.

Hinson, E. Glenn. "Pastoral Authority and the Priesthood of Believers from Cyprian to Calvin." *Faith and Mission* 7 (1989) 6–23.

Hodge, Charles. *Systematic Theology*. Vol. 1. Grand Rapids: Eerdmans, 1973.

Hodgson, Leonard. *The Doctrine of the Trinity*. Croall Lectures, 1942–43. London: Nisbet, 1943.
Hoehner, Harold W. *Ephesians: An Exegetical Commentary*. Grand Rapids: Baker Academic, 2002.
Hoekendijk, Johannes Christiaan. *The Church Inside Out*. Philadelphia: Westminster, 1966.
Holmes, Stephen R. "Towards a Baptist Theology of Ordained Ministry." In *Baptist Sacramentalism*, edited by Anthony R. Cross and Philip E. Thompson, 247–62. Milton Keynes: Paternoster, 2003.
———. "Trinitarian Missiology: Towards a Theology of God as Missionary." *IJST* 8.1 (2006) 72–90.
Hooker, Morna. "Did the Use of Isaiah 53 to Interpret His Mission Begin with Jesus?" In *Jesus and the Suffering Servant: Isaiah 53 and Christian Origins*, edited by W. H. Bellinger and William Farmer, 88–103. Harrisburg, PA: Trinity, 1998.
———. *Jesus and the Servant: the Influence of the Servant Concept of Deutero-Isaiah in the New Testament*. London: SPCK, 1959.
Hornbeck, J. Patrick. *What Is a Lollard?: Dissent and Belief in Late Medieval England*. New York: Oxford University Press, 2010.
Horton, Michael S. *The Christian Faith: A Systematic Theology for Pilgrims on the Way*. Grand Rapids: Zondervan, 2011.
———. "The Church after the Parachurch." *MR* 2 (2012) 50–53.
Hubmaier, Balthasar. *Balthasar Hubmaier, Theologian of Anabaptism*. Edited by John Howard Yoder and H. Wayne Pipkin. Scottdale, PA: Herald, 1989.
Hugenberger, Gordon. "The Servant of the Lord in the 'Servant Songs' of Isaiah: A Second Moses Figure." In *The Lord's Anointed: Interpretation of Old Testament Messianic Texts*, edited by Philip Satterthwaite and Gordon Wenham, 105–40. Grand Rapids: Baker, 1995.
Hunsberger, George. "The Newbigin Gauntlet: Developing a Domestic Missiology for North America." In *The Church Between Gospel and Culture: The Emerging Mission in North America*, edited by George R. Hunsberger and Craig Van Gelder, 3–25. Grand Rapids: Eerdmans, 1996.
———. "Proposals for a Missional Hermeneutic: Mapping a Conversation." *Missiology* 36 (2011) 309–21.
Hurtado, Larry W. *Lord Jesus Christ: Devotion to Jesus in Earliest Christianity*. Grand Rapids: Eerdmans, 2003.
Husbands, Mark. "The Trinity Is Not Our Social Program: Volf, Gregory of Nyssa, and Barth." In *Trinitarian Theology for the Church: Scripture, Community, Worship*, edited by Daniel J. Treier and David Lauber, 120–41. Downers Grove, IL: InterVarsity, 2009.
Husbands, Mark, and Daniel J. Treier, eds. *The Community of the Word: Toward an Evangelical Ecclesiology*. Downers Grove, IL: InterVarsity, 2005.
Hütter, Reinhard. *Suffering Divine Things: Theology as Church Practice*. Grand Rapids: Eerdmans, 2000.
Irenaeus. *Against Heresies*. Translated by A. Roberts and W. H. Rambaut. *ANF* 1.309–568. Buffalo, 1885–1896. Electronic ed.
Issler, Klaus. "Jesus' Example: Prototype of the Dependent Spirit Filled Life." In *Jesus in Trinitarian Perspective*, edited by Klaus Issler and Fred Sanders, 189–225. Nashville: B&H, 2007.

Istavridis, Vastil. "The Orthodox World." In *The Layman in Christian History: A Project of the Department on the Laity of the World Council of Churches*, edited by Stephen Neill and Hans Ruedi Weber, 276–97. Philadelphia: Westminster, 1963.
Jeffcoat, James R. "Martin Luther's Doctrine of Ministry." PhD diss., Drew University, 1989.
Jenson, Philip. *Graded Holiness: A Key to the Priestly Conception of the World*. Sheffield: Sheffield Academic, 1992.
Jeremias, Joachim. "ἀμνός, ἀρήν, ἀρνίον." In vol. 1 of *TDNT*, 338–41.
Jobes, Karen. *1 Peter*. BECNT. Grand Rapids: Baker Academic, 2005.
John of Damascus. *Writings*. Translated by Frederic Hathaway Chase. Vol. 37. FC. New York: Fathers of the Church, 1958.
Johnson, Keith L. "The Being and Act of the Church: Barth and the Future of Evangelical Ecclesiology." In *Karl Barth and American Evangelicalism*, edited by Bruce L. McCormack and Clifford B. Anderson, 201–26. Grand Rapids: Eerdmans, 2011.
Jones, L. Gregory. "Baptism: A Dramatic Journey into God's Dazzling Light: Baptismal Catechesis and the Shaping of Christian Practical Wisdom." In *Knowing the Triune God: The Work of the Spirit in the Practices of the Church*, edited by James Joseph Buckley and David Yeago, 147–77. Grand Rapids: Eerdmans, 2001.
———. *Embodying Forgiveness: A Theological Analysis*. Grand Rapids: Eerdmans, 1995.
———. *Transformed Judgement: Toward a Trinitarian Account of the Moral Life*. Nortre Dame, IN: University of Notre Dame, 1990.
Justin Martyr. *Dialogue with Trypho*. Edited by Michael Slusser. Translated by Thomas Halton. Vol. 3. FC. Washington, DC: Catholic University of America Press, 2003.
———. *Saint Justin Martyr: The First Apology, The Second Apology, Dialogue with Trypho, Exhortation to the Greeks, Discourse to the Greeks, The Monarchy; or the Rule of God*. Vol. 6. FC. New York: Fathers of the Church, 1948.
Kant, Immanuel. *Religion and Rational Theology*. Edited by Allen W. Wood and George Di Giovanni. New York: Cambridge University Press, 1996.
Kärkkäinen, Veli-Matti. "The Calling of the Whole People of God into Ministry: The Spirit, Church, and Laity." *Studia Theologica* 53 (1999) 144–62.
———. *Spiritus Ubi Vult Spirat: Pneumatology in Roman Catholic-Pentecostal Dialogue (1972–1989)*. Helsinki: Luther-Agricola-Society, 1998.
Kaufman, Stephen. *Targum Jonathan to the Prophets: The Jewish Literary Aramaic Version of the Prophets from the Files of the Comprehensive Aramaic Lexicon Project (CAL)*. CD-ROM. Cincinnati, OH: Hebrew Union College, 2005.
Kavanagh, Aidan. *The Shape of Baptism: The Rite of Christian Initiation*. Collegeville, MN: Liturgical, 1978.
Kidder, Annemarie S. *Making Confession, Hearing Confession: A History of the Cure of Souls*. Collegeville, MN: Liturgical, 2010.
Kilmartin, Edward. *The Eucharist in the West: History and Theology*. Edited by Robert Daly. Collegeville, MN: Liturgical, 1998.
Koch, Klaus. "Messias und Sündenvergebung in Jesaja 53, Targum: ein Beitrag zur der Praxis der aramäischen Bibelübersetzung." *JSJ* 3.2 (1972) 117–48.
Köstenberger, Andreas J., and Scott R. Swain. *Father, Son, and Spirit: The Trinity and John's Gospel*. Downers Grove, IL: InterVarsity, 2008.
Kreider, Alan. "Baptism, Catechism, and the Eclipse of Jesus' Teaching in Early Christianity." *TynBul* 47 (1996) 315–48.

———. "Beyond Bosch: The Early Church and the Christendom Shift." *IBMR* 29 (2005) 59–68.

———. "Changing Patterns of Conversion in the West." In *Origins of Christendom in the West*, 3–46. New York: T. & T. Clark, 2001.

———. "'They Alone Know the Right Way to Live': The Early Church and Evangelism." In *Ancient Faith for the Church's Future*, edited by Mark Husbands and Jeff Greenman, 169–86. Downers Grove, IL: InterVarsity Academic, 2008.

———, ed. *The Origins of Christendom in the West*. New York: T. & T. Clark, 2001.

Küng, Hans. *The Church*. Translated by Ray and Rosaleen Ockenden. New York: Sheed and Ward, 1967.

———. "Paradigm Change in Theology: A Proposal for Discussion." In *Paradigm Change in Theology: A Symposium for the Future*, edited by Hans Küng and David Tracy, 3–33. New York: Crossroad, 1989.

———. *Theology for a New Millennium*. New York: Doubleday, 1988.

———. "What Does a Change of Paradigm Mean?" In *Paradigm Change in Theology: A Symposium for the Future*, edited by Hans Küng and David Tracy, 212–19. New York: Crossroad, 1989.

Kupp, David. *Matthew's Emmanuel: Divine Presence and God's People in the First Gospel*. New York: Cambridge University Press, 1996.

Laansma, Jon. "Hebrews and the Mission of the Earliest Church." In *New Testament Theology in Light of the Church's Mission: Essays in Honor of I. Howard Marshall*, edited by Jon Laansma, Grant R. Osborne, and Ray Van Neste, 327–46. Eugene, OR: Cascade, 2011.

———. *"I Will Give You Rest": The "Rest" Motif in the New Testament with Special Reference to Mt 11 and Heb 3–4*. WUNT 98. Tubingen: Mohr Siebeck, 1997.

Lang, Bernhard. *Sacred Games: A History of Christian Worship*. New Haven: Yale University Press, 1997.

Latourette, Kenneth Scott. *A History of Christianity*. New York: Harper, 1953.

Lattke, Michael. *Odes of Solomon: A Commentary*. Translated by Marianne Erhardt. Minneapolis: Fortress, 2009.

Laurance, John. *Priest as Type of Christ: The Leader of the Eucharist in Salvation History According to Cyprian of Carthage*. New York: Peter Lang, 1984.

"Lausanne Occasional Paper 22: Christian Witness to the Urban Poor." 1980. Online: http://www.lausanne.org/all-documents/lop-22.html

Leithart, Peter. "Attendants of Yahweh's House: Priesthood in the Old Testament." *JSOT* 85 (1999) 3–24.

———. *Blessed are the Hungry: Meditations on the Lord's Supper*. Moscow, ID: Canon, 2000.

———. *Defending Constantine: The Twilight of an Empire and the Dawn of Christendom*. Downers Grove, IL: InterVarsity, 2010.

———. "Infant Baptism in History: a Tragicomedy." In *The Case for Covenantal Infant Baptism*, edited by Gregg Strawbridge, 246–62. Phillipsburg, NJ: P&R, 2003.

———. *The Priesthood of the Plebs: A Theology of Baptism*. Eugene, OR: Wipf & Stock, 2003.

Letham, Robert. *The Holy Trinity: In Scripture, History, Theology, and Worship*. Phillipsburg, NJ: P and R, 2004.

Leuchter, Mark. "The Priesthood in Ancient Israel." *BTB* 40 (2010) 100–10.

Levenson, Jon. "On the Promise to the Rechabites." *CBQ* 38.4 (1976) 508–14.

———. *Theology of the Program of Restoration of Ezekiel 40-48.* Cambridge, MA: Scholars Press for the Harvard Semitic Museum, 1976.

Levering, Matthew. *Christ and the Catholic Priesthood: Ecclesial Hierarchy and the Pattern of the Trinity.* Chicago: Hillenbrand, 2010.

———. *Sacrifice and Community: Jewish Offering and Christian Eucharist.* Malden, MA: Blackwell, 2005.

Lewis, C. S. *The Discarded Image an Introduction to Medieval and Renaissance Literature.* Cambridge: Cambridge University Press, 1964.

Lindbeck, George A. "Scripture, Consensus, and Community." In *Biblical Interpretation in Crisis: The Ratzinger Conference on Bible and Church*, edited by Richard John Neuhaus, 74–101. Grand Rapids: Eerdmans, 1989.

Littel, Franklin H. "From 'Christendom' to Christian Renewal." In *The People of God: Essays on the Believers' Church*, edited by Paul A. Basden and David S. Dockery, 315–27. Nashville, TN: Broadman, 1991.

Lohse, Bernhard. *Martin Luther's Theology: Its Historical and Systematic Development.* Translated by Roy A. Harrisville. Minneapolis: Fortress, 1999.

Loimeier, Roman. "Is There Something like 'Protestant Islam'?" *Die Welt des Islams* 45.2 (2005) 216–54.

Longenecker, Bruce. *Remember the Poor: Paul, Poverty, and the Greco-Roman World.* Grand Rapids: Eerdmans, 2010.

Lubac, Henri de. *Medieval Exegesis, Vol. 3: The Four Senses of Scripture.* Grand Rapids: Eerdmans, 2009.

———. *The Splendor of the Church.* San Francisco: Ignatius, 1999.

Lucass, Shirley. *The Concept of the Messiah in the Scriptures of Judaism and Christianity.* New York: T. & T. Clark, 2011.

Luter, Boyd. "'Worship' as Service: The New Testament Usage of Latreuō." *Criswell Theological Review* 2 (1988) 335–44.

Luther, Martin. *D. Martin Luthers Werke: Kritische Gesamtausgabe.* 97 vols. In 112 parts. Weimar: Böhlau, 1883–1985.

———. *Luther's Works.* Edited by Jaroslav Pelikan and Helmut T. Lehmann. 56 vols. Philadelphia: Fortress, 1955–86.

Luz, Ulrich. *Matthew: A Commentary.* 3 Vols. Continental Commentaries. Minneapolis: Augsburg Fortress, 1989.

Macchia, Frank D. "Baptized in the Spirit: Toward a Global Theology of Spirit Baptism." In *The Spirit in the World: Emerging Pentecostal Theologies in Global Contexts*, edited by Veli-Matti Kärkkäinen, 3–20. Grand Rapids: Eerdmans, 2009.

MacDonald, Nathan. "A Trinitarian Palimpsest: Luther's Reading of the Priestly Blessing (Num 6:24–26)." *Pro Ecclesia* 21 (2012) 299–313.

MacIntyre, Alasdair. *After Virtue: A Study in Moral Theory.* 2nd ed. Notre Dame, IN: University of Notre Dame Press, 1984.

Mallen, Peter. *The Reading and Transformation of Isaiah in Luke-Acts.* New York: T. & T. Clark, 2008.

Markschies, Christoph. "Jesus Christ as a Man Before God: Two Interpretive Models for Isaiah 53 in the Patristic Literature and Their Development." In *The Suffering Servant: Isaiah 53 in Jewish and Christian Sources*, edited by Bernd Janowski and Peter Stuhlmacher, translated by Daniel Bailey, 225–334. Grand Rapids: Eerdmans, 2004.

Marshall, Bruce D. "Trinity." In *The Blackwell Companion to Modern Theology*, edited by Gareth Jones, 183–203. Blackwell Companions to Religion. Malden, MA: Blackwell, 2004.
Marshall, Christopher. "One for All and All for One: The High Priesthood of Christ, the Church, and the Priesthood of All Believers in Hebrews." *JCBRF* 129 (1992) 7–13.
Marshall, I. Howard. *1 Peter*. Downers Grove, IL: InterVarsity, 1991.
Martens, Elmer. "Impulses to Mission in Isaiah: An Intertextual Exploration." *BBR* 17 (2007) 215–39.
Martin, Troy. *Metaphor and Composition in 1 Peter*. Atlanta, GA: Scholars, 1992.
McDonnell, Kilian. *The Baptism of Jesus in the Jordan: The Trinitarian and Cosmic Order of Salvation*. Collegeville, MN: Liturgical, 1996.
McGrath, Alister. *Christianity's Dangerous Idea: The Protestant Revolution--A History from the Sixteenth Century to the Twenty-First*. New York: HarperOne, 2007.
Meadors, Gary T., ed. *Four Views on Moving Beyond the Bible to Theology*. Grand Rapids: Zondervan, 2009.
Melito of Sardis. *Sur la Pâque et fragments*. Edited by Othmar Melito. Vol. 123. SC. Paris: Cerf, 1966.
Merrill, Eugene. "Royal Priesthood: An Old Testament Messianic Motif." *Bibliotheca sacra* 150 (1983) 50–61.
Michalski, Melvin. *The Relationship Between the Universal Priesthood of the Baptized and the Ministerial Priesthood of the Ordained in Vatican II and in Subsequent Theology: Understanding "essentia Et Non Gradu."* Lewiston, NY: Mellen University Press, 1996.
Mikolaski, Samuel. "The Contemporary Relevance of the Priesthood of All Christians." *Southwestern Journal of Theology* 30 (1988) 6–14.
Mikoski, Gordon. *Baptism and Christian Identity: Teaching in the Triune Name*. Grand Rapids: Eerdmans, 2009.
Minear, Paul Sevier. "Disciples and the Crowds in the Gospel of Matthew." *ATR* 3 (1974) 28–44.
———. "The House of Living Stones: A Study of 1 Peter 2:4-12." *Ecumenical Review* 34.3 (1982) 238–48.
———. "Ontology and Ecclesiology in the Apocalypse." *NTS* 12 (1966) 89–105.
Moe, Olaf Edvard. "Der Gedanke des allgemeinen Priestertums im Hebräerbrief." *TZ* 5 (1949) 161–69.
Molinos, Miguel de. *Miguel de Molinos: The Spiritual Guide*. Translated by Robert P. Baird. Paulist, 2010.
Montover, Nathan. *Luther's Revolution: The Political Dimensions of Martin Luther's Universal Priesthood*. Eugene, OR: Pickwick, 2011.
Moo, Douglas. *The Epistle to the Romans*. Grand Rapids: Eerdmans, 1996.
Moss, Charlene. *The Zechariah Tradition and the Gospel of Matthew*. BZNW. New York: de Gruyter, 2008.
Motyer, J. A. *The Prophecy of Isaiah: An Introduction and Commentary*. Downers Grove, IL: InterVarsity, 1993.
Mullins, Edgar Young. *The Axioms of Religion*. Edited by R. Albert Mohler. Nashville, TN: Broadman & Holman, 1997.
Murdock, James, trans. *The Syriac New Testament Translated into English from the Peshitto Version*. 1893rd ed. Orig. 1883. Piscataway, NJ: Gorgias, 2001.

Murphy, Nancey C., Brad J. Kallenberg, and Mark Nation, eds. *Virtues and Practices in the Christian Tradition: Christian Ethics After Macintyre.* Harrisburg, PA: Trinity, 1997.

Muthiah, Robert A. *The Priesthood of All Believers in the Twenty-First Century: Living Faithfully as the Whole People of God in a Postmodern Context.* Eugene, OR: Wipf and Stock, 2009.

Neill, Stephen. *A History of Christian Missions.* Rev. ed. Baltimore: Penguin, 1987.

Nelson, Richard D. *Raising up a Faithful Priest: Community and Priesthood in Biblical Theology.* Louisville: Westminster John Knox, 1993.

Newbigin, Lesslie. "The Christian Layman in the World and in the Church." *National Christian Council Review* 72 (1952) 185–89.

———. *Come Holy Spirit: Renew the Whole Creation.* Selly Oak Colleges Occasional Paper. Birmingham, England: Selly Oak Colleges, 1990.

———. "Ecumenical Amnesia." *IBMR* 18 (1994) 2–5.

———. *The Gospel in a Pluralistic Society.* Grand Rapids: Eerdmans, 1989.

———. *The Household of God: Lectures on the Nature of the Church.* London: SCM, 1953.

———. "Lay Presidency at the Eucharist." *Mid-Stream: The Ecumenical Movement Today* 35 (1996) 177–82.

———. "Ministry and Laity." *National Christian Council Review* 85 (1965) 479–83.

———. *One Body, One Gospel, One World: The Christian Mission Today.* London: International Missionary Council, 1958.

———. *The Open Secret: An Introduction to the Theology of Mission.* Grand Rapids: Eerdmans, 1995.

———. "Speaking the Truth to Caesar." *Ecumenical Review* 43.3 (1991) 372–75.

———. *Unfinished Agenda: An Updated Autobiography.* Grand Rapids: Eerdmans, 1993.

———. "An X-Ray to Make God Visible in the World." *Reform* (December 1990) 7.

Newell, Samuel W. "Many Members: The Relation of the Individual to the People of God." *Interpretation* 5 (1951) 413–26.

Newman, Elizabeth. "The Priesthood of All Believers and the Necessity of the Church." In *Recycling the Past or Researching History?*, edited by Philip E. Thompson, Anthony R. Cross, and Stephen Brachlow, 50–66. Studies in Baptist History and Thought. Milton Keynes, UK: Paternoster, 2005.

Ng, Andrew Wai Man. "Watchman Nee and the Priesthood of All Believers." ThD diss., Concordia Seminary, 1986.

Nicholls, Bruce J., ed. *In Word and Deed: Evangelism and Social Responsibility.* Grand Rapids: Eerdmans, 1985.

Nichols, Aidan. *Christendom Awake: On Re-Energizing the Church in Culture.* Grand Rapids: Eerdmans, 1999.

Niebuhr, Reinhold. *The Nature and Destiny of Man: A Christian Interpretation.* New York: Scribner's, 1949.

Nikolajsen, Jeppe Bach. "The Distinctive Identity of the Church: A Constructive Study of the Post-Christendom Theologies of Lesslie Newbigin and John Howard Yoder." PhD diss., Norwegian School of Theology, 2010.

Nimmo, Paul. *Being in Action: The Theological Shape of Barth's Ethical Vision.* New York: T. & T. Clark, 2007.

Noll, Mark. *Turning Points: Decisive Moments in the History of Christianity.* Grand Rapids: Baker, 1997.

Noll, Ray Robert. *Christian Ministerial Priesthood: A Search for Its Beginnings in the Primary Documents of the Apostolic Fathers.* San Francisco: Catholic Scholars, 1993.

O'Brien, Peter. *The Letter to the Hebrews.* PNTC. Grand Rapids: Eerdmans, 2010.

O'Collins, Gerald, and Michael Keenan Jones. *Jesus our Priest: A Christian Approach to the Priesthood of Christ.* Oxford: Oxford University Press, 2010.

O'Connor, James T. *The Hidden Manna: A Theology of the Eucharist.* San Francisco: Ignatius, 2005.

O'Donovan, Oliver. *The Desire of the Nations: Rediscovering the Roots of Political Theology.* New York: Cambridge University Press, 1996.

Öberg, Ingemar. *Luther and World Mission: A Historical and Systematic Study with Special Reference to Luther's Bible Exposition.* Translated by Dean Apel. St. Louis: Concordia, 2007.

Oden, Thomas C. *Classic Christianity: A Systematic Theology.* New York: HarperOne, 2009.

———. *Corrective Love: The Power of Communion Discipline.* St. Louis, MO: Concordia, 1995.

Oepke, Albrecht. "μεσίτης, μεσιτεύω." In vol. 4 of *TDNT*, 598–624.

Origen. *Homélies Sur Le Lévitique.* Edited by Marcel Borret. 2 vols. SC 286. Paris: Cerf, 1981.

———. *Homilies on Leviticus: 1–16.* Translated by Gary Barkley. Vol. 83. FC. Washington DC: Catholic University of America Press, 1990.

———. *Origen Against Celsus.* Translated by Frederick Crombie. ANF 4:395–670. Buffalo, 1885–96. Electronic ed.

Orr, David. "Educating for the Priesthood of the Faithful." *Worship* 83.5 (2009) 431–57.

———. *The Gift of the Priesthood to the Faithful: A Study of the Theme as Evidenced in the Use of 1P 2:9 in the Patristic and Liturgical Traditions of the Latin Roman Church.* Rome: Pontificium Athenaeum S. Anselmi, 1991.

———. "The Giving of the Priesthood to the Faithful." In *Priesthood: The Hard Questions*, edited by Gerald Gleeson, 61–77. Newtown: Downer, 1993.

Osborne, Grant. *Matthew.* ECNT. Grand Rapids: Zondervan, 2010.

———. *Revelation.* Grand Rapids: Baker Academic, 2002.

Osborne, Kenan. "Envisioning a Theology of Ordained and Lay Ministry: Current Issues of Ambiguity." In *Ordering the Baptismal Priesthood: Theologies of Lay and Ordained Ministry*, edited by Susan Wood, 195–227. Collegeville, MN: Liturgical, 2003.

———. *Ministry: Lay Ministry in the Roman Catholic Church, Its History and Theology.* New York: Paulist, 1993.

———. *Orders and Ministry: Leadership in the World Church.* Maryknoll, NY: Orbis, 2006.

Oswalt, John. *The Book of Isaiah: Chapters 40–66.* NICOT. Grand Rapids: Eerdmans, 1998.

Owen, John. *Communion with the Triune God.* Edited by Kelly M. Kapic and Justin Taylor. Wheaton, IL: Crossway, 2007.

Owens, L. Roger. *The Shape of Participation: A Theology of Church Practices.* Eugene, OR: Cascade, 2010.

Packer, J. I. "A Puritan Perspective: Trinitarian Godliness According to John Owen." In *God the Holy Trinity: Reflections on Christian Faith and Practice*, edited by Timothy George, 91–108. Grand Rapids: Baker Academic, 2006.

Palmer, Paul. "The Lay Priesthood: Real or Metaphorical?" *Theological Studies* 8 (1947) 574–613.

Pannenberg, Wolfhart. *Systematic Theology*. Translated by Geoffrey W. Bromiley. 3 Vols. Grand Rapids: Eerdmans, 1991.

Pao, David. *Acts and the Isaianic New Exodus*. Grand Rapids: Baker Academic, 2002.

Parrett, Gary, and J. I. Packer. *Grounded in the Gospel: Building Believers the Old-Fashioned Way*. Grand Rapids: Baker, 2010.

Pelikan, Jaroslav. "The Bible and the Word of God." In *Luther the Expositor*, 48–70. St. Louis: Concordia, 1959.

———. *The Christian Tradition: A History of the Development of Doctrine*, 5 Vols. Chicago: University of Chicago Press, 1975–91.

———. "Once for All the Sacrifice of Himself (Heb 9:26)." In *Luther the Expositor*, 237–60. St. Louis: Concordia, 1959.

———. *Spirit Versus Structure; Luther and the Institutions of the Church*. New York: Harper & Row, 1968.

Perrin, Nicholas. *Jesus the Temple*. Grand Rapids: Baker Academic, 2010.

Petterson, Anthony. *Behold Your King: The Hope for the House of David in the Book of Zechariah*. LHBOTS 513. New York: T. & T. Clark, 2009.

Philibert, Paul J. *The Priesthood of the Faithful: Key to a Living Church*. Collegeville, MN: Liturgical, 2005.

Pitts, William. "The Priesthood of All Christians in The Baptist Heritage." *SwJT* 30 (1988) 34–45.

Plato. *The Statesman; Philebus*. Translated by Harold N. Fowler and W. R. M. Lamb. Vol. 164. LCL. Cambridge: Harvard University Press, 1995.

———. *Timaeus, Critias, Cleitophon, Menexenus [and] Epistles*. Vol. 234. LCL. Cambridge, MA: Harvard University Press, 1981.

Pliny. *Letters*. Edited by W. C. L. Hutchinson. Translated by William Melmoth. Vol. 2. LCL. Cambridge, MA: Harvard University Press, 1915.

———. *Letters, and Panegyricus*. Translated by Betty Radice. Vol. 2. LCL. Cambridge: Harvard University Press, 1969.

Pohl, Christine D. *Living into Community: Cultivating Practices That Sustain Us*. Grand Rapids: Eerdmans, 2012.

Pontius. "St. Cyprian." In *Early Christian Biographies Lives of: St. Cyprian, by Pontius St. Ambrose, by Paulinus St. Augustine, by Possidius St. Anthony, by St. Athanasius St. Paul the First Hermit, St. Hilarion*. Translated by Roy Deferrari. New York: Fathers of the Church, 1952.

Power, David Noel. "Priesthood Revisited: Mission and Ministries in the Royal Priesthood." In *Ordering the Baptismal Priesthood: Theologies of Lay and Ordained Ministry*, edited by Susan Wood, 87–120. Collegeville, MN: Liturgical, 2003.

Powery, Emerson. *Jesus Reads Scripture: The Function of Jesus' Use of Scripture in the Synoptic Gospels*. Boston: Brill, 2003.

Poythress, Vern. "'Hold Fast' versus 'Hold Out' in Philippians 2:16." *WTJ* 64 (2002) 45–53.

Procksch, Otto. "ἅγιος—ἁγιάζω—ἁγιασμός ἁγιότης—ἁγιωσύνη." In vol. 1 of *TDNT*, 88–115.

Pseudo-Dionysius. *Pseudo-Dionysius: The Complete Works*. Translated by Colm Luibheid, CWS. New York: Paulist, 1987.

Putnam, Robert D. *Bowling Alone: The Collapse and Revival of American Community*. New York: Simon & Schuster, 2000.

Rae, Murray. "Baptism of Christ." In *The Person of Christ*, edited by Murray Rae and Stephen Holmes, 121–37. New York: T. & T. Clark, 2005.

Raiser, Konrad. *Ecumenism in Transition: A Paradigm Shift in the Ecumenical Movement?* Geneva: WCC, 1991.

———. "Is Ecumenical Apologetics Sufficient? A Response to Lesslie Newbigin's 'Ecumenical Amnesia.'" *IBMR* 18.2 (1994) 50–51.

Rea, James Edward. *The Common Priesthood of the Members of the Mystical Body: An Historical Survey of the Heretical Concepts of the Doctrine as Compared with the True Catholic Concept*. SST 101. Washington, DC: Catholic University of America, 1947.

Redding, Graham. *Prayer and the Priesthood of Christ: In the Reformed Tradition*. New York: T. & T. Clark, 2003.

Reventlow, Henning. "Basic Issues in the Interpretation of Isaiah 53." In *Jesus and the Suffering Servant: Isaiah 53 and Christian Origins*, edited by W. H Bellinger and William Farmer, 23–38. Harrisburg, PA: Trinity, 1998.

Robertson, Duncan. *Lectio Divina: The Medieval Experience of Reading*. Collegeville, MN: Liturgical, 2011.

Rogers, Mark. "A Dangerous Idea? Martin Luther, E.Y. Mullins, and the Priesthood of all Believers." *WTJ* 72 (2010) 119–43.

Roldán, Alberto. "The Priesthood of All Believers and Integral Mission." In *The Local Church Agent of Transformation: An Ecclesiology for Integral Mission*, edited by Tetsunao Yamamori and C. René Padilla, translated by Brian Cordingly. Buenos Aires: Kairós, 2004.

Rooke, Deborah. "Kingship as Priesthood: The Relationship between the High Priesthood and the Monarchy." In *King and Messiah in the Ancient Near East: Proceedings of the Oxford Old Testament Seminar*, edited by John Day, 187–208. JSOTSup 270. Sheffield: Sheffield Academic Press, 1998.

Root, Michael. "Freedom, Authority, and the Priesthood of All Believers." In *Critical Issues in Ecclesiology: Essays in Honor of Carl E. Braaten*, edited by Alberto L. García and Susan K. Wood, 88–104. Grand Rapids: Eerdmans, 2011.

Ryan, Laurance. "Patristic Teaching on the Priesthood of the Faithful." *ITQ* 29 (1962) 25–51.

Safrai, Shmuel. "Spoken and Literary Languages at the Time of Jesus." In *Jesus' Last Week*, edited by Steven Notley, Marc Turnage, and Brian Becker, 225–44. Boston: Brill, 2006.

Sanders, Fred. *The Deep Things of God: How the Trinity Changes Everything*. Wheaton, IL: Crossway, 2010.

———. *The Image of the Immanent Trinity: Rahner's Rule and the Theological Interpretation of Scripture*. New York: Peter Lang, 2005.

Sanneh, Lamin O. *Translating the Message: The Missionary Impact on Culture*. Maryknoll, NY: Orbis, 2009.

Saucy, Robert L. *The Church in God's Program*. Chicago: Moody, 1972.

Sawyer, John. *The Fifth Gospel: Isaiah in the History of Christianity*. New York: Cambridge University Press, 1996.

Schleiermacher, Friedrich. *The Christian Faith*. Edited by Hugh Ross Mackintosh and J. S. Stewart. New York: T. & T. Clark, 1928.

Schlier, Heinrich. "Die 'liturgie' des apostolischen Evangeliums (Rom 15:14–21)." In *Martyria, Leiturgia, Diakonia: Festschrift für Hermann Volk, Bischof von Mainz, zum 65. Geburtstag*, edited by Hermann Volk, Rudolf Haubst, and Karl Rahner, 247–59. Mainz: Matthias-Grunwald-Verlag, 1968.

Schneider, Johannes. "προσέρχομαι." In vol. 2 of *TDNT*, 683–84.

Scholer, John. *Proleptic Priests: Priesthood in the Epistle to the Hebrews*. JSNTSup 49. Sheffield: Sheffield Academic Press, 1991.

Schultz, Richard. "How Many Isaiahs Were There and What Does It Matter? Prophetic Inspiration in Recent Evangelical Scholarship." In *Evangelicals and Scripture: Tradition, Authority, and Hermeneutics*, edited by Vincent Bacote and Laura Miguélez, 150–70. Downers Grove, IL: InterVarsity, 2004.

———. "The King in the Book of Isaiah." In *The Lord's Anointed: Interpretation of Old Testament Messianic Texts*, edited by Philip Satterthwaite and Gordon Wenham, 141–65. Grand Rapids: Baker, 1995.

———. "Servant, Slave." In *NIDOTTE*, 1183–98.

Schüssler Fiorenza, Elisabeth. "Cultic Language in Qumran and in the NT." *Catholic Biblical Quarterly* 38.2 (1976) 159–77.

———. *Priester für Gott: Studien zum Herrschafts- und Priestermotiv in der Apokalypse*. Neuetestamentliche Abhandlungen. Münster: Aschendorff, 1972.

Schweizer, Eduard. "Glaubensgrundlage und Glaubenserfahrung in der Kirche des allgemeinen Priestertums: 1 Peter 2:1–10." In *Kirche und Volk Gottes: Festschrift für Jürgen Roloff zum 70. Geburtstag*, edited by Martin Karrer, Wolfgang Kraus, and Merk Otto, 272–83. Neukirchen-Vluyn: Neukirchener, 2000.

Segura C., Harold. "La misión como liberación integral: Jesús, modelo sin igual." *Kairós* 38 (2006) 23–40.

Seidensticker, Philipp. *Lebendiges Opfer (Röm 12, 1): Ein Beitrag zur Theologie des Aposteles Paulus*. Neutestamentliche Abhandlungen. Münster Westf: Aschendorff, 1954.

Seitz, Christopher. "Isaiah and the Search for a New Paradigm: Authorship and Inspiration." In *Word Without End: The Old Testament as Abiding Theological Witness*, 113–29. Grand Rapids: Eerdmans, 1998.

Selwyn, Edward. *The First Epistle of St. Peter: The Greek Text with Introduction, Notes and Essays*. New York: Macmillan, 1947.

Senn, Frank C. *The Witness of the Worshiping Community: Liturgy and the Practice of Evangelism*. New York: Paulist, 1993.

Siggins, Ian D. Kingston. *Martin Luther's Doctrine of Christ*. New Haven: Yale University Press, 1970.

Smith, Gary. *Isaiah 40–66*. Nashville: B&H Academic, 2009.

———. "Paul's Use of Psalm 68:18 in Ephesians 4:8." *JETS* 18 (1975) 181–89.

Smith, Gordon T. *A Holy Meal: The Lord's Supper in the Life of the Church*. Grand Rapids: Baker Academic, 2005.

Smith, James K. A. *Thinking in Tongues: Pentecostal Contributions to Christian Philosophy*. Grand Rapids: Eerdmans, 2010.

Smith, Joseph Fielding. *Doctrines of Salvation: Sermons and Writings of Joseph Fielding Smith*. Edited by Bruce R. McConkie. Salt Lake City: Bookcraft, 1954.

Smith, Ted A. "Theories of Practice." In *The Wiley-Blackwell Companion to Practical Theology*, edited by Bonnie J. Miller-McLemore, 244–54. Malden, MA: Wiley-Blackwell, 2012.

Snyder, Howard A. *The Community of the King*. Downers Grove, IL: InterVarsity, 2004.

———. "Pietism, Moravianism, and Methodism as Renewal Movements: A Comparative and Thematic Study." PhD diss., University of Notre Dame, 1983.

Sommer, Benjamin. *A Prophet Reads Scripture: Allusion in Isaiah 40-66*. Stanford, CA: Stanford University Press, 1998.

Southern, R. W. "The Church of the Dark Ages." In *The Layman in Christian History: A Project of the Department on the Laity of the World Council of Churches*, edited by Stephen C. Neill and Hans Ruedi Weber, 88–110. Philadelphia: Westminster, 1963.

Spener, Philipp. *Pia desideria*. Translated by Theodore G. Tappert. Philadelphia: Fortress, 1964.

Spijker, Willem Van't. *The Ecclesiastical Offices in the Thought of Martin Bucer*. Translated by John Vriend and John Bierma. New York: Brill, 1996.

St. Hilary of Poitiers. *The Trinity*. Translated by Stephen McKenna. Vol. 25. FC. New York: Fathers of the Church, 1954.

Stackhouse Jr., John G., ed. *Evangelical Ecclesiology: Reality or Illusion?* Grand Rapids: Baker Academic, 2003.

Stedman, Ray C. *Body Life: The Church Comes Alive*. Glendale, CA: Regal, 1972.

Stevens, R. Paul. *The Other Six Days: Vocation, Work, and Ministry in Biblical Perspective*. Grand Rapids: Eerdmans, 2000.

Stewart, Bryan Alan. "'Priests of My People': Levitical Paradigms for Christian Ministers in the Third and Fourth Century Church." PhD diss, University of Virginia, 2006.

Stott, John R. W. *Christian Mission in the Modern World*. Downers Grove, IL: InterVarsity, 1975.

———. *Confess Your Sins: the Way of Reconciliation*. Waco, TX: Word, 1965.

———. "The Living God is a Missionary God." In *Perspectives on the World Christian Movement: A Reader*, edited by Ralph D. Winter and Steven C. Hawthorne, 3–9. 3rd ed. Pasadena, CA: William Carey Library, 1999.

———., ed. *Making Christ Known: Historic Mission Documents from the Lausanne Movement, 1974-1989*. Grand Rapids: Eerdmans, 1997.

Stout, Tracey Mark. *A Fellowship of Baptism: Karl Barth's Ecclesiology in Light of His Understanding of Baptism*. Princeton Theological Monographs. Eugene, OR: Pickwick, 2010.

Strehle, Stephen. *The Egalitarian Spirit of Christianity: The Sacred Roots of American and British Government*. New Brunswick, NJ: Transaction, 2009.

Stromberg, Jacob. "An Inner-Isaianic Reading of Isaiah 61:1–3." In *Interpreting Isaiah: Issues and Approaches*, edited by David Firth and H. G. M. Williamson, 261–72. Downers Grove, IL: InterVarsity Academic, 2009.

Studzinski, Raymond. *Reading to Live: The Evolving Practice of Lectio Divina*. Collegeville, MN: Liturgical, 2009.

Tanner, Kathryn. "The Trinity." In *The Blackwell Companion to Political Theology*, edited by Peter Scott and William T. Cavanaugh. Blackwell Companions to Religion. Oxford: Blackwell, 2006.

———. "Theological Reflection and Christian Practices." In *Practicing Theology: Beliefs and Practices in Christian Life*, edited by Miroslav Volf and Dorothy C. Bass, 228–42. Grand Rapids: Eerdmans, 2002.

Tanner, Norman P., ed. *Decrees of the Ecumenical Councils*. Vol. 2. Washington, DC: Georgetown University Press, 1990.

Tertullian. *Writings of Tertullian*. Translated by S. Thellwall and Peter Holmes. ANF Vol 3. 5–392. Buffalo, 1885–1896. Electronic ed.

Thayer, Anne T. *Penitence, Preaching, and the Coming of the Reformation*. Burlington, VT: Ashgate, 2002.

Thümmel, Hans Georg. "Versammlungsraum, Kirche, Tempel." In *Gemeinde ohne Tempel*, edited by Beate Ego, Armin Lange, and Peter Pilhofer, 489–504. Tübigen: Mohr Siebeck, 1999.

Tie, Lok-Hung. "The Priesthood of All Believers as a Unifying Motif in the Ecclesiology of James Leo Garrett, Jr." PhD diss., Southwestern Baptist Theological Seminary, 2010.

Torjeson, Karen Jo. "Clergy and Laity." In *The Oxford Handbook of Early Christian Studies*, edited by Susan Ashbrook Harvey and David G. Hunter, 389–405. New York: Oxford University Press, 2008.

Torrance, Thomas. "A New Reformation?" In *Theology in Reconstruction*, 259–83. Grand Rapids: Eerdmans, 1966.

———. *Royal Priesthood: A Theology of Ordained Ministry*. 2nd ed. New York: T&T Clark, 1993.

———. *Theology in Reconstruction*. Grand Rapids: Eerdmans, 1966.

Tranvik, Mark D. "Luther on Baptism." In *Harvesting Martin Luther's Reflections on Theology, Ethics, and the Church*, edited by Timothy J. Wengert, 23–37. Grand Rapids: Eerdmans, 2004.

Treier, Daniel J. *Introducing Theological Interpretation of Scripture: Recovering a Christian Practice*. Grand Rapids: Baker Academic, 2008.

———. *Virtue and the Voice of God: Toward Theology as Wisdom*. Grand Rapids: Eerdmans, 2006.

Tutu, Desmond. *No Future Without Forgiveness*. New York: Doubleday, 2000.

Vanhoozer, Kevin. *The Drama of Doctrine: A Canonical Linguistic Approach to Christian Theology*. Louisville: Westminster John Knox, 2005.

———. "A Drama-of-Redemption Model: Always Performing?" In *Four Views on Moving Beyond the Bible to Theology*, edited by Gary T. Meadors, 151–99. Grand Rapids: Zondervan, 2009.

———."Evangelicalism and the Church: The Company of the Gospel." In *Futures of Evangelicalism: Issues and Prospects*, edited by Craig Bartholomew, Robin Perry, and Andrew West, 40–99. Grand Rapids: Kregel, 2003.

———. *First Theology: God, Scripture and Hermeneutics*. Downers Grove, IL: InterVarsity, 2002.

———. *Is There a Meaning in This Text? The Bible, the Reader, and the Morality of Literary Knowledge*. Grand Rapids: Zondervan, 1998.

———. "Theological Method." In *Global Dictionary of Theology*, edited by William A. Dyrness, Veli-Matti Kärkkäinen, Juan Francisco Martinez, and Simon Chan, 889–98. Downers Grove, IL: InterVarsity Academic, 2008.

———. "Triune Discourse: Theological Reflections on the Claim that God Speaks." In *Trinitarian Theology for the Church: Scripture, Community, Worship*, edited by Daniel J. Treier and David Lauber, 25–78. Downers Grove, IL: InterVarsity, 2009.

———. "The Voice and the Actor: A Dramatic Proposal about the Ministry and Minstrelsy of Theology." In *Evangelical Futures*, edited by John G. Stackhouse Jr., 61–106. Grand Rapids: Baker, 2000.

Vanhoye, Albert. *Old Testament Priests and the New Priest: According to the New Testament*. Translated by J. Bernard Orchard. Petersham, MA: St. Bede, 1986.

Volf, Miroslav. *After Our Likeness: The Church as the Image of the Trinity*. Grand Rapids: Eerdmans, 1998.

———. "Theology for a Way of Life." In *Practicing Theology: Beliefs and Practices in Christian Life*, edited by Miroslav Volf and Dorothy C. Bass, 245–63. Grand Rapids: Eerdmans, 2002.

———. "The Trinity and the Church." In *Trinitarian Soundings in Systematic Theology*, edited by Paul Louis Metzger, 153–74. New York: T. & T. Clark, 2005.

———. *Work in the Spirit: Toward a Theology of Work*. New York: Oxford University Press, 1991.

Vos, Geerhardus. "The Priesthood of Christ in the Epistle to the Hebrews." Orig. 1907. In *Redemptive History and Biblical Interpretation: The Shorter Writings of Geerhardus Vos*, edited by Richard Gaffin, 126–60. Phillipsburg, NJ: P&R, 1980.

———. *The Teaching of the Epistle to the Hebrews*. Edited by Johannes Vos. Grand Rapids: Eerdmans, 1956.

Voss, Hank. "Exalted Clergy, Egalitarianism, or Equipping? Implications for Christian Leadership From Ephesians 4:11–12." MA thesis, Talbot School of Theology, 2003.

———. "From 'Grammatical-historical Exegesis' to 'Theological Exegesis': Equipping Evangelical Theological Exegetes." *ERT* (Forthcoming).

Wagner, J. Ross. *Heralds of the Good News: Isaiah and Paul in Concert in the Letter to the Romans*. NovTSup 101. Leiden: Brill, 2002.

Wainwright, Geoffrey. *Eucharist and Eschatology*. 3rd ed. Peterborough: Epworth, 2002.

———. *Lesslie Newbigin: A Theological Life*. New York: Oxford University Press, 2000.

Waltke, Bruce, James Houston, and Erika Moore. *The Psalms as Christian Worship: An Historical Commentary*. Grand Rapids: Eerdmans, 2010.

Ware, James. *The Mission of the Church in Paul's Letter to the Philippians in the Context of Ancient Judaism*. Boston: Brill, 2005.

Warneck, Gustav. *Outline of a History of Protestant Missions from the Reformation to the Present Time*. Edited by George Robson. Edinburgh: Oliphant Anderson & Ferrier, 1906.

Watts, John. *Isaiah*. WBC. Waco, TX: Word, 1987.

Watts, Rikk. "Isaiah 40–55: Consolation or Confrontation? Isaiah 40–55 and the Delay of the New Exodus." *Tyndale Bulletin* 41 (1990) 31–59.

———. "Isaiah in the New Testament." In *Interpreting Isaiah: Issues and Approaches*, edited by David Firth and H. G. M. Williamson, 213–33. Downers Grove, IL: InterVarsity Academic, 2009.

———. *Isaiah's New Exodus in Mark*. Grand Rapids: Baker, 2000.

Webb, Robert. "Jesus' Baptism by John: Its Historicity and Significance." In *Key Events in the Life of the Historical Jesus: A Collaborative Exploration of Context and Coherence*, edited by Darrell Bock and Robert Webb, 95–144. WUNT. Tübingen: Mohr Siebeck, 2009.

Webber, Robert E. *Ancient-Future Evangelism: Making your Church a Faith-Forming Community.* Grand Rapids: Baker, 2003.

Webster, John. *Barth's Ethics of Reconciliation.* New York: Cambridge University Press, 1995.

———. "'Eloquent and Radiant': The Prophetic Office of Christ and the Mission of the Church." In *Barth's Moral Theology: Human Action in Barth's Thought,* 125–50. Grand Rapids: Eerdmans, 1998.

———. "The Ethics of Reconciliation." In *The Theology of Reconciliation,* edited by Colin E. Gunton, 109–23. New York: T. & T. Clark, 2003.

———. *Holiness.* Grand Rapids: Eerdmans, 2003.

———. "Ministry and Priesthood." In *The Study of Anglicanism,* edited by Stephen Sykes and John Booty, 285–96. London: SPCK, 1988.

———. "One Who Is Son: Theological Reflections on the Exordium to the Epistle to the Hebrews." In *The Epistle to the Hebrews and Christian Theology,* edited by Richard Bauckham, et al., 69–94. Grand Rapids: Eerdmans, 2009.

Wells, Jo Bailey. *God's Holy People: A Theme in Biblical Theology.* JSOTSup 305. Sheffield: Sheffield Academic, 2000.

Wengert, Timothy J. *Priesthood, Pastors, Bishops: Public Ministry for the Reformation and Today.* Minneapolis: Fortress, 2008.

Wenschkewitz, Hans. *Die Spiritualisierung der Kultusbegriffe: Tempel, Priester und Opfer im Neuen Testament.* 4. Leipzig: Angelos, 1932.

Wess, Paul. *Ihr alle seid Geschwister: Gemeinde und Priester.* Mainz: Matthias-Grünewald, 1983.

West, Cornel. *Prophesy Deliverance! An Afro-American Revolutionary Christianity.* Philadelphia: Westminster, 1982.

Westermann, Claus. *Isaiah 40-66: A Commentary.* Philadelphia: Westminster, 1969.

White, Michael. *The Social Origins of Christian Architecture.* 2 Vols. Valley Forge, PA: Trinity, 1996.

Wilken, Robert Louis. *The Spirit of Early Christian Thought: Seeking the Face of God.* New Haven: Yale University Press, 2003.

Wilkins, Michael. *Discipleship in the Ancient World and Matthew's Gospel.* 2nd ed. Grand Rapids: Baker, 1995.

Williams, George Huntston. "Christology and Church-State Relations in the Fourth Century: Part I." *Church History* 20.3 (1951) 3–33.

———. *The Radical Reformation.* Philadelphia: Westminster, 1962.

Williamson, H. G. M. "Recent Issues in the Study of Isaiah." In *Interpreting Isaiah: Issues and Approaches,* edited by David G. Firth and H. G. M. Williamson, 15–39. Downers Grove, IL: InterVarsity Academic, 2009.

Wilson, Jonathan R. *God so Loved the World: A Christology for Disciples.* Grand Rapids: Baker Academic, 2001.

———. *Gospel Virtues: Practicing Faith, Hope and Love in Uncertain Times.* Downers Grove, IL: InterVarsity, 1998.

———. *Why Church Matters: Worship, Ministry, and Mission in Practice.* Grand Rapids: Brazos, 2006.

Wingren, Gustaf. *The Christian's Calling: Luther on Vocation.* Edinburgh: Oliver and Boyd, 1958.

Winter, Ralph. "Two Structures of God's Redemptive Mission." In *Perspectives on the World Christian Movement: Reader*, edited by Ralph D. Winter and Steven C. Hawthorne, 220–30. 3rd ed. Pasadena, CA: William Carey Library, 1999.

Witmer, Stephen. *Divine Instruction in Early Christianity*. WUNT 2. Tübingen: Mohr Siebeck, 2008.

Wood, Susan. "Baptism as a Mark of the Church." In *Marks of the Body of Christ*, edited by Carl E. Braaten and Robert W. Jenson, 25–43. Grand Rapids: Eerdmans, 1999.

———. *One Baptism: Ecumenical Dimensions of the Doctrine of Baptism*. Collegeville, MN: Liturgical, 2009.

———, ed. *Ordering the Baptismal Priesthood: Theologies of Lay and Ordained Ministry*. Collegeville, MN: Liturgical, 2003.

Wright, Christopher J. H. *The Mission of God: Unlocking the Bible's Grand Narrative*. Downers Grove, IL: InterVarsity, 2006.

———. "The World in the Bible." *ERT* 34.3 (2010) 207–19.

Wright, David. "At What Ages Were People Baptized in the Early Centuries?" In *Infant Baptism in Historical Perspective: Collected Studies*, 61–67. Eugene, OR: Wipf & Stock, 2007.

———. "Augustine and the Transformation of Baptism." In *Infant Baptism in Historical Perspective: Collected Studies*, 68–88. Eugene, OR: Wipf & Stock, 2007.

———. "Baptism: Where Do We Go from Here?" In *Infant Baptism in Historical Perspective: Collected Studies*, 377–84. Eugene, OR: Wipf & Stock, 2007.

———. "The Meaning and Reference of 'One Baptism for the Remission of Sins.'" In *Infant Baptism in Historical Perspective: Collected Studies*, 55–60. Eugene, OR: Wipf & Stock, 2007.

———. *What Has Infant Baptism Done to Baptism?: An Enquiry at the End of Christendom*. Waynesboro, GA: Paternoster, 2005.

Wright, N. T. *After You Believe: Why Christian Character Matters*. New York: HarperCollins, 2010.

———. *Jesus and the Victory of God*. London: SPCK, 1996.

———. *The New Testament and the People of God: Christian Origins and the Question of God*. Vol. 1. Minneapolis: Fortress, 1992.

Yarnell, Malcolm B. "Changing Baptist Concepts of Royal Priesthood: John Smyth and Edgar Young Mullins." In *The Rise of the Laity in Evangelical Protestantism*, edited by Deryck Lovegrove, 236–52. New York: Routledge, 2002.

———. "Congregational Priesthood and the Inventio or Invention of Authority." *JBTM* 3 (2005) 110–35.

———. "The Priesthood of All Believers: Rediscovering the Biblical Doctrine of the Royal Priesthood." In *Restoring the Integrity of Baptist Churches*, edited by Thomas White, Jason Duesing, and Malcolm Yarnell, 221–45. Grand Rapids: Kregel, 2008.

———. "Reformation Development of the Priesthood of All Believers." ThM, Duke University, 1996.

———. *Royal Priesthood in the English Reformation*. New York: Oxford University Press, Forthcoming.

Yarnold, Edward. *The Awe-Inspiring Rites of Initiation: The Origins of the RCIA*. New York: T. & T. Clark, 1994.

Yeago, David. "The New Testament and the Nicene Dogma: A Contribution to the Recovery of Theological Exegesis." In *The Theological Interpretation of Scripture:*

Classic and Contemporary Readings, edited by Stephen Fowl, 87–100. Cambridge, MA: Blackwell, 1997.

Yieh, John. *One Teacher: Jesus' Teaching Role in Matthew's Gospel Report*. Berlin: de Gruyter, 2004.

Yoder, John Howard. *Anabaptism and Reformation in Switzerland*. Edited by C. Arnold Snyder. Translated by David Carl Stassen. Anabaptist and Mennonite Studies. 1962 and 1968. Reprint, Kitchener, ON: Pandora, 2004.

———. "The Basis of Barth's Social Ethics." 1–11 Midwestern Section of the Karl Barth Society, Elmhurst, IL, September 30, 1978.

———. *Body Politics: Five Practices of the Christian Community Before the Watching World*. Scottdale, PA: Herald, 2001.

———. "The Constantinian Sources of Western Social Ethics." In *The Priestly Kingdom: Social Ethics as Gospel*, 135–147. Notre Dame, IN: University of Notre Dame Press, 1985.

———. "The Disavowal of Constantine: An Alternative Perspective of Interfaith Dialogue." In *The Royal Priesthood: Essays Ecclesiological and Ecumenical*, edited by Michael G. Cartwright, 242–61. Grand Rapids: Eerdmans, 1994.

———. *For the Nations: Essays Evangelical and Public*. Grand Rapids: Eerdmans, 1997.

———. *The Fullness of Christ: Paul's Revolutionary Vision of Universal Ministry*. Elgin, IL: Brethren, 1987.

———. "To Serve our God and Rule the World." In *The Royal Priesthood: Essays Ecclesiological and Ecumenical*, edited by Michael G. Cartwright, 127–40. Grand Rapids: Eerdmans, 1994.

Zizioulas, John D. *Being as Communion: Studies in Personhood and the Church*. Crestwood, NY: St. Vladimir's Seminary, 1985.

Subject Index

Achtemeier, Paul, 30–31, 33–34
Adam, 6n27, 9, 16, 16, 89
Adam, as Priest-king, 16n90, 84n74, 198n90
Afanasiev, Nikolay, 2n9, 4, 229n93, 249, 264
Ambrose, 5n22, 121, 123n105, 251
Anizor, Uche, xv, xviii, 16, 133n13, 141–42, 146n90, 228, 259
anointing, Jesus, 17, 18, 28, 29, 30, 32, 37, 39, 40, 45–46, 49, 57n38, 75, 76; 77, 78, 79, 80, 82, 84, 85, 87, 89, 93, 135, 167, 215n28, 219, 221, 241
anoint/ anointing, priesthood, 29n11, 47, 63, 64, 66, 69–70, 75, 105, 220, 221, 234, 250, 253, 254,
Apostolic Tradition, 4, 249
appropriation, doctrine of, 187–188, 193–195
Aquinas, Thomas, xxv, 5n22, 77n29, 111, 123n105, 187n25, 189, 193, 215n28, 236, 255, 262
Aramaic Levi Document, xxi, 76n23
Arnold, Clinton, xvii, 229n90
Athanasius, 193
Attridge, Harold, 95
Augustine, xxvi, 5n22, 8, 12n60, 20n105, 32n32, 53, 113, 119, 121–22, 124, 126–27, 135n30, 181, 187–89, 190n41, 199n93, 219, 222, 224, 251–52

Baptism, xii, 2, 4–6, 7n33, 9, 13, 18, 22–23, 32, 34n42, 40n96, 43–44, 72–79, 82–84, 86, 92, 95–96, 98n171, 104, 114, 117–24, 126, 134–35, 137–38, 140, 142, 144–45, 148, 152–54, 156, 158, 164, 167–70, 177, 187n24, 203–5, 209–10, 213–24, 226, 228, 231, 236–39, 242, 249–54, 258, 261, 263–65
Baptism, Eucharist, Ministry, 120n78
Barna, George, 203–4
Barth, Karl, xii, xxii, 5, 11, 22–23, 64n84, 66n102, 79, 89n105, 127, 152, 154–72, 175–77, 183n8, 187–91, 194–95, 199n94, 201, 203, 206–8, 210n2, 213n16, 215–16, 218–21, 223–24, 226–27, 230n95, 233, 236, 242, 244n6, 259, 261
Barth, Hans-Martin, 1, 20, 133n13, 133n15, 134, 149n105, 149n106, 156n2, 215n27, 259, 261, 262, 263, 267,
Basil the Great, 121, 189n33
Bass, Dorothy, 211–12, 214n24, 217
Bauckham, Richard, 31n24, 34n48, 41n101, 60n60, 76n24
Beale, G. K., 7n37, 16, 28, 61n63, 84n74, 94, 194, 198n90, 214
Beasley-Murray, George, 79n42
Beaton, Richard, 57n44, 74n5, 76n24, 80
Bellarmine, Cardinal Robert, 153–54, 260
Benedict, St., 122–23, 227, 252
Best, Ernest, 4, 16, 31, 40n92, 96
Beuken, W. A. M., 55–56, 63–64, 67–69
Blenkinsopp, Joseph, 55n28, 67–69, 74n6, 85n82

297

Subject Index

Blocher, Henri, 53n14, 186n19, 188n28, 194n67
Block, Daniel, xviii, 56–57
Boff, Leonardo, 215n27, 267
Bonhoeffer, Dietrich, 232
Bosch, David, 11n58, 13, 18–19, 122n101, 125–27, 150–54, 160n26, 260
Bradshaw, Paul, 4n17, 249
Brent, Allen, 113–15, 250
Bucer, Martin, 150, 259
Bulley, Colin, 10n49, 45n126, 86n83, 93, 104, 113, 116n67, 248–49, 264

Caesarea, 112, 122n102, 250
Calvin, John, 20n105, 36, 65n90, 70, 145–46, 152, 159–60, 183n11, 201, 226, 259
Carey, William, 21, 154, 262
Catechism of the Catholic Church, 173n120
character indelibilis, 138, 266
Childs, Brevard, 55n28, 64–65, 67n109
Chilton, Bruce, 27–28, 58–59, 87, 248
Christendom, xiii, 11–13, 19, 21–22, 103, 117–19, 122–23, 125–26, 128, 131, 151–52, 156, 160n26, 170, 172, 175–76, 206–7, 233, 242–44
christocentric-only, 182–84, 206
Christocentric-Trinitarian, 23, 172, 182–85, 198–99, 206, 208, 219, 233, 242–44
Chrysostom, John, 21n108, 75n16, 78n39, 93n133, 121, 251
church discipline, xii, 23–24, 210, 215–16, 225, 229, 231–32, 236, 239, 242, 259
Citizenship, 22, 117, 149
Clarke, Andrew, 45n126
Clement of Alexandria, 88n97, 104, 109n27, 123n103, 249
Clement of Rome, 8, 22, 103, 106–7, 109, 112, 117, 128, 248
Clericalism, 158, 216n30, 264
Concerning the Ministry, 130n1, 141, 216

Congar, Yves, 5n23, 9n44, 28n5, 32n31, 46, 112n39, 148n99, 174, 200–201, 224–25, 231n107, 244, 253–54, 265–66
Constantine, 8, 13, 20–22, 104, 106, 108, 117–19, 122–28, 160n26, 175, 250
Cooke, Bernard, 111, 114n53, 148, 250, 252–53, 266
Corriveau, Raymond, 30–31, 63n77, 91–92, 224n65, 237n143
Cyprian, 8, 19–22, 104, 106, 108, 112–17, 120n79, 124, 128, 237, 250

Dabin, Paul, 5, 8, 15, 19, 29n7, 44n118, 49, 52n1, 79n40, 104, 219n44, 247, 249–55, 258, 260–63
Daly, Robert, 28, 37, 41n106, 44–45, 82n61, 93n135, 237n141, 248–49
Davies, John, 16, 34n45, 65–67, 77n25, 81–82, 87n93, 182n5
Davis, Don, xvii, 15, 213n14
Didache, 123, 248
Didascalia Apostolorum, 250
Didymus the Blind, 197n84
Dionysius, -Pseudo, 8, 107, 110–12, 122, 252
Drobner, Hubertus, 110–11, 251

Eastwood, Cyril, 16, 19–20, 52, 95n148, 113n47, 116, 147, 182n4, 248–56, 259–62
ecclesiology, xii–xiii, 2–3, 11–13, 23, 89n106, 110, 115, 125, 127, 133, 145, 155–57, 159, 161–62, 165, 169–73, 175–77, 184–85, 187, 190–91, 201, 204n118, 206, 222, 233n117, 235n132, 241, 243, 261, 263–64, 266–67
Eden as Sanctuary, 18, 50, 67, 71, 77, 84, 89, 174,
Elliot, John, 4n14, 15, 29, 31–33, 36–37, 40–42, 64–65, 91n118, 164n54, 205n124
Emery, Gilles, 187–88, 190n41, 192–93
Emser, Hieronymus, 132, 139, 257
Ephrem the Syrian, xv, 251

Subject Index 299

Eucharist, 22, 36, 111n38, 113–16, 120n78, 131n4, 137, 142, 144, 175n126, 207, 214–15, 217–18, 236–39, 250, 253, 255–56, 258–59, 263–65
Eusebius of Caesarea, 8, 107, 108, 109, 111, 112, 118, 123, 124, 250

Faivre, Alexandre, 22n115, 105–7, 248–52
Farrow, Douglas, 7, 36n64, 80, 89
Father, God, vi, 4n14, 12, 23, 34, 36, 40n98, 46, 47, 48, 76, 77, 78, 83, 87, 88, 88, 89, 134, 139, 155, 165, 167, 168, 175, 182, 183, 184, 185, 187, 188, 189, 192, 193, 194, 195, 197, 198, 199; 200, 206, 207, 208, 209, 218, 219, 220, 221, 222, 223, 225, 226, 233, 239, 242, 243, 259, 261
Ferguson, Everett, 79n40, 236n135
Flett, John G., xviii, 11n57, 155n1, 162n44, 169, 171n106, 190–91, 207n135
Fox, Zeni, 265
Francis of Assisi, 215n27, 255

Garrett, James Leo, 19–21, 113n47, 115–16, 167n77, 219n40, 223–24, 250–51, 264, 267
Gelder, Craig, Van., 204
George, Timothy, 9, 150n110, 203, 259, 263
Gignilliat, Mark, 60n60, 66n97, 87n95, 93n129
Goheen, Michael, xviii, 12–13, 171–73, 175n126, 184–85, 204n118, 233n117, 235n132
Gratian, Emperor (d. 383), 118n74, 251
Gratian, Italian Monk (d. 1179), 111, 115, 116, 125, 127,128, 130, 131, 252,
Gregory the Great, 111, 115–16, 125, 127–28, 130–31, 252
Guder, Darrell, xviii, 10–12, 127, 162n44, 176, 198n87, 217
Gupta, Nijay, 31n20, 35, 39–40, 92n122, 205n125

Gurtner, Daniel, 77n28, 82–84, 247
Gutiérrez, Gustavo, 238n150, 267

Habets, Myk, 77n30, 221n51
Hays, Richard, 18n91, 123
Hellerman, Joseph, 88, 115n59, 248, 250
Hilary of Poitiers, 188–89
Himmelfarb, Martha, 16, 32n34, 41n99, 81n56
Hippolytus, 99, 152, 159, 176, 185, 206, 211, 262
Horton, Michael, 201–2
Hubmaier, Balthasar, 231–32, 257

Investiture Controversy, 254
Irenaeus, 77n31, 85–86, 104, 109, 221n51, 227n78, 249
Islam, 182
issler, Klaus, 197n85

Jerome, 121, 251
Justin Martyr, 32, 50, 52, 104, 106, 109, 120, 249
Justinian, Emperor, 110, 122–23, 125, 128, 252

von Karlstadt, Andreas, 258
Kärkkäinen, Veli-Matti, 223n59, 230n93, 263–64, 267
Kilmartin, Edward, 115–16, 131n4, 237n141, 255–56, 258, 265
Kreider, Alan, 13n66, 19n96, 122n101, 124–25, 127n131, 252
Küng, Hans, 2n9, 5n23, 18–19, 23, 37, 62n70, 67n108, 230–31, 266

Lausanne Covenant, vi, 175, 264
lectio Divina, xii, 23–24, 142, 146, 210, 213, 215–16, 225–28, 236, 239, 242
Leithart, Peter, 20, 28–30, 32n33, 37n71, 46–47, 74–75, 78–79, 93, 96, 106n16, 108n22, 112, 117–18, 120–21, 127–28, 160n26, 167–68, 187n24, 202n109, 204n119, 206–7, 209, 211, 219n40, 236, 249–51, 254, 267

Subject Index

Levering, Matthew, 72–73, 111n38, 237n141, 252, 255, 264
Lord's Supper, xii, 23–24, 82, 144, 150, 158, 168, 204, 210–11, 215–16, 223n61, 236–39, 242
Lumen Gentium, 5–12, 129–53, 225n68
Lubac, Henri de, 5, 140n65, 191n51, 226n75, 264
Luther, Martin, 129–153

Macintyre, Alasdair, 210–13
Melchizedek, 6–8, 18, 46, 56, 72–75, 78, 80–81, 85, 88–89, 94–95, 98–99, 106, 113, 117, 135–37, 140, 182–83, 185, 198n90, 200, 225, 241, 251
Melito of Sardis, 104, 249
Michalski, Melvin, 5n25, 263–67
ministry, 3n11, 34n51, 90n113
missio dei, xii-xiii, xv, 2–3, 6, 10–12, 21, 23, 99, 171, 176, 182, 184–85, 198, 208, 217, 222–23, 226, 233, 242
Mormonism, 2–12, 21, 23, 99, 171, 176, 182, 182n5, 184–85, 198, 204, 208, 217, 222–226, 233, 242
Muhammad, 253
Muthiah, Robert, 156n2, 176n135, 187n23, 203n112, 212, 215n26, 217n34, 219n40, 244n5, 264–65, 267

Newbigin, Lesslie, xii, 1–2, 10n50, 12–13, 21, 23, 127, 155–56, 161–62, 166n74, 170–77, 181–82, 184–86, 197–99, 201, 203–4, 206–7, 211, 221n53, 233–35, 243, 262, 264
Nimmo, Paul, 169–70, 221n54

Oden, Thomas, 5n22, 231n108
Odes of Solomon, 42, 89, 248
ordained leadership, 200
Origen, xv, 5n22, 8, 65n90, 96n158, 103–5, 107n17, 109, 113n48, 126–27, 250
Orr, David, xviii, 117n71, 221n53, 249, 251–54, 260, 264, 267

osborne, Kenan, 19–20, 35n58, 87, 90n114, 94, 106, 118–19, 125n115, 231n107, 249–50, 252, 254–55, 262–63, 266–67
Owen, John, 188n27, 192, 261

Paul, Apostle, 8, 10, 18, 28, 30–31, 35–36, 38–39, 41–49, 53n13, 58, 60–61, 64, 87n95, 91, 99, 107–10, 190, 195, 205, 210, 216, 224, 247
Peasant's Revolt, 133, 144, 148, 151, 160, 234n120, 257
Pelikan, Jaroslav, 12n60, 27n1, 141n69, 220n45, 227n81, 231n104, 237n142, 249, 254, 257
perichoresis, 187–88, 190–91, 218, 265
Perrin, Nicholas, 28, 81, 84n78, 87, 95n148, 235n130
Peter, 28–32, 34–41, 43–44, 47, 49–51, 88–89, 91, 106–7, 115, 126, 134, 140n65
Plato, 110, 112n42, 114
Pliny, 7n35
Powell, Edward, 144–46, 228n83, 258
practice, 23, 42, 95n147, 120, 125, 140–43, 148, 158, 160, 168, 183, 185, 188, 193–96, 198, 210, 213, 215–16, 225–27, 236–39, 242, 259, 262
prayer, 148, 168, 238
Priesthood of all believers, xii, 17, 21, 23–24, 28, 33, 37, 43–47, 50, 125–26, 143, 146, 149, 151, 162–63, 197, 210, 215–16, 225, 233–39, 242
proclamation, 207
propaganda, 187, 193
properties, 218

Sanders, Fred, 183–84, 193n61, 196n77, 206–7, 228n87
Sanneh, Lamin, 228n84
Schleiermacher, friedrich, 150, 190, 205
Scholer, John M., 15–16, 30n12, 39n90, 47n134, 62n69, 96–98, 167n77

Subject Index   301

Schüssler Fiorenza, Elizabeth, 15, 40n92, 48n136, 65–67, 94n142, 244n4, 267
Shehata, Maged, 52, 54, 57–58, 80, 86, 92
Smith, Gordon T., 55n25, 61–62, 67n109, 212n10, 221n53, 237–39
Snyder, Howard A., 145n86, 161n33, 183n11, 215n27, 261, 267
soul competency, 9, 150, 203, 263
spirtual sacrifices, 134n24, 145n86, 147n95, 153, 161n33, 259, 261
Stott, John R. W., 175, 231n108
Stout, Tracey, 155n1, 168–69

Tanner, Kathryn, 190–91
telos, 9, 50, 212–14, 222, 225, 239
temple, xi-xii, 16–18, 28–36, 39–40, 42–50, 52, 56–57, 59–64, 67–70, 74, 77–78, 81, 83–89, 91–92, 94, 97n164, 103, 106–10, 112, 115, 119, 123, 140, 143, 147, 168n90, 182, 187, 194, 196–98, 200, 202, 205–6, 223–24, 229, 235, 241, 244, 247–49, 251
Tertullian, xv, 4–5, 8, 89n106, 104, 109, 113–14, 120–21, 126, 219, 221n49, 249
Tie, Lok-Hung, 21n109, 267
Torrance, Thomas, 16, 19–20, 52, 164n58, 176, 196n78, 203n113, 205n124, 223n60, 265
Treier, Daniel, xi, xviii, 2n8, 216n30, 225n69, 228n88, 231
Trent, Council of, 260
Tutu, Desmond, 231n108

Vanhoozer, Kevin J., xviii, 13–15, 18n92, 23n119, 49, 188–90, 192n56, 197, 206n127

Vatican II, 5, 19–20, 175, 200, 219, 225, 237n142, 252, 261, 263–65
Volf, Miroslav, 187–88, 190–92, 196n81, 210, 212n11, 214n24, 229–30, 236n134, 260, 267
Voss, Hank, xi-xiii, 228n88, 230n98, 247–55, 257–62, 264, 267

Waldo, Peter, 255
Walton, John H., xviii
Ware, James, 34n47, 38, 60n60, 64n89, 67n110, 92, 234n122
Webster, John, 10n50, 169, 221n50, 230–31
Wells, Jo Bailey, 16, 33–34, 57n41, 60n59, 67n105, 137n42, 214n24, 231n106
Wengert, Timothy, 134n24, 140n65, 145n84, 259, 261, 267
Wess, Paul, 116n68, 266
Willingen Conference, 171
Wilson, Jonathan R., 212–14
Wood, Susan, 5n21, 219, 222
Wright, Christopher, 16n84, 34n45, 198
Wright, David, 120–21
Wright, N. T., 16, 214n22
Wycliffe, John, 19–21, 127, 231n107, 256

Yarnell, Malcolm, xviii, 16, 19–21, 131n6, 135n29, 144–46, 150n112, 157n4, 203n114, 219n40, 228n83, 255–60, 263, 267
Yoder, John Howard, 48, 107, 127, 151, 157n5, 160n26, 176, 212, 214–16, 224, 229, 231–33, 248, 257, 265

Zizioulas, John, 5n20

Scripture Index

Genesis	16, 37n71, 59n53
1–3	67n112
1–2	16
1:6	84
1:26–27	198n90
3	18, 84, 89
3:24	84
12:1–3	51, 67n105
12:3	135n32, 137
14	137
14:17–20	135n32
14:18	81
14:18–20	95n149
14:19	198n90

Exodus	16, 65
4:22–23	66n102
12:3–27	88
12:29	66n102
13:2–16	66n102
15:25–26	57n42
17:10–13	57n42
19–24	84n78
19:6	2, 4n14, 16, 17, 28, 34, 41, 42, 50–52, 56n30, 60, 62, 65, 66n102, 67, 70–71, 70n124, 73, 75, 86n85, 92n121, 135n32, 164n53
19:22	6n27, 66n102
19:26	66n102
23:3–8	35n61
25:31–37	94n141
26:31	84
28:29–30	44n116, 95n147, 225n70
28:30	227
28:35–36	168n92
29:1	35n56
29:4–9	82n57
29:4	75n13, 96n154
29:20–21	96n154
29:21	35n56, 57n45
30:30	29n11
32:11–14	36n68, 57n42
32:29	35n56
32:30–34	36n68
33:11	57n42
33:12–23	36n68
34:8–9	36n68
37:17–24	94n141
39:29	94n142
40:12	75n13

Leviticus	8, 96n158, 103, 105, 107n17, 227
4:1–21	58n45
4–5	59n52,
4:3	29n11, 82n57
4:5	29n11
4:16	29n11
5:9	58n45
6:13	82n57
6:15 LXX [ET 22]	29n11

Leviticus *(continued)*

8:6	75n13
8:30	35n56
10:10	227
10:10–11	47n134
14:7	58n45
16	82n57
16:2	82n64
16:12	82n64
16:30–34	82n65
17:8–13	64n83
26:11	31n21

Numbers   16, 59n52, 97, 216n29

1:51	97n164
3:10	97n164
3:38	97n164
3:11–13	66n102
3:40–51	66n102
4:15	98n165
6:24–26	189
8:1–4	94n141
8:14–19	66n102
8:18	70n122
8:19	70
16:40	98n165
18:4	97n164
18:7	82n64, 97n164
27:21	227

Deuteronomy   53

10:8	44n123
14:28	235n129
15:18	235n129
17:12	44n123
17:15–20	43n57
18:14	57
18:15	44n123
18:7	44n123
21:5	44n123
21:15–17	66n102
22:2 LXX	60
27:14–26	47n134
31:9–11	47n134

Joshua

1:1	79

Judges

20:28	44n123

1 Samuel

2:35	75n14
2:35	78n37
12:16	94n139
14:35–37	57n42
23:1–3	57n42
28:6–7	57n42
30:8	57n42

2 Samuel   57n42

2:1	57n42
5:19	57n42
5:23	57n42
7:11–16	59n53
7:13	31
7:14 LXX	31
7:14	31n21

1 Kings   84n78, 94n139

22:7	57n42

2 Kings   47

1 Chronicles

14:10	57n42
14:14	57n42
17:11–14	59n53
22	59n53

2 Chronicles

7:1–2	84n78
10:1	59n53
28:6–10	59n53

Scripture Index

Ezra
227
7:10   47n134

Job
125

Psalms
4, 6, 7, 7n30, 7n33, 7n34, 17, 18, 29n11, 30, 36, 36n64, 47, 51, 53, 56n35, 57, 57n38, 57n40, 57n41, 70n123, 73, 75n17, 76, 77, 79, 80, 80n44, 81, 81n51, 81n54, 82, 82n60, 85, 86, 88, 94n143, 95, 121n96, 129, 130n1, 136, 136n33, 136n37, 159, 159n19, 167, 186, 220, 226, 241, 244,

2:2	77n25, 77n26
2:7	76, 76n20
2:8	95
5:7 (LXX 5:8)	32n32
22:1	195n74
22:2	58n51
22:31	69n118
23 (LXX 22)	32n32
27:4 (LXX 26:4)	32n32
51:17	135n32
68:18	70
82:4	135n32
84:10 (LXX 83:11)	32n32
99:6	57n41
110	7, 79n40, 183
110:1	81, 87, 95
110:3	183n11
110:1–4	225n70
110:4	66, 76n20, 95n149, 132, 135, 136, 183
118:22	30, 30n15
118:26	30n15
119:18	226
132:10–12	81n54
139:7	197

Isaiah
7, 7n37, 15, 16n84, 17, 18, 27, 30, 34, 34n47, 35, 36, 36n66, 39, 41, 41n101, 43, 46, 50, 51, 52, 53, 54, 54n15, 54n16, 54n20, 54n22, 55, 55n24, 55n25, 55n28, 56, 56n29, 56n31, 56n34, 57, 57n38, 57n44, 58, 58n48, 58n49, 58n50, 58n51, 59, 59n52, 59n54, 59n57, 59n58, 60, 60n58, 60n60, 61, 61n63, 62, 62n72, 62n73, 63, 63n77, 64, 64n82, 65, 65n90, 65,92, 65n96, 66, 66n97, 66n102, 67, 67n109, 67n110, 68, 68n113, 69, 69n120, 70, 70n123, 71, 72, 73, 74, 74n5, 74n6, 75n17, 76, 76n24, 77, 79, 80, 80n45, 82, 82n62, 83, 83n66, 85, 85n82, 87n95, 88, 91, 92, 93, 93n129, 95, 99, 118, 126, 196, 200, 218, 200, 235, 241, 244

2:2–3	61
2:3	47n134, 61n64
6:1–8	34
6:9–10	58n51
11:1–3	77
11:1–4	221
27:8	58n51
28:16	30
32:14–17	63n76
37:5	55n24
37:35	54n18, 57n40
41:8	55n28
42:1	80
42:1–4	57n44, 80
42:1–7	68n115
42:1–9	64n83
42:6	64n88, 67, 77n32, 168
42:7	67, 76
42:12	36n66
43:5	55n28
43:10	55

Isaiah (continued)

Reference	Pages
44:3	55n28
45:1	29n11
48:20	69n118
49:6	74n116
49:8	93
49:13	64n88
49:19	55n28
50:6	54n15, 82n58
50:9	36n66
50:11	58n51
52–53	36n66
52:3	36n66
52:11	8n40, 31, 31n21, 98n165
52:12	54
52:13	17, 54, 77
52:13—53:12	57n38
52:15	44n121, 57, 68n115
53:3–12	54n15
53:4	36n66
53:4–12	68n116
53:5	36n66, 59n55, 59n56
53:6	36n66, 62n71
53:7	82n58
53:9	36n66
53:10	17, 36n66, 51, 55, 55n28, 56n30, 58, 58n47, 71, 73, 83, 87, 88, 99
53:11	50, 55, 58n48, 83
53:11 LXX	36n66
53:12	17, 36n66, 44n116, 51, 53n10, 58n48, 77, 80, 83, 87
53:15	118
53:54–66	88
54:1	68
54—66	73
54:3	55n28
54:11–17	61n63, 69, 68n116
54:13	70, 88, 126n121, 135n32, 143, 146, 227
54:17	55, 61
55:3–5	66n99
56:1	67
56:1–8	62, 112
56:6	62n70
56:6–7	34, 63n77, 68n115, 70, 68n116
56:7	64n88, 81, 81n53
56:4–8	66n104
56:6–7	69
56: 6–8	42
57:1	67n122
57:15	60n59, 68n116
58:6	67
58:8	64n83
58:10	64n83
59:6	64n82
59:21	63n76, 64, 66, 68n116
59:21—60:3	69, 70, 126
60:3	69, 94n144, 68n115
60:5	64n88
60:7	60n59, 62n71, 66n100
60:10	62n71
60:14	66n99
60:21	60n59, 66n99
61:1	29n11, 67
61:1–3	65, 66
61:1–11	66n104, 68n115, 68n116
61:3	66n100
61:6	34, 41n99, 42, 44, 50, 62n71, 65, 65n90, 65n93, 66, 66n102, 66n104, 70, 73, 75, 91, 92n121, 99, 106, 118, 126, 135n32
61:7	64n88, 70
61:10	66n100
63:6	67n112
66:1–3	68n116
66:1–6	60n59
66:2	235
66:14	56, 67, 68, 68, 69
66:14–17	69
66:14–21	62
66:18	69
66:18–21	62, 67, 68, 68
66:19	69, 68n115
66:20	30n15, 66n104, 69, 69n115 69n119

66:21	33n36, 34, 42, 66n104, 68n116, 69, 70, 70	**Jonah**	206
66:22	69, 135n32	**Zephaniah**	
66:22–24	67n112, 68, 71	3:10	70n124
66:24	58n51		
		Haggai	70n124
Jeremiah	16, 57n38, 61, 70, 81n53		
		Zechariah	16, 33n36, 41n101, 43, 57n38, 67n110, 70, 71, 79, 80, 81n49, 82, 88
7:4–11	81n53		
18:18	47n134		
30:1—33:26	56n35		
31:31	61		
31:31–34	81n53	3:1–9	81n50
31:32–34	61, 64n82	6:12	30n15,
31:33–34	61	7:3	47n134
31:34	61	14: 16–21	67n110
		6:9–10	81n49
Ezekiel	16, 57n38, 57n39, 70n124, 125	6: 9–15	81n49
		14:16–21	81n50
6:19	75n13	**Malachi**	43
7:26	47n134		
9:4	31n24	1:9	43
20:34	31n21	1:10	205
37:20–29	57n39	1:11	70n124
44:4	30n15	2:1–9	70n124
		2:7	143, 227
Daniel	53, 57n38, 82, 82n60, 94, 125	2:7–9	47n134
		2:19	135n32
7:13	70n124	**Matthew**	18, 50, 57n44, 61, 71, 72, 73, 74, 77n32, 79, 80, 82, 83, 84, 85, 86, 87, 88, 89, 90, 91, 99, 106, 123, 214, 219, 220, 247
7:14	70n124		
9:25	29n11		
9:26	29n11		
Hosea	16		
4:4–9	70n124		
6:6	60n59, 86, 87,	1–2	82n57, 83n67
		1:1	87n90
Joel	30n15, 70n124	1:6	87n90
		1:11	87n90
2:17	70n124	1:16	87n90
2:28–29	70n124	1:57–59	75n17
4:18	30n15		

SCRIPTURE INDEX   307

Matthew *(continued)*

Reference	Page
3	78n33
3:3	75n14
3:7	74n8
3:13—4:1	209, 219
3:13-17	74, 74n7, 87n90, 221n52
3:13	238
3:15	53n10, 78n37, 123, 220
3:16-17	76
3:16	77, 84
3:17	77n27, n32, 80
5-7	88
5:3	235
5:14	161
5:16	47
5:17	78n37
5:22-24	88n101
5:34-35	53n11
5:35	80
5:47	88n101
6:9	195n73
6:10	238
6:14-15	238
7:2	58n51
7:3-5	88n101
7:15	228n85
8:2-4	86n88
8:17	80n48, 87n95
9:2-8	86n88
9:9-13	86, 238
10	74n6, 91
10:40-42	196
10:40	88
11:2-15	79
11:2-6	234
11:5	53n11
11:11	221
11:11-13	74
11:11-14	78n36
11:23	53n11
12	86
12:1-8	18, 85, 86, 90, 92
12:1	53n11
12:5	86
12:6	86, 60n59, 81n54, 86, 87, 109n28, 123
12:9-14	
12:15-21	80, 82
12:18-21	80
12:18	77n32
12:21	80
12:23	80, 82
12:41	81n54
12:42	81n54
12:49-50	88, 88n101
13	91
13:11	88, 90
13:13-15	53n11
13:16	88n104, 90
13:23	88n104, 90
13:51-52	88n104, 90
13:57	82n59
14:5	82n59
15:1-20	86n84
15:7-9	53n11
15:17-20	86n88
16:13-20	89
16:18-19	89
16:14	82n59
16:18	30
16:21	54n15
16:24-27	90
17:5	77n27, 77n32, 80
17:8	84
17:12	78n36
17:22-23	54n15
18	231
18:15-20	89, 90n112, 109n28, 231
18:15	88n101
18:18	47n132, 91
18:20	89n106, 90, 91, 238
18:21-35	
18:21	88n101
18:35	88n101
20:18-19	54n15
20:27-28	
20:28	53n10, n11, 54n15, 87
21:4-5	81n49
21:9	81
21:11	82n59

21:12–13	81	28:19–20	74n6, 79, 90n112, 91, 152, 189
21:13	53n11	28:19	69n118, 78n33, 123, 168
21:15	81		
21:25	78, 78n36		
21:46	82n59	28:20	199n93, 91
22:41–46	36, 77n25, 80, 81, 87n90		
22:41	77n25	**Mark**	78n36
22:42	77	1–6	72n2, 86
22:44	81	1:1–12	182
23:8–12	87, 89, 90n116	1:9–11	74n7
23:8–10	61n68, 88	1:10	84
23:8	28n1, 88n101, 123	1:12	185, 197
23:37	82n59	1:24	86
24:4–5	228n85	1:39–45	86n88
24:29–30	53n11	1:40–45	86
25:1–13	239	2:1–12	86
25:31–46	88	2:23–28	86
25:40	88n101, 196	3:14	94n139
26:3	77n25	4:12	58n51
26:6–13	78	5:25–34	86
26:26–30	82	5:35–43	86
26:28	53n10, 58n48, 80n48, 82, 83, 238	7:14–23	86n84
		8:31	54n15
26:39	195n74	9:12	53n10
26:42	195n74	9:31	54n15
26:52	58n51	9:48	58n51
26:54	78n37	10:33–44	54n15
26:57–69	81n56, 87n90	10:38–39	79n42
26:57	77n25	10:45	53n10, 54n15, 196
26:63	77n25, 80n48, 81n57, 82n58, 82n60, 87	14:23	58n48
		14:24	53n10
26:64		14:36	195n74
26:67	80n48, 82n58	15:28	58n48
26:68	77n25	15:34	58n51
27:11	81n57, 82n60	15:38	96n155
27:14	82n58	16:15	174, 198n90, 235
27:30	82n58		
27:42	82n60	**Luke**	58n48, 63, 65
27:46	58n51, 195n74	2:32	64n84
27:51—28:20	83n67	2:46–52	77
27:51	77n27, 83, 84, 91, 91n120, 96n155	3:21–22	74
		3:22	64n81
27:62	77n25	3:38	18, 89
28:20	88n101, 199n93	4	54n15
28:16–20	74, 221n52	4:1	64n81, 197
28:18–20	89		

Luke (continued)

4:14	64n81
4:16–44	234
4:17–27	53n10, 65n90, 66, 67, 197
4:18	64n81
4:26–27	67
9:22	54
10:21	195n74
10:29–37	88n99
11:2	195n73
11:22	53n10
11:31	64n84
14	135
14:23	126, 127
18:31–33	54n15
22:16	239n153
22:20	53n10, 238
22:24–27	58n48
22:27	53n10, 196
22:37	53n10, 58n48, 77, 80n48
23:34	195n74
23:45	96n155
23:46	195n74
24:48–49	198n92

John

	35, 61, 82, 85, 91n120, 95, 99, 140, 195n74, 214, 238
1:29–34	74n7
2:13–22	95n147
4:4–42	95n147
4:20–24	194n70
5:37	197
6:35	239
6:45–46	61n68
6:45	135n32, 143, 146, 228n85
7:39	197
10:4	228n85
11:41	195n74
12:8	53n11
12:27–28	195n74
12:41	53
12:49–52	82n59
13	82n62, 238
13:1–17	53n11, 95n147
13:10	75n13
13:12–20	196n80
13:13	28n1
13:15	196
14–16	130n1, 139
14:6	189n34
15:4	135n32
15:7	52n11
15:8	139
15:26–27a	197, 198n92
15:26	195
16:13	47n133
17	82n62, 95n147
17:1–26	195n74
17:21	160
18:15	95
18:37	197
19:23–25	94n142
20:19–21	95n147
20:21–23	89, 199n93
20:21	2, 177
20:22–23	89n105
20:23	232

Acts

	60, 63
1:8	64n81, 123, 198n92, 234
2	34n52, 84n78
2:4	64n81
2:30	81n54
2:33	36n64
2:34	36n64
2:36	94n139
2:38–39	36n81
3:13	40n98
3:26	40n98
4:26–27	77n25
4:27	29n11, 40n98
4:30	40n98
4:36	48
5:28	28n1
5:32	47n133
6:7	48
6:10	47n133

Scripture Index 311

8:26–39	34n52, 58n46, 60n61, 63, 112	8:34	6n29, 36n64, 44n116, 185, 225n70
8:39	63n74, 64n88	9–11	43
9:15	163	9:33	30
10:36–38	64n81, 78n36	11:1	43
10:38	77n26	11:13	45n126
11:26c	90	11:36	189n34
13:1	28n1	12	44, 229
13:2	47n133	12:1–8	28n3, 37, 41, 43, 44, 47, 50, 91
13:46–47	64n84	12:1–2	41, 43, 44, 122, 168n92, 224
13:47–48	64n88	12:1	17, 30, 36, 38n78, 40n97, 44, 45n123, n125, 47, 92, 93, 134, 135n32, 139, 143, 148, 158n9, 187n24, 196, 211, 214, 217, 224
17:19	28n1		
17:28	186		
17:34	110		
20:28	181n2, 230		
Romans	30n19, 36n62, 38, 42		
1–11	44		
1–6	224	12:3–8	41, 44n120
1–3	43	12:3	34, 44
1:7	45n127	12:4	44, 45n126, 92
1:8–15	43n113	12:7	28n1
1:9	10n51, 38, 43, 44, 92n121, 108n25	12:8	230
		14:12	44
3–4	43	15:14–33	43n113
3	92	15:14	231
3:25	92n123	15:16	8n40, 10n51, 37n72, 38, 43, 44, 45n123, 45n124, 70, 92n121, 108n25
5–7	43		
5:2	36n62, 43n115		
6	92		
6:3–4	79n42	15:21	44n121
6:3	92n123	15:27	45n124
6:10	36n69	15:31	44n122, 45n126
8:9–16	44n123	16:26	71
8:9a	30		
8:11	30	**1 Corinthians**	42n108
8:14	47n133		
8:15–17	195	1:2	181n2
8:15	185	1:24	189
8:18–25	174	2:13	47, 61
8:24	58n49	3:16–17	92n121, n122
8:26	226	3:16	30, 109n28
8:29	185	5:6–8	92n121
		5:7	34n48
		6:19–20	92n121, n122,

1 Corinthians *(continued)*

6:19	187n24
8:6	189
9:13–14	10n51, 93n136, 108n25
10:16	92n123, 239
11:16	181n2, 238
11:20–34	83
11:23	92n123
11:24	237
11:25	238
12	229
12:4–6	196n80
12:7	201, 229
12:11	189, 201
12:12–31	187n24
12:28	28n1
14:16	107n18
14:26	30n14
15:3–4	58n47
15:3	82n63
15:25	91n119
16:15	45n126

2 Corinthians   42n108, 93

1:21	93n133
2:14–15	92n121, 93
3:6	56n35, 93, 238
3:16	93
4:1	45n126
5:14—6:10	87n95, 93
5:17—6:4	92
5:17–20	93
5:18	45n126
6	92
6:2	93
6:15–18	31, 93
6:16—7:1	44n122, 92n121, n122, 108
6:16	31n21, 44n123
6:17	8n40, 31n21, 98n165
6:18	31n21
9:12	92n121

Galatians

2:20	163n51
3	135n32
3:27–28	117
3:28	213

Ephesians   30n18, 38, 42, 190n45

1:7	94n140
1:20	6n29, 36n64, 91n119
2:6	91n119, 94n140
2:8	30
2:9–10	212, 229, 236n134
2:14–16	92n123
2:18–22	30, 44n123, 92n121, n122, 109n28
2:18	30, 36n62, 43n115
2:19	30
2:20	30n14
2:21	31
2:22	31
3:12	44n115
4:1–4	236n134
4:4	47
4:6	189n34
4:7–12	70
4:11–16	202n109
4:11–12	135n32, 229, 230
4:11	28n1
4:12	30n14, 32, 45n126, 47, 196, 201, 229, 230
4:13	193n65, 230
4:15	231
4:16	30n14, 31
4:24	190n45
5:1–2	44n122, 47, 92n121
5:1	190
5:2	38n78, 92n123, 93n136
5:4	238n146
5:19	42n109
5:25–27	92n121, n123
6:4	47

Scripture Index 313

6:5–8	47
6:6–7	236

Philippians — 38, 42

1:1	230
2:4–11	39
2:5–7	196
2:14–18	38, 47, 64, 196n79, 234
2:15–16	94n144, 234
2:15	126n121, 210
2:16–17	38n78
2:16b–18	92
2:16	38
2:17	44n121, 92n121, n123
2:25	44n122
3:5	43
3:20	167
4:17	45n123
4:18	92n121, 93n136

Colossians

3:1	91n119
3:16	42n109, 47, 227, 231
3:23–24	236
4:3	47n132

1 Thessalonians

4:9	61n68
5:21	228n85

1 Timothy

1:12	45n126
2:1	44n116
2:5	35, 40n98
2:6	159
3:1–7	230
3:2	230
3:15	181n2
5:17	202

2 Timothy — 42

3:17	229n90
4:3	28n1
4:5–6	38n83
4:5	45n126
4:6	44n122

Titus

1:5–9	230
1:9	28n1
2:1	28n1

Hebrews — 7, 8, 16, 18, 30, 38, 41, 42, 49, 73, 80n44, 81n54, 83, 85, 88n101, 91, 95–100, 105, 114, 118, 132, 134, 136, 141, 247

1:1–5	95
1:1–4	7n33
1:3	36n64, 95, 136n33
1:5–13	76n20
1:8	136n37
1:13	136n33
2:10–11	195
2:17	82n57
3:13	231
3:14	50n143
4:14—10:25	95n152
4:14—10:18	95
4:14–16	62n69
4:14	56n32
4:16	97n161
5:1	35, 39, 207
5:5–8	76
5:5–6	7n33, 36n64
5:5	76
5:6–10	95n149
5:6	136n33
5:7	76n22
5:10	136n33
5:11	98
5:12	47, 62n69
6:2	98n171

Hebrews (continued)

6:19–20	97n162
6:19	83n69, 96n155
6:20	75, 95n149, 136n33
7:1–17	95n149
7:3	46n129
7:4–10	75n18
7:11	136n33
7:12	41, 56n35
7:14–17	98
7:15	136n33
7:17	136n33
7:21	136n33
7:25	44n116, 58n49, 97n161, 225n70
7:27	37n72, 39n90, 56n32
8–12	61
8:1	136n33
8:6	35n59
9:2	94n141
9:3	83n69, 96n155
9:8	83n69
9:12	39n90, 97n162
9:13–21	58n45
9:15	35n59
9:24	97n162, 225n70
9:25	97n162
9:26	12n60, 39n90, 114
9:28	37n72, 39, 56n32, 59n58, 99
10:1	97n161
10:10	39n90
10:11	44n119
10:12	114, 136n33
10:13	136n33
10:15–16	43n112
10:15	47n133
10:19–22	93
10:19–25	62, 62n69, 79n40, 95, 167, 226
10:19–20	83n69
10:19	44n115, 97n162
10:20	96n155
10:22	58n45, 75n13, 97n161
10:24	196n80
10:25	98n171
10:26—13:25	96
11:6	97n161
11:28	58n45
12:2	50n143, 136n33, 234
12:18	97n161
12:22	97n161
12:23	98
12:24	35n59, 58n45
12:28—13:17	207
13:7	202
13:13	207
13:15–16	38nn78, 39, 40n97, 44n123, 96, 114, 135n30
13:15	36, 37n72, 47, 194n70
13:16	96n157
13:7	202
13:20–21	39
13:21	229n90

James

3:1	28n1
5:16	196n80

1 Peter

	30, 33, 39, 42, 45, 95, 105, 118, 194, 247
1:2	35, 45n123, 50, 58n45, 96n156, 194n72
1:3	32, 40n98, 194n72
1:5	50
1:12	47n133, 69n118
1:15–16	37n76
1:17	34
1:18	36n66
1:19	36n66
1:21	35n61, 194n72
1:23	32
2	223n62
2:3	107

2:4–9	15, 17, 28, 29, 32, 33, 38, 40, 41, 43, 48, 50, 91, 106, 109n28, 131, 134n25, 135, 141, 173, 202, 205n124, 209, 219, 223, 241, 244	3:18	35n61, 36n66, 44n115, 194n72
		3:21	32n35, 35n61, 40n98
		3:22	36, 194n72
		4:10–11	41, 47n132, 229
		4:10	32, 34, 44, 183n11, 196
2:4	30, 194n72	4:11	33, 34, 35n61, 40n98, 194n72
2:5	4n14, 29, 30, 31, 32, 33, 34, 35, 36n62, 37, 38, 40, 42, 44n119, n120, n123, 45, 47, 106, 115, 139, 194, 196, 223, 231	4:14	40n98
		4:16–17	40n98
		4:16	90
		4:17	31n24
		4:19	39n86
		5:10	40n98, 194n72
2:6–7	29	5:14	40n98

2 Peter

1:3	35n61

2:6	30, 33, 40	
2:7	30, 238	
2:8	40	
2:9	4n14, 23, 32, 33, 34, 35, 36n66, 37, 38, 42, 44n121, 47, 48, 64n84, 65n90, 69n118, 92n121, 94n144, 105, 115, 121, 126, 134, 136, 156, 161, 163–66, 176, 185, 187, 198n92, 207, 216n31, 230, 233	

1 John

1:5	69n118
2:20	61n68, 93, 166
2:27	61n68, 93, 166
4:11–12	196n80
5:6	197

Jude

20	126

2:12	35, 37, 38, 126
2:15	39n86
2:20	39n86
2:21–25	40n98, 50n143
2:22	36n66
2:23	36n66
2:24	35n61, 36n66, 37n72, 60n58, 238
2:25	36n66
3:1–2	47
3:1	37, 38
3:6	39n86
3:12	37
3:13	36n66
3:15	35, 38, 47
3:16	40n98
3:17	39n86

Revelation

	15, 80n44, 94, 118, 248
1:5–6	50n144, 214n19
1:5	94, 197
1:6	4n14, 17, 28n2, 33, 36, 42, 47, 70n122, 75n13 v.r. NA26, 92n121, 94, 107n17, 135n32, 187n24, 194n70, 241
1:12–20	239

Revelation (continued)

1:13	94
2:7	47n133
2:29	226
3:21	214n19
5:9–10	50n144, 194n71, 214, 214n19, 237
5:10	4n14, 17, 28n2, 42, 92n121, 94, 135n32, 223, 241
5:13	195n75
7:14	35
7:15	35, 45n123, n125, 50n144, 94, 214n19, 223n58, 226
15:3	99
15:6	94n142
19:7	223n58, 239n153
20:4–6	214n19
20:6	4n14, 17, 28n2, 42, 50n144, 92n121, 94, 121, 135n32, 223n58, 241
21–22	67n112
21:3–4	50n144
21:16	97n163
21:18–21	61n63
21:22–26	50n144
22:3–4	94n138
22:3	50n144
22:17	237

www.ingramcontent.com/pod-product-compliance
Lightning Source LLC
Chambersburg PA
CBHW070013010526
44117CB00011B/1542